Tropical Gothic in Literat

Tropical Gothic examines Gothic within a specific geographical area of 'the South' of the Americas. In so doing, we structure the book around geographical coordinates (from North to South) and move among various national traditions of the gothic (Mexico, Argentina, Brazil, etc.) alongside regional manifestations of the Gothic (the U.S. south and the Caribbean) as well as transnational movements of the Gothic within the Americas. The reflections on national traditions of the Gothic in this volume add to the critical body of literature on specific languages or particular nations, such as Scottish Gothic, American Gothic, Canadian Gothic, German Gothic, Kiwi Gothic, etc. This is significant because, while the Southern Gothic in the U.S. has been thoroughly explored, there is a gap in the critical literature about the Gothic in the larger context of region of 'the South' in the Americas. This volume does not pretend to be a comprehensive examination of tropical Gothic in the Americas; rather, it pinpoints a variety of locations where this form of the Gothic emerges. In so doing, the transnational interventions of the Gothic in this book read the flows of Gothic forms across borders and geographical regions to tease out the complexities of Gothic cultural production within cultural and linguistic translations. *Tropical Gothic* includes, but is by no means limited to, a reflection on a region where European colonial powers fought intensively against indigenous populations and against each other for control of land and resources. In the cases of other regions, vast populations of slaves were transported here, endowing these lands with a cultural heritage that all the nations involved are still trying to comprehend. The volume reflects on how these histories influence the Gothic in this region.

Justin D. Edwards is Professor of English at the University of Surrey. He has taught at the universities of Wales, Copenhagen, Montreal and Quebec. Among his books are *Gothic Passages: Racial Ambiguity and the American Gothic* (2003), *Gothic Canada: Reading the Spectre of a National Literature* (2005), *Grotesque* (with Rune Graulund, 2013), as well as co-editor (with Agnieszka Soltysik Monnet) of *Gothic in Contemporary Literature and Popular Culture: Pop Goth* (2012).

Sandra Guardini Vasconcelos is Professor of English Literature and Comparative Literature at the University of São Paulo, where she obtained her MA and PhD in Literary Theory and Comparative Literature. She has edited several books, has published articles and chapters and is the author of *Puras Misturas. Estórias em Guimarães Rosa* (1997), *Dez Lições sobre o Romance Inglês do Século XVIII* (2002), and *A Formação do Romance Inglês: ensaios teóricos* (2007), for which she won the 2008 Jabuti Prize (Literary Theory and Criticism). She is curator of the João Guimarães Rosa Archive, at the Instituto de Estudos Brasileiros (USP).

Routledge Interdisciplinary Perspectives on Literature

For a full list of titles in this series, please visit www.routledge.com.

31 **Rethinking Empathy through Literature**
Edited by Meghan Marie Hammond and Sue J. Kim

32 **Music and Identity in Postcolonial British South-Asian Literature**
Christin Hoene

33 **Representations of War, Migration, and Refugeehood**
Interdisciplinary Perspectives
Edited by Daniel H. Rellstab and Christiane Schlote

34 **Liminality and the Short Story**
Boundary Crossings in American, Canadian, and British Writing
Edited by Jochen Achilles and Ina Bergmann

35 **Asian American Literature and the Environment**
Edited by Lorna Fitzsimmons, Youngsuk Chae, and Bella Adams

36 **Transnational Feminist Perspectives on Terror in Literature and Culture**
Basuli Deb

37 **Children's Literature, Domestication, and Social Foundation**
Narratives of Civilization and Wilderness
Layla AbdelRahim

38 **Singularity and Transnational Poetics**
Edited by Birgit Mara Kaiser

39 **National Poetry, Empires and War**
David Aberbach

40 **Technologies of the Gothic in Literature and Culture**
Technogothics
Edited by Justin D. Edwards

41 **Global Ecologies and the Environmental Humanities**
Postcolonial Approaches
Edited by Elizabeth DeLoughrey, Jill Didur, and Anthony Carrigan

42 **Theoretical Schools and Circles in the Twentieth-Century Humanities**
Literary Theory, History, Philosophy
Edited by Marina Grishakova and Silvi Salupere

43 **Gender, Race, and American Science Fiction**
Reflections on Fantastic Identities
Jason Haslam

44 **Space and the Postmodern Fantastic in Contemporary Literature**
The Architectural Void
Patricia García

45 **New Directions in 21st-Century Gothic**
The Gothic Compass
Edited by Lorna Piatti-Farnell and Donna Lee Brien

46 **Latin American and Iberian Perspectives on Literature and Medicine**
Edited by Patricia Novillo-Corvalán

47 **Institutions of World Literature**
Writing, Translation, Markets
Edited by Stefan Helgesson and Pieter Vermeulen

48 **Narrative Theory, Literature, and New Media**
Narrative Minds and Virtual Worlds
Edited by Mari Hatavara, Matti Hyvärinen, Maria Mäkelä, and Frans Mäyrä

49 **Women Writers and the Occult in Literature and Culture**
Female Lucifers, Priestesses, and Witches
Miriam Wallraven

50 **Technology, Literature, and Digital Culture in Latin America**
Mediatized Sensibilities in a Globalized Era
Edited by Matthew Bush and Tania Gentic

51 **Race and Popular Fantasy Literature**
Habits of Whiteness
Helen Young

52 **Subjectivity and the Reproduction of Imperial Power**
Empire's Individuals
Daniel F. Silva

53 **Ireland and Ecocriticism**
Literature, History and Environmental Justice
Eóin Flannery

54 **Security and Hospitality in Literature and Culture**
Modern and Contemporary Perspectives
Edited by Jeffrey Clapp and Emily Ridge

55 **New Perspectives on Detective Fiction**
Mystery Magnified
Edited by Casey A. Cothran and Mercy Cannon

56 **Vulnerability and Security in Human Rights Literature and Visual Culture**
Alexandra Schultheis Moore

57 **Globalizing Literary Genres**
Literature, History, Modernity
Edited by Jernej Habjan and Fabienne Imlinger

58 **War Gothic in Literature and Culture**
Edited by Agnieszka Soltysik Monnet and Steffen Hantke

59 **Ageing, Gender and Illness in Anglophone Literature**
Narrating Age in the Bildungsroman
Heike Hartung

60 **Tropical Gothic in Literature and Culture**
The Americas
Edited by Justin D. Edwards and Sandra Guardini Vasconcelos

Tropical Gothic in Literature and Culture

The Americas

Edited by Justin D. Edwards
and Sandra Guardini
Vasconcelos

Routledge
Taylor & Francis Group
LONDON AND NEW YORK

First published 2016 by Routledge

2 Park Square, Milton Park, Abingdon, Oxfordshire OX14 4RN
52 Vanderbilt Avenue, New York, NY 10017

Routledge is an imprint of the Taylor & Francis Group, an informa business

First issued in paperback 2019

Library of Congress Cataloging-in-Publication Data

Names: Edwards, Justin D., 1970– editor. | Vasconcelos, Sandra Guardini T., editor.
Title: Tropical gothic in literature and culture: the Americas / edited by Justin D Edwards and Sandra Guardini Vasconcelos.
Description: New York: Routledge, 2016. | Series: Routledge interdisciplinary perspectives on literature; 60 | Includes bibliographical references and index.
Identifiers: LCCN 2015035804 | ISBN 9781138915862 (alk. paper)
Subjects: LCSH: Gothic revival (Literature)—History and criticism. | Gothic revival (Literature)—America. | America—In literature. | Tropics—In literature.
Classification: LCC PN3435 .T77 2016 | DDC 809.3/876—dc23
LC record available at http://lccn.loc.gov/2015035804

ISBN: 978-1-138-91586-2 (hbk)
ISBN: 978-0-367-87356-1 (pbk)

Typeset in Sabon
by codeMantra

Contents

Introduction

Tropicalizing Gothic

Justin D. Edwards and Sandra Guardini Vasconcelos

In the Mexican film *Cronos* (1993), a mysterious device designed to provide its owner with eternal life resurfaces after 400 years, leaving a trail of destruction in its path. When opened, the device stabs the handler, and the incision stimulates youthful vigor and a vampire's need for blood. Directed by Guillermo del Toro, who went on to make the Gothic horror films *Devil's Backbone* (2001), *Pan's Labyrinth* (2006) and the American mainstream vampire superhero action movie *Blade II* (2002), *Cronos* is part of a tradition of vampire narratives in the American tropics. This tradition stretches from the civatateo of Aztec mythology to the tale of the azeman in Surinam to the oral stories of the peuchen in Chile to the lobisomem of Brazilian folklore to the soucouyant and volant in the Anglophone and Francophone Caribbean. *Cronos* is also part of a significant Gothic cinematic tradition in the tropics of the Americas. This group includes, among many others, vampire films such as *Vampiros* (2004) by the Puerto Rican director Eduardo Ortíz and *Sangre eternal* (*Eternal Blood*, 2002) by Jorge Olguin from Chile, as well as the Colombian films *Pura sangre* (*Pure Blood*, 1982) by Luis Ospina and *Carne de tu carne* (*Flesh of Your Flesh*, 1983) by Carlos Mayolo. In fact, Mayolo refers to his vampire movie and his haunting work *La mansión de Araucaíma* (*The Manor of Araucaíma* 1986) as 'Gótico tropical' (tropical Gothic) films that revolve around 'la estructura del gótico', a gothic structure in a tropical setting (9).

In the American tropics, these Gothic figures adapt to their social, cultural and political context. *Cronos* includes a sixteenth-century alchemist in Veracruz, a reference to the Spanish search for gold in the region. In *Pura sangre,* the literal vampire is placed alongside a metaphoric vampire who owns a Colombian sugar plantation and who sucks the life out of his workers. In *Vampiros* the urban setting of San Juan foregrounds a tropical Gothic cityscape in Puerto Rico. This process might be categorized as what Fernando Ortiz, Ángel Rama and Mary Louise Pratt call transculturation, which merges the acquisition of another culture (acculturation) with the uprooting of a previous culture (deculturation) to engender new cultural phenomena. Indeed, transculturation often arises out of colonial conquest and subjugation, particularly in a postcolonial era when indigenous cultures articulate historical and political injustices while struggling to regain a sense of cultural identity. This gives the power of transformative cultural agency to the colonized subject by transforming, appropriating, adapting and 're-writing' the modes and genres from the North Atlantic, sometimes engendering texts of resistance by revising models for articulating local experience and culture in the American tropics.

An extension of transculturation is what some cultural and literary critics call tropicalization, a process of troping and infusing a particular space, place, region or nation with an assortment of qualities, metaphors, ideas and principles that are disseminated and maintained through literary texts, historical narratives, film and media (Aparicio 2–4). This form of tropicalization is a reversal of North Atlantic discourses that tropicalize the southern Other through fixed definitions and stereotypes; instead, it includes self-identified tropicalization that resists the externally driven discourses of exoticization. In his work on early Latin American Gothic writing, Gabriel Eljaiek-Rodríguez argues that Gothic can be understood in relation to transculturation and tropicalization. He writes,

> The *tropicalization* of the Gothic works in a similar manner as the process of *transculturation* [...], an intercultural and bidirectional dynamic, a two-way flow of information, knowledge, and cultural products. The mechanism revives Gothic images and themes, while at the same time employing images and imaginaries that are related to the colonial and postcolonial relationship of Europe and the United States with Latin America (and vice versa), ideas that situate extreme otherness and monstrosity in the southern part of the continent. (14)

In this context, Gothic adapts to a new geography through a process of appropriation to engender autochthonous texts that do not simply abandon North Atlantic Gothic but problematize and alter it to fit a unique location. Gothic thrives off local popular cultures and, through its adaptations, re-emerges to underscore politically charged ghosts and monsters that return the colonial Other to the center of Empire and foreground the unease and complications of Gothic figures. Thus the seemingly contradictory expression 'tropical Gothic' thrives in regions ostensibly untouched by the dark tropes of the North Atlantic Gothic tradition. Sunlit and humid conditions form a hotbed where Gothic figures—ghosts, zombies, vampires—move freely through plantations, houses and tropical cities, haunting the bright landscape and forming the basis for tropical chills.

The uniqueness of Gothic in the American tropics arises out of the social, cultural, economic and geographical complexities of the region. The indigenous cultures that existed long before European invasion include their own ghosts, just as the violence of colonization engendered a haunted history often incorporated into the tropical Gothic text. For the colonist, the 'settling' of the 'unsettled' land brings with it a sense of the uncanny wherein the homely blurs into the unhomely, an unstable ground that, for a colonial culture, is intensified in the twentieth-century political assertions of independence. The region also comprises countries and nations grouped together under geographical or linguistic labels such as the Caribbean, Anglo-America and Latin America, as well as North, Central and South America. This is further complicated by regional diasporas that have led to hyphenated expressions of identity—such as Haitian-Quebecois or Mexican-American—which gesture to affiliations with at least two national territories.

While these double or multiple identities underscore the linguistic and cultural variety that characterizes this vast territory, the countries and nations comprehended within the idea of the 'tropics' share the common experience of having been forged from various European colonial and imperial projects. In their history, in the shared experience of extermination of indigenous peoples, slavery and exploitation of their riches and natural resources lies a past that needs surfacing, revisiting, confronting and critiquing. The ghosts from this violent past were often silenced or driven to the margins in the texts that have helped to construct the national literatures in the nineteenth century or have taken new forms in the treatment of a troubled and troubling present, riddled with *coups d'état*, military dictatorships, persecution and torture. They keep returning from those margins or loiter in contemporary cultural productions as a strategy to excavate what has been concealed or repressed. This common history, however, does not obliterate the specific nature of each historical experience and context throughout the American tropics. Representations of the tropical and sub-tropical world encompass a complex geography, topography and historical process, with substantial differences from region to region. These representations have been shaped through time in travel writing, iconography, literary texts and the cinema. The appropriation of Gothic tropes by travelers, filmmakers and writers to address the cultural and historical experience of life in the tropics is far from being misplaced in this environment and context. It plays an important role in the construction of an idea of the tropics and needs to be interrogated as to its different meanings, a challenge met by each of the essays in this collection.

In geographical terms, the American tropics includes that region of the continent within the boundaries of the so-called 'torrid zone' that comprises two parallels of latitude: the Tropic of Cancer (about 23.5° N of the equator) and the Tropic of Capricorn (about 23.5° S of the equator). Like other parts of the terrestrial globe, the neighboring regions around the American equator comprise sub-tropical geographic and climatic zones located roughly between the tropic circle of latitude (the Tropic of Cancer and Tropic of Capricorn) and the 38th parallel in each hemisphere. Yet what is known as the tropical belt is far from a homogeneous region, from the point of view of its topography and vegetation. Though it is generally associated with heat, eternal summer, a lush flora, torrential rains and a rich fauna, some of its areas are savannahs, with scattered tree growth and seasonal rainfall, while others are typically affected by long periods of serious droughts, with direct consequences for their economy and Human Development Index (HDI).

Our focus on tropical Gothic in the Americas includes both the tropics and sub-tropics, extending from the southern region of the mainland U.S. territories through Mexico and the Caribbean into Central and South America. In their literary geography of the American tropics, Fumagalli, Hulme, Robinson and Wylie offer a helpful definition of this region and its significance for literary and cultural critics. They write,

> Not a tightly defined geographical designation, American Tropics refers to a kind of extended Caribbean, including the south-eastern USA, the Atlantic littoral of Central America, the Caribbean islands, and north-eastern South America [...]. This area shares a history in which the dominant fact is the arrival of millions of white Europeans and black Africans (with devastating impact for indigenous populations). It shares an environment that is tropical and sub-tropical. And it shares a socio-economic model (the plantation), whose effects lasted at least well into the twentieth century. (2)

Drawing on this general definition, we aim to signpost the various traditions of Gothic in the region by illustrating how North Atlantic Gothic tropes have been transported to these tropical and subtropical zones as a way of addressing the violence and inequality that 'haunts' this part of the Americas. A land of contrasts—economic, political, social, cultural, environmental—and a description French sociologist Roger Bastide once offered of Brazil but easily extended to this whole vast region, the tropical and subtropical Americas are as much what scientific exploration and knowledge have made them as a symbolic construction that allows for the appropriation of the Gothic, as the literary texts and films discussed in this collection evince.

Traditionally, the tropical world has been synonymous with extravagance and excess; it resonates with sensuality and exoticism, while it is simultaneously riddled with diseases and lurking dangers. In early colonial times, the tropics were seen as an empty and unknown territory, a space not yet filled by colonization and thus a realm of disorder, barbarism and savagery. It was often described as the land of the devil, which needed to be tamed and ordered (Lima 58) by the impact and imprint of European culture and civilization (Bates). From the European colonists and travelers in the past to the contemporary film and media industries, images of both paradise and hell have time and again been associated with the tropics and sub-tropics (Freyre). Out of the encounter between the Old and the New Worlds, or out of the contrast between the urbanized areas and the hinterland, arose a vision that could both idealize and demonize those lands that lay beyond and hid secrets and mysteries yet to be unraveled. These ambivalences have continued to permeate the different constructions of the tropical and sub-tropical zones, both from a local and peripheral point of view, by the different projects of nation-building, national identity and the foreign gaze.

The construction of Otherness is a textual strategy that has been engaged in as much from within as from without, with Gothic tropes, motifs and trappings used to deal with this unfamiliar and often indecipherable territory for colonists, settlers, travelers in the past, writers and, more recently, filmmakers living in metropolitan centers. The chapters in this book engage with the idea of tropical Gothic in the Americas and represent—as much as 15 essays can—the rich diversity of Gothic produced within this geographical area. The volume thus offers a survey of Gothic across the region, from New Orleans to Mexico City and Port-au-Prince to São Paulo.

The essays that follow expose the continuities and discontinuities that characterize the appropriations and acclimatization of the Gothic in the tropical and sub-tropical Americas from the nineteenth century to the present, and in various genres and cultural forms, from novels and short-stories to films and computer games. In common with classical Gothic texts and settings, they enact the fear of the unknown, the unsettling past with its secrets and 'ghosts', as well as the social and political issues of gender, race and identity formation, cultural anxieties involving class and difference, but also memory and nationhood. Empire and colonialism, which lie at the heart of the tropics' historical experience, now take on new forms and make their appearance in global tourism. Spheres of private experience like subjectivity, sexuality and the body, all of which have haunted Gothic narratives from their early days, are themes that also appear in the selection of tropical Gothic texts, films and games discussed in this collection. There is continuity between Gothic tropes from other regions and those found in the American tropics. What each one of the essays in this collection claims, however, is that tropical Gothic texts in the Americas have been mobilized in order to deal with the particular nature of the imperial and historical experience in this part of the world. The American tropics have been Gothicized, in Enrique Ajuria Ibarra's apt formulation, so as to flaunt the violence that has characterized their historical process from the very early days of colonization. In more recent times, popular revolts, military dictatorships, economic speculation and exploitation have produced their share of violence and anxiety, which can explain and justify the Gothic treatment of materials, settings and plots. Zombies have replaced the specters of classical Gothic; imperialist and economic interests have assumed less concrete, insidious forms, though they are ever more powerful in their transnational character, rapacity and aggressiveness. As Jeffrey D. Sachs has argued, almost all of the tropical countries in the world remain underdeveloped and rank among the poorest even at the start of the twenty-first century. Each chapter explores the uses of the Gothic in a wide variety of materials in order to confront this disturbing past and present.

The essays in this collection interrogate the various aspects of these reworkings and have been organized in three sections, which bring to the forefront thematic continuities and common perspectives in their treatment of the Gothic. What would then seem to be a geographical dispersal of Gothic appropriations over a large spatial continuum proves to be evidence of recurrences and overlapping. Their connections and disconnections have more to do with the specificities of the different colonial projects and historical forces that have shaped each of the national traditions in that vast area than with an essentialist identity of destiny. Transplantation and movement are, in this sense, pivotal to all the essays and offer an overarching approach that does not strictly obey chronology and geography, allowing for their ordering in clusters around common topics and concerns.

The first section, 'Tropical Undead', brings together essays that deal with zombies, zombieism and voodoo, as they have migrated from West Africa to haunt the sub-tropical American South and the Caribbean and been mythologized as part of a culture of death and conjure rituals that seek to settle accounts with these regions' black heritage and the haunting history of slavery. It opens with Justin D. Edwards's mapping of the Tropical Gothic, wherein he demonstrates how, in its transnational migration, the Gothic has traveled across geography, nation and history and negotiated with local cultural forms and practices like hybridism, cannibalism, and mongrelization. His essay offers a frame for the whole collection by foregrounding how in different traditions and locales over the vast expanse of the tropics the experience of displacement and dislocation has produced fresh readings of the Gothic to address relevant issues common in, and at the same time specific to, their colonial past or problematic present. As Edwards argues, fundamental to this relocated Gothic are the transfers and cultural translations that the process of concrete and metaphorical circulation of goods (in this case, books and literary works) and ideas have enabled.

In 'The Zombie Tropocalypse: Entropic (Digital) Disaster in the Hot Zone', Rune Graulund's discussion of what zombies have signified over time and how they have been appropriated by contemporary cultural forms suggests that, in spite of 'the incessant repetition and recirculation of the zombie throughout the late twentieth and early twenty first centuries', zombies are marked by difference. Rather than death, they represent a 'figure of excessive life' and have changed from a 'tropical reality' to a 'global monstrosity', adaptable to various contexts and circumstances, as evidenced in their invasion of many different media, fields and cultural manifestations. The entropic and apocalyptic world depicted in films, computer games and TV shows, where these creatures proliferate and spread like an infectious disease, is nothing but the representation of the system we live in, where the reproduction of capital, its colonization of all spheres of life, and the endless circulation of goods are the nightmare which is becoming increasingly difficult to escape.

A step back in time, the experience of a nightmarish, but now unfamiliar environment and unhealthy climate suffuses the accounts by European and American travelers. As Owen Robinson illustrates, the challenge to make sense of a reality and culture related to 'the mythology of death' is pervaded by an impending atmosphere of doom, fear and anxiety. The imaging and imagining of nineteenth-century New Orleans are as much its own creation as the result of these travelers' confrontation with their unhomely experiences. Likewise, Elizabeth Rodriguez Fielder examines how elements of West African religious and cultural traditions were incorporated into William Faulkner's and Tennesse Williams's representations of life in the South and re-appropriated by the Black Arts Movement of writers of the 1970s and 1980s. This was done in ambivalent ways and in the politicization of these traditional practices, wherein the supernatural is instrumental in a critical reading of cultural nationalism within the circum-Atlantic. Zombification also features as a tool in Haitian culture's negotiation of identity, which moves beyond nationality to become racialized, as Kelly Gardner suggests, by taking on contemporary meanings of zombification as a critique of capitalism, consumerism and technology.

Digital culture has become a place where questions of identity and Otherness may be addressed. In a videogame like *Dead Island*, for instance, the player is invited to adopt an avatar and experience the action through the eyes of a protagonist in the game. Johan Höglund's essay explores how the gamer is transformed into a tourist who is motivated by series of quests and, through role-playing, has the choice of playing as a one-hit U.S. rap star, a vacationing football player, a female Chinese desk clerk/government spy or an Australian Aboriginal policewoman. Here, Höglund discusses the tropical tourist industry as a type of neo-colonial practice, arguing that the game can be understood as a form of American imperial Gothic in the tropics and, as such, it works in ways similar to both the U.S. and British imperial Gothic of the late nineteenth century.

Character identification in computer and video games allows for a vicarious experience of Otherness and often works as a strategy to simulate the real-life encounter of colonizer and colonized. Predominantly visual and reliant on a different kind of medium, these games mobilize and reinterpret Gothic tropes to create a fictional world wherein one can apprehend contemporary concerns regarding neo-colonialism and Empire. Although they seem to be merely games, intended simply for the entertainment of players, these can be read metaphorically as enactments of political anxieties and the power dynamics of globalization as an extension of nineteenth-century forms of imperialism.

Gothic as a way of addressing specifically socio-political content is the cornerstone of the essays in the second section of this collection. In order to explore Mexico as a Gothic site, David Punter focuses on Laura Esquivel's two novels *Like Water for Chocolate* and *Malinche*, both of which provide a series of discursive intersections that shed light on the complexity of Mexican history. His main concern in his piece is the tropic and topic rewritings of history, and how to find a discourse that will give an account of those 'distortions' of history with which the Gothic, in many of its modes, so often deals. The processes of identification and distantiation from the forces of Mexico's 'legendary' past are, he asserts, different and put a separate slant on such primary cultural loci as the fatal translational encounter, between ruler/priest and conquistador, which some have seen as at the root of Mexican history.

From the ghosts of the past we move on to Gothic visions of the future. In her reading of three Mexican literary dystopias, Inés Ordiz Allonso-Collada explores how Mexico's terrifying present (ruined urban landscapes, economic crises, social inequality and environmental degradation) is translated into the horrifying, apocalyptic future of a country ruled by the masters of monstrous technology. Science fiction, combined with the motifs and structures of a gothic aesthetic, foreshadows a barbaric time when Mexico City will be the site of environmental destruction, while evoking a past of pre-Hispanic myths and sacred places. In this Cybergothic fiction, the country is a dystopic place where the haunting of history engenders a site of chaos and catastrophe.

The ruins of Mexico's past are the setting of Carter Smith's film adaptation of Scott Smith's novel *The Ruins*, a tourist adventure narrative that features a carnivorous plant capable of mimicking human and technological sound. The film establishes a clear dialectic between civilization and nature, the homely and the unhomely, as young American tourists decide to visit an ancient Mayan archaeological site that, though not inherently Gothic, is reconstructed to heighten the audience's awareness of horror and anxiety. Enrique Ajuria Ibarra explores how the monstrosity of body horror in *The Ruins* is a key factor for illustrating fantasies of perilous danger in a foreign land. The film, he argues, structures Otherness artificially by means of Gothic conventions and rather than creating a form of Mexican gothic, it Gothicizes unfamiliar, exotic elements in order to narrate and display a spectacular fascination for foreign Otherness in the form of dark and unknown tropical fears.

Antonio Alcalá's and Ilse Büssing's essays move beyond the threats lurking in a strange and baffling natural environment into urban settings. Here, large and old buildings are inhabited by ghostly presences, memories and the secrets of the past. In the heart of Mexico's capital, wherein three centuries of Spanish colonial rule have not erased the marks of Aztec Tenochtitlan, the fiction of Carlos Fuentes adapts the Gothic mode in order to deal with Mexican national identity. While Alcalá explores how Fuentes makes use of spaces located near the city's downtown neighborhood in order to tease out the implications of the uncanny Gothic events his protagonists experience, Ilse Büssing compares Fuentes's 'La Buena Compañia' with Julio Cortázar's 'Casa Tomada' to investigate how the house is represented as a prison or an uncanny space that destabilizes domesticity. The tension between the homely and the unhomely permeates these two stories: traumas in the family resurface as specters to haunt siblings or close relatives as the characters confront their complicated pasts. Reading the Argentinian writer's short story from this private and personal perspective should not exclude, however, the possibility of a political interpretation of the claustrophobic atmosphere that invades the two characters' family house. Cortázar published this story in 1969, during the fierce military dictatorship that controlled Argentina for many years; thus, we might read the family relationships in the story as allegories for political and social relations within the homeland. The mysterious noises that progressively invade all areas of the house, imprisoning the brother and sister and forcing them into increasingly confined spaces until they give up altogether, mirror the oppression and suppression of individual freedom imposed by the regime that ruled Argentina during this period.

Gothic tropes and conventions have given, and continue to give, vent to the demonic aspects of individual and collective experiences in the American tropics and configure narrative strategies to articulate national and historical issues that have haunted this region for generations. Imaging and imagining the troubled and troubling process of construction of nations and literatures in the tropics have always entailed the negotiation of endogenous and exogenous tensions and the re-appropriation of foreign suggestions to very specific uses. This relates directly to the Brazilian writer Álvares de Azevedo (described by some as 'the Brazilian Byron'), who incorporates dark morbidity and ultra-Romanticism in his work. As Cilaine Alves Cunha claims, there is a transgressive model of tormented beauty in Azevedo's writing, whose demonic heroes embody the processes of degeneration and the violation of limits that represent an evident contrast with any aesthetically uplifting experience. She goes on to suggest that his *A Night in the Tavern* draws on significant Gothic features to raise controversies about the social construction of Brazilian literature and the subsequent rise of literary nationalism. No less meaningful is the role allotted to women in his narrative: they are assaulted by humiliations, indignities and violence. Perverse sexuality also permeates Azevedo's work and introduces an unprecedented dimension into Brazilian Romanticism.

The body is sometimes the receptacle for an alien organism. We find this in Smith's *The Ruins* and in Azevedo's work, wherein the body is represented as a vessel for transgressive sexual practices (necrophilia and incest) and the subjugation of women's bodies within a patriarchal society. Rita Schmidt's essay represents a counterpoint to this representation of women in her discussion of the transculturation of the European Gothic mode in four novels by women. She argues that the difference of women's texts engendered at the nation's margins—as the nation's Other—lies in a narrative economy that subverts the celebratory collective histories of nationality embedded in canonical texts by men. By appropriating gothic tropes, these women writers offer alternative understandings of history and politics in the countries where these novels were produced. Patriarchal power is at the heart of this strand of female Gothic; in these works of fiction, identity and gender are inscribed in a web of violence, racialization and sexuality. The body thus becomes a political statement in the work of these four nineteenth-century women writers who subvert the received ideas about nation building and romance.

Two novels by José de Alencar, one of the founders of the Brazilian novel, are discussed in the essay by Sandra Guardini Vasconcelos. She argues that the appropriation of Gothic tropes by Alencar is instrumental in the representation of Brazilian rural life as a space that is prone to violence and excess, and therefore as the Other of the 'civilised' and Europeanized capital of the country. Outside the metropolis, the history of slavery and miscegenation is pivotal to challenging the dominant discourses of Brazilian identity and nation in the novelist's work as conceptions of nationhood devoid of conflict and tension. Alencar's depiction of Brazil as a sunlit, tropical country is tinged by shadows and gloom as his plots enact, if marginally, some of the harsh aspects of Brazilian life in the nineteenth century.

Referring to texts produced more than a century later, Daniel Serravalle de Sá explores Brazilian Gothic cinema and how this medium includes the seemingly irreconcilable imagery of gloominess and sunniness alongside Gothic motifs. The films by Brazilian filmmakers Walter Hugo Khoury and José Mojica Marins (alias Zé do Caixão) are connected here in a protocol of reading that favors a specific aesthetic and iconography of Anglo-American extraction and also understands Gothic as a useful framework to address socio-political contexts, metaphorical connotations and contradictions in the plots of the films. Sexuality and politics emerge once again as pivotal concerns in the works of the two filmmakers who resort to gothic motifs and tropes to illuminate the violent aspects of recent Brazilian history and convey the horror of the military dictatorship. The metanarrative of the nation is once again challenged as these films address the traumas associated with gender, class, and racial difference.

Bibliography

Aparicio, Frances, and Susana Cháez-Silverman. *Tropicalizations: Transcultural Representations of Latinidad*. Hanover: University Press of New England, 1997. Print.

Bastide, Roger. *Brasil: terra de contrastes*. São Paulo: Difusão Europeia do Livro, 1959. Print.

Bates, Marston. *Where Winter Never Comes: A Study of Man and Nature in the Tropics*. New York: Scribner's, 1952. Print.

Eljaiek-Rodríguez, Gabriel. 'Semillas de maldad. Early Latin American Gothic'. *Studies in Gothic Fiction 3.2* (2014): 13–23. Online.

Freyre, Gilberto. 'O Brasil como civilização europeia nos trópicos'. In: *Novo Mundo nos Trópicos*. São Paulo: Editora Nacional e Editora da USP, 1971. Print.

Fumagalli, Maria Cristina, and Peter Hulme, Owen Robinson and Lesley Wylie. Introduction. *Surveying the American Tropics: A Literary Geography from New York to Rio*. Ed. Fumagalli, Maria Cristina, Peter Hulme, Owen Robinson and Lesley Wylie. Liverpool: Liverpool University Press, 2013. 1–21. Print.

Lima, Nísia Trindade and Mader, Maria Elisa S. *Um sertão chamado Brasil*. Rio de Janeiro: Renavan/IUPERJ, UCAM, 1999. Print.

Mayolo, Carlos. Interview. In *Valle de pelicula: retrospectiva del audiovisual vallecaucano*. Cali: Columbia, 2007. 1–16. Print.

Sachs, Jeffrey D. Tropical Underdevelopment, NBER Working Paper n. 8119, February 2001, http://www.nber.org/papers/w8119. Print.

Section I

Tropical Undead

1 Mapping Tropical Gothic in the Americas

Justin D. Edwards

Space, place and region have always been central to Gothic literary and cultural production. We see this in the labyrinthine underground spaces found in eighteenth-century English novels by, among others, Horace Walpole and Ann Radcliffe or in the tombs and claustrophobic spaces of nineteenth-century short stories by Edgar Allan Poe and Charlotte Perkins Gilman. We see it in how the Catholic nations of Southern Europe become significant places for the development of eighteenth-century Gothic plots about cross-dressing monks and bleeding nuns just as the dark forest and untamed frontier of the United States become meaningful places for the rise of national Gothic narratives in the wake of European-Aboriginal conflict and genocide. And we see this in how the European regions associated with the sublime become unsettling terrains that reflect eighteenth-century revolutionary political upheavals just as the images of decay and grotesquery in the regional U.S. Southern Gothic become important geographical markers for signifying difference, degeneration and chattel slavery. In all of these locations, Gothic texts explore dislocations and a sense of the unhomely in the homeland is caused by the transformation of geographic space into alienating or incorporating sites. Gothic thus casts a dark shadow over the nationalist projects that arise out of European Enlightenment thought, Romanticism and imperialist projects, signaling remote geographies that lie beyond the stable landscapes of rationality and logic.

Like Southern Europe or the East, the American tropics have long been sites of difference for Anglophone Gothic novelists. Monstrous threats from this region can be found in texts as diverse as Charles Brockden Brown's *Ormond; or, the Secret Witness* (1799), Charlotte Smith's *Letters of a Solitary Wanderer* (1800), Cynric Williams's *Hamel, the Obeah Man* (1827), Charlotte Brontë's *Jane Eyre* (1847), Herman Melville's *Benito Cereno* (1855), Florence Marryat's *Blood of the Vampire* (1897) and others.[1] These texts interrogate the location of the Other and its relationship to national identities in England or the United States, worrying about what happens when the nation admits, or is infiltrated by, Otherness so that the homeland becomes an alien nation. In these narratives, the threat of Otherness posed by the American tropics comes to consolidate national identities by imagining models of difference that might form a means of resistance to foreign dangers. These Gothic texts, then, reflect anxieties about the displacements of national identities and how the monstrous Other might be identified as originating from a specific location—in this case, the tropics—and thus regulated and geographically contained. At the same time, though, these texts also betray an anxiety about how the threat of invasion can never be fully eradicated. Or, to put this another way, the Other is located and defined as geographically removed and simultaneously internalized as a way of defining the nation *and* a potential threat to national identity.

This chapter moves beyond Gothic texts from England or the United States that identify the monstrous Other as located in, or emanating from, the American tropics. In the American tropics, there is a long tradition of figures associated with Gothic—tyrannical villains, ghosts, blood-sucking cannibals, the undead—that move across geographic and national borders as well as historical periods. This is not to say that these figures are static, for they shift and change according to various historical or cultural contexts within the American tropics. But it is significant that these Gothic figures travel across the region in conjunction with the movements of people and the transnational flows of cultural production disseminated in oral narratives, novels, films, TV, visual culture and new media. Thus, it is important to reflect on how tropical Gothic in the Americas alters in relation to migrations or displacements that can, in some cases, engender social dislocations, cultural changes, traveling ideas and narrative shifts. Such movements across regions can help us to reflect historically on the pressure of transnational passages (slavery, colonization, neo-colonialism, etc.) and how gothic narratives have migrated and transformed aesthetic, ideological and political landscapes. Mapping these narrative movements in the unique geographical place of the American tropics offers insights into how different Gothic tropes intersect and overlap in a region where transnationalism, multiculturalism, syncretism and mongrelization have had a profound influence on cultural production.

Hybrids, Mongrels, Cannibals

In his short story 'Monstro', the Dominican-American writer Junot Díaz depicts an apocalyptic scenario wherein the people of Hispaniola are threatened by a mysterious disease called 'La Negrura' (The Darkness). The disease portends global disaster as the unnamed narrator describes, in retrospect, the spread of a black mold that grows on its 'viktims'. As the virus spreads, the infected—referred to as 'the Possessed'—lose cognition and, in a zombified state, come together to form large crowds before violently attacking the uninfected population. In his essay 'Apocalypse' (2011) Diaz comes to terms with what the Haitian earthquake 'revealed [...] about Haiti, our world, and even our future'. 'Monstro' explores how catastrophe generates profits for some and death for others, particularly in the wake of ineffective disaster responses from a global politico-economic Empire that has no interest in empowering the islands of the Caribbean archipelago. At the end of the story, the narrator and the other protagonists travel to the border that separates Haiti from the Dominican Republic. Their intention is to photograph the giant cannibal-zombies that are conquering the island in order to document how the world they knew, or thought they knew, has ended.

The cannibal and the zombie are not foreign to writing from or about the American tropics. Peter Hulme shows how European narratives of pre-Columbian America included cannibalism as a way of marking 'the world beyond European knowledge' and registering a horror that would fuel a 'civilizing mission' (3). Likewise, Anne Schroder and others have tracked how the Caribbean zombie has migrated to the U.S. and become a popular creature in Gothic film, TV and fiction. Schroder reads some of these texts as depicting the lurid figure of the U.S. zombie as historically linked to the Afro-Caribbean bogeyman (in films like Victor Halperin's 1932 *White Zombie* and Jacques Tourneur's 1943 *I Walked with a Zombie*). She argues that the depiction of the American tropics—specifically the Caribbean—in these films portrays this as a place outside 'modernity', emancipation or sovereignty (9–20). The shift from the Afro-Caribbean zombie to the U.S. zombie is clear: in Caribbean folklore, people are scared of becoming zombies, whereas in U.S. narratives people are scared of zombies. This shift is significant because it maps the movement from the zombie as victim (Caribbean) to the zombie as an aggressive and terrifying monster who consumes human flesh (U.S.). In Haitian folklore, for instance, zombies do not physically threaten people; rather, the threat comes from the voduon practice whereby the sorcerer (master) subjugates the individual by robbing the victim of free will, language and cognition. The zombie is enslaved.

'Monstro' moves fluidly from the zombie as a symbol of Caribbean slavery to the U.S. zombie of B-movie schlock. Its many references to other texts and narratives include appropriations and rejections of appropriations through transnational contexts and the mixture of globalized popular genres from Gothic-horror to sci-fi to humor-lite. This does not elide the Hispaniola context: the characters are rooted to the place even while they participate in a cosmopolitan position of privilege, which enables them to move seamlessly between Haiti, the Dominican Republic and the United States. Gothic aesthetics are used to deal with socio-political contexts in order to articulate concerns about a re-incursion of barbarism both as a manifestation of life on the island and a by-product of the hyper-capitalist Empire that faces self-destruction in the apocalypse. The story, then, draws on the various tropes of zombies and cannibals to highlight the value of life and the struggles for survival. 'The metaphors that genres have established (mostly off the back of our experiences as people of color: the eternal other)', says Díaz in an interview with Edwidge Danticat, 'can be reclaimed and subverted and expanded in useful ways that help clarify and immediateize our own histories, if only for ourselves' (Danticat 4).

The tropical Gothic of 'Monstro' is part of a varied and articulated process based on the palimpsest of cross-references to engender a mongrel text. This entails transcultural affiliations that exude ambiguity: the text is in a way doubly undecidable because it exposes the effects of numerous identifications that cannot simply be understood in the dualities and mergers associated with hybridity. In other words, it would be reductive to situate the text in a reading practice informed by hybridity wherein two different elements are combined to form something new through that hyphenated and now overdetermined word 'cross-fertilization'. Even to speak of hybridity as an adjective—the Caribbean's hybrid post-conquest culture—is inadequate because it implies an originality or uniqueness that erases the mixed characters of all cultures, suggesting that a 'pure' and 'untainted' culture might exist outside of an imaginary nation, region or place. A more nuanced way of reading the tropical Gothic text is in terms of mongrelization. This is not to invoke the derogatory meaning of 'mongrel' as a variation of that which is not a genuine or inferior thing of dubious origin (as in 'the architecture was a kind of bastard suggesting Gothic but to true Gothic'). Nor does it refer to a text that deviates from a norm or standard. Rather, it calls attention to the problematic readings of texts in search of the 'genuine', the 'norm' or the 'origin'. The mongrel text is a multiply constituted work, as every text is, but it also includes an unsettled negotiation that cannot be easily resolved. In its crossing of different types, the mongrel text has no definable type. This is the 'real' mongrel text: the *mongreal*.

Díaz's cannibals are mongrels. They are of course real. We have no doubt. After all, 'the Possessed' fly into what the narrator describes as a 'berserk murderous blood rage. No pleading with the killers or backing them down; they just kept coming and coming, even when you pointed a gauss gun at them, stopped only when they were killed'. Even after 'The Detonation Event' that is meant to contain the outbreak, there are 'forty-foot-tall cannibal motherfuckers running loose on the Island'. Yes, they are all too real. But as a mongrel text, these zombie-cannibals also encode the text with the metaphor of cultural cannibalism and tropicália. In this context, cannibalism is appropriated as an anti-colonist project for critiquing, and at times absorbing, transcultural affiliations born out of the power dynamics of expansionist imperial politics. Here, the trope of cannibalism is read as a postcolonial reclamation of power wherein the colonized group uses agency to subvert the power of colonizers. Although the postcolonial project is questioned by the representation of contemporary forms of Empire in Díaz's story, the paradigm of cultural cannibalism has a tropical trajectory that can be found at least as early as 1928 in 'Manifesto Antropófago' ['The Cannibal Manifesto'] by the Brazilian modernist poet Oswald de Andrade. In this witty text, Oswald articulates a positive re-evaluation of the cannibal idea as a cultural norm that tries to address European conquest, postcolonial politics, indigeneity and the complexities of attempting to construct a Brazilian national culture. Cannibalizing a Dada publication of two small press issues, *Cannibale* (1920), Oswald's playful cultural cannibalism challenges the dualities of, among other things, modern/primitive, genuine/derivative, normal/abnormal to appropriate the colonizing European inscription of the Americas—particularly the American tropics—as a barbarous land of monstrous creatures in need of civilization. Oswald's cannibalization of European modernism, Rousseau, Montaigne and Shakespeare ('Tupi, or not tupi that is the question') is an eating of Europe without the ingestion: he is not what he eats; he is not a blurry copy of a European poet. His proposal is to ingest the European cultural legacy and digest it under the form of Brazilian art. He is the devourer *and* the mongrel; he takes what he can get wherever he can get it: 'Só me interessa o que não é meu. Lei do homem. Lei do antropófago' [I am only interested in what's not mine. The law of men. The law of the cannibal.]

Seeing this from a different perspective, the Haitian zombie has been 'cannibalized' by American Gothic-horror cinema to create a monstrous figure that is conflated with that other 'savage' stereotype, the cannibal. Indeed, by the time the zombie flows into the North Atlantic consciousness, the cannibal already exists as a shadowy, yet powerfully evocative figure, of Otherness on the periphery of 'civilization'. The zombie takes on the colonial features ascribed to the cannibal in the popular imaginary of the colonial powers wherein conquest narratives have, at least since the Early Modern period, linked the 'Native' to the flesh-eating cannibal. As zombiedom spreads, the 'living dead' become bestial hordes ravening to devour human flesh; or as the critic Steve Beard put it, films by George Romero and his contemporaries were 'responsible for the familiar incarnation of the zombie as a ghoulish cannibal', for giving the figure 'extra bite' (Beard 30–31; Warner 357–68).

The mongrelization of the zombie is illustrated through a reading of Sarah Juliet Lauro and Karen Embry's 'Zombie Manifesto' (2008), which highlights a surprising flexibility and versatility in the dense and multiple layers of signification that have accrued to the figure of the zombie through its history of varied usage. After all, Lauro and Embry conjure a genealogy of zombie narratives from the Haitian *zombi* to the North American *zombie* to an emerging posthuman *zombii*. The Haitian zombie that was reconfigured as the U.S. cinematic zombie was in its Caribbean form 'a somnambulistic slave singly raised from the dead' but has now become 'evil, contagious, and plural' in its various North Atlantic screen manifestations (88). The very idea of a 'zombie manifesto' is absurd and, like all manifestos since Marx, it must be read with at least a touch of irony. If zombies lack agency and consciousness, how can this category of the undead be reconciled with the kinds of political, ethical or artistic principles that are proclaimed through the genre of a manifesto? This question addresses a conceptual instability at the core of our understanding of zombies. Throughout Lauro and Embry's classification of various zombie figures and contexts, they move between the interwoven categories of zombification as an actual state and as a figurative description of specific kinds of (non)subjectivity. Drawing on Derridean discourse, they view the zombie as an 'ontic/hauntic object'—a definition that succinctly articulates the conjunction and easy slippage between material and abstract notions of the zombie-as-mongrel (86; note 6, 86).

Any cartography of tropical Gothic must take place in relation to migrations and displacements that have, in some cases, engendered social dislocations, cultural changes, traveling ideas and narrative shifts. In his mapping of Gothic, David Punter identifies the nature of Gothic as a 'para-site' that is related to various migrations. He writes,

> Gothic exists in relation to mainstream culture in the same way as a parasite does to its host, and [...] Gothic writing can often be seen as a perversion of other forms, albeit a perversion which, as perversions do, serves to demonstrate precisely the inescapability of the perverse in the very ground of being. But I also mean to suggest that it is, in fact, impossible to see this relation as merely one-way: the parasite supports the host as much as vice versa, as the paradigmatic daylight world survives only in its infolding of the spectral world of desire. (3)

Here, site-specificity and Gothic para-sites suggest a series of deterritorializations that can help us to reflect historically on the pressure of monumental transnationalist shifts (economically, politically, geographically) and how Gothic narratives have migrated and transformed aesthetic, ideological and political landscapes. Mapping these movements in the unique historical geography of the American Tropics offers insights into how different Gothic narratives intersect and overlap. In addition, such migrations and displacements offer myriad dislocated sites of contestation to the hegemonic, homogenizing forces of conquest, colonization and contemporary forms of Empire. These movements can help us rethink the rubrics of nation and narration, nationalism and mongrelization, while refiguring the relations of citizens across national borders and languages in a specific region.

Transfers, Translations, Circulations

A key way of mapping Tropical Gothic is in relation to the various historical, economic and material processes associated with the transnational flow of culture that began when the first eighteenth-century European Gothic novels were disseminated in the Americas (Vasconcelos). This transfer, which sometimes included a complicated set of cultural and linguistic translations, is a starting point for reflecting upon new paradigms in the field of Gothic studies. The critical incorporation of transfers that take place as a result of European imperial projects in the Americas entails the rejection of a mononational paradigm but also, and more particularly, the rejection of a monolingual framework that has so powerfully influenced and sustained readings of Gothic in Anglophone institutions. As a way of avoiding this pitfall, Sandra Guardini Vasconcelos demonstrates how, after the 1821 suspension of censorship in Brazil, the free circulation of books, magazines and newspapers in the bookshops, libraries and circulating libraries of Rio de Janeiro included English Gothic novels by Walpole, Radcliffe, Lewis and others. The circulation of these novels, along with other novels written in French or Portuguese, offered significant and influential models for the rise of the Brazilian novel in the latter half of the nineteenth century (212–20). Following Vasconcelos, there must be a critical response to a significant set of questions arising out of Glennis Byron's work on globalgothic. How can Gothic studies be planetary if it is monolingual, if it operates within the *lingua franca* of any given era, if it reproduces the linguistic hegemonies of modernity's imperial legacies, or if it remains contained within the confines of global English today (Introduction 2)? Recently, scholars have begun to address this question; what is at stake here is a transnational reconceptualization of Gothic that takes into account the processes of transfer, cultural and linguistic translation and the way Gothic texts from the eighteenth century to the present have generated the production, reproduction and circulation of Gothic forms and traditions in various geographical locations.[2]

The concept of 'circulation', rather than mere transfer, expands centripetally toward a genuine understanding of the dissemination of Gothic in the Americas by expanding emphasis on the transference of texts from one place to another and, in some cases, from one language to another. This then opens up reading possibilities that allow for nuanced considerations of the mongrelization and creolization of cultural practices over a vast range of major and 'minor' literatures, cinemas and visual cultures, as well as big-budget videogames, TV series and films. The concept of 'circulation' as used by the cultural anthropologists Benjamin Lee and Edward LiPuma in 'Cultures of Circulation: The Imaginations of Modernity' (2002) is particularly helpful for conceiving of the process of circulation as a 'constitutive act' in the generation, dissemination and interpretation of cultural forms (192). Following their formulation, circulation is not simply a form of exchange that transmits meaning. Rather, it is a key process in the flow of capital within an Empire—global capitalism or the European colonial project that formed the basis for contemporary forms of globalization—that carries with it the seeds of its own destruction. They conceive of the 'cultures of circulation' as a performative and constitutive process that is 'created by the interactions between specific types of circulating forms and the interpretive communities built around them' (192). Circulation, then, acts as a means by which Gothic moves through the constitutive and performative practices related to cultural and linguistic translations to generate various forms of transfers that articulate the circulation of Gothic in the American tropics and articulate a space of mediation between different national traditions, languages and cultures.

The transnational movement of Gothic is grounded in circulations that relate to the processes of cultural translations. In the specific location of the American tropics, the transatlantic transfer and circulation of Gothic has always been caught up in the cultural encounter that was engendered through the continued history of colonization and European imperialist projects. Yet Gothic can be said to move intelligibly (rather than just physically) from one cultural space to another only in a state of translation and, by extension, dynamic transfiguration of Gothic across circulatory matrices. One must also take into account the materiality (rather than just the meaning) of Gothic that acknowledges transatlantic flow as part of a culture that is moving and transformative as it touches down in various locations.

Latin American Gothic is particularly significant in the circulation of Gothic in the tropics. Alejandro Jodorowsky's *The Holy Mountain* (1973), for instance, includes the terrifying and bizarre images of soldiers shooting innocent people as birds fly from their bullet-hole wounds, Gothic-grotesque scenes such as the conquest of Mexico re-enacted by toads and a witch-doctor-alchemist who turns human feces into gold. These scenes combine to create the mélange of surreal, psycho-magical-realist and Gothic-grotesque images, enabling the viewer to image what would happen if Salvador Dali, Michelangelo Antonioni, David Cronenberg and George Romero had all dropped acid together and made a movie. Here, transatlantic transfers are evident: modernist European surrealism, 1970s psychedelic-pop, pseudo-spiritualism and a strand of the Gothic-grotesque that echoes the Southern U.S. Gothic of Carson McCullers and Flannery O'Connor. Likewise, Gustavo Hernández's *La casa muda* (*The Silent House,* 2010) includes a series of transfers wherein European Gothic imagers, particularly those often associated with the uncanny, are combined with Uruguayan oral storytelling. Set in a small village in Uruguay, a father and daughter are staying in a cottage they have been asked to repair; upon hearing a voice from the upper floor, the father ventures up the stairs to investigate, but he never returns. The uncanny plot and the Gothic space of the haunted house combine with art-house avant-garde, for Hernández asserts that the film was made in real time using one continuous 88-minute take. Finally, a particularly interesting example of Gothic circulation in Latin American cinema is Alejandro Brugués's *Juan de los Muertos* (*Juan of the Dead*, 2010). Billed as the first Cuban zombie film, *Jaun of the Dead* is of course a parody of Edgar Wright's *Shaun of the Dead* (2004), which is itself a parody of George Romero's *Dawn of the Dead* (1978). A parody of a parody, *Juan* is a mongrel text that mixes the genres of comedy, thriller, Gothic and horror to portray an apocalyptic Havana overrun by zombies identified by the Cuban authorities as dissidents funded by an aggressive imperialist Empire, the United States.

It would be wrong to ignore the local specificities of Latin American Gothic films, for each work is politically and socially located in a particular national and regional context. However, Latin American Gothic cinema often resides on the borders between diverse genres, filtering several non-naturalistic kinds of narrative (thriller, Sci-fi, fantasy, crime, etc.) while embracing parody by means of comedic techniques or aesthetic experimentation. This is partly due to the constitutive and performative circulations of Western European, North American and 'non-Western' Gothic texts in the region—texts that combine with specific contexts in Latin America to reveal a syncretism whereby the tropical Gothic work is linked to local histories of colonization, cosmopolitanism, multiculturalism and transnationalism. The syncretism here is thematic and formal. The transnational Gothic theme of cannibalism comes together with the reptilian re-enactment of the conquest of Mexico; the thematic intersection of the Gothic and the uncanny joins with Uruguayan folklore about a haunted house; the British parody of an iconic U.S. zombie outbreak movie is displaced and re-located in early twenty-first century Havana. These films include narrative strategies and cinematic techniques associated with both North Atlantic films and non-Western forms: spaces such as the Aztec pyramids become sites of bloody terror; rural Uruguayan cottages are transformed into mysteriously haunting places of suspense and fear. Revolution Square is overrun by zombies who must be killed (again) if the protagonists are to survive. It is always difficult—if not impossible—to identify an ideal (uncorrupted) genre, but in Latin American Gothic cinema the combination of genres calls attention to its 'impurity', cannibalization and mongrelization. Lacking a crystalized 'genre culture', Latin American filmmakers are often forced to bend to the demands of a foreign market, for full-fledged commercial and critical success is usually judged on acclaim within a North Atlantic context.

Trans-Gothic

A striking example of this is *Kilómetro 31* (2006), a Mexican Gothic-horror film directed by Rigoberto Castañeda. The film mixes the familiar North Atlantic Gothic tropes of doppelgangers, haunted houses, uncanny occurrences, mysterious disappearances and vengeful ghosts with the Mexican legend of The Crying Woman (La Llorona). Although there are variations on the legend, the basic story of La Llorona revolves around a beautiful woman, Maria, who drowns her children in a fit of madness before taking her own life in a river near Mexico City. In the afterlife, she is not permitted into heaven until she has found her children, so she is forced to wander the earth, trapped between life and death, searching in vain for her dead children and crying, *¡Ay, mis hijos!* (Oh, my children!). In some versions of the story, she haunts the rivers and lakes of Mexico; in other versions, she kidnaps wandering children who resemble her offspring. In *Kilómetro 31*, she is transformed from a tragic ghost into a monstrous figure who possesses her victims and is driven by murderous violence. 'The use of La Llorona', writes Glennis Byron in her reading of Castañeda's film, 'may, for example, reveal something about the ways in which a figure of folklore, here one common to Central and South America, is appropriated, commodified and turned from a regionally specific bogeywoman into a Gothic figure for an international audience' ('Global' 374–75).

Indeed, the plot of *Kilómetro 31* revolves around a car accident that leaves a young woman, Agata, in a coma. Her identical twin sister, Catalina, is haunted by her catatonic sibling and, through telepathy, believes Agata is screaming for help from her comatose state. She investigates the highway, goes to KM 31 where the accident occurred and discovers that a series of violent deaths have transpired at this location. She also finds that KM 31 is the site of mysterious disappearances and stories about poltergeists that stalk the highway and prey on unsuspecting travelers.

Much of the action and dialogue takes place in or around moving cars, and the focal point of the road is a 'trans' space where transportation, travel and movement exist between points of departure and arrival, thus mirroring the place between life and death inhabited by La Llorona and the comatose Agata. Thus, Gothic in *Kilómetro 31* does not just arise in a strange place—somewhere other, different, distant, marginal, mysterious—but also in a place of transition that confounds the distinction between here and there, this place and that other place. In several scenes, the solidity of the road is itself transitional: it transforms into the fluidic space of the river, thus conflating the road and river as forms of transportation and places of death. This is significant because it links the drowning figures of La Llorona folklore to a modern transportation system. But it is also noteworthy that Omar, Agata's boyfriend, discovers that those who built the road decided to pave over the Mixcoac River, diverting the water into Mexico City's extensive sewer system.

In the Gothic cartography of *Kilómetro 31*, the road and the river are mapped in relation to the subterranean tunnels under the city. The underground passages of the urban sewers hence echo the dark labyrinths found beneath castles or abbeys in eighteenth-century Gothic novels where the underworld is often a counter-site, a site of repression, contestation and inversion. This is not just the space of primal terrors buried in the unconscious or the psychodrama of an individual's search for enlightenment. It is also a place that represents the cumulative pressure related to a haunted history delineated by trauma, violence and death. In Castañeda's film, the buried passages—what lies beneath—are where the past has been suppressed and sent underground, literally covered by the asphalt and concrete of the modern metropolis. Like the doubling of the identical twins, the sewer system is a mirrored space, reflecting both the particular culture that created it and, more generally, a desire to face what has been suppressed.

Omar uncovers the history of the Mixcoac River by reading a map from Mexico's colonial period. The surface of the river, he finds, had long been diverted underground. By reading these maps, Omar calls attention to how the European mapping of Mexico functions as part of the symbolic and material appropriation and transformation of the land. The colonial map takes the place of all previous representations of the landscape and becomes the authoritative text that legitimizes Spanish power over the territory. Cartography is never a passive form of colonial administration; after all, before the place can be controlled, it must be categorized, conceptualized and comprehended. This engenders an abstraction of space where locality and proximity are subordinated to the lines of colonial property and the experience of the local person is pushed underground and subordinated to the surface effects of power through the abstract set of lines, boundaries and borders on the map. Behind these lines is a world of unspoken but evident possibilities, silences and absences so there is a divergence between what is read on the map and the gaps that remain unfilled, gaps left behind in the wake of the political agenda behind the mapping endeavor. 'Cartographic discourse is', writes Graham Huggan, 'characterized by the discrepancy between its authoritative status and its approximate function, a discrepancy that marks out the recognizable totality of the map as a manifestation of the desire for control rather than as an authenticating seal of coherence' (127).[3]

The superimposition of power by the colonial administration in the American tropics is partly achieved through epistemic violence wherein the local culture, belief systems, languages and narratives are eradicated or forced to become covert. Like other texts, the sway of the map is directed as much through its representational force as through its overt representations. The map is a significant symbol of power that moves from a mere record drawn by the European cartographer toward an image of the location permeated with a politically driven ontology. Questions thus arise about who produces knowledge and how those in power appropriate and condition the production of knowledge. This is significant because, like the river that has been physically pushed under the surface of the land, the history of La Llorona at KM 31 has been suppressed. Even the Mexican police officer, Martin, who has investigated more than 20 distressing crashes at this location, has no knowledge of the history of the river or its connection to local folklore. In fact, the suppressed history is only revealed when Catalina and Nuño visit the haunted house—El Encanto—in the wooded area adjacent to the road and meet an old woman, who is later revealed to be a ghost. The ghost casts the La Llorona players on the imperial stage; during the colonial period, she says, a Spanish officer arrived at a Mexican village by the Mixcoac River and saw a beautiful young woman. The Spaniard was, she continues, unable to have children with his wife, so he pursued the young Mexican woman, with whom he bore a child. When the young woman learned her lover was married, she threw herself and her child into the river; they both drowned, and the ghost of the child now wanders the river/road seeking out young women as the ghost of the mother cries out in the darkness.

This scene revolves around the return of that which has been supressed. The old woman cannot rest in peace; she returns to pass on the tale that has been lost in a modern era that has pushed the landscape and folklore underground in the ideological wake of progress and modernity. The colonial setting of her story is part of this paradigm: the history of conquest haunts the land and the 'settling' of Mexico by the Spanish and engenders an 'unsettled' postcolonial nation that is scarred by the traumatic history of physical and epistemic violence in the suppression or comprehensive eradication of people, communities, languages, cultures and belief systems. The ghost thus warns against a repetition of the past, for she tells her story to Catalina (a young Mexican woman) and her love interest, Nuño (a Spaniard living in Mexico). Within the symbolic logic of this scene, the specter is a sign of instability, insecurity and colonization; indeed, the ghost is a sign of the land itself and the land's history, signifying how the nation cannot escape the ghosts of colonization. The haunted house, El Ecanto, is a synecdoche for the familiar and homely nation that moves fluidly into the realm of the unfamiliar and the unhomely as the destabilization of the nation leads to the most terrifying and threatening ghosts that return to haunt the characters from the graves of the national plot. The effects of marginalization, ostracization and oppression haunt the history of this site with violent acts that refuse to be hidden.

Texts such as 'Monstro' and *Kilómetro 31* map a mongrel form that conjugates North Atlantic Gothic with specific locations in the American tropics. Simultaneously inside and outside of a North Atlantic Gothic tradition, these texts reveal a catalysis and cross-culturalism by confounding location and embracing movement, while also bearing witness to the transculturality within the power dynamics of Empire. Tropical gothic leads us away from problematic notions about 'purity' or 'authenticity' and toward the recognition that Gothic travels and then becomes cannibalized within specific locations. In this, North Atlantic Gothic conventions merge with the local folklore of the American tropics not as a 'progress' or an arrival but as a process, a continuous activity of becoming mongrel.

Notes

1. For other texts related to this strand of Gothic, see Lizabeth Paravisini-Gebert's 'Colonial and Postcolonial Gothic: The Caribbean' in *The Cambridge Companion to Gothic Fiction* edited by Jerrold Hogle (229–57).
2. For examples of criticism and scholarship pertinent to addressing Byron's question, see Angela Wright's *Britain, France and the Gothic, 1764–1820: The Import of Terror*; *Popular Revenants: The German Gothic and Its International Reception, 1800–2000* edited by Andrew Cusack; and *Transnational and Postcolonial Vampires: Dark Blood* edited by Tabish Khair and Johan Höglund.
3. According to the geographer J. B Harley, 'The cartographic processes by which power is enforced, reproduced, reinforced and stereotyped consist of both deliberate and "practical" acts of surveillance and less conscious cognitive adjustments by map-makers and map-users to dominant values and beliefs. The practical actions undertaken with maps: warfare, boundary making, propaganda, or the preservation of law and order, are documented throughout the history of maps. On the other hand, the undeclared processes of domination through maps are more subtle and elusive. These provide the "hidden rules" of cartographic discourse whose contours can be traced in the subliminal geometries, the silences, and the representational hierarchies of maps' (303).

Bibliography

Andrade, Oswald de. 'Manifesto Antropófago'. 1928. Accessed 23 May 2015. http://www.tanto.com.br/manifestoantropofago.htm. Online.

Beard, Steve. 'No Particular Place to Go'. *Sight and Sound* 3.4 (April 1993): 30–33. Print.

Byron, Glennis. 'Global Gothic'. *A New Companion to the Gothic*. Ed. Punter, David. Oxford: Blackwell, 2012. 369–78. Print.

———. Introduction. *Globalgothic*. Ed. Byron, Glennis. Manchester: Manchester University Press, 2013. 1–10. Print.

Castañeda, Rigoberto. Dir. *Kilómetro 31* Mexico: Yume Pictures, 2006.

Cusack, Andrew, and Barry Murnane. Eds. *Popular Revenants: The German Gothic and Its International Reception, 1800–2000*. London: Camden House, 2012. Print.

Danticat, Edwidge. 'Junot Díaz'. *Bomb 101* Fall 2007. Web. 12 June 2012. Online.

Díaz, Junot. 'Apocalypse: What Disasters Reveal'. *Boston Review* May/June 2011. Web. 10 June 2012. Online.

———. 'Monstro'. *The New Yorker* 4–11 June 2012. 107–18. Print.

Harley, J. B. 'Maps, Knowledge, Power'. *The Iconography of Landscape*. Ed. Cosgrove, Denis, and Stephen Daniels. Cambridge: Cambridge University Press, 1988. 277–303. Print.

Huggan, Graham. *Territorial Disputes: Maps and Mapping in Contemporary Canadian and Australian Fiction*. Toronto: Toronto University Press, 1994. Print.

Hulme, Peter. 'Introduction: The Cannibal Scene'. *Cannibalism and the Colonial World*. Ed. Barker, Francis, Peter Hulme and Margaret Iversen. Cambridge: Cambridge University Press, 1998. 1–38. Print.

Khair, Tabish, and Johan Höglund. Eds. *Transnational and Postcolonial Vampires: Dark Blood*. Basingstoke: Palgrave, 2012. Print.

Lauro, Sarah Juliet, and Karen Embry. 'A Zombie Manifesto: The Nonhuman Condition in the Era of Advanced Capitalism'. *Boundary* 2 (Spring, 2008): 85–108. Print.

Lee, Benjamin, and Edward LiPuma. 'Cultures of Circulation: The Imaginations of Modernity'. *Public Culture* 14.1 (2002): 191–213. Print.

Paravisini-Gebert, Lizabeth. 'Colonial and Postcolonial Gothic: The Caribbean'. *The Cambridge Companion to Gothic Fiction*. Ed. Hogle, Jerrold. Cambridge: Cambridge University Press, 2003. 229–57. Print.

Punter, David. 'Introduction: Of Apparitions'. *Spectral Readings: Toward a Gothic Geography*. Ed. Byron, Glennis and David Punter. Basingstoke: Palgrave, 1999. 1–10. Print.

Schroder, Anne. 'Zombie Fictions: Possession, Consumption and Zombification in Recent Caribbean and U.S. Literature'. PhD Dissertation. University of Essex, 2011. Print.

Vasconcelos, Sandra Guardini T. 'From the French or Not: Transatlantic Contributions to the Making of the Brazilian Novel'. In *Books between Europe and the Americas: Connections and Communities, 1620–1860*. Ed. Howsam, Leslie and James Raven. Basingstoke: Palgrave, 2011. 212–32. Print.

Warner, Marina. *Phantasmagoria: Spirit Visions, Metaphors, and Media into the Twenty-First Century*. Oxford: Oxford University Press, 2006. Print.

Wright, Angela. *Britain, France and the Gothic, 1764–1820: The Import of Terror*. Cambridge: Cambridge University Press, 2013. Print.

2 The Zombie Tropocalypse

Entropic (Digital) Disaster in the Hot Zone

Rune Graulund

Zombies are all over the place: 'zombies are everywhere, lurching in some places and running in others'; 'the zombie is ubiquitous in popular culture' (Riley 194; Lauro and Christie 1). The spread of the zombie has been so complete that it is often likened to a plague. As 'a figure of contagion', the zombie has prompted a feedback mechanism of 'repetition and recirculation' that has entered into a 'complex and interpenetrated genealogy of zombie films, television, comics, games, and literature' (Boluk and Lenz 3). Zombies feed off one another and spread the plague ever further so that no form of cultural expression has been left untouched by the contagion: 'Zombie fictions, along with many returns on screen, in games and graphic fiction, are on the rise', Fred Botting wrote in 2012 (25). In 2015 this observation seems like an understatement. Peak Zombie cannot be far off.

Botting has a valid point. Unlike a plague, which will die out or mutate as its reaches its zenith, zombies just keep on living and living and living. In the following, I track the continuous rise as well as the incessant repetition and recirculation of the zombie throughout the late twentieth and early twenty-first centuries. I do this in order to form the basis for a somewhat different argument than the typical classifications of the zombie as 'living dead', 'walking dead', or 'undead'. I do not seek to frame the spread of the zombie as a plague, a disease, a virus or some other life-threatening disaster that results in the death of countless people; rather, I suggest that, as a trope, the zombie is often represented as *a force of life*, not death. Indeed, the zombie is a figure of *excessive life*—life that is so profuse and so vibrant that it refuses to back off, to stay down and stay dead, regardless of how many times we shoot it down, cut it down to size, slash it, hack at it or burn it.

From this perspective, the zombie shares many characteristics with the tropical region from which it first originated. Accordingly, the tropical zombie is a fitting trope for reflecting on Gothic production in the cross-national context of 'the South' in the Americas. In what follows I engage with the history of the zombie as a figure that originated in a particular national and historical context (Haiti), as well as a figure that emerged from a broadly defined tropical region (the Caribbean). Yet the zombie has never been content to remain in this region. Therefore, I also trace the historical and geographical aspects of a move away from the zombie's tropical roots, turning it into a global phenomenon. In doing so, I do not seek to erase the zombie from the environment where it took its first tottering steps; instead, I seek to examine the various means of mediating the tropical zombie (film, television, computer games) and exploring what tropical zombies can tell us about the zombie apocalypse in general.

Haiti to Hollywood (and Beyond): From Tropical Reality to Global Monstrosity

The zombie is not new, nor is this the first zombie craze. 'Zombies existed long before they first shuffled their way across the silver screen', writes David Flint, a claim backed up by scores of academic articles and books published on the zombie in recent years (9). Indeed if we trace the zombie back to its embryonic form in African mythology prior to its transatlantic transferal to the Caribbean, the zombie is an ancient creature. However, the zombie as we know it came into being through an amalgam of African mythology and European colonial encounters. As Sarah Juliet Lauro and Karen Embry write in 'A Zombie Manifesto' (2008), one 'cannot take up the figure of the zombie without acknowledging its appropriation from Haitian folklore' (96). Consequently, a history of the zombie must recognize its original form (as specific to Haiti) and that 'the ideology connected to them [zombies] is directly linked to the political and social life of postcolonial Haiti [in that] it is a creature born of slavery, oppression, and capitalist hegemony' (Bishop 37).

I am not interested in giving a full history of the zombie here. However, it is important to note that, in the context of the American tropical gothic, the zombie is a unique monster. This so for three reasons: first, the zombie is, according to Kyle William Bishop, *geographically* distinct in that it is 'a fundamentally American creation' (12). Unlike the vampire, the werewolf or the ghost, the lineage of the zombie cannot be traced back to a Gothic European tradition. Second, the zombie is distinct in the Eurocentric canon of monsters because it is, from a temporal perspective, a relatively new phenomenon; in Europe and the US, this monster only came into being in the twentieth century. Third, the zombie is 'the only supernatural foe to have almost entirely skipped an initial literary manifestation' (Bishop 12–13). Whereas almost 'every vampire movie owes something of its mythology to Bram Stoker, and the reanimated dead have clear ties to Mary Shelley', the zombie 'has no germinal Gothic novel from which it stems, no primal narrative that established and codified its qualities or behaviors' (13).[1]

While the monstrous zombie is unique, it is also malleable. It can adapt to almost any situation; so much so, in fact, it is at risk of losing any *specific* meaning. Like many monsters, zombies 'are disturbing hybrids whose externally incoherent bodies resist attempts to include them in any systematic structuration' (Cohen 6). In revealing 'ways of becoming that are not known, not domesticated, and not appropriated by the existing discourses of power', monsters can help us decipher and understand the culture in which they are created (Levina and Bui 7). Yet the problem with the zombie is that there are now so many 'keys' available to it; the zombie can unlock many doors, leading us pretty much anywhere. Zombies have been claimed by academics working in a bewildering array of fields: international politics (Drezner), biopolitics (Mbembe), global capitalism (McNally), agribusiness (Newbury), computer science (Anitha), philosophy (Tanney), porn studies (Hyland and Shorey), ecology (Lauro), psychology (Mahoney), music and dance (Bruhm) and political activism (Zealand), to name just a few.

What we *can* say about the zombie is that it is infectious as well as highly adaptive. We see this most clearly expressed in the move from a local to a global environment. With the zombie, we witness the transferal of a deeply entrenched political and religious entity, a creature born from the particulars of 'rich religion of the Haitian traditional society' and, beyond Haiti, a ubiquitous 'metaphor' that can represent 'various social concerns' (Davis 11; Lauro and Embry 87). The zombie, once indigenous to the hot and sweltering tropics, now takes on any imaginable environment. From the arctic wastelands of *Dead Snow* (2009) to the desert of *El Desierto* (2014), from the swamps of *Swamp Zombie* (2005) to the forest of *Severed: Forests of the Dead* (2005), the cinematic zombie has spread far and wide since it first piqued Hollywood's interest at the beginning of the twentieth century. As seen in *Zombi 2* (1979) or *Last Days on Mars* (2013), even the abyss of the sea and the inhospitable void of space have been invaded by zombies. The zombie has thus shifted from the embodiment of the local political, religious and racial contexts of a postcolonial nation (Haiti) to a cypher for almost any imaginable subject in a rapidly globalizing and interconnected 'globalgothic' world (Byron 1–3; Botting and Edwards 11–15). This expansive evolutionary history has also expressed itself in a transfer from one specific medium—cinema—to a wide range of other media. Whether it is of a visual nature as in adverts, the textuality of fiction, the visual-textual nature of graphic novels or the audio-visual-interactive nature of computer games, 'zombies [have] resonated so pervasively in the popular imagination and media' that the tropical origin is often forgotten (Leverette and McIntosh iix). In the following, I tease out a limited selection of such media and a selection of texts in order to map the changing patterns of the tropical zombie from its inception to today.

Voodoo Visuals: Tropical Zombies in Film and Television

Once it migrates from the Caribbean to the U.S., the zombie enters the typical environments and haunts of the classic European gothic tradition (the graveyard, the ruin, the deserted countryside), as well as more modern manifestations of the contemporary uncanny (the city, the suburbs, the shopping mall). In its early cinematic manifestations, the zombie was still linked to the tropics: Victor Halperin's *White Zombie* (1932), 'the first zombie film', is set in Haitian locations like the plantation and the sugar cane mill, and the tropical landscape forms the geographical backdrop to the film

(McIntosh 4). Similarly, *Revolt of the Zombies* (1936), Halperin's second zombie film, revolves around the quest for a zombie recipe hidden in the humid swamps and jungles of Cambodia. Similarly, Jacques Tourneur's *I Walked with a Zombie* (1943), another early zombie film, is set on the Caribbean island of Saint Sebastian. Whether in Haiti (*White Zombie*), elsewhere in the Americas (*I Walked*) or in Asia (*Revolt*), all three of these films take place in a tropical setting. Unlike later manifestations of the zombie as 'undead', 'living dead', or 'walking dead', these films share an overarching vision of the zombie as not so much 'dead' as 'possessed' by some kind of malignant human intelligence, a belief that can be traced back directly to Haitian folklore. With the zombified figures acting as enslaved puppets (rather than cadavers brought back to life), they can also be potentially *re*turned to their previous selves with consciousness and cognition. Here, the turn of the zombie *trope* is not irrevocable.

After the initial push of zombies into Hollywood film, the cinematic zombie undergoes a hiatus in popularity. When it came back into vogue through George Romero's *Night of the Living Dead* (1968), 'the seminal work that forever transformed how zombies are portrayed', it was transplanted from its Caribbean setting (McIntosh 8). Romero's film is set in rural Pennsylvania, first in a graveyard, then in the countryside and finally in an abandoned farmhouse. In contrast to earlier zombie films, there was little left of the Haitian zombie, with no more than the mindless husks of the zombie body in Romero's film linking it to a Haitian context. Significantly, the *turn* experienced by the infected—the human-turned-zombie—is therefore represented by Romero as permanent. The zombies may 'look like people but behave like animals'; a state of affairs, and a state of being, from which they cannot return (Romero 1968).

In Lucio Fulci's *Zombi 2* (1979), a savvy attempt to capitalize on the success of *Night of the Living Dead*, the zombie's link to the tropics is not entirely erased. Set partly in New York but mainly on the fictional tropical island of Matool (actually St. Thomas, Virgin Islands), *Zombi 2* returns the zombie to its tropical home. Significantly, Fulci's zombies are not the possessed but still-living humans of Haitian folklore and early Hollywood films; instead, Fulci's zombies are supernatural monsters who do not feel pain and are only motivated by basic needs. This can be seen in an underwater battle between a zombie and a shark, a classic example of 'the silliness that fans and genre critics associate with the Italian zombie film' (O'Brien 63). The zombie, impervious to pain and fear, and with no need for oxygen, engages in hand-to-hand combat with the shark, temporarily getting the upper hand as he manages to bite off one of the shark's fins. The contest ends evenly, with the shark biting off the zombie's arm, at which point the zombie continues on his underwater journey.

The shark versus zombie scene is mainly introduced to pander to audience desire: the scene links Romero's bloodthirsty zombies to Steven Spielberg's equally ravenous shark in *Jaws* (1975). Still, Fulci returns the zombie to a tropical island setting where the contrasts between light and dark, verdant vegetation and rotting flesh, playful tourism and extremely graphic violence, are a clear departure from the bland landscape of Romero's rural Pennsylvania. In fact, Romero himself returns the zombie to the tropical setting in *Day of the Dead* (1985), the third instalment in his zombie series. In *Day*, Romero includes beaches, brightly lit cities and the fertile yet murky swamplands of tropical Florida.[2]

As with Fulci, it is unclear whether this return to the tropics is a reference to the zombie's historical connection to Haiti. It is likely that the location was chosen simply for the effect of the extreme contrast of the tropics as a place of fun, life and light, but also a place of death, despair, destruction and darkness. Regardless, the film's opening shot is a flyover of a lush, tropical landscape and a seemingly pleasant tropical city; by the film's conclusion, wherein the survivors of the zombie apocalypse find refuge on a deserted tropical island, the allusions to tropical gothic are therefore rife. Infested by the zombie horde, the otherwise inviting tropical landscape and cityscape turn out to be as menacing as a classic European gothic setting that is obscured by fog, shade and darkness.

Over the years, the tropical zombie has made forays into other visual media. Originally a graphic novel and later a computer game, *The Walking Dead* TV series (2010–) surprised the TV industry and audiences by becoming a mainstream hit. Once appealing solely to teenagers and a few twisted aficionados, *The Walking Dead* elevated the zombie to the status of family entertainment, thus making the violent dismemberment of rotting corpses as acceptable as courtroom dramas and romantic comedies. However, *The Walking Dead* does not carry the markers of the tropical zombie as overtly as *Day of the Dead* (palms, jungles, swamps) or *Zombi 2* (calypso beats, palms, beaches, nude bodies, sharks). Set in sub-tropical Atlanta and northern Georgia, the tropics here are less extreme but therefore, from the perspective of a mainland U.S. perspective, a more homely place. As in most Southern U.S. gothic, the environment offers a distinct visual experience from the dark and gloomy settings of traditional gothic cinema. The viewer is routinely treated to vistas of lushly opulent forests and fields, a vitalism that stands in stark contrast to not only the rotting hordes of undead but also the dark shadows of standard gothic.

Season Three of the series capitalizes on the Southern sub-tropical gothic setting. The protagonists, a ragged group of survivors, spend considerable time clearing out and reinforcing an old prison to turn it into a secure home. This homemaking is a matter of somewhat tedious routine, on occasion ruptured by scenes of combat wherein the characters are placed in high-risk scenarios. Some of the menial tasks would certainly be considered out of the ordinary; for instance, the killing and dismembering of countless zombies and the burning of the leftover bodies (and body parts) in bonfires. But the monotony, carried out on a daily basis, makes it prosaic and everyday despite its horrific nature. Similarly, the backbreaking toil of turning the soil of the prison's yard gestures to the South's troubled agrarian history. The plantation house is replaced by a modern high-security prison; the white overseers are replaced by the grey-skinned zombies and the black slaves by a multiracial mélange of voluntary workers. Yet the shadow of slavery continues to haunt this place. The prison setting automatically invokes images of surveillance, power and imprisonment. In addition, the planting, weeding and harvesting is carried out with hoes, scythes and spades; the human laborers do not have access to tractors, harvesters or plows. Therefore, the agricultural tools of Southern history haunt the zombie-infested land of the present. The problem of enforced labor is however most effectively evoked by the zombie hordes who watch over the surviving humans from outside the prison gates. Significantly, though, the zombie is not the slave who toils the soil (as in the Haitian context); in *The Walking Dead* it is the non-zombies (the not-slaves) who are forced into backbreaking labor from which they cannot hope to make a profit. Their only wage, the sole yield of the hundreds of hours invested in the drudgery of tending the field under the hot glare of the sun, is the chance to live another day. Accordingly, the lives, and the quality of life, of the human survivors are not very different from the zombies that are kept at bay.

Zombi 2, *Day of the Dead*, and *The Walking Dead* deal with geographically diverse settings (a fictional Caribbean island, Florida and Georgia). Yet they are all set in the same region: the hot zone of the American tropics. Romero's and Fulci's films foreground the contrast between light and dark, life and rot offered by the tropical gothic, but they are not so interested in the history and culture of the American tropical settings. By contrast, *The Walking Dead* is linked to a specifically Southern gothic tradition. It does not always invoke the tropical setting simply as an aesthetic backdrop. Nevertheless, because of the apocalyptic thrust of zombie narratives, the primary focus of all three texts is not the past but the present and the future; hence, the specificities of historical contexts are not always significant.[3]

Life, Flesh and Byte: Tropical Zombies in Computer Games

The twentieth-century U.S. invention of the zombie as a monstrous figure is a progeny of cinema. But the ubiquity of the zombie in twenty-first-century popular culture is not limited to one medium. Computer games have helped to proliferate the zombie, including the tropical zombie. Computer games often focus on aspects of zombie life and zombie killing that are of particular importance for the trope of the zombie as *excess life*. This trope is particularly prominent when the game is set in a tropical setting.

The zombie too has spread like a virus through the computer game industry. Because the zombie is part of a swarm, 'neither individuals nor living beings', the zombie is well suited to be a video-game foe that can be eradicated in droves (Botting, 'Love Your Zombie' 20). We see this illustrated, for instance, in *Plants and Zombies* (2009–), one of the best-selling game app franchises of recent years. As a so-called tower defense game, the game mechanics revolve around the placement of a range of defensive mechanisms so that a swarm of intruders—zombies—cannot invade the stronghold defended by the player. In this, the game mimics the fortress mentality of Romero's *Night of the Living Dead, Dawn of the Dead*, and *Day of the Dead*, wherein several human survivors attempt to fortify themselves in a house (*Night*), a mall (*Dawn*) and a military bunker (*Day*). In computer games, though, the gamer is actively in charge of keeping the zombies 'out' by erecting various fortifications and dispatching the zombies (usually in vast numbers) as they attempt to enter the fortified domain. We see a similar scenario expressed in the most popular video game genre: the first-person shooter. Indeed first-person shooter franchises like the *Call of Duty* games revolve around a specific formula: if bored, add zombies. By offering zombie scenarios as downloadable extra content to games that nominally deal with human villains (Nazis, terrorists, rogue state soldiers), the designers of the franchise routinely seek to breathe fresh (rotting?) life into games that might have otherwise gone stale.

There is something inherently ludic to the zombie; it so often acts as a faceless and therefore 'ideal enemy [which] invite[s] the player to blow them away without guilt or a second thought' (Krzywinska 153). This is also seen in survival horror games. While the stress of the survival horror game is placed on the survival of the player (not the eradication of an enemy), the successful survival horror game—such as *Resident Evil* (1996) or *State of Decay* (2013)—depict zombies as horrific figures that must be exterminated in numerous ways.[4] Here, zombies are slashed and hacked to pieces, burned and squashed, riddled with bullets and blown apart with explosives; the player is not faced with guilt or concern for the zombie's humanity, past or present, for it is 'a monster that can be killed guilt-free' (McIntosh 13).[5]

Dead Island (2011), *Dead Island: Riptide* (2013) and *Dead Rising 3* (2013) are part of a tradition of the zombie as excess, and faceless, life. All three games are set in the tropics, and their titles are testament to a recent turn toward tropical gothic in gaming. Moreover, by representing the trope of the tropics as a zone of excess life, *Dead Island, Dead Island: Riptide* and *Dead Rising 3* raise questions about life and death, living and killing; questions that go far beyond the concern of completing the games' tasks of surviving and escaping a zombie-infested tropics. Indeed, as Evan Calder Williams remarks in relation to cinema, 'zombie films are not about the living dead, at least not in any direct way. They are about *surplus-life*, the new logic of excessive existence: something has given us all too-much-life, an inability to properly die in a system that no longer knows where or when to quit' (92). The same can be said of the tropical zombie in computer games. In a tropical environment, where life is often perceived to be overwhelming, the latent tendency in the zombie-as-monster of having 'all-too-much-life' is foregrounded and highlighted. In the lush and bright tropical environment, the zombie's status as a faceless force of perversely persistent life is reinforced, to the degree that the encroaching vegetation and wildlife that threaten to occupy the remains of civilization in the zombie post-apocalypse are linked to the zombie horde.

Dead Rising 3 offers an illustrative example of this in its core design. The game designers assert that the game is the next evolutionary step in zombie gaming because of the sheer number of zombies that can be exterminated. According to the game's official website, *Dead Rising 3* offers 'more zombies than ever before. Get ready for a new generation of zombie thrills, where you'll find an overwhelmingly [sic] horde of blood thirsty zombies that never stop coming' (http://www.xbox.com/en-US/xbox-one/games/dead-rising-3#zombies). This is an assertion that holds true. As one reviewer of the game puts it, 'When I finally completed *Dead Rising 3*, the kill counter in the corner of my screen read 26,978 [and] that's a really big number. It's like killing one zombie per second for seven and a half hours. I have never seen this many zombies on screen at once in any game' (Stapleton n.pag.). Set in a sub-tropical location, the fictional city of Los Perdidos is a slightly futuristic version of contemporary Los Angeles. Here, the player's annihilation of thousands of zombies takes place against a backdrop of bright sunlight, palm trees and the iconic architecture of La-La Land. In fact, some of the game's promotional material includes a Facebook update by one of the earlier *Dead Rising* game protagonists, Frank West, describing how he was about to pack his belongings and head for 'a break in paradise'. This sense of a holiday mood, of taking 'a break' and 'having fun', is reiterated throughout the game in the eclectic and silly weaponry the player can use in the quest to escape the zombie-filled streets. In addition to the standard zombie-movie arsenal of axes, chainsaws, crowbars, baseball bats and other forms of potentially lethal household items, *Dead Rising 3* offers an impressive, sometimes ridiculous, array of articles used as zombie-killing implements, including teddy bears with machine guns, booby trapped buffet carts, and lethal 'super massagers' (an array of dildos jerry-rigged to a leaf blower). Killing zombies becomes a relaxing pastime, a 'break' from everyday life wherein the gamer can engage in extraordinary, often absurd, acts of violence. According to the reviewer cited above, 'I love the many ways in which they fall apart. You can chop them in half (horizontally or vertically!) blow off limbs and heads, and even take out chunks of torso. They put on quite a show. They're fun and easy to kill' (Stapleton n.pag.).

The tension between a 'fun' tropical holiday and a zombie-infested hell is also played up in *Dead Island* and its sequel *Dead Island: Riptide*. In both games, the story is set on a tropical island in a luxury resort, albeit one that is infested with zombies. Adopting the role as one of four characters, the player fights countless zombies in order to collect resources and survive long enough to complete a series of tasks that will allow the player to leave the island. The game is not significantly different from other games in the genre. Yet there is an interplay between, on the one hand, the verdant jungle full of life and the brightly lit beaches presented as luxuriously exotic and inviting and, on the other, the extremely graphic and violent acts of killing. In this,

Dead Island and *Dead Island: Riptide* offer interesting perspectives on the trope of the tropical zombie: the zombie is a source of life, not death, in the jungle of zombieland. That is, the zombie is a source of excess life that may be 'slow', as well as 'fairly easy to kill', but it is also a (life) force that cannot be stopped because it is 'tenacious and will never relent' (Paffenroth 5).

Dead Island, *Dead Island: Riptide*, and *Dead Rising 3* include coinciding, though ultimately rather different, versions of the zombie tropocalypse. The first version gives the gamer-tourist the option of going on a holiday of death, a trip to a tropical location that offers a dark yet pleasurable touristic site wherein the bright tropical holiday setting simultaneously enhances and diminishes the horror of the zombie's digital byte. The second version is less visible but nevertheless a dark undercurrent beneath the 'fun'; these games might also be read as 'dark vitalism' (Woodard 11). The portrayal of the horror arises out of a world that is not ruled by the highly organized order of human civilization but by primal urges and uncontrolled appetites. Many zombie computer games, regardless of their specific settings, perform the digital equivalent of a funfair shooting gallery, but *Dead Rising 3*, *Dead Island* and *Dead Island: Riptide* stress the dark vitalism of eradication and highlight the surplus of life in an extreme manner.

As a digital site of dark tourism, the virtual paradises of Los Perdidos and Banoi offer the gamer a playground wherein the act of exterminating and dismembering thousands of zombies provides a perverse pleasure: it can lead to satisfaction and relaxation in the face of an ever-increasing body count that will never end. In this, it is however important to ponder who exactly is enjoying the tropical zombie apocalypse as a getaway and a temporary release from the stress of 'our' daily lives. As Johan Höglund states in this volume, 'the game [*Dead Island*] ultimately imagines tropical tourism as a form of colonial consumption of the global, tropical south'. From a North American and European perspective, the tropical location is often seen to be a place one travels to temporarily, a place where the tourist can purchase and consume pleasures before returning to his everyday life 'back home'. However, in zombie games such as *Dead Island*, *Dead Island: Riptide*, and *Dead Rising 3*, the tropical environment is particularly effective for emphasizing the 'new logic of excessive existence' that is, according to Evan Calder Williams, the guiding paradigm of contemporary life. We are surrounded by a 'slow entropic loss of energy and profit' rather than a sudden and cataclysmic collapse (Williams 5).

Hot Disaster and the Eternal Return: Apocalyptic Visions and Entropic Tropes

Other monsters have threatened to take over the world, but the zombie comes the closest to achieving this goal. Paradoxically, though, zombies have no plan for world domination, no desire to topple governments, no need to eradicate humankind in order to exert their power. In his *Theories of International Politics and Zombies*, Daniel W. Drezner points out that, by comparison to zombies, 'there are far fewer narratives of vampires trying to take over the world' (Drezner 9). Zombies do not *try* to take over the world: they 'just do it', in an uncaring and incessant way. Indeed the problem with zombies, and the zombie apocalypse, is that they are not the *end* of the world. They might just *be* the world, in all its mindless, aimless, disordered being. From this perspective the (digital) zombie tropocalypse is consistent with narratives that present the contemporary world as in a chronic state of disaster and disorder. From Naomi Klein's *The Shock Doctrine: The Rise of Disaster Capitalism* (2007) to Zlavoj Žižek's *Living in the End Times* (2010) and Jared Diamond's *Collapse* (2005), there are many influential thinkers who see disaster, collapse and apocalypse as defining our age. Accordingly, one might ask, 'when the world as such cataclysmically manifests itself in the form of disaster, how do we interpret or give meaning to the world?' (Thacker 3). To put this another way, what happens when apocalyptic narratives become part of our everyday lives?

In *Writing the Apocalypse* (1993), Lois Parkinson Zamora makes a distinction between an 'apocalyptic' vision and an 'entropic' vision: 'The promise inherent in the apocalyptic vision, the radical transformation of old worlds into new, is absent in the entropic vision' (5). There is no 'promise' in the entropic vision because 'entropy posits the encroachment of chaos and sameness on all systems of organization and differentiation' (57). The entropic vision presents no swift and spectacular collapse at the end of which a new world order can emerge. Nor does the entropic vision stand out in the spectacular display of collapse found in apocalyptic narratives. This is particularly important for apocalyptic narratives set against a tropical backdrop; according to Zamora, 'the jungle eats at the city from the outside' and 'the jungle signals [...] the steady loss of organization in the civilizations upon which it relentlessly encroaches' (72, 71). As vines and creepers, critters and creatures overwhelm the civilization that has for a short time existed in the disturbingly verdant and unruly jungle, the law of entropy reasserts its rule. Eventually subsumed by the lumbering and unrelenting onslaught of excess life, the backdrop eventually merges with the foreground as all trace of human life is slowly erased.

The 'end' of the tropical zombie apocalypse can thus be written into a tradition of entropic disaster narratives that is different from apocalyptic visions. In the move from a geographically specific tropical location (Haiti) on to a generalized and often fictionalized hot zone of tropical excess (Matool, Banoi, Los Perdidos), we can gain insight into the process of a monstrous figure that has become one of, if not indeed *the*, most pervasive monster of our time. As the zombie has gone global, despite its ability to mutate into and take on many meanings, it has always signaled the 'steady loss of organization' that Zamora calls entropic, not apocalyptic. For in the apocalypse, we see a simultaneous *collapse* and the promise of a *renewal*. The promise of restoration and reorganization is rare in zombie films and zombie computer games.

The cinematic and ludic visions of the zombie tropocalypse are the most extreme example of a greater (tropical) trend around the world. From conquistadores like Hernán Cortés to Victorian explorers like Henry Morton Stanley and through to our own time, the tropics have repeatedly been portrayed as the space where the 'civilized' white (European) traveler encounters unruly and overabundant life forms that cannot be tamed, managed or eradicated. Joseph Conrad's *Heart of Darkness* (1899), Louis-Ferdinand Céline's *Journey to the End of the Night* (1932), Claude Levi-Strauss's *Tristes Tropique* (1955) and Francis Ford Coppola's *Apocalypse Now* (1979) illustrate the futility of trying to control and conquer the tropics. Physical violence (Conrad and Coppola), colonial attempts at management (Céline) and description and categorization (Levi-Strauss) fail in the face of the unruly entropic disorder of the tropics. It is no wonder, then, that zombie films and zombie computer games return to the tropics from where the zombie was born. In the move from a specific early-twentieth-century American context to a global twenty-first-century vision, the zombie tropocalypse is part of a much older tradition that associates the tropics with disorder but also the chaotic resilience of life at its most tenacious. For what are we left with when we strip the zombie trope to its core? A death and life cycle wherein life is eradicated but keeps coming (back), albeit in increasingly disorganized forms that gradually break down any kind of human order. The *trope* of the zombie apocalypse is, then, a trope that never 'turns' or ends. Rather, it is a regression to the basics of the second law of thermodynamics, which is also known as the law of entropy, according to which 'the world acts spontaneously to minimize potentials' (http://www.entropylaw.com/entropy2ndlaw.html).

Notes

1. The latter point is especially important for my argument. Spreading from its Haitian origin to Hollywood, early zombie classics like *White Zombie* (1932), *Revolt of the Zombies* (1936) and *I Walked with a Zombie* (1943) took their inspiration from a textual source, namely William Seabrook's study *The Magic Island* (1929). Seabrook's book, a travelogue of his trip to Haiti, was instrumental in bringing the zombie to the attention of Hollywood directors who were seeking out new forms of monstrosity. But it is important to note that the zombie is a monster that, in a Eurocentric context, began in the medium of film, not in literary texts.
2. Much of the film takes place underground, in a military bunker situated in the Everglades. Nevertheless, in the film's opening shot, as in its conclusion, where the survivors of the zombie apocalypse find refuge on a deserted tropical island, there are several allusions to a tropical strand of gothic.
3. For more on this distinction between the apocalypse itself and its aftermath, see Claire P. Curtis's *Postapocalyptic Fiction and the Social Contract* (1–16).
4. Survival horror is defined as games 'characterized by horror iconography (undead creatures, serial killers, darks settings, etc.), with a gameplay emphasis on surviving rather than on combat' and focus on the discovery and rationing of

resources (Andersen and Shimabukuro 88). While the player will dispatch hundreds, perhaps even thousands, of zombies in a game like *State of Decay*, there is a significant difference in terms of pacing, for the combat is neither constant, nor necessarily central, as it is in a first-person shooter game.

5. Viewing the zombie as absolute other has been, in recent years, countered by games like *The Last of Us* (2013) and the video game version of *The Walking Dead* (2012). The detailed and often ambiguous depictions of the human turning into a zombie are central to the mechanics of these games. The player is faced with ethical choices regarding what he considers to be humane acts in a world that has gone to seed (or rather rot). Nevertheless, in the survival horror game, zombies usually exist so they can be exterminated.

Bibliography

Andersen, Kara, and Karra Shimabukuro. '*Little Red Riding Hood's Zombie BBQ* and the European Game Industry.' *Transnational Horror across Visual Media: Fragmented Bodies*. Ed. Och, Dana, and Kirsten Strayer. New York: Routledge, 2014. 86–100. Print.

Anitha, G. 'Reliable Determination of Zombies Based on Entropy Variation.' *Journal of Computer Applications* 5 (10 February 2012): 257–60. Digital.

Bishop, Kyle William. *American Zombie Gothic: The Fall (and Rise) of the Walking Dead in Popular Culture*. Jefferson: McFarland Press, 2010. Print.

Boluk, Stephanie, and Wylie Lenz. 'Introduction: Generation Z, the Age of Apocalypse.' *Generation Zombie: Essays on the Living Dead in Modern Culture*. Eds. Boluk, Stephanie and Wylie Lenz. Jefferson: McFarland, 2011. 1–17. Print.

Botting, Fred. 'Love Your Zombie: Horror, Ethics, Excess.' *The Gothic in Contemporary Literature and Popular Culture*. Ed. Edwards, Justin D., and Agnieszka Monnet. New York: Routledge, 2012. 19–36. Print.

Botting, Fred. 'Globalzombie: From White Zombie to World War Z.' *Globalgothic*. Ed. Byron, Glennis. Manchester: Manchester UP, 2013. 188–201. Print.

Botting, Fred. *Gothic 2nd Edition*. New York: Routledge, 2014. Print.

Botting, Fred, and Justin D. Edwards. 'Theorising Globalgothic'. *Globalgothic*. Ed. Byron, Glennis. Manchester: Manchester UP, 2013. 11–24. Print.

Bruhm, Steven. 'Michael Jackson's Queer Funk.' *Queering the Gothic*. Ed. Smith, Andrew, and William Hughes. Manchester: Manchester UP, 2009. 158–76. Print.

Byron, Glennis. 'Introduction'. *Globalgothic*. Ed. Byron, Glennis. Manchester: Manchester UP, 2013. 1–10. Print.

Christie, Deborah, and Sarah Juliet Lauro. 'Introduction.' *Better off Dead: The Evolution of the Zombie as Post-Human*. Ed. Christie, Deborah, and Sarah Juliet Lauro. New York: Fordham UP, 2011. 1–4. Print.

Cohen, Jeffrey Jerome. 'Monster Culture (Seven Theses).' *Monster Theory: Reading Culture*. Ed. Cohen, Jeffrey Jerome. Minneapolis: University of Minnesota Press, 1996. 3–25. Print.

Curtis, Claire P. *Postapocalyptic Fiction and the Social Contract*. Lanham: Lexington Books, 2012. Print.

Darabont, Frank. *The Walking Dead*. AMC Studios, 2011–2014. 64 episodes. Television.

Davis, Wade. *The Serpent and the Rainbow: A Harvard Scientist's Astonishing Journey into the Secret Societies of Haitian Voodoo, Zombis, and Magic*. New York: Simon & Schuster, 1985. Print.

Dead Island. Techland, Deep Silver. 2011. Video game.

Dead Island: Riptide. Techland, Deep Silver. 2013. Video game.

Dead Rising 3. Capcom Vancouver, Microsoft Studios. 2013. Video game.

Diamond, Jared. *Collapse: How Societies Choose to Fail or Survive*. London: Penguin, 2006. Print.

Drezner, Daniel W. *Theories of International Politics and Zombies*. Princeton: Princeton UP, 2011. Print.

Flint, David. *Zombie Holocaust: How The Living Dead Devoured Pop Culture*. London: Plexus, 2009. Print.

Fulci, Lucio, dir. *Zombi 2*. Variety Film Production, 1979. 91 min. Film.

Halperin, Victor, dir. *White Zombie*. United Artists, 1932. 67 min. Film.

Halperin, Victor, dir. *Revolt of the Zombies*. Academy Pictures, 1936. 65 min. Film.

Hyland, Jeff, and Eric Shorey. "You Had Me at 'I'm Dead'': Porn, Horror, and the Fragmented Body. *Transnational Horror across Visual Media: Fragmented Bodies*. Ed. Och, Dana, and Kirsten Strayer. New York: Routledge, 2014. 176–90. Print.

Klein, Naomi. *The Shock Doctrine: The Rise of Disaster Capitalism*. New York: Picador, 2007. Print.

Krzywinska, Tanya. 'Zombies in Gamespace: Form, Context, and Meaning in Zombie-Based Video Games.' *Zombie Culture: Autopsies of the Living Dead*. Edited by Shawn McIntosh and Marc Leverette. Lanham: The Scarecrow Press, 2008. 153–68. Print.

Lauro, Sarah Juliet. 'The Eco-Zombie: Environmental Critique in Zombie Fiction' *Generation Zombie: Essays on the Living Dead in Modern Culture*. Ed. Boluk, Stephanie, and Wylie Lenz. Jefferson: McFarland, 2011. 54–66. Print.

Lauro, Sarah Juliet, and Karen Embry. 'A Zombie Manifesto: The Nonhuman Condition in the Era of Advanced Capitalism'. *Boundary* 2 (Spring, 2008): 85–108. Digital.

Leverette, Marc, and Shawn McIntosh. 'Giving the Living Dead Their Due'. *Zombie Culture: Autopsies of the Living Dead*. Ed. McIntosh, Shawn, and Marc Leverette. Lanham: The Scarecrow Press, 2008. vi-xiv. Print.

Levina, Marina, and Diem-My T. Bui. 'Introduction: Toward a Comprehensive Monster Theory in the 21st Century.' *Monster Culture in the 21st Century: A Reader*. Ed. Levina, Marina, and Diem-My T. Bui. London: Bloomsbury, 2013. 1–13. Print.

Mahoney, Phillip. 'Mass Psychology and the Analysis of the Zombie: From Suggestion to Contagion.' *Generation Zombie: Essays on the Living Dead in Modern Culture*. Ed. Boluk, Stephanie, and Wylie Lenz. Jefferson: McFarland, 2011. 113–29. Print.

Mbembe, Achille. 'Necropolitics.' *Public Culture* 15.1 (2003): 11–40. Digital.

McIntosh, Shawn. 'The Evolution of the Zombie: The Monster That Keeps Coming Back.' *Zombie Culture: Autopsies of the Living Dead*. Ed. McIntosh, Shawn, and Marc Leverette. Lanham: Scarecrow Press, 2008. 1–18. Print.

McNally, David. *Monsters of the Market: Zombies, Vampires and Global Capitalism*. Leiden: Brill, 2011. Print.

Newbury, Michael. 'Fast Zombie/Slow Zombie: Food Writing, Horror Movies, and Agribusiness Apocalypse.' *American Literary History* 24.1 (2012): 87–114. Digital.

O'Brien, Brad. 'Vita, Amore, e Morte—and Lots of Gore.' *Zombie Culture: Autopsies of the Living Dead*. Ed. McIntosh, Shawn, and Marc Leverette. Lanham: Scarecrow Press, 2008. 55–70. Print.

Paffenroth, Kim. *Gospel of the Living Dead: George Romero's Visions of Hell on Earth*. Waco: Baylor UP, 2006. Print.

Riley, Brendan. 'The E-Dead: Zombies in the Digital Age.' *Generation Zombie: Essays on the Living Dead in Modern Culture*. Ed. Boluk, Stephanie, and Wylie Lenz. Jefferson: McFarland, 2011. 194–205. Print.

Romero, George, dir. *Night of the Living Dead*. Image Ten, 1968. 96 min. Film.

Romero, George, dir. *Dawn of the Living Dead*. Laurel Group Inc., 1978. 118 min. Film.

Romero, George, dir. *Day of the Dead*. Dead Films, 1985. 100 min. Film.

Seabrook, William. *The Magic Island*. Emeryville: Marlowe & Company, 1989. Print.

Stapleton, Dan. 'High-Def Zombie Slaughter.' http://www.ign.com/articles/2014/09/04/dead-rising-3-apocalypse-edition-review. Accessed 12 March 2015.

Tanney, Julia. 'On the Conceptual, Psychological, and Moral Status of Zombies, Swamp-Beings, and Other 'Behaviourally Indistinguishable' Creatures.' *Philosophy and Phenomenological Research* 69.1 (2004): 173–86. Digital.

Thacker, Eugene. *In the Dust of this Planet*. Winchester: Zero Books, 2011. Print.

Tourneur, Jacques. *I Walked with a Zombie*. RKO Radio Pictures, 1943. 69 min. Film.

Williams, Evan Calder. *Combined and Uneven Apocalypse*. Winchester: Zero Books, 2010. Print.

Woodard, Ben. *Slime Dynamics*. Winchester: Zero Books, 2012. Print.

Zamora, Lois Parkinson. *Writing the Apocalypse: Historical Vision in Contemporary U.S. and Latin American Fiction*. Cambridge: Cambridge UP, 1993. Print.

Zealand, Christopher. 'The National Strategy for Zombie Containment: Myth Meets Activism in Post-9/11 America.' *Generation Zombie: Essays on the Living Dead in Modern Culture*. Ed. Boluk, Stephanie, and Wylie Lenz. Jefferson: McFarland, 2011. 231–47. Print.

Žižek, Zlavoj. *Living in the End Times*. London: Verso, 2010. Print.

3 'The Head-Quarters of Death'

Early Nineteenth-Century New Orleans as Gothic Nexus

Owen Robinson

New Orleans is a problematically Southern city famously in touch with its own mythology of death. It has played an important part in the history and culture of both the U.S. South and the Caribbean. It is increasingly acknowledged in scholarship as belonging to both and figuring crucially in the critical tendency to see the South and the Caribbean as parts of a wider 'extended Caribbean' or 'American tropics'. It shares with other sites in that wider region a rich and often discussed tradition of zombie imagery and mythology, tied in with its voodoo heritage. Similarly, vampires are widespread in New Orleans' popular literature. Perhaps inevitably, much of this feeds into commercialized and profitable forms, and the French Quarter is full of tourist-trapping voodoo shops and 'Haunted New Orleans' tours, while the city's cemeteries, its 'cities of the dead', remain among its greatest draws for visitors. As with many other facets of its past and present, there is a romantic exuberance to much of New Orleans' engagement with death and deathliness that sits in intriguing ways with the macabre, at times horrific subject matter.

So idiosyncratic is New Orleans, in Southern and other contexts, that it does not fit in easily with generic notions of 'Southern Gothic', or Southern literature and culture more generally, particularly as it developed in the twentieth century. Looking further back, however, enables us to see the gothic credentials of New Orleans and its surroundings figured in some intriguingly transnational ways and in some perhaps surprising sources. This essay will consider accounts of New Orleans and its surroundings written by European and American travelers and temporary residents for whom New Orleans was a stop on itineraries taking in other areas of the wider Caribbean. These pieces were written between the Louisiana Purchase of 1803 and the outbreak of the U.S. Civil War in 1861. Parallels and links with other Caribbean places are drawn regularly, and gothic elements are frequently identified in descriptions of topography, atmosphere and death with the awful presence of yellow fever in particular lending an air of horror mixed with willful denial and romantic escapism.

This essay will begin by examining the writings of a number of European travelers to the city in the early decades of the nineteenth century. These provide fascinating, often chilling depictions of the treacherous swamps and overwhelming sense of confusion and decay in and around the city, while also noting the fluctuations between isolation and communication with the outside world. In many cases, New Orleans is a stop on a route that includes travel throughout the Americas, and it is posited as the site of myriad influences, as well as a point of crucial contact between North America and the rest of the hemisphere, indeed the world. The allegiances, politics and intentions of these accounts are as varied as the city itself, but they all register New Orleans as a transitional, transnational place: if it has only recently become 'Southern', as such, its continuing status as a northern site in wider 'plantation America', with the transatlantic importance this implies, renders it a global South, indeed. In the remit and space here, I cannot of course present anything like a comprehensive survey of this material. My intention is to examine ways in which such texts, individually and collectively, introduce or develop gothic elements to the narrative of the city and its immediate and wider surroundings that lay the groundwork for the more famous and deliberately gothic literature that followed in the later nineteenth century and beyond.

The years and decades following the Louisiana Purchase are a particularly fascinating period in New Orleans' history, not least because they allow us to view the city as a focal point for the colonial and imperialist shifts and movements in the Americas in the nineteenth century. In them, crucially, we can also consider the changing role of the United States as it seeks to consolidate and expand its position—its existence, indeed—in the wider region as it approaches the internal but transnationally crucial trauma of the Civil War. Doreen Massey, in her writing on place, suggests that

> There is the specificity of place which derives from the fact that each place is the focus of a different *mixture* of wider and more local social relations. There is the fact that this very mixture together in one place may produce effects which would not have happened otherwise. And finally, all these relations interact with and take a further element of specificity from the accumulated history of a place, with that history itself imagined as the product of layer upon layer of different sets of linkages, both local and to the wider world. (70)

New Orleans, and indeed Louisiana, had already experienced the administration of France, from its foundation in 1718 to 1762, and Spain, which somewhat grudgingly held control from then until 1800, before the French fleetingly took over again before selling the entire vast territory to the youthful United States in the Louisiana Purchase of 1803. The relationships and tensions that this fairly intense turnover of identities produced in the early nineteenth century were perhaps most famously engaged with in the 1870s and '80s work of George Washington Cable, applying the perspective of the skilled post-Reconstruction era novelist and sketch-writer to the earlier, comparable period. But some of what Cable and his like charted later can already be seen, in some sometimes disconcerting ways, in the accounts of travelers and visitors to the city, writers coming from the United States and the wider Americas but also from various countries in Europe, not least France. These contribute intriguingly to the ongoing *narrative* of the city: as history, they are perhaps not the most reliable sources, but they nonetheless speak as important voices in the narrative construction of New Orleans. The writers' versions of the city are affected by their own national and political allegiances and attitudes, of course, but also by such factors as their direction of approach (from North or South, land or sea, river or lake) and their reasons for traveling (trade, leisure, migration, etc.). All of these points, as well as the stage of 'Americanization' the city is deemed to be in at a given point after the Purchase, crucially shape the city that is given to us, as well as its status in the Americas as a whole.

One of the earliest post-Purchase European travelers to write of his impressions of New Orleans was the French naturalist C. C. Robin, who traveled in Louisiana and the Caribbean extensively between 1802 and 1806, first arriving in New Orleans around the time of the Purchase. Robin, not to be confused with the more famous Abbé Robin, approached from the direction of Lake Pontchartrain, reaching the city via the Bayou St. John. Nowadays, this affords pleasant strolls in the vicinity of City Park but in 1803 meandered through a forbidding land,

> everywhere flooded by the water of the stream and lake; stagnant, or at best showing a current so slow as to be barely perceptible. Only here and there are places that are not flooded. These stagnant waters swarm with reptiles, especially alligators... They are shaded by tall trees which are, however, crowded and deformed and covered from their tops to the ends of their branches with a lugubrious covering of a plant parasite, a kind of greyish moss which hangs down in festoons up to seven feet long, which causes the branches to bend under their weight. This covering conceals most of the foliage and gives to these wild places a strange air of sadness. (30)

The sense of decay and ruination that surrounded the city is palpable in Robin's description, and it is as if the weary traveler was being warned away. The very land itself was treacherous, through scarcely being land at all, inundated as it perpetually is, the lack of firm foundation underfoot matched by the lack of definition in the trees above. The danger was real as well as sensory, the waters patrolled by fearsome beasts, the air and surroundings foul and unhealthy. To even reach New Orleans, then, Robin implies, one must be determined and not easily deterred. Robin goes on to say that as one further travels down the bayou, the land does eventually become inhabitable. This area between the lake and the old city is today heavily populated, the below-sea-level swamps having been drained and built upon during the twentieth century. Thus, these descriptions of treacherous, stagnant floodwaters cannot help but seem horribly prescient of the horrors of Hurricane Katrina—not least because many of these same trees (or their descendants), with their now cherished covering of 'Spanish moss', were felled by the storm: City Park alone lost over two thousand live oaks. Back in 1803, this sense of devastation continues as Robin reaches the city itself, what is now known as the French Quarter, to find the streets to be 'soaked', 'impassable' 'chasms' after three months of rain (31). Navigation is made no easier by the lack of street signs, the confusion arising from which Robin explicitly links into the period's political and demographic changes: the outgoing regime, he suggests, would have done well to bequeath such handy tools to 'a city so populous and so visited'. If this is, in part, the frustrated European visitor speaking, Robin also notes that this is a manifestation of collective unease directly arising from issues of the city's identity: 'Everyone thus suffered from the uncertainty of what would be the effects of the new order, and hardly dared to make the simplest assumptions. However, the city every day acquired new population, European Frenchmen, fugitives from San Domingo and Anglo-Americans' (31–2). This at once notes the particular quality of this moment of transition for the city and registers its ongoing relationship with the wider colonial movements of the region. The city may itself be struggling to orient itself to strange new times, but the effect on the outsider is more unsettling still. Having journeyed through a sodden, sinister wilderness, the effectively island city itself offers no comfort, no solidity. There is a paradox, perhaps, in Robin's noting how 'much-visited' such an evidently difficult-to-reach place is, a paradox that he does not address.

Similar tropes of portentous arrival and discovery of bustling internationalism are found in the narrative of Alex Mackay, a lawyer from London traveling to New Orleans in the mid-1840s. Mackay also arrives from the north, via Lake Pontchartrain, but by this time a fragile railway now operates between the lake and the expanding city:

> I was, at length, then, fairly in the delta of the Mississippi, and its aspect was as gloomy and repulsive as I had been prepared to find it. The tract, through which the railway led, was as flat as a bowling-green, but seemingly saturated with water. The road led straight through a dense growth of timber, such as is found in most of the American swamps, the cypress and cedar abounding on either side, with here and there some clumps of palmettos interspersed amongst them. As we proceeded at the rate of about twenty miles an hour, the tremulous ground seemed to quiver beneath our feet. The railway is short, but its construction must have been a work of no little difficulty. It was dusk ere we came in sight of the city, and seen from a little distance through the uncertain twilight, it looked like a dark and ponderous exhalation surging slowly from the swamps around it. (286)

Another grim approach, then, but by this much later stage mixed with admiration for the human (specifically U.S. American) incursion upon this unforgiving terrain. Mackay's language does much to emphasize the sensory effects of the approach: the ground 'quivers beneath our feet', and the distant New Orleans itself is figured as a somewhat sinister miasma breathed out from the swamps. Notwithstanding its ghostly aspect, this was actually a rather accurate identification of the city's relationship to the semi-ground upon which it is built: its founder Bienville struggled to wrest the original settlement from the swamp in 1718, and his successors have had effectively similar struggles ever since. The city has always been caught in the paradox of being a colonial and economic necessity in a near-impossible setting, both entirely of and effectively alien to the conditions of its site. Mackay goes on to depict a city that has thrived in the decades since it came under U.S. administration. Shifting his focus to a view from the Mississippi, he notes:

> In bending to the right, the river forms a species of bay, in the recess of which New Orleans is nestled. Nothing can be more imposing than its position, as you approach it by the stream. Almost the entire length of the noble amphitheatric front which it presents to you is in view; the rows of warehouses and other commercial establishments, which follow each other in rapid succession, extending for nearly three miles along the margin of the river. In front of these, and close to the quays, or to the Levee, as the spacious promenade dividing the city from the river is here called, are numerous vessels of all kinds, and bearing the flags of almost all nations. (288)

So far from the flooded chaos that Robin noted upon his arrival in a city confused as to its multinational identity back in 1803, New Orleans' aspect was now 'noble' and 'imposing'. It is interesting to note that the grandeur of the city is figured here in specifically commercial terms, which is perhaps in keeping with Mackay's regard for the railway's apparent triumph over the dismal swamps. Just as in Robin's account, the world is here in Mackay's opening impressions—but here its ships and flags are noted before its people. In each case, though, it is interesting to note that the grimness and difficulty of the traveler's arrival, or at least his direction of travel, is matched against the multitudes, and their ocean-going ships, who have arrived from the other direction with less evident trouble and ambiguity. A lack of fixity is still to the fore, however, as, so soon after becoming part of the United States, New Orleans' myriad otherness is thoroughly marked.

Two travelers approaching from the south rather than the north offer comparable but differently inflected first impressions. Like Robin and Mackay, Edouard de Montulé and Elisée Reclus come to Louisiana via the Gulf of Mexico. Whereas the two writers I've discussed already took the shortcut via Lake Pontchartrain to the north, Montulé in 1816–17 and Reclus in 1855, head up the Mississippi itself, retracing something like the journeys of the earliest European explorers in the region. While their respective descriptions of the terrain are in some ways similarly waterlogged and bleak, their southerly approach by the river—and as such implicitly from the sea and the wider Americas—involves another vital element. It either enabled or commented upon the importance of news and communication, the dialogic connection between New Orleans and the world to its south that is so vital to its survival, prosperity and identity. They also highlight the city's being prey to dangers that recognize no national boundaries. When the boat that Montulé is traveling on upriver from Balize is grounded some way to the south of the city, he explores his surroundings. On his return:

> I discovered that Mr. Stoward, the consignee of our boat, was aboard. He spoke French about as well as I spoke English; however, we understood each other well enough for him to invite me into his cabriolet. We left, then, around five o'clock for New-Orleans. At our starting point there was the beginning of a levee and a passable road. We stayed at a rather good inn, six or seven leagues from that city. There a corpulent man vigorously insisted in mumbling French, that I provide him news, since I had come from Jamaica; he urged me so strongly that I satisfied him.[1]

We don't find out what news he imparted, or whether it is truthful, but as expressed it seems enough to grant his passage. Whether political, commercial or personal—news of any sort could be highly valued in New Orleans—Montulé becomes important because of the asserted certainty, specifically because he 'recently came from Jamaica', of his ability to convey information from one of the other key Caribbean nodal points. This certainty is at odds with the 'faintness' of Europeans' impressions of New Orleans itself, according to Montulé—a point itself somewhat at odds with many contemporary New Orleanians' insistence on 'European' identity, at least in part to counteract the gradual 'Americanization' of the city following the Louisiana Purchase.

Writing some 40 years later, the Swiss anarchist and geographer Reclus recounts a somewhat related experience but, like Mackey's in relation to Robin's, bearing the marks of the gradual technologization of the region. Entering the watery world of the Gulf's meeting with the Mississippi, he describes how 'the cane rose twenty feet above my head, and only allowed a narrow view of the sky and … an electric telegraph wire':

> Science seems out of place in the wilderness of Louisiana, and this wire that mysteriously transmits thoughts seemed all the more strange in that it passes above these reeds, far from all cultivated fields, between stagnant marshes and a muddy river. Such is the march of civilisation in the United States: here, on soggy ground that is not even part of

> the continent yet, but only the residue of waves, the telegraph is the first work of humans. Before having disturbed this earth with pickax or plow, the American already has his thoughts circulating here—or at least his calculations. As soon as a ship arrives at Balize, this wire announces to the Orleanian merchants how many barrels of salt, immigrants, or bolts of cotton fabric are contained in the cargo. Rarely does an employee come to examine the condition of the wire's insulation. It sways amid the high stalks of cane, and so long as a speculator does not have it cut, it transmits the news quite well. Sometimes, wild cattle wandering through the thicket knock down the poles with their horns, but as long as electricity flows obediently through the wire, no one even thinks of putting them back up. These wandering cows belong to the *Islingues*, semi-barbaric people who are descended from the *Islenots* or *Canariotes* so numerous in Cuba and in the other Antilles. (41)

This wonderful passage, at once sardonic and full of wonderment, speaks to a number of crucial factors, not least the U.S. 'march of civilisation' otherwise known as manifest destiny. The apparent triumph of the United States is measured here by the fact that this is scarcely even a physical victory over both nature and other powers, but rather an intellectual one—or, perhaps, a commercial one. In a sense, this is a manifestation of the idea of America, as much as its ideas, as such, being transmitted over the 'wilderness' that is, of course, rendered wild no longer through being thus overlaid with talk. At the same time, the image of the telegraph registers that this cultural claim is not and cannot be made in isolation, that the march of U.S. civilization, however apparently dominant, and the prosperity and importance of New Orleans, was still contingent upon the rest of the world, on both human and natural terms. The wire's fragility is palpable in Reclus's vivid description, its integrity and condition registered entirely by the communication that passes along it and gives it meaning. Communication could be interrupted by self-interested 'speculators' or by cattle belonging to colonized people whose colonized forebears could be found in places with which the wire itself now so vitally enabled communication, through enabling efficient trade. But the balance of power with regard to information had shifted in the 40 years since Montulé's account: whereas he, a visiting European, was eagerly embraced as a conveyor of Caribbean tidings, Reclus now stands extraneously and watches the United States, and New Orleans specifically, manage the narrative for itself. Knowledge is power, indeed, and while its transmission might still be delicate in some ways, New Orleans evidently finds it good to talk.

Within the city, many travelers' accounts continue this often uncomfortable relationship between its inhospitable and unsettling nature and atmosphere and the perhaps paradoxical fact of its internationalism, its being a nexus in the wider American Tropics. Much attention is given to the unhealthy climate and atmosphere, and at times this is specifically linked to the city's population or certain groupings within it—almost always different from the writer's own demographic and probable target audience. Writing in 1851, the self-styled 'Manhattaner in New Orleans', A. Oakey Hall, tells us that 'One section of New Orleans, the First Municipality, is the old city, left to the tender mercies of the French and Creole population; narrow, dark, and dirty (meaning either their city or the people)' (35). On one level, this was not an untypical attitude toward New Orleans' Creole population from an 'American' perspective—such prejudice can often be found in the writings of 'American' New Orleanians as well as travelers from elsewhere in the U.S. But Hall's very explicit identification of what we now call the French Quarter with its majority population emphasizes the impression of a section that is unfamiliar and alien and perhaps dangerous to outsiders. Its 'narrowness' suggests both the claustrophobia-inducing streets and buildings and the asserted insularity of the implicitly foreign people within them, the gloom and squalor encapsulating both the physicality and the mentality of the place. We can find similar assertions of the Vieux Carré's otherness in the writings of European travelers, too, particularly, probably unsurprisingly, those not from a Francophone background. The British lawyer Alex Mackay, for instance, notwithstanding the generally positive and commercially oriented aspect of his account (which mostly focuses on its 'American' aspects), discusses the swampy ground, its deleterious effect on the built environment and 'dismal' effect this has on his mood (295–96) and the apparent architectural and demographic separation of the city's sections:

> The dividing line between them is Canal-street, a broad and spacious thoroughfare, lined throughout with trees, dividing the two quarters from each other, as Tottenham-court-road separates the east from the west in London. On one side of this line the aspect of the town is totally different from its aspect on the other… not only exhibiting a marked difference in architecture, but also a difference of race. You not only, in crossing Canal-street, seem to bound from one century into another, but you might also fancy that you had crossed the boundary line between two coterminous nations. (296–97)[2]

Again, then, the otherworldliness of the Creole city is emphasized in physical, racial and temporal terms, Mackay a stranger in a strange land: to cross Canal Street into the Vieux Carré is to journey into the past, a past here literally figured as a foreign country.

Travelers sometimes imbue some of New Orleans' best-known landmarks with a sense of dread and death—and not just the obvious candidates for such, like the fabled above-ground cemeteries, the 'cities of the dead', but also its centers of commerce and international exchange. Hall, for instance, describes the famous St. Charles Hotel in detail:

> The very left behind forgotten trunks, piled in a store room to the bar hard by, could tell a thousand wondrous tales. From yonder window

> has cast many a stranger his last look-upon busy life, and lain down on his pillow to die; thoughts of his far off home and expecting friends making doubly painful the last bitter hour. In this or that room the gambler lodger has laid his plots, or woven his web of cunning, which were to ruin or ensnare those for whom parental solicitude were vainly expended. These halls and corridors are full of echoes, and thronged with shadows; echoes of mirth; echoes of sorrow; shadows of human life; their original essence and substance, part of the past, and perhaps an injunction for the present, to remember. (15)

The alienation of the imagined dying 'stranger' is extreme. Dying in a residence that, however opulent, is transient by nature, he was separated from both the 'busy life' of this strange city, and the distant home—which could be anywhere, remembering New Orleans' port status—and the people there that defined him through association and expectation. This is a single, imaginatively constructed death, but it is universalized and enlarged by Hall to stand for the disturbingly estranged passing of 'many'. Given the danger represented by the purported plotting gamblers to the hotel's residents, even those who escaped lonely death were doomed to 'ensnarement' of a different kind by New Orleanian agents who preyed on the uninitiated outsider. And the 'wondrous tales' of all of these and 'a thousand' others 'could' be told by the forgotten luggage—could be, but weren't, as the cases and trunks stood mute, unopened, silently eloquent in their frustrated travels and tales, effectively unmarked or at least unread graves. Yet all these 'human lives, and the stories of them, were ongoing absent presences, haunting the famous hotel, the stories and their aftermath, however unregarded, continually unspooling across time.

The sense of death and decay, and the vexed relations between native and stranger, is sometimes figured in more ostensibly practical terms relating to New Orleans' appalling sanitary conditions. To give an illustrative example, Thomas Wharton, a British-born architect long resident in the United States, writing his journal in the 1850s, discusses the seemingly endless influx of new arrivals as being on a ride toward inevitable doom in a city seemingly falling apart under the pressures of its own filth and fever and civic weakness:

> Upwards of 2000 passengers from foreign ports have arrived within 2 days, and thousands are said to be waiting on the other side for some friendly Charon to ferry them over. And a fatal ferry boat it promises to be to many of them during the fervid months of the coming summer, with no Quarantine laws, no sanitary arrangements worth a straw, a feeble city government, an inefficient police, and an embarrassed city finance. The Lord help the unacclimated stranger, and the citizen too, whom business ties here for the summer. (25)

This mix of social criticism and portentous use of mythical horror registers the city's problems as both tangible and overwhelming, blending political comment with poetic license. In this imagining, the terror seemed inescapable. Even when reflecting on a rare reprieve from the punishing climate, Wharton could not help noting both the rarity of the relief and the feeling that even this is a trial of sorts:

> The fine breeze today is very refreshing, tho' being due north at noon, rather trying to thin southern blood. Months have passed without a breeze, save once or twice. Day by day and night by night, the same still, stagnant calm. No motion to carry off the gases of a populous, damp and almost tropical city. (145)

Recalling Mackay's external sense of New Orleans seeming a grim exhalation from the surrounding swamps, Wharton's view here from within the city was even bleaker. The combination of demography and oppressive humidity in this 'almost tropical city' creates a toxic stasis that seems to lock one in, physically and mentally, to a place that seems contrary to human existence. Even as its population increased inexorably, it was a place in part defined by its position and relation to other places in terms of trade and immigration but contrarily determined to isolate and close in upon itself. The sense of doom, again, seemed almost absolute.

In no way is this combination of physical, mental and spiritual foreboding stronger than with regard to yellow fever. Perhaps the most extreme example of these gothic-tinged descriptions and fantasies becoming horrific reality, yellow fever was an all-too-physical manifestation of the difficulties of New Orleans' geographical position and climate and had a profound effect on the mind and spirit of the city. Yellow fever was a very real horror that afflicted New Orleans from the late-eighteenth century until the early twentieth century, when the link to its spreading by mosquitoes was finally established. In that time, over 40,000 New Orleanians lost their lives to the disease, in epidemics that varied in frequency and ferocity: the very worst outbreak was in the summer of 1853, when some 10,000 people died—that is, 10 percent of the population. Even when it struck less fiercely, in terms of fatalities, the widespread fear and the awful manner in which the sufferers died or sometimes recovered, paralyze the city with dread and putrefying corpses and people of all ages succumbing to the hysteria, severe jaundice and black vomit that are among yellow fever's symptoms. The city's buildings would be marked with yellow cards to indicate fever therein, and during the early days of photography, grieving relatives would line up with their recently deceased loved ones to pose for memorial portraits. All in all, New Orleans' long nineteenth century was one gruesomely marked by Yellow Jack's rampages. Travelers to the city provide vivid descriptions and reflections that presage better-known accounts in the work of later writers like George Washington Cable, William Wells Brown, Lafcadio Hearn, Mark Twain, Baron Ludwig von Reizenstein and, more recently, Josh Russell.[3]

As previously noted, many of these travelers came to New Orleans as a stop in an itinerary that took them to various places in the Americas—particularly the tropical and sub-tropical Americas—arriving in the city either across the surrounding dismal swamps or via the tortuous and scarcely less forbidding Mississippi itself. As such, some came upon yellow fever in the city having already encountered it elsewhere in the wider Caribbean region. Edouard de Montulé, for instance, arrived in New Orleans having studiously and with some difficulty avoided the fever in his travels across the Caribbean and the Gulf of Mexico, scrapping plans to visit Martinique and Guadeloupe, and realizing that friends in Saint Thomas viewed him as a dead man walking as long as he stayed in this 'little city' in which 'twenty persons a day were dying' (37). While the causes of yellow fever were far away from discovery at this stage in the early nineteenth century, Montulé drew attention to the phenomenon of its being transported from colony to colony around the region: to travel here was to play a high-risk game of tag with Mister Jack. Other writers drew attention to the myriad rumors and whispers of the fever's arrival from elsewhere. The architect Benjamin Latrobe, for instance, wrote in a journal entry in 1919 that a vessel had arrived from Havana that was suspected to harbor yellow fever. A temporary quarantine was introduced, but not before two infected sailors were rumored to have reached the city before dying, thereby sparking a whispering campaign of fear and, indeed, a very real outbreak of the fever in the city (146). Nearly 40 years later, Thomas K. Wharton charted reports of outbreaks in various distant places, and told us that 'All eyes turn Eastward in expectation of exciting tidings by the next steamer ...' (84). Individually and collectively, such accounts contributed greatly to the sense of a city that was at once isolated by its treacherous surroundings and beset on all sides by fearful dangers, it being only an inevitable matter of time before the fever laid waste to New Orleans again. Like the hurricanes that terrorize and devastate the entire region of the American Tropics, yellow fever recognizes and is limited by no national borders, particularly in a region so lax with regard to quarantine. Wharton, writing as another epidemic looms in the summer of 1855, noted that:

> It is not unlikely that the confined hold of a vessel lying at the Levee might generate the disease during the summer months of this latitude even without communication with a sickly tropical port. Still a rigid quarantine would be of immense value to this city by excluding a vast amount of morbific influence which every summer flows freely into it, and aggravates the danger of a naturally unwholesome atmosphere. (88)

This, in combination with the disquiet provoked by the causes of the disease being unknown, undermined any sense of security brought about by now being part of the increasingly powerful United States: the transnational disease rendered nation effectively irrelevant, particularly when the nations concerned valued trade and profit over public health.

Within the city itself, the apprehension gradually mounted as the summer fever season approached. A. Oakey Hall described that, after a winter trying to forget or ignore the killer that was all too likely to strike again, 'when cloaks and thick coats disappear, and pedestrians contemptuously kick about the stray lumps of coal occasionally met with; and the suns of latter May crisp the tops of new carriages, discussions upon the fever are agitated' (66). Even the fear caused by the unknowable but inevitable outside threat was overshadowed by the accounts of conditions when the fever actually does strike, however. Numerous travelers and new or temporary residents provide grim litanies of the toll upon the city. Benjamin Latrobe, writing in 1819, charted the steadily increasing numbers of dead and sick, and the disease at times seemed omnipresent: 'I have had many opportunities of knowing correctly the symptoms of the disorder as they appear this year … Most of my workmen were attacked with different degrees of violence. The sober lived; the drunken died with few exceptions.' While this amateur prognosis was probably more reflective of personal inclination than medical evidence, this in itself is suggestive of the numerous narratives the fever provoked. Latrobe's account of the 1819 epidemic also gives vivid accounts of the sufferings of those who survived, writing of 'violent vomiting, of yellow, & green, & slimy matter. Pains in the head & back & limbs succeeded.' Sweats could be so violent that 'cloaths [*sic*] are soaked through & through' (148). Latrobe himself went on to suffer such symptoms, but was not so fortunate as those he discussed: he was to die from the fever the following year.

Wharton's New Orleans journal covers nine years (1853–1862), and he pays witness to several epidemics of varying severity during those years and his understanding as to who was most vulnerable varies likewise. At times, he notes that newcomers to the region were particularly susceptible: for instance, in 1858, he recounts a report from an acquaintance: 'Mr. Thiel, buried a servant yesterday of fever, she was a new comer from Germany and he says her death struggles were perfectly frightful' (48). The sense of New Orleans as a strange, unknowable place that presents strange, unknowable danger to the outsider is registered in chilling terms here. At other times, when the fever was at its most vicious and unforgiving, even such selectivity seems abandoned, and the verdict was that no one in New Orleans was safe. In 1858, Wharton noted that 'Creoles are no longer considered safe': in a city in which Creoles were considered the indigenous population (except by neighboring Native Americans, of course), such a verdict was an ominous marker of the fever's reach at such times (179).

Perhaps the most vivid accounts of yellow fever from the travelers and temporary residents of New Orleans that I have been discussing are by the 'Manhattaner', A. Oakey Hall. In part, this is because he was unabashed about his literary intentions and made clear that he had little interest in medical matters *per se*:

> I have no intention of boring the literary world with a diagnosis of the disease which accompanies cholera and plague in the catalogue so often pondered by nervous people. But having had an encounter with

> 'Yellow Jack,' I deem it not ungenerous upon my part to say a few things about him; especially as he is at times no unimportant sojourner of the Crescent City. (65)

Hall cites personal experience rather than medical expertise as his authority, although he is quick to qualify even this by noting that he was at a disadvantage during their encounter. 'Not that I know his birth and origin; not that I am in possession of full particulars regarding his nurture or education; not that I am intimately acquainted with his domestic habits; not that I have phrenologized him and discovered his most secret characteristics' (65–66). Hall is not the first to anthropomorphize the fever as 'Yellow Jack', and this name was not exclusive to New Orleans, but he did so very effectively in gothic terms. The Yellow Jack that Hall encountered and went on to portray is gallingly rootless and unknowable (or at least, at this stage, unknown), resisting attempts to read him or to pin him down—it was no easier to comprehend him than it was to keep him at bay. Yellow Jack is only identifiable through his victims: he himself had no physical form, and yet his physicality is appallingly visceral as realized in the afflicted.

In Hall's telling, Yellow Jack has sinister agents, too, in the form of Board of Health officials and incompetent or corrupt doctors, as well as the city's newspapers. The officials toured the city, profoundly affecting the city's mood depending on what they said or how they looked:

> The yearly members of the Board of Health become characters for ocular interest as they walk about the streets. Their nods and winks and various gestures are scrutinized with great care; and should any of them be suffering under dyspepsia or any other complaint productive of a long face and sour speech, an article on Yellow Fever is sure to get into the Gazettes, either editorially or by favor of some 'X. Y. Z.' correspondent. (67)

Mister Jack's reach manifests through the spreading of fear as much as through his death toll, and when a board member's disagreeable visage is translated into fever symptoms by the newspapers, the city is paralyzed accordingly. There is not escape from this facet of the terror. Even when the Board declares that the fever is present 'only sporadically' and therefore is not an epidemic, the citizens of New Orleans are lulled into a false sense of security (Hall also wryly reflects, 'Very fine logic all this, but one naturally asks what difference does it make whether one dies sporadically or otherwise!') (67). But when the Board members *do* use the word 'epidemic', New Orleans becomes a ghost town:

> Girod-street, and Julia-street, and the New Shell road, and Circus-street, and Rue de Conti are dotted through the day with hearses and carriages on their way to the Protestant Yard, or the Cypress Grove, or

> the Cemetery of St. Louis. An ominous looking cart stands at the door of the Charity Hospital. Physicians' gigs rattle around. The list of daily interments head [*sic*] the editorials in each gazette as being the most interesting item for home and interior subscribers. (68)

In a sense, then, the Board of Health and other health/death-oriented people become Yellow Jack's agents again, but this time in terms of terror. As Hall writes it, all it took is an official to utter one dread word. The streets would turn into death drives and the papers turn from irresponsible denial of fever—shamelessly favoring commercial interest over public safety, in trying to hide facts that might encourage business to leave the city—into frenzied organs of fear and panic. One might counter that the officials and journalists are rather damned if they do and damned if they don't, here, but in terms of imagery, Hall's narrative was compelling. The city's doctors also figured not as reassuringly healing presences, but rather as agents of doom: patients' recovery is as dependent upon their doctors' relationship with quack apothecaries as upon anything else. But really, as Hall describes it, recovery is largely a matter of luck, and the bodies nominally responsible for public health, treatment and information are corrupt agents of the dread figure that ruled the city.

Death pervades this water-bound, waterlogged city to such a degree that even the elements of respite are underwritten with it. Notwithstanding the inhospitable climate that Hall and others so often describe, he notes that even pleasant conditions are treacherous:

> That which renders the presence of yellow fever in the city, and its rod of power as laid upon patient backs, doubly disagreeable, is the almost invariable accompaniment of unsuspiciously fine weather; clear skies, and cooling night breezes. To have a pestilence brooding in the common summer weather of New Orleans, is like suffering a malicious drowning in the waters of Lake George, near its most romantic neighborhoods. (71)

This sense of elements of beauty, of reprieve, being covers for Yellow Jack's activities is echoed by Wharton, also writing in the 1850s:

> It was the loveliest of moonlights when we walked home and it was hard to persuade ourselves that such a radiant atmosphere should instinct with the seeds of death. The mortality by fever is still about 70 per day. Many, however, are strangers who persist in rushing to the city in quest of situations, which is simply suicide. (179; underlined in original)

Wharton and Hall's respective wonder and frustration at deceptive pleasure and self-deceptive commercialism is a further keys to understanding how

New Orleans came to be figured during these early-to-middle decades of the nineteenth century as, in the words of another traveler writing in 1831, Henry Tudor, 'the head-quarters of Death' (Kelman 91). The writings of these travelers and newly arrived residents offer a cumulative account of a city steeped in tangible elements of an extremely difficult time and place. They also did much to establish New Orleans as a place suffused with death and decay, gloomy desolation and deceptive beauty, the terrifying presence of deadly disease and its figurative and physical agents. This side of the city has become almost omnipresent in today's understanding of it, so popular is its particular twist on the gothic in Southern and American term. These earlier writers, however, while perhaps not deliberately seeking to infuse this fascinating city with gothic sensibility, effectively did so, all in the context of its conditional, fragile place in the wider hemispheric American scene.

Notes

1. See Edouard de Montulé, *Travels in America 1816–1817*, trans. Edward D. Seeber (Bloomington: Indiana UP, 1951). A much truncated contemporary translation is held in the Louisiana Collection at the Tulane Special Collections, published as E. Montule, *A Voyage to North America, and the West Indies, in 1817* (London: printed for Sir Richard Philips and Co., 1821). In terms of selection and the translation itself, this early version is inferior but nonetheless interesting in itself for registering the particular interests of contemporary British readers.
2. Joseph G. Tregle discusses how the model of Canal Street, as a strict dividing line between Creole and 'American' society in the decades following the Louisiana Purchase, offered both in contemporary accounts such as Norman's and in much other comment before and since, is essentially false, as there was actually a great deal of personal, economic and cultural interchange between the communities, and members of each lived on either side of this purported border (Joseph G. Tregle, Jr., 'Creoles and Americans,' in Arnold R. Hirsch and Joseph Logsdon (eds.), *Creole New Orleans: Race and Americanization* (Baton Rouge: Louisiana State University Press, 1992), 164–65).
3. I think in particular of Cable's *Dr. Sevier*, Brown's *Clotel*, Hearn's many newspaper articles of the 1870s and 1880s, Twain's *Life on the Mississippi*, Reizenstein's *The Mysteries of New Orleans* and Josh Russell's *Yellow Jack*, but there are many more examples. I have discussed traveler's accounts in relation to Russell's novel in Owen Robinson, "Magic Portraits Drawn by the Sun': New Orleans, Yellow Fever, and the sense(s) of death in Josh Russell's *Yellow Jack*,' in *Transatlantica*, 2001, issue 1, http://transatlantica.revues.org/5393.

Bibliography

Campanella, Richard. *Bienville's Dilemma: A Historical Geography of New Orleans*. Lafayette: Center for Louisiana Studies at the University of Louisiana, 2008. Print.

Cresswell, Tim. *Place: A Short Introduction*. Oxford: Blackwell, 2004. Print.

Hall, A. Oakey. *The Manhattaner in New Orleans; or, Phases of 'Crescent City' Life*. New York: J. S. Redfield; New Orleans: J. C. Morgan, 1851. Print.

Hirsch, Arnold R., and Joseph Logsdon, Eds. *Creole New Orleans: Race and Americanization*. Baton Rouge: Louisiana State University Press, 1992. Print.

Kelman, Ari. *A River and Its City: The Nature of Landscape in New Orleans*. Berkeley: University of California Press, 2006. Print.

Latrobe, Benjamin Henry Boneval. *Impressions Respecting New Orleans: Diary & Sketches, 1818–1820*. Ed. Wilson, Samuel, Jr. New York: Columbia University Press, 1951. Print.

Mackay, Alex. *The Western World; or, Travels in the United States in 1846–47: Exhibiting Them in their Latest Development Social, Political, and Industrial; Including a Chapter on California. With a New Map of the United States, Showing their Recent Acquisitions, and a Map of California*. 3 vols. London: Richard Bentley, 1849. Print

Massey, Doreen. 'A Global Sense of Place'. *Place: A Short Introduction*. Ed. Cresswell, Tim. Oxford: Blackwell, 2004. Print.

Montule, E. *A Voyage to North America, and the West Indies, in 1817*. London: printed for Sir Richard Philips and Co., 1821. Print.

Montulé, Edouard de. *Travels in America 1816–1817*. Trans. Seeber, Edward D. Bloomington: Indiana UP, 1951. Print.

Reclus, Elisée. *A Voyage to New Orleans: Anarchist Impressions of the Old South*. 1860. Trans and Ed. Clark, John, and Camille Martin. Thetford, VT: Glad Day Books, 2004. Print.

Robin, C. C. *Voyage to Louisiana, 1803–1805*. Abridged and Trans. Landry, Stuart O., Jr. New Orleans: Gretna, 1966. Print.

Robinson, Owen. "Magic Portraits Drawn by the Sun': New Orleans, Yellow Fever, and the Sense(s) of Death in Josh Russell's *Yellow Jack*.' *Transatlantica* (2001). http://transatlantica.revues.org/5393. Online.

Wharton, Thomas K. *Queen of the South: New Orleans, 1853–1862, the Journal of Thomas K. Wharton*. Ed. Wilson, Samuel, Jr., Patricia Brady and Lynn D. Adams. New Orleans: Historic New Orleans Collection, 1999. Print.

4 A 'Litany Seeking a Text'

The Specter of Conjure in the Sub-Tropical Southern Gothic

Elizabeth Rodriguez Fielder

On a Sunday evening in February 2012, the Infinite Theater of New York produced Tennessee Williams' *Orpheus Descending* in the Paris-Yates chapel on the campus of the University of Mississippi. Director Nick Potenzieri brought together the original main actors with local Mississippi cast members on this tour of Williams' home state, which was also the inspiration for many of Williams' plays including *Orpheus*. With an altar for a stage and a lack of audience in the pews, the chapel added an eerie ambience to an already somewhat surrealist play. Interrupting the expository action in the initial scene, the character referred to as the Conjure Man entered trembling and mumbling down the aisle, costumed in 'tattered garments ... fantastically bedizened with many talismans and good-luck charms of shell and bone and feather', true to Williams' original stage directions. He startled the audience made up of mostly academics and local senior citizens who—gathering from their expressions—probably assumed that a mentally unstable person had wandered onto campus looking for solace in the chapel. The setting served to heighten the action Williams wrote into the play: as the actors on stage playing churchgoing Delta ladies shrieked in horror, the all-white audience in the pews also reacted in shock when they saw a black man with 'cryptic signs in white paint' (Williams 301) on his face, holding a bone toward the altar. Time momentarily collapsed in Mississippi as the Conjure Man disrupted the all-white space in the chapel and unsettled its audience.

The scene in Mississippi dramatizes the ability for conjure to interrupt and destabilize community boundaries. This essay offers conjure as a device used by authors to create a passageway through which one gains access to an indefinable South—the sub-tropical region that amorphously straddles the U.S. South and the Caribbean. I use the term conjure to represent a multivalent network of folk traditions and practices that also go by voodoo, vodou, hoodoo, Obeah, root-working, juju and many other names that suggest different permutations and locations. In essence they all represent an alternative system of knowledge, what Leigh Anne Duck observes as 'a realm of difference that is not meant to be incorporated into the public sphere, but to be preserved as a kind of understanding which originates not from the center but from the margins of a community' (286–87). These unknown rituals and traditions stem from a circum-Atlantic community that reveals itself through signs along the literary and culture landscape of the Caribbean, South America and the U.S. South. Symbols of conjure intersect not only the black-white racial boundary in fictional geographies such as Williams' Two River County and William Faulkner's Yoknapatawpha County, but also the Southern political border of the United States to offer more global vision of the South. The modernist writers shared their vision of this porous border retroactively with another generation of authors in the 1970s and 1980s that include Ishmael Reed, Toni Cade Bambara, Toni Morrison, Erna Brodber, and Paule Marshall to name a few. They also used the gothic trope of conjure to create a 'geography jazz' in their fiction that would destabilize the boundaries of identity.[1]

The focus on conjure recalls not only African, but also Caribbean and U.S. Southern hybridized rituals and religions and thus shifts the perspective of U.S. literature and positions the Southern region as North (of the tropics). From this perspective, the South becomes a liminal space of cultural blending, a border region. New Orleans—as a place and a symbol of cultural confluence—lies at the epicenter of the sub-tropical region that is the Caribbean, the Gulf Coast and the U.S. South and extends beyond in all directions. Ishmael Reed embodies this cultural migration in 'Jes Grew', an ambiguous cultural movement with the power to 'end Civilization As We Know It' (*Shrovetide*, 3) and in his poem 'Neo-HooDoo Manifesto' where he gives the historical context that positions hoodoo as both present and hidden: 'the power of hoodoo challenged the stability of civil authority in New Orleans and was driven underground where to this day it flourishes in the Black ghettos throughout the country' (Reed, *Conjure* 20). *Conjure* reveals a hemispheric network that exposes the U.S. Southern border for what it really is: a fluid space, a mysterious archipelago that hybridizes water and land. Within this space, alternative cultures that express different systems of economy, identity, belief and medicine create a mythology around conjure. Despite a lack of full understanding provided by any of the authors, or even anthropologists such as Zora Neale Hurston, this mythology has been preserved as a 'consequence' of circum-Atlantic memory, as Joseph Roach observes, where 'the unspeakable cannot be rendered forever inexpressible' (4).[2] The inexpressible emerges on the page as uncanny or misunderstood signs and—like the Conjure Man—they disrupt text and evade authorial explanation.

The Southern gothic as literary trope invites misunderstanding of these unknown spaces signposted with mysterious, almost unreadable signs on the landscape. In Faulkner's 'Pantaloon in Black' the unreadable sign emerges as the circum-Atlantic ritual of decorating a grave with 'objects insignificant to sight but actually of a profound meaning and fatal to touch, which no white man could have read' (*Go Down Moses* 132). At other points in his fiction, he uses a hog bone to signify conjure, akin to the bone the Conjure Man waves at the audience and actors in *Orpheus*. By offering symbols rather than clear explanation, Faulkner employs what Jessica Adams defines as '[p]erformative language' that can 'play a crucial role in the assignment, representation, codification, and resistance of circum-Atlantic identities' (Adams et al. 9). Faulkner depends more on the motions and actions of the characters to convey what cannot be articulated through text so that characters in authority misread the signs of conjure, which mirrors Beulah's inability to understand the Conjure Man in *Orpheus*. The authors describe unknown landscapes and misunderstood symbols and thus repudiate some of their authorial knowledge. The power of conjure lies in its inability to be fully understood by authors and explained through text.

These literary representations challenge assumed perceptions of conjure folk traditions as something backward or autochthonous—the folk is ethereal, yet active within a contemporaneous geography and temporality. Ever evolving and hybridizing, conjure interrogates the process of community formation that seeks to categorize, separate and remain static, a process exemplified through segregation and the legacy of Jim Crow racism. Thus the 'folk' actually represents progress as it changes forms and adapts, while modern society seeks to maintain the status quo. Examples of modern adaptations include Hurston's description of how conjure can be used to settle a lawsuit in 'Hoodoo in America' (343) and Rider, the possessed saw-mill worker in Faulkner's 'Pantaloon in Black', who slits the throat of a crooked industrial foreman. The loa[3] in *The Salt Eaters* that 'ride buses just the same's they ride brooms, peoples, carnival floats' (Bambara, *The Salt Eaters* 43) and Denmark Vesey in Reed's poem 'The ghost in Birmingham', who haunts present-day Birmingham by 'attending mass meetings, coming up behind each wave of protest, loading a pistol' (Reed, *Conjure* 3) provide further examples. These images of ghosts are indeed *un*dead as their actions impact the contemporary scene within which they appear. The scenes that conjure interrupts in Faulkner and Williams—and one could link this back to Charles Chesnutt's *The Conjure Woman*—are modern scenes of commerce in the South. There is a sense that conjure 'never went underground: it merely put on a mask' (*Mumbo Jumbo* 10) and that the conjuring real provides a literary axis for a continuum of images across generations of literature.

Conjure—as a literary device—collapses the cultural and temporal differences between seemingly different modes: on one hand the Southern Gothic modernism of Williams and Faulkner and on the other, the postmodernist Black Arts Movement[4] stylistics of Reed and Bambara. As Teresa A. Goddu argues in *Gothic America: Narrative, History, and Nation*, the gothic does not act as an ahistorical 'escapist retreat' (2) but rather 'registers its culture's contradictions, presenting a distorted, not a disengaged, version of reality' (3). I would add that in the case of the texts that I examine here, the accuracy of 'historical representation' collapses under the ambiguity of conjure as a practice and threatens the very idea of representation. In the field of Southern literature—or rather the swamp of the Southern gothic—conjure opens discussion about how the Southern gothic was used and continues to be used to question the process of inclusion and exclusion that constitutes the formation of a community.

Conjure enabled authors to take a stand against segregation in 1955 and then criticize identity politics in 1980 because ambiguity offered the best method with which to approach the complexity of race in the sub-tropical region. In *Orpheus*, conjure breaks down the boundaries between racial oppression and other forms of human cruelty that Williams described as the meaning of the play: 'the acceptance of prescribed answers that are not answers at all, but expedient adaptations or surrender to a state of quandary' (*Orpheus* 288). Decades later, Bambara's *The Salt Eaters* fictionalized that 'state of quandary' in a community center in Georgia as she used conjure to critique identity politics and to suggest that a community acts as an ambiguous space that refuses to conform to any identity category. Thus, conjure as a specter of the Southern gothic enables us to gaze more directly at supernatural ambiguity—and its equally elusive textual representations—as a political act of resistance.

The gesture to collapse time between these authors is not that difficult, as they wrote on more-or-less a twentieth-century continuum from the 1930s to the 1980s, not to mention that they all passed through New Orleans physically and in their literary influence. Both Faulkner and Williams lived in and wrote about the city and Reed wrote about experiencing Mardi Gras with Bambara. Their work rotates along the axis of this sub-tropical region, moving images of conjure from New Orleans up the arterial flow of the Delta into small towns of the U.S. South and the nation as a whole. However, they also move along an arch of *access* where their outsider status complicates their ability to understand fully the supernatural processes they describe in their work. As Zora Neale Hurston proves in her anthropological writings on hoodoo and folklore, one cannot easily join the alternate networks in which conjure and other supernatural folk traditions operate. Despite her subject identity as a black Southerner, the 'Catholic hoodoo doctor of New Orleans' receives her 'reluctantly' with 'distrust in his eyes' (Hurston 357). Perhaps it is unnecessary to state that the same applied to Williams and Faulkner, however, Reed and Bambara faced difficulties even with their subject identities as African Americans and a positive interest in conjure practices. Despite Reed's prolific writing about conjure and New Orleans, he admits that the ritual of the Black Indians during Mardi Gras was 'unintelligible to [him]' (*Mumbo Jumbo* 30). Bambara revealed in an interview that she does not understand the supernatural complexity of conjure, even within her own book: 'I'm not there yet. I don't understand it yet' (*Deep Sightings* 235). Conjure's spectral presence within the text reflects a *lack* of access; as the authors misunderstand the images in their texts, they give conjure the agency to interrupt and destabilize their narratives.

Williams depicted a global South in his plays and located the Latin and Black French Quarter of New Orleans as its epicenter that, as he claims, 'provided me with more material than any other part of the country' (qtd in

Holditch et al. 61). He spread this cultural and ethnic diversity into the U.S. South, including the Gulf Coast Louisiana town in *The Rose Tattoo* where the 'setting seems almost tropical' with 'palm trees [and] tall canes with feathery fronds and a fairly thick growth of pampas grass' (132) or the 'tropical jungle' set of Sebastian's garden in *Suddenly Last Summer*. The latter location takes place in a 'mansion of Victorian Gothic style in the Garden District of New Orleans', yet Williams describes the 'jungle-garden' as being of a 'prehistoric age of giant fern-forests when living creatures had flippers turning to limbs and scales to skin' *(Suddenly Last Summer* 239). The pre-historical, tropical flora and fauna juxtapose symbols of modernity that attempt to contain it. Examples include the highway in *The Rose Tattoo* and the process by which the garden's 'savage nature' in *Suddenly Last Summer* is categorized and artificially maintained by the late Sebastian who feeds his insectivorous plants with fruit flies flown in from a genetics lab in Florida.

Williams' allusions to a pre-historic or primitive time aligns with what Chris Baldick and Robert Mighall refer to as a gothic anachronism. In this, 'Gothic novels thrive on anachronistic emphases, and their narrative effects derive from the clash between 'modernity' and 'antiquity', whether the former finds itself misplaced in the latter or the latter lives beyond its proper scope and survives into the present' (279). They argue that Catholic-European spaces such as Italy allowed for an outside observer to experience a different time. Williams replicates these exotic locations in the U.S. South, as Marion Magid facetiously notes:

> A European whose knowledge of America was gained entirely from the works of Tennessee Williams might garner a composite image of the U.S.: it is a tropical country whose vegetation is mostly man-eating; it has an excessive annual rainfall [...] it had not yet been converted to Christianity but continues to observe the myth of the annual death and resurrection of the sun god. ...
>
> (qtd. in Winchell 162)

However, Sebastian's tropical garden nuances this view of gothic anachronism, for the autochthonous flora represents organic and living entities. The highway in *The Rose Tattoo* and Sebastian's horticulture divide and contain the natural growth, just as the flies from the genetic laboratory symbolize science's attempt to understand and control the natural course of genetic mutation. Williams' 'gothic anachronisms'—represented by wild country, conjure, or the Italian Catholic immigrants in the South—are mobile and alive in the present. Here the temporal tension described as a tenet of gothic literature by Baldick and Mighall align with a parallel theme in Southern literature: in contrast to a 'sense of Gothic space [that] remains subterranean' (Ellis xvi), folkways coexist within modern society and force us to recognize contemporary unknowns. The gothic interrupts not as an anachronism, but rather as evidence of alternative (not past) systems of knowledge.

In *Orpheus*, the social and legal structure of Two River County provides the artificial boundaries that contain and control the population. Yet New Orleans is ever present in the Mississippi Delta town as the characters move between the bars and jazz clubs of the Vieux Carré up through the Delta juke joints with facility and ease. The ethnic diversity and Catholicism inherent to New Orleans migrate literally and symbolically up the Mississippi River—a process embodied by Lady Torrence, the Sicilian wife of the white Southern racist, Jabe Torrence. Lady's Italian family emigrated to the South and built a vineyard in an otherwise dry county. The play also evidences the trail of blues music migration represented by the musician Val Xavier, who follows a path parallel to that of the Conjure Man. Both Val Xavier and the Conjure Man are emblematic of how migration results in ethnic and cultural blending—Val brings blues music to the small town, and the Conjure Man's voodoo rituals combine with his Choctaw cry, as he is half-Choctaw in the play.

Members of the community are threatened by this diversity traveling up the Delta and attempt to enforce their boundaries through the color line of the Jim Crow South. The plot is common, but its victims are unexpected as Williams conflates exclusion along racial, gender and class lines in the play and extends them out, oppressing characters cross-culturally. The Italian immigrants are somewhat accepted until they sell liquor to the black community, resulting in a white mob resembling the Ku Klux Klan burning down the vineyard. Even Carol Cutrere, the white debutante, is not immune to excommunication when she challenges the status quo of racism. A former 'Christ bitten-reformer' and activist against racism, Carol has been cast out of the county for 'lewd vagrancy' (Williams, *Orpheus Decemding* 310) because of a protest against an unfair trial and state-sanctioned lynching of a black man. Her expulsion robs her of her gender-based identity as a debutante, which she then mocks by appearing in a campy hyper-feminine style with overdone makeup—a grotesque version of the Southern Belle. Although she is legally barred from entering Two River County, she continues to do so throughout the play just as the Conjure Man ignores Jim Crow segregation and enters the general store. Their lack of citizenship renders them external to the community even though they continue to invade the county. However, Carol reverses the direction of invasion by positioning *modernity* as the invasive species on the Southern landscape: 'Something is still wild in the country! This country used to be wild, the men and women were wild and there was a wild sort of sweetness in their hearts, for each other, but now its sick with neon, like most other places …' (364). It is the invasion of neon and its brightness that is corrupting the dark country—an authentic place to which she and the other 'fugitive kind' belong. However, when Carol mentions her car that facilitates her movement between New Orleans and the small Delta town in Mississippi, she offers a confusing perspective of modernity, one that facilitates her personal freedom and yet makes efforts to contain it.

The outsider status of the Conjure Man and Carol Cutrere enables their mobility and grants them access to certain freedoms because their identities are difficult to define. When the Conjure Man enters the store, one of the women runs up the stairs out of fear that he will 'mark' her baby (301), a superstitious belief that instills in him unusual power. Another woman, Beulah, cannot place him and resorts to a spectrum of names: '*Hey, old man, you! Choctaw! Conjure man! Nigguh!*' (302). When he enters the store holding out a bone, Carol is able to communicate with him telepathically and exhibits a knowledge of conjure: 'No, I don't want to touch it. It isn't clean yet, there's still some flesh clinging to it ... Yes, I know it's a breastbone of a bird but it's still tainted with corruption' (301). Then Carol instructs the Conjure Man on how to rid it of its corruption as a performance of translation to the reader/audience and as a means to publicly align herself with conjure practices. 'Leave it a long time on a bare rock in the rain until every sign of corruption is burned and washed away from it, then it will be a good charm, a white charm, but now it's a black charm Uncle. So take it away and do what I told you with it' (301–302). Carol's detailed knowledge and the Conjure Man's subsequent sign of 'obeisance' positions Carol within the realm of conjure. In a concluding act of solidarity, they repulse the Delta ladies with their 'Choctaw cry' that Williams describes as a 'series of barking noises that rises to a high sustained note of wild intensity' (302). Carol conflates the tropical conjure practices of New Orleans and the local Choctaw cry with the modernity of her car, displacing these rituals as something 'past' and hybridizing them together as a means to access empowerment. The struggle against Jim Crow in the small Southern community expands out in concentric circles, while encompassing resistances to patriarchy, economic structures, Protestant Christianity and other systems of dominance. The play represents oppression as a systemic process rather than something that can be separated into isolated issues, and it questions the idea of community formation as part of this systemic process. By exposing signs of 'subjugated knowledges', to borrow a phrase from Foucault, within a space of the unknown, Williams could build unusual bridges, such as the connection between the Conjure Man and Carol as marginal outsiders to the community and make resistance stronger through intersectionalism.

Characters in *Orpheus* exist within a prism of victimization policed by community exclusion in Two River County where Italians, Southern debutantes and even white males (Val Xavier) are expunged through acts that connote racial violence when they challenge the status quo. Val Xavier articulates the connection between social outliers through the language of commerce: 'there's people bought and sold in this world like carcasses of hogs in butcher shops ... there's just two kinds of people, the ones that are bought and the buyers' (319). This language of buying and selling of bodies based on sex and marriage repeats throughout the play and suggests that the underlying system of human trafficking that established the segregated community structure in Mississippi continues to haunt characters in the play's present. However, the presence of conjure suggests an alternative system that resists the dominant power structure of buying and selling and destabilizes the core of this value system. At the end of the play, after Lady's confectionary has been burned down by Jabe Torrence with Val immolated within, the Conjure Man scavenges through the debris and finds Val's snakeskin jacket. Carol barters her gold ring for it and through this act signals their alternate system of values: 'Wild things leave skins behind them, they leave clean skins and teeth and white bones behind them, and these are the tokens passed from one to another, so that the fugitive kind can always follow their kind ...' (374). This non-verbal communication through objects instills in them a covert, unknown value, and the method by which these exchanges happen destabilizes the system of commerce in which the rational community is set. The unknown objects on the grave in Faulkner's 'Pantaloon in Black' work toward the same result: a secret system of signs that demarcate separate economies of knowledge. As Roberto Esposito observes within the philosophical context of Ferdinand Tönnies and Max Weber, 'community is a "property" belonging to subjects that join them together ... They have in common what is most properly their own; they are owners of what is common to them all' (2–3). However, the presence of 'tokens passed from one to another' and other unreadable objects that contain secret power remind members of the dominant community that objects can assume different property values and that through this shadow economy the concept of ownership diffuses. As Alphonso Lingis argues, this alternative community always exists alongside the 'rational community' and is 'not simply absorbed into the rational community; it recurs, it troubles the rational community, as its double or its shadow' (10). Thus, the dominant community of Two River County must continue to enforce a definition that they can never fully achieve. Characters such as the Conjure Man and Carol exist as social outliers beyond the system of buying and selling and yet they are highly mobile and empowered through a mysterious folk practice with its own economic structure. Conjure is more than a subversive practice, it signals a separate hemispheric world existing within the U.S. South.

The presence of conjure and its potential to defy the community becomes in itself a form of protest. At the conclusion of *Orpheus*, the 'fugitive kind' conjurers—Carol and the Conjure Man—ignore the sheriff's command, 'Don't no one move, don't move! ... Stay here!' as Carol laughs at him and continues her movement out the door. The curtain closes as the Conjure Man gives the audience a 'secret smile' (375). As Williams exemplifies with Carol Cutrere, conjure has the ability to interrupt the color line as it adapts to the location, a racial ambiguity that parallels the Catholic New Orleans ambiguous identity of the famous voodoo priestess Marie Laveau. Literary representations of conjure such as Williams' Carol Cutrere, Faulkner's characters Jesus and Rider, Charles Chesnutt's Aunt Peggy and the descriptions in Zora Neale Hurston's writings share little in common—perhaps except their 'wider range of mobility within the community' (Martin 61) and across the Southern landscape. They represent the movement in and out of narratives, geographic locations and racial categories. Their alternatives to the black and white binary that exists within the subtropical region argued that no community could be contained and that structures have always existed in resistance to segregation.

The alternate modes of knowledge that appear in the texts of the modernist writers reincarnate themselves in the writing of another wave of authors that used conjure as a literary device in their Southern-gothic remix, what Ishamel Reed theorized as Neo-HooDooism. Reed understood conjure in terms of an 'American "pantheon"' of hoodoo that 'borrows from Haiti, Africa and South America' (*Conjure* 22). While acknowledging in his Neo-HooDoo Manifesto that 'Africa is home of the loa', Reed focuses on the transitional quality of voodoo's 'remarkable ability to blend with other religions, even those considered its rivals' (1978: 9) as well as Neo-HooDoo's 'Black Red ... And occasionally White' (1972: 25) ethnic makeup. The tropical gothic trope shifts from challenging the boundaries of the small Southern town to an otherness that Stuart Hall recognized as 'the negation of everything the West stood for' (Hall 221). Reed and Bambara built out from the models of Sebastian's garden and Two River and Yoknapatawpha Counties in ambitious works that challenge a variety of bounded community spaces. Even though they reached wider in their scope, their continuum with Faulkner and Williams maintains the geographic jazz of the subtropical South and manifests conjure through fragmented images and ambiguous writing.

Through Reed and Bambara, the specter of conjure continues as a method by which to pull the past into the present and define this subtropical circum-Atlantic South as a cultural and literary mestizo. Reed and Bambara were writing simultaneous to the emergence of black and ethnic nationalism as social movements shifted toward a strong identity-based politics. Yet, conjure and its folkways question the sustainability of separatism and the essentialist tendencies within identity politics. The amorphous folk tradition that aligns itself with region rather than ethnicity/race interposes activist communities that depend on separate identities in order to function. Williams' description of *Orpheus* as a 'surrender to the quandary' contextualizes a paradox that Reed articulates in his poem 'Neo-HooDoo Manifesto' when he refers to hoodoo as a 'litany seeking a text' (*Conjure* 25). Reed combines manifesto with poetry and subverts both genres by claiming that hoodoo exists without textual means of communication. Here, the ability for conjure to take on its own agency and undermine literary form sends out a controversial political message against separatist-style activism.

Manifesto writing makes a strong political declaration often through the 'we' voice that stands in for an imagined group of people. Therefore, the manifesto becomes a useful tool for the nationalist paradigm of self-presentation. The concept of 'we' or 'us' bridges the process of communal formation with that of identity politics and nationalism, what Robert Carr in *Black Nationalism in the New World: Reading the African-American and West Indian Experience* views as a 'macrotheoretical literature' in which 'terms for defining an "us" whose difference from 'them' is chaotically described' (6). The carefully maintained nationalist community is always in danger of becoming a replication of the 'the protean capitalist nation creating a state as its supreme representation' (5). As nationalism seeks to define itself and solidify a race-based identity, the ambiguity and lack of political solidarity within the folk pose a threat to the newly established order: the 'new black subject' emerging in the circum-Atlantic space of activism during the 1960s and 1970s. Thus, many poets and writers disparaged folkways and criticized conjure as inauthentic 'mumbo-jumbo just like Hollywood would do it' in favor of 'hard organizing' (Cook 196).[5] Reed and Bambara, on the other hand, recognized the importance of these practices within a wider, hemispheric network and looked for ways to reconcile politics and spirituality through literary expression. They placed confrontations with the folk as a central issue in their writing and forced readers to confront their own lack of cultural awareness or interaction with these alternative systems.

In Bambara's *The Salt Eaters,* figures representing the 'new black subject' come face-to-face with those who practice conjure and engage in the alternative folk structures that have always existed within *and without* the nation, challenging its political and economic borders. Conjure complicates nationalism by defying the spirit of the manifesto and cohesive definition and thus forces characters in the novel to realize that identity-based politics replicates the very system they are fighting against. Returning to Williams' image of Sebastian's garden, the struggle to define and preserve community as a kind of cultural horticulture prevents the hybridization and adaptation of nature that could make resistance powerful. Bambara creates a method out of conjure by creating scenes and images that reconcile both realms—the realm of the supernatural and the realm of political-realism—and argues for this method as necessary for social change.

In *The Salt Eaters*, conjure acts as a specter of hidden knowledge systems of healing through a ceremony that takes place at the Southwest Community Infirmary in the fictional town of Claybourne, Georgia. The healing centers on Velma, an activist who has collapsed under the pressure of her role as intermediary between the separate political factions. Velma's attempt at suicide symbolizes the self-destruction of the community in its inability to cohere together in the face of its continuous adherence to identity politics. Generations of the community and their different political ideologies are physically present at the healing, and Bambara floods the narrative with voices that interrupt the narrative in fragments of ambiguous character voices. Some voices speak from beyond the grave through a medium without a clear explanation to the reader of who they are or where they are from; the narrative confusion is symbolic of the chaos of community activism present in the novel. Conjure haunts the narrative by suggesting points of black identity that are not understood by members of the urban, political or academic black communities and serves as constant reminder of the tension between political organization and unorganized oral tradition. The ritual at the heart of *The Salt Eaters* is so confusing that it fictionalizes Reed's poetic image of a 'litany without a text;' not even Bambara fully understood the ceremony. Bambara claimed in an interview 'I don't know nothing about that book. I'm still reading it' (1996: 237), and thus she positioned herself as a reader, leaving us to wonder who—or what—is writing the text? Bambara saw the purpose of her fiction—alongside Julie Dash's film *Daughters of the Dust* and Paule Marshall's novel *Praisesong of a Widow*—as a 'process to liberate the imperialist eye' (151). All three works, and to this list I would add Reed's poetry and Erna Brodber's novels, show ways in which conjure manipulates characters and text into bizarre imaginative spaces and can act as an antidote to the replication of the capitalist-dominant system. Bambara's fractured narrative in *The Salt Eaters* forces us to rethink the utopian vision of community activism reflected in manifestos. In the alternative vision that Bambara provides, community is not always a binding strength but rather something that also contains possibility for the same kind of harmful exclusion that occurred in *Orpheus*.

Despite the generational divides, Bambara attempts to collapse the past into the present condition: 'Everyone seemed to be pulling in the same direction then. But that of course was selective memory, a chump way to excuse the self from the chaos of the moment, longing for a past or for a future as if there were no continuum' (*Deep Sightings* 98). The continuum critiques fractional activism as not being an effective means of protest unless it can adapt and embrace the flexibility of time and identity. Velma's desire for death is placed in terms of stasis and immobility: 'Her grandmother would be pleased, her godmother Sophie too. "Girl, be still", they'd been telling her for years, meaning different things' (20). The novel connects stillness to the metaphor of Lot's wife, who in the Biblical story turns to a pillar of salt as a result of looking backward at the collapse of Sodom. If Velma and the community continue the backward gaze to inform their current condition and if they do not leap forward into an unknown new space, they will be ossified and too static to make social change. Salt acts as a metaphor for the process of healing, it is used against snakebite to 'neutralize the venom', and yet, as one of the matriarchal characters explains, 'To neutralize the serpent's another matter'. The answer is never offered, however, and Velma cites the inability for previous lessons to apply to her current situation, even the information garnered from reading slave narratives or from her idols from the tradition of black activism such as Ida B. Wells, Malcolm X and John Coltrane. Velma realizes that even though she '[t]hought she knew how to build resistance' (258), the lessons of the past do not adequately fit the cause in the novel: a labor strike against a chemical plant that calls for intersectional and coalition activism. The Transchemical plant emerges as the new modern oppressive force of nuclear energy and evolves from Carol Cutrere's 'sick with neon' modernity to threaten environmental damage across the spectrum of humanity. The suggestion that an antidote could be as harmful as venom parallels identity politics as a process that is simultaneously useful and harmful as a method of resistance.

Thus when the main healer, Minnie Ransom, asks Velma 'Are you sure you want to be well?' (3), she is presenting the question of change to the entire community. Separatist political factions fracture the community, and therefore in order for it to become whole it will have to reach across those boundaries. The backward gaze that holds onto the past is a safer, better-known process than the alternative: 'people sometimes believed that it was safer to live with complaints, was necessary to cooperate with grief, was all right to become an accomplice in self-ambush' (107). In an argument between two activists, the usually loud and abrasive Ruby refuses to acknowledge the importance of coalition politics in order to resist the environmental threat and abusive labor practices of the Transchemical plant. She claims that 'all this ecology stuff is a diversion' to which her fellow activist Janice retorts, 'They're connected. Whose community do you think they ship radioactive waste through, or dig up waste burial grounds near? Who do you think they hire for the dangerous dirty work at those plants? What parts of the world do they test-blast in? And all them illegal uranium mines dug up on Navajo turf—the crops dying, the sheep dying, the horses, water, cancer, Ruby, cancer' (242). Janice builds the connections between environmental destruction and the pathways of race and class-based persecution in the community. Nuclear energy represents a more ambiguous force of oppression not quite understood by the community and thus calls on a similar structure of resistance. The voices of the loa that appear throughout the novel represent the antidotal mirror to nuclear power: they both consist of mysterious unseen forces to which only an elite few have access, and their processes of creation and destruction are anterior to race-based politics.

And yet, the loa do not provide a simple answer within the novel. The supernatural voices conjured by Minnie Ransom in the healing process interrupt the narrative and create confusion for the reader as well as the characters; conjure acts as a disorienting and uncomfortable presence in the text. However, Velma does find a place where she can obtain a 'breakthrough' moment where the spiritual and political click universally. In a flashback she finds herself in a swamp—another tropical-gothic location—waiting for 'some steamy creature to arise dripping and unbelievable from the marshes' (170).Velma is actually in Georgia, a few minutes from where she grew up, but its lushness is reminiscent of the tropics: 'the site of metamorphosis. River rain, underground spring, marsh ... Things were active around her ... Time not speeding up but opening up to take her inside' (171). A series of correlations emerge in her mind that assuage her fear: 'Panic. Pan. Pan-Africanism. All of us. Every. God. Pan. All nature. Pan. Everywhere. She was grinning, as she always grinned when she was able to dig below the barriers organized religion erected in its push toward a bogus civilization' (170). In the swamp marsh Velma feels universality not as panic-inducing but 'occurring to her rather than ... haunting her' (170), and she finds solace in the gothic-tropical setting where the 'unbelievable' creature that arises is a new perspective, an alternative view outside the structures of society. However, the underside for Velma, the other aspect of her 'pan' perspective is its transience: 'She found no words. Nor a brief passage of music. Nothing stayed fixed and available for later ... the marsh visit had failed to inform her ... Whatever has occurred, stayed behind' (172). The knowledge she gains in the marsh does not translate to her daily life in the community by resisting translation. Like Carol Cutrere's wild country, the swamp is under threat by a modernity that seeks to understand and categorize the ambiguity of this indescribable, amorphous knowledge.

This same paradox happens with the journalist Campbell, whose intense independent study of mythology and nuclear energy (rather than swamp musing) has led him to the conclusion that 'all the systems were the same at base—voodoo, thermodynamics, I Ching, astrology, numerology, alchemy, metaphysics, everybody's ancient myths—they were interchangeable, not at all separate much less conflicting.' He comes to the same conclusion as Velma in the marsh and has the same reaction exclaiming, 'How simple universal knowledge is after all, he grinned' (210). Naturally, he faces Velma's same problem of articulating or translating this universal knowledge into conceptual thought. As much as he can 'couch principles of thermonuclear dynamics in the language of down-home Bible-quoting folks', he has difficulty getting it on paper. 'Damballah, he wrote, represents, he wrote, and scratched that out, Damballah is similar to, he wrote, and scratched that out, Damballah is the first law of thermodynamics and is the Biblical wisdom and is the law of time and is, Campbell wrote, everything that is now has been before and will be again in a new way, in a changed form, in a timeless time' (249). Campbell's manic writing is confusing and oxymoronic, and his pride in being able to make connections fails him, a parallel to Velma's inability to retain the knowledge gained in the swamp. The cryptic message of regeneration—that forward movement depends on adaptation and change—serves to open more questions on what that 'changed form' is, or what the pragmatic steps are to his theory.

Velma's experience and Campell's theory reveal that this universal system of knowledge has existed all along in the swamp and in Damballah. The loa in *The Salt Eaters* are the 'laws alive' that are not relegated to the past but are 'prettyin up to hop a bus to New Orleans' (43) for Carnival. Bambara suggests that the adaptation of the loa and the ability for Voodou, hoodoo, Neo-HooDoo, conjure and other manifestations of the folk that insured its survival through time is the pattern from which intersectional connections emerge. The temporal confluence of methods of activism has strong political possibilities, as Bambara articulates in her reflections on the process of writing *The Salt Eaters*:

> I was trying to figure out as a community worker why political folk were so distant from the spiritual community ... I wondered what

> would happen if we could bring them together as Bookman brought them together under Toussaint, as Nan brought them together in Jamaica. Why is there that gap? Why don't we have a bridge language so that clairvoyants can talk to revolutionaries? (235)

A bridge language emerges throughout the novel as a combination of Bambara's narrative and the performative writing emerging through images of conjure. Bambara fictionalizes a microcosm of intersectional politics with the Seven Sisters, a group of women activists from a variety of ethnic groups—Sister of the Yam, Plantain, Rice, etcetera—that share and argue over their experiences. The Sisters do not offer any solution within the novel, but their conversation opens the potential for shared experience, even if it is in danger of slipping into palaver. When one of the Sisters, Cecile, starts explaining the fire rites of 'macumba, condomble, obeah, shango, lucumi, sanitaria, winti, voodoo' (223), it sparks memories for another Sister, Mai. She says: 'Perhaps the contrast of Mai's story and Cecile's, the two family stories rubbing against each other in Mai's mind ... something had flashed a light around in the jumble of those old told-to's' (221). Even though it is based on difference, the stories enable Mai to reach back through the silence of the generation that suffered through the Japanese and pan-Asian internment camps where they 'ke[pt] themselves alive with stories' (222). Like loa interrupting the narratives, the stories shared between the Seven Sisters serve as reminders of orality as a parallel to intersectional politics where both have the ability to open up pathways between personal and political connections. This becomes a common trope in the connection between the folk and the Black Arts Movement writers who sought to reclaim and adapt 'juju' and the oral tradition on the text. Sonia Sanchez in her poem titled 'now poem. for us' describes the effort for the Black Arts Movement generation to 'record them talken their ago talk/for our tomorrows [...] let them tell us about their juju years/so ours will be that much stronger' (Adoff 70). The difference between Sanchez's poem and *The Salt Eaters* is that Velma does not reach to the past; the juju exists both then and contemporaneously; Faulkner's adage 'there is no such thing as was—only is' meets Bambara's 'timeless time' of Damballah.

At the conclusion of the novel, Velma is healed through music and dance. While this momentarily confuses the healer, the loa communicating with Minnie urge to 'Let her go' (264) and succumb to dancing. The music to which she dances is a combination of an old blues standard 'Wild Woman Don't Have the Blues' and Charlie Parker with Coleman Hawkins doing 'Now Is the Time' simultaneously. This blend of blues and bebop and the dancing that follows heals Velma using a discordant cacophony of sounds—the temporal overlapping of jazz styles. The ritual blends conjure, dance and blues and gathers up the literary fabric into an arcade of sounds and movement with parallels to Reed's poetry that defines Neo-HooDoo as a 'Dance and a Music closing in on its words' (Reed, *Conjure* 25). The

Choctaw cry shared by Carol Cutrere, the Conjure Man and Val Xavier's blues guitar, Nancy's noise that 'was like singing and it wasn't like singing' in Faulkner's 'That Evening Sun' (31) (a title lifted from the famous blues standard 'St. Louis Blues'); Zora Neale Hurston's Bahamian Fire Dance at the conclusion of *The Great Day*; Katherine Dunham's intersections of dance and Haitian voodoo in *Island Possessed*; Avery Johnson's dancing at the Big Drum ceremony at the conclusion of Paule Marshall's *Praisesong for the Widow*; and many other moments that show how conjure forces text to adapt to sound, vision and movement. Conjure becomes an axis point on which the sub-tropical region above the Tropic of Cancer turns and as a literary device; it becomes a point of access for authors to understand the potential for 'other' communities.

The healing ritual in *The Salt Eaters* adapts through jazz and dance and maintains a shroud of mystery over its process through multiple fragmented interjections in the narrative. Indeed, on this gathered fabric of collapsed moments within the Southern gothic of the sub-tropical region, the specter of conjure fractures texts and demands authors to express themselves through indefinable images—as litanies without texts. Within these fragmentations—that can be read as visual or aural interruptions in texts—frequencies of resistance emerge as community structure breaks down and new bridges form, such as the connections made here between iconic white male writers of the Southern gothic tradition and black radical writers aligned with the Black Arts Movement. Ever undoing efforts to define and separate, images of conjure communicate together above the authors' authorial agency where categories such as modernism, postmodernism and Southern gothic become outdated tautologies for loa messing around with texts.

Notes

1. The term 'geography jazz' is from Carolina Hospital's poem of the same name found in *Little Havana Blues: A Cuban American Literature Anthology*. Virgil Suarez and Delia Poey, ed. (Houston: Arte Publico Press, 1996).
2. For more detailed discussion on the circum-Atlantic, see Roach; Paul Gilroy's *The Black Atlantic: Modernity and Double Consciousness*. (Cambridge: Harvard University Press, 1993; Adams et al., 2007).
3. Loa refers to the gods or spirits in the vodou or voodoo traditions.
4. I selected Reed and Bambara not only because they are major figures within the Black Arts Movement but also because their work advocated multiculturalism. See James E. Smethurst *The Black Arts Movement: Literary Nationalism in the 1960s and 1970s* (Chapel Hill: University of North Carolina Press, 2005) and Bambara's introduction to *This Bridge Called My Back: Writings by Radical Women of Color* Gloria Anzaldúa and Cherrie Moraga eds. (New York: Kitchen Table Press, 1985).
5. See also Richard Wright's *Black Power* for a skeptical view of folk religion and as superstitious belief. For more on the lineage of African Americans who rejected folk traditions, see Martin.

Bibliography

Adams, Jessica, Michael Bibler, Cecile Accilien, Eds. *Just Below South: Intercultural Performance in the Caribbean and the U.S. South*. Charlottesville and London: University of Virginia Press, 2007. Print.

Adoff, Arnold, Ed. *The Poetry of Black America: Anthology of the 20th Century*. New York: Harper Collins, 1973. Print.

Baldick, Chris, and Robert Mighall. 'Gothic Criticism' in *A New Companion to the Gothic*. Ed., Punter, David. West Sussex: Blackwall Publishing Ltd, 2012. 267–87. Print.

Bambara, Toni Cade. *The Salt Eaters*. First Vintage Contemporaries Edition. New York: Vintage Books, 1992. Print.

———. *Deep Sightings and Rescue Missions: Fiction, Essays, and Conversations*. Ed. Morrison, Toni. New York: Pantheon Books, 1996. Print.

Carr, Robert. *Black Nationalism in the New World: Reading the African-American and West Indian Experience*. Durham: Duke University Press, 2002. Print.

Cook, Ann. 'Black Pride? Some Contradictions' *The Black Woman: An Anthology*. Ed. Bambara, Toni Cade. New York: Washington Square Press, 1970. Print.

Duck, Leigh Anne. '"Go There Tuh Know There": Zora Neale Hurston and the Chronotype of the Folk,' *American Literary History* 13.2. 2001. 265–94. *JSTOR*. Accessed 9-1-2014. Web.

Edwards, Justin D. *Gothic Passages: Racial Ambiguity and the American Gothic*. Iowa City: University of Iowa Press, 2002. Print.

Ellis, Jay. 'On Southern Gothic Literature.' *Southern Gothic Literature*. Ed. Ellis, Jay. Ipswich, MA: Salem Press, 2013. xvi–xxxiv. Print.

Esposito, Roberto. *Communitas: The Origin and a Destiny of Community*. Trans. Campbell, Timothy. Stanford: Stanford University Press, 2010. Print.

Faulkner, William. 'That Evening Sun' (1931). *Selected Short Stories*. New York: Random House, 2012. 76–98. Print.

———. *Absalom, Absalom!* (1936). New York: Random House, 1986. Print.

———. *Go Down Moses* (1940). New York: Random House, 1990. Print.

Goddu, Teresa A. *Gothic America: Narrative, History, and Nation*. New York: Columbia University Press, 1997.

Hall, Stuart 'The West and the Rest: Discourse and Power' *Formations of Modernity*. Ed. Hall, Stuart, and Bram Gieben Cambridge, UK: Polity Press, 1992. 185–227. Print.

Holditch, Kenneth W., and Richard F. Leavitt, Eds. *Tennessee Williams and the South*. Jackson: University Press of Mississippi, 2002.

Hull, Gloria T. "What It Is I Think She's Doing Anyhow': A Reading of Toni Cade Bambara's The Salt Eaters.' *Conjuring Black Women, Fiction, and Literary Tradition*. Ed, Pryse, Marjorie, and Hortense J. Spillers. Bloomington: Indiana University Press, 1985. 216–32. Print.

Hurston, Zora Neale. 'Hoodoo in America' *The Journal of American Folklore* 44.174. (1931), 317–417. *JSTOR*. Accessed 9-1-2014. Web.

Lingis, Alphonso. *The Community of Those Who Have Nothing in Common*, Bloomington and Indianapolis: Indianapolis University Press, 1994. Print.

Martin, Kameelah L. *Conjuring Moments in African American Literature: Women, Spirit Work and other Such Hoodoo*. New York: Palgrave MacMillan, 2012. Print.

Reed, Ishmael. *Conjure: Selected Poems 1963–1970*. Amherst: University of Massachusetts Press, 1972. Print.

———. *Mumbo Jumbo*. New York: Avon Books, 1978. Print.

———. *Shrovetide in Old New Orleans*. Garden City, NY: Doubleday and Company, Inc., 1978. Print.

Roach, Joseph. *Cities of the Dead: Circum-Atlantic Performance*. New York: Columbia University Press, 1996. Print.

Williams, Tennessee. *The Rose Tattoo* (1951). *Five Plays by Tennessee Williams*. London: Secker and Warburg, 1962. 125–216. Print.

———. *Orpheus Descending* (1955). *Five Plays by Tennessee Williams*. London: Secker and Warburg, 1962. 283–374. Print.

———. *Suddenly Last Summer* (1958). *Five Plays by Tennessee Williams*. London: Secker and Warburg, 1962. 237–82. Print.

Winchell, Mark Royden. *Reinventing the South: Versions of a Literary Region*. Columbia, MS: University of Missouri Press, 2006. Print.

5 'They Are Not Men, Monsieur … They Are Zombies …'

The Construction of Haitian Identity and the Work of the Left Hand

Kelly Gardner

The concept of zombification first entered the popular imagination during the American occupation of Haiti by means of William Seabrook's quasi-anthropological study, *The Magic Island* (1929). Seabrook's colorful descriptions of Voodoo rituals and eerie revelations of soulless corpses slaving in the sugarcane fields functioned as the inspiration for both the short-lived stage play *Zombie* (1932) as well as the more successful, and arguably foundational, Halperin film *White Zombie* (1932). Seabrook's depiction of Haitian life and the Halperins' embellished reimagining of Haitian Voodoo[1] became the exogenous lens through which American audiences regarded Haitian reality (Degoul 24). This chapter will examine the historical context from which the zombie emerged and the manner in which authentic accounts of Haiti, and zombieism itself, were sensationalized in cinematic depictions in order to construct a primitive Haitian identity. Furthermore, an engagement with imagological concepts will discuss how an endogenous auto-image of Haitian identity was established in response to the Western exogenously constructed hetero-image of Haitian savagery. It revealed that, above all else, while the past century has experienced numerous manifestations of this malleable figure as an 'empty signifier' (Laclau 76), the notion of *identity* occupies the very essence of zombieism.

As a figure of contemporary horror, the monstrous zombie has roots in the sweltering heat of the Caribbean rather than the darkened forests of his feted European brethren. Emerging from tales of Haitian Voodoo, the zombie owes much of its notoriety to the American trepidation of Haiti as the first independent black republic. Initiated by the Haitian Revolution, tales of Voodoo and zombification disseminated slowly through the Americas before dispersing to Europe. Apprehension regarding Haiti and her subsequent independence transmuted into apprehension of Voodoo and its association with cannibalism, thereby foregrounding the assumption of Haitian primitivism and savagery in the American imagination. However, Chera Kee notes that following the U.S. occupation of Haiti from 1915 to 1934, a fear of cannibalism was replaced with a fear of zombies, and the cannibalistic discourse of the nineteenth and twentieth centuries regarding Haitian Voodoo was replaced with a highly racialized discourse perpetuated by early zombie films (Kee 9–10). As the zombie continues to develop into the Gothic figure of contemporary representations, often void of any reference to its Haitian history, it has become apparent that the racialized discourse it once inhabited has transformed into a discourse of Othering[2] in its appropriation of 'a more diffuse definition of the Self and the Other' (Kee 10). Accordingly, the evolution of the zombie, as well as the evolution of the films it inhabits, instigated by the shift in representation initiated by George A. Romero and his *Dead* series[3], has demonstrated the new emphasis placed on the instability of the boundary between 'us' and 'them', and subsequently between 'self' and 'other'. The zombies were no longer distinguishable by nationality and race, as every member of the population became susceptible to infection by a zombie virus. Countries, communities and families were depicted in a state of turmoil as survivors took up arms to defend themselves against zombified family members, friends and neighbors. The recent emergence of the 'zombie self' in contemporary zombie-themed literature, film and television reflects a shift toward a discourse of identity detectable in the early discussions of Haitian identity in zombie and Voodoo-related investigations. Isaac Marion's novel *Warm Bodies* (2010), the 2013 film adaptation of the same name and the Bafta award-winning series *In the Flesh* (2013) created by Dominic Mitchell all explore the development of zombie sentience, which raises questions regarding a zombie selfhood[4]. In order to appreciate this development in contemporary zombie representation, it is vital that one first examine the origins of the zombie figure in the early American imagination. Thus our attention must first be redirected to nineteenth-century Haiti and the threat posed by American intervention on Haitian identity.

Haiti and Voodoo

On the 1st of January, 1804, Jean-Jacques Dessalines proclaimed the independence of Saint-Domingue following over a decade of slave revolts inspired by the French Revolution. As a result, Haiti was declared 'the first black-ruled independent nation in the Western Hemisphere'. (Kee 10) Yet, in spite of this, then U.S. President Thomas Jefferson, as well as the prominent leaders of the majority of European nations, refused to recognize the independence of Haiti as a new republic. Voodoo ceremonies played a vital role in the rebellion, as they served as an environment in which the instigators of the revolution could assemble and discuss objectives with their supporters. Historically, the Bois Caïman Voodoo ceremony of August 1791 is credited as the event that initiated the revolution. Serving as both a religious ceremony and tactical political assembly, Bois Caïman ensured that the root of Haitian independence and, as a result, Haitian identity itself, became securely tied to Haitian Voodoo (Dubois 99). In effect, this central link between the Revolution and Voodoo provided antagonists to Haitian Independence with 'a means to disparage revolutionary ideas by linking them to a supposedly barbaric, superstitious belief system' (Kee 10). Similarly, the violence of the

Revolution was portrayed as 'racialized violence' specifically targeting the white populace of Haiti, a claim that served to reinforce the opinion that, as David Brion Davis notes, 'slave emancipation in any form would lead to economic ruin and to the indiscriminant massacre of white populations' (4). The purposeful refusal to accept the independence of Haiti by the U.S. and most of Europe resulted in Haiti's relative isolation from the rest of the trading world, and thus imaginative stories regarding this black-ruled republic were able to spread without refute. Kee notes, 'Haiti's revolution deprived white Europeans and Americans of the ability to 'civilize' the black world formerly known as Saint-Domingue' (11). Thus, in order to justify American occupation, Haiti was demonized, compelling therefore the intervention of the 'civilizing forces of the white world' (Kee 11) to act as redeemers in order to negate the revolution.

Sensationalized reports of Voodoo spread unchecked and unverified. Haiti was depicted as the carcass of a once boundless colonial beast, the promise of French colonialism slain by the primitive savagery of superstitious Voodoo, by black magic controlled by black hands. The former slave population of Haiti was regarded as de-evolved natives, their rejection of the colonial civilizing process was seen as proof of their inherent animality and their subsequent return to an African ignorance (Kee 12). Following the assassination of Jean-Jacques Dessalines on 17 October 1806, Haiti was a divided state. Henri Christophe ruled the Kingdom of Haiti in the north, while Alexandre Pétion ran the republic in the south. Successor to Pétion, Jean-Pierre Boyer succeeded in reuniting the north and south and ruled the island from 1822 until 1843 when he was forced out of office. However, in the lead up to and following the departure of Boyer, Haiti found herself once more in a state of upheaval. Successive coups and increasing poverty had resulted in Haiti being viewed as an example of self-destruction, a self-destruction that threatened to breach the border and infect the Americas. Therefore, in an attempt to stabilize the situation, 1915 saw the beginning of the U.S. occupation of Haiti. Kee indicates that 'to most Americans, the United States occupied Haiti under the pretence of civilising it' (13), and therefore the sensationalized renditions of Haitian Voodoo, with particular emphasis on the maliciousness of black magic and the barbarism of Voodoo, became integral to justifying the occupation and maintaining national support for the necessity for America to civilize her animalistic neighbor.

Haitian Zombie

It was in 1819 that the word 'zombie' first made its appearance in *The Oxford English Dictionary*. However, it was not until Lafcadio Hearn published the article 'The Country of the Comers-Back' (1889) in *Harper's Magazine* that whispers of the walking dead began to circulate the English-speaking world of North America (Russell 9). An amateur anthropologist, Hearn discovered that the inhabitants of Martinique in 1887 were not forthcoming with information regarding these *corpse cadavres* and that, more worryingly, those who were willing to share relayed 'contradictory anecdotes, vague stories and superstitious mumblings' that proved 'more confusing than illuminating.' (Russell 9). It was Hearn's inability to discover the truth of the zombie myth or, at least, his inability to discover a single coherent first-hand account of zombieism, that led to his eventual article for *Harper's Magazine* colorfully detailing his expedition to the Caribbean. Only the merest hint of zombies was enough to provoke interest and intrigue in the notion of the returning dead, the Comers-Back.

Despite Hearn's article, it was not until 1929 that the notion of zombieism took hold of the American imagination with the publication of William Seabrook's anthropological account of Haiti, *The Magic Island*. Seabrook, whose colorful background and enigmatic anthropological research practices cemented his position as one of the 'Lost Generation' of writers, inhabited the island in an attempt to embed himself in Haitian culture. Befriending locals and engaging with practitioners of Voodoo, Seabrook familiarized himself with the cultural folklore and Voodoo rituals of the island. In a chapter entitled '... Dead Men Working in the Cane Fields', Seabrook detailed a conversation he had with a Haitian farmer named Polynice, 'I recalled one creature I had been hearing about in Haiti, which sounded exclusively local—the zombie' (Seabrook 94). This emphasis on locating the zombie as 'exclusively local' established the zombie as the product of Haiti. Seabrook explains:

> The zombie, they say, is a soulless human corpse, still dead, but taken from the grave and endowed by sorcery with a mechanical semblance of life—it is a dead body which is made to walk or act and move as if it were alive. (94)

The method, as documented by Seabrook, is as follows:

> People who have the power to do this go to a fresh grave, dig up the body before it has had time to rot, galvanize it into movement, and then make of it a servant or slave, occasionally for the commission of some crime, more often simply as a drudge around the habitation or the farm, setting it dull heavy tasks, and beating it like a dumb beast if it slackens. (94)

Polynice recounts a story wherein he describes the zombies as 'vacant-eyed like cattle' (Seabrook 96). Furthermore, Seabrook himself recounts his own personal experience with zombies, who 'continued dumbly to work' in an 'unnatural and strange' manner, noting: 'They were plodding like brutes, like automatons [with] the eyes of a dead man, not blind, but staring, unfocused, unseeing' (101). Seabrook's physical description of zombies, as well as the connection drawn between the zombie and slave labor, served as the archetype for future depictions of the zombie.

The sensationalized link made between Haiti and the zombie coincided with the beginning of the Great Depression in 1930. The figure became contemporarily relevant as a moral critique of capitalist exploitation as the dispossessed population of the United States came to identify with the powerlessness of the zombie workforce. Similarly, the social financial turmoil initiated by the depression resulted in the worsening of racial tensions, whereby 'stereotypes of colour', Kee notes, 'thrived in this sort of environment' (14). At that time, Hollywood utilized actors of color to portray marginalized characters and thus the prospect of an entirely marginalized island posed a promising opportunity for the entertainment industry. Removed from the reality of Haitian life, Voodoo existed outside the 'norm of whiteness' and could therefore be embellished as monstrous. As a nation of slaves 'zombies were faceless masses: a new means of robbing the Other of its individuality in order to keep it as the Other' (Kee 14).

Inspired by Seabrook's *The Magic Island*, Kenneth Webb lifted the zombie from the pages of the travelogue and placed it on the stage in New York. *Zombie* the stage play opened in 1932 and despite having a limited run, Webb's contribution to the zombie trope was twofold. First, adhering to Seabrook's account, the zombie, as a figure of color, was associated with disposable slave labor, tirelessly toiling at the will of the controlling master. In his review of the play, J. Brooks Atkinson identified with the theme of exploitation and noted that, 'If zombies are those who work without knowing why and who see without understanding, one begins to look around among one's fellow countrymen with a new apprehension. Perhaps those native drums are sounding the national anthem'.[5] Second, Webb acknowledged the unspoken socio-political fear of miscegenation that had arisen in the American imagination through his depiction of a white female as the victim of both the zombified black male figure and his Voodoo master known as a Houngan. The staged exotic barbarism of Voodoo and its practitioners threatened to corrupt the sanctitude of white American femininity. Without overtly casting a black actor in the role of manipulative Houngan, the threat of 'blackness' was instead projected onto the enactment of Voodoo practices, thereby tarring the religion as a malicious endangerment to American values (Kee 15). While this self-proclaimed 'Play of the Tropics' garnered extra publicity with the enlistment of two Haitian immigrants as a more authentic replacement for actors in blackface, Webb's script lacked the dramatic flair required to establish the zombie as a veritable figure of horror (Russell 20). In spite of this, Victor and Edward Halperin recognized the horrific potential of the zombie and enlisted Garnett Weston as the screenwriter for the zombie's Hollywood debut. As a documented figure of fact, the zombie existed outside of the realm of copyright, therefore when the Halperins released the feature-length film *White Zombie* a few months after the final stage performance of *Zombie* in 1932, Webb's legal claims of infringement were viewed as nothing more than disparagement. Weston's familiarity with Seabrook's account of Haiti, having already penned an inspired short story 'Salt Is Not for Slaves', resulted in a depiction of the zombie that replicated the mystique and horror of Seabrook's original ghouls, with an added element of Hollywood sensationalism. And in casting Béla Lugosi, fresh from his title role in Tod Browning's *Dracula* (1931), in the role of Voodoo master Murder Legendre, the Halperins ensured that *White Zombie* catapulted the figure into the Gothic imagination (Russell 20).

Despite its status as an independent production, *White Zombie* had sought to expand on the themes introduced by Webb in *Zombie*. However, Russell notes that an aggressive marketing campaign was used to 'play up the veracity of the events depicted in the film' (Russell 22) by stating that the film was based on factual evidence and events. In the buildup to the film's opening night on July 29, 1932, the advertising campaign reached a crescendo as is evident in an excerpt from *The 1922 Film Daily Year Book of Motion Pictures*:

> When *White Zombie* was ushered into the Rivoli Theatre in New York, all Broadway was startled by the sudden appearance of nine zombies on the boardwalk erected above the marquee of the theatre. Thousands packed the sidewalks and gasped with amazement as the nine figures, faithfully garbed and made-up to simulate actual members of the *White Zombie* cast, went through a series of thrilling dramatic sequences [...] The doll-like figures of the girls were dressed in white flowing robes and the men looked as if they had been dug up from the ground with wooden splints on their legs and battered facial expressions [...] crowds gathered all day, lured there not only by the drama enacted above the theatre but by the *White Zombie* sound effects records which included the screeching of vultures, the grinding of the sugar mill and the beating of tom toms and other nerve wracking sounds. (Alicoate 101)

Onlookers were immersed in a sensory explosion of Haitian exotica, wherein the 'otherness' of Haiti, her people and her secrets were exploited and embellished in an attempt to sell movie-theater tickets. In effect, Haitian identity became a commodity or, rather, the American construction of a sensationalized Haitian identity became a commodity. Due to the emphasis that had been placed on the anthropological legitimacy of the film, America's already polluted perception of Haiti thus became further distorted.

The 'white zombie' of the film is Madeleine Short (Madge Bellamy), a young, newly married American woman who becomes a zombie after drinking poison administered by the wealthy plantation owner, Charles Beaumont (Robert Frazer). Beaumont, having obtained the poison from the Houngan, Murder Legendre (Béla Lugosi), quickly regrets his decision to transform Madeleine into a zombie once he realizes his zombified bride is nothing more than an unresponsive automaton. Legendre refuses to return Madeleine to life, choosing rather to zombify Beaumont and take Madeleine for himself. Legendre's zombification of Madeleine had various implications.

First, the concept of zombification existed as an aspect of the primitivism associated with Haiti. Therefore, Madeleine's susceptibility to Legendre's Voodoo implies, Kee would suggest, 'that a primitive nature lurked inside the civilized white person' (Kee 17). Legendre's decision to betray Beaumont and claim Madeleine for himself spoke to the white societal fear of miscegenation that was prevalent during the 1930s. It is through Legendre's claim to the white woman that conventional boundaries between Self and Other begin to collapse. The traditional colonial roles of white master and black slave are reversed as the 'whiteness' of the 'civilized' Western world is breeched by the primitivism of black magic for, as Gyllian Phillips notes, 'Legendre threatens to infect whites with the contagion of native magic and pharmacology by transforming them into zombies' (27). Haiti is therefore instantiated as a land of primitivism, sacrifice and Voodoo wherein the young white American female requires rescuing from the racially impure hands of the Houngan and zombieism. As Degoul notes, 'The American imagination appropriates, then, a theme that issued from the Haitian imagination, racializes and eroticizes it, all the while associating it in quasi-symbolic fashion with the Haitian situation, with Negro Haitianness more broadly, as marked by witchcraft' (27).

White Zombie begins with a scene taken directly from Seabrook's *The Magic Island* wherein Madeleine and her soon-to-be husband, Neil (John Harron), witness a Voodoo burial ceremony occurring in plain view along the roadside. The scene immediately sets the tone of the narrative, catapulting both characters and viewers into the unfamiliar exoticism of the Haitian way of life. Madeleine asks, 'Driver, what is it?' to which he answers, 'It's a funeral, Mademoiselle. They're afraid of the men who steal dead bodies'. The carriage continues on down the road until it stops next to a stranger, Murder Legendre, to ask for directions. Legendre ignores him and instead, stares transfixed at Madeleine until the driver notices a group of shuffling figures heading towards the carriage. 'Zombies!' the driver yells, before hastening the horses onwards. Later, the driver explains, stating 'They are not dead, monsieur. They are dead bodies. Zombies! The living dead. Corpses taken from their graves and made to work in the sugar mills and fields at night'. This explanation drives to the very still undead-heart at the core of zombieism: *They are not men*. The zombies depicted in both *Zombie* and *White Zombie* are portrayed as having been stripped of their identity and, subsequently, their humanity. Herein it is possible to identify the American attraction to the zombie in the 1930s as stemming from the possibility to 'cast an entire group of people as beings without humanity' (Kee 17). Human beings are reduced to automata, toiling tirelessly and endlessly, the definitive other; void of selfhood, existing only as a nonentity. A definitive scene in *White Zombie* further illustrates the insignificance of the dehumanized figure as a working zombie silently tumbles into the sugar mill where his body is obliviously ground up with the sugar cane by his unresponsive comrades. The scene, as a critique of slavery, not only signifies the capitalist system's exploitation of workers but is also indicative of the white sugar as a product of the capitalist system, being stained with the blood of disposable labor, which echoes Marx's notion of the capitalist mode of production. 'Capital comes dripping from head to foot, from the very pore, with blood and dirt' (834). However, the central force of horror within *White Zombie* is not emphasized as originating in the capitalist system, but rather with the Houngan, Murder Legendre. It is his extensive knowledge of Voodoo that gives him the power to de-humanize men in the creation of zombies.

Haitian Identity: Exogenous and Endogenous

The construction of the zombie as a specifically Haitian figure of horror originated, as previously explored, in the ethnographic and anthropological investigations of Western researchers exploring the social and cultural systems of Haiti. Thus, the zombie has been fabricated as a figure of Haitian folklore, as opposed to purely a feature of Haitian folklife (Bishop 41). Therefore, Bishop suggests, the figure should 'be approached as both a disciplinary subject and the resulting product of such academic investigations' (41). However, in his recent anthropological research on Haiti, Franck Degoul indicates that there is perhaps an additional aspect to consider when investigating the connection between the zombie and Haiti. Most notably, 'the way the practice is thought of and practiced by Haitians' (Degoul 25) encapsulates the Haitian image, self-produced as a response to the sensationalized image created by outside perceptions of Haiti.

Degoul utilizes the term 'exogenous' when referring to the construction of the Haitian image by Western authors. The term 'exogenous' becomes integral to this investigation as it is vital to regard these interpretations of Haiti as emerging from 'outside the sociocultural Haitian context' (Degoul 24), established 'through the interpretive prism that defines zombification and witchcraft as unfailingly linked' (24). The imagological notion of 'hetero-image' is the construction of a national 'image', namely of Haiti, as assembled from an external perspective and therefore differing greatly from the 'auto-image' created internally, endogenously, by Haitians. Degoul maintains that the 'auto-image' of Haiti was constructed, by Haitians, in response to the negative 'hetero-image' propagated by sensationalized reports of primitive Voodoo folklore. Therefore, the concept of zombieism can be explored from two perspectives: first, from the perception of foreign visitors to Haiti and second, as a product of the 'Haitian indigenous movement, born precisely in reaction to the American occupation' (Degoul 27). As previously mentioned, the primitive image of Haiti perpetuated by American forces was used to justify the necessity of the American occupation of Haiti in an attempt to 'civilize' the devolved, and de-evolved, nation. While Seabrook's *The Magic Island* ignited the spark of the American fascination with Voodoo and zombies, an alternative textual analysis of Seabrook's interactions with Haitian natives exposes the way in which his Haitian interviewees presented notions of Voodoo and zombies in a manner that allowed for and invited the perpetuated sensationalism in the construction of the Haitian hetero-image, in order to facilitate the simultaneous construction of a powerful and purposeful depiction of an Haitian auto-image in opposition. A similar comparison can be drawn with a more recent ethnographic exploration of Haitian Voodoo and zombieism, Wade Davis' *The Serpent and the Rainbow* (1985). Davis, an ethnobotanist, travelled to Haiti with the intention of dispelling the supernatural myth behind the creation of zombies. While his anthropological investigation conducted a measured approach of the island, its inhabitants and their culture, the 1988 horror film of the same name, inspired by the book and directed by Wes Craven, presented an account of Haiti that used its basis on factual research to justify the veracity of sensationalized depictions of Voodoo and zombies. The relationship between *The Serpent and the Rainbow* and its cinematic adaptation suggests that the representation of Haitian identity and its connection to Voodoo continues to dominate American perceptions of Haiti. This echoes Najman's statement that 'The great powers, which had never accepted the birth of the completely new black republic, would instantly associate Vaudou and witchcraft before making the zombie the incarnation of the 'bad Haitian' (249).[6] The practice of zombification is established as a symbol distinguishing the difference between the cultures of the civilized white American from that of the barbaric black Haitian. In so doing, this difference is racialized and reduced to a matter of nature, which results in implying an inherent Haitian mysticism.

As a 'black' country, Haiti was categorized by its association to Africa and the imported primitive practices of Voodoo. As a result, zombification was constructed as the reigning emblem of an inherited tradition, 'a sign of the Negro atavism that pushed the Haitian to cruelty, as revelatory of his incapacity to access the 'civilization' to which, at the time, the Americans were trying to guide him' (Degoul 28). As opposed to recognizing the exogenous origins of this perception of Haitian identity as being informed by a Western imagination that held it to Western ideals, zombieism is maintained as an intrinsic element of the Haitian reality, 'Haiti: it is Vaudou; Vaudou: witchcraft; and witchcraft… zombification' (Degoul 29).

Consequently, this exogenous perception influenced the way in which the endogenous portrayal of Haitian identity was adapted in order to take advantage of the flawed impression of Haitian abilities. Haiti, Degoul notes, 'defended itself by means of zombification' (29), using techniques unique to Haiti and exploiting existing superstitions regarding Haitian mysticism. 'Americans make weapons, but us, our weapon is the principle of zombification!' Claudel, an informant of Degoul's, explains, 'In the same way, if we cannot zombify you, if we see that we cannot zombify you, we'll try another route that we call 'pyès', that we call 'powders''[7] (Degoul 31–32). The Haitian association with zombification as established and documented in travelogues during the early years of the American occupation, such as in Seabrook's *The Magic Island*, created an 'emblem of Negro Haitian savagery' (Degoul 32) that was positively reappropriated by Haitians in the construction of an auto-image that confirms the American trepidation of an intrinsic Haitian mysticism. Seabrook describes his informant Polynice as 'rational' (94), as the least credulous of the 'negroes' interviewed, as 'too intelligent to believe [the superstitions] literally true' (93). And yet, Polynice remarks 'Superstition? But I assure you this of which you now speak is not a matter of superstition. Alas, these things—and other evil practices connected with the dead—exist. They exist to an extent that you whites do not dream of, though evidences are everywhere under your eyes' (94). Polynice's suggestion that the existences of Haitian 'evil practices' are outside of the 'white' sphere of experience implies that the Haitians are in possession of a certain kind of knowledge imperceptible to white visitors, an inherent Haitian knowledge. In an interview with a Houngan named Max Beauvoir, Wade Davis is told of Haiti: 'This is a land where things are not the way they seem' (Davis 47). The racialized knowledge of zombieism is utilized as a cultural trait 'to mark a fundamental difference between Haiti' (Degoul 32) and white visitors to her shore as a defining affirmation of Haitian identity.

Zombification, exogenously, was established as a demonstration of Haitian primitivism and used as the basis for the separation between American 'self' and Haitian 'other'. Sensationalized accounts of zombieism in film, *White Zombie* and *The Serpent and the Rainbow*, projected the hetero-image of a savage Haitian mysticism into the realm of the Western audience, whereby attention was redirected back toward Haiti. Positively reappropriated, the exogenous sign of Haitian barbarism becomes an endogenous indicator of Haitianness, implying a unique knowledge of practices outside the realm of Western perception—a knowledge that Degoul identifies as 'completely Haitian and jealously protected' (34). Western attempts to access this specifically Haitian knowledge are depicted in both films as being detrimental to the men involved. In *White Zombie* Charles Beaumont enlists the power of Murder Legendre: using the Houngan's potion to zombify Madeleine, Beaumont appears to have accessed the world of Voodoo knowledge. However, following his expressed displeasure and disappointment with the zombified Madeleine, he is promptly poisoned by Legendre and reduced to the state of a mere white zombie. Similarly, in *The Serpent and the Rainbow*, Dennis Allan journeys to Haiti with the intention of discovering the secret active ingredient in a drug used to make zombies. Allan's attempt to gain this closely guarded knowledge results in him being arrested (twice), having his scrotum nailed into a chair and being framed for murder, held at gunpoint, zombified, buried alive, embroiled in a battle of feuding Houngans and finally having to rely on the assistance of his 'Jaguar spirit' to defeat an evil Houngan in a hallucinogenic final scene. The knowledge is never wholly attained.

These films, and the travelogues on which they are based, depict a purposeful journey to Haiti with the objective of gaining insight into the fiercely protected knowledge at the heart of Haitian Voodoo. As Other, the Western seeker enters the realm of Haitian mysticism with the intention of gaining an understanding of the fundamental basis of Haitian identity. The Houngans of these narratives allow the Western Other a participatory role in their private practices, proving the authenticity of their abilities without revealing the true source of their powers. The Western seeker finds himself immersed in Haitian alterity, while failing to define or comprehend the basis or magnitude of this uniquely Haitian power. In his anthropological research of the subject, Degoul explains that 'the desire demonstrated by certain 'blancs' to be initiated into its rites, takes on the quality of suspicious intrusions into the very core of their Haitianness' (36). An intrusion into the very source of the construction of Haitian identity, the acquisition of such knowledge would threaten the Haitian ability to maintain control of 'that which the Haitian national identity is founded on, and which gives it its strength and power' (Degoul 37).

Conclusion

The difference, therefore, between 'self' and 'other', in these examples, extends beyond differences of nationality into the very essence of nature and of race. In the same way that the Haitian was depicted as lacking a natural capacity to appropriate the civilizing practices offered by the French colonialists and then the American occupiers, now the white American is positioned as 'other' with a racialized incapacity to comprehend or possess the Haitian mysticism of Voodoo. Voodoo practices, particularly that of zombification, operating in a manner of 'explicitly racialized Haitianness' (Degoul 38) surpass their original conception and become significant factors in the construction of a 'collective Haitian Identity' (38). The exogenous image constructed of zombieism as a notion of barbaric Haitianness is positively reappropriated in the endogenous conception of a uniquely Haitian national identity informed by its inherent understanding of, and participation in, a knowledge of Voodoo and its practices to serve as a strategic defense against the imposing control of American powers.

While, on the one hand, the figure of contemporary zombie cinema has been stripped of its exoticism following Romero's extrication of the figure from Haiti and enabling, as Chris Vials notes, 'a more progressive bent within the genre' (42). The relocation of the figure from the exotic to the domestic has allowed the zombie to function as a somewhat 'empty signifier' in that the term 'can [now] be attached to the most diverse social contents' based on an absence of a 'content of its own' (Laclau 76). The zombie has become a figure of malleable meaning, extending beyond the realm of the Gothic into corporate, political and legal discourse. Words like zombie banks, zombie funds, zombie investors and zombie computers circulate in a world far removed from the folkloric origins of the term. The zombie is used to critique capitalism, consumerism, the threat of miscegenation, obsessive technology trends, overzealous science, and the concept of a zombie apocalypse has even been utilized in training templates for large scale catastrophe planning and by the Centers for Disease Control and Prevention as a tongue-in-cheek approach to engage with a wider audience. Within contemporary literature, there has been an increasing shift from the threat of a zombie apocalypse to the emergence of zombie sentience, wherein zombie protagonists navigate the 'living' landscape as an 'other', negotiating the construction of identity in consideration of their own 'selfhood'. This, though greatly detached from the exoticism of Haiti, implies that notions of identity remain an integral aspect of zombieism.

Notes

1. When Voodoo practices are used with malicious intent, those practices are referred to as: 'the work of the left hand.'
2. On the most basic level, the Other can be understood as that which deviates from what is considered the idealized cultural norm within a society. The Other is positioned externally to the Self; additionally, in terms of groups of people, the Other can function as the group on to which another group can project its fears and insecurities, in line with Julia Kristeva's theory of Abjection. See: Kristeva, Julia. *Powers of Horror: An Essay on Abjection*. Trans. Leon S. Roudiez. New York: Columbia UP, 1982.
3. The first three in the *Dead* series being *Night of the Living Dead* (1968), followed by *Dawn of the Dead* (1979), and *Day of the Dead* (1985) concluding the original trilogy.
4. For examples in literature see: Browne, S. G. *Breathers: A Zombie's Lament* (New York: Broadway, 2009). As well as the *White Trash Zombie* series by Diana Rowland: Rowland, Diana. *My Life as a White Trash Zombie* (New York: Daw, 2011).
5. Atkinson, J. Brooks. Rev. of *Zombie,* by Kenneth Webb. *New York Times*, 11 February 1932, clipping in *White Zombie Production Code File*. The Margaret Herrick Library of the Academy of Motion Picture Arts and Sciences.
6. This quotation is taken from the translated version, which appears in Degoul, Franck. "We Are the Mirror of Your Fears': Haitian Identity and Zombification.' *Better off Dead: The Evolution of the Zombie as Post-human*. Ed. Deborah Christie and Sarah Juliet Lauro. Trans. Lore, Elisabeth M. (New York: Fordham UP, 2011), 27.
7. 'Powders' are also mentioned by Wade Davis in *The Serpent and the Rainbow*, see page 185 for Davis's expansion on the subject from an anthropological context.

Bibliography

Alicoate, Jack. *The 1933 Film Daily Year Book of Motion Pictures*. New York: Wid's Films and Film Folk, 1933. Print.

Atkinson, J. Brooks. Rev. of *Zombie,* by Kenneth Webb. *New York Times*, 11 February 1932, clipping in *White Zombie Production Code File*. The Margaret Herrick Library of the Academy of Motion Picture Arts and Sciences.

Bishop, Kyle William. *American Zombie Gothic: The Rise and Fall (and Rise) of the Walking Dead in Popular Culture*. North Carolina: McFarland, 2010. Print.

Browne, S. G. *Breathers: A Zombie's Lament*. New York: Broadway, 2009. Print.
Davis, David Brion. 'Impact of the French and Haitian Revolutions.' *The Impact of the Haitian Revolution in the Atlantic World*. Ed. Geggus, David P. Columbia: U of California, 2001. 3–9. Print.
Davis, Wade. *The Serpent and the Rainbow*. New York: Simon and Schuster, 1997. Print.
Dawn of the Dead. Dir. George A. Romero. Perf. David Emge and Ken Foree. United Film Distribution Company, 1979. DVD.
Day of the Dead. Dir. George A. Romero. Perf. Lori Cardille and Joseph Pilato. United Film Distribution Company, 1985. DVD.
Degoul, Franck. "We Are the Mirror of Your Fears': Haitian Identity and Zombification.' *Better off Dead: The Evolution of the Zombie as Post-human*. Ed. Christie, Deborah, and Sarah Juliet Lauro. Trans. Elisabeth M. Lore. New York: Fordham UP, 2011. 24–38. Print.
Drezner, Daniel W. *Theories of International Politics and Zombies*. Princeton, NJ: Princeton UP, 2011. Print.
Dubois, Laurent. *Avengers of the New World: The Story of the Haitian Revolution*. Cambridge, MA: Belknap of Harvard UP, 2004. Print.
Hearn, Lafcadio. *The Country of the Comers-Back*. Redditch: Read, 2011. Print.
Hurston, Zora Neale. *Tell My Horse: Voodoo and Life in Haiti and Jamaica*. New York: Perennial Library, 1990. Print.
Kee, Chera. ''They Are Not Men... They Are Dead Bodies!' From Cannibal to Zombie and Back Again.' *Better off Dead: The Evolution of the Zombie as Post-human*. Ed. Christie, Deborah, and Sarah Juliet Lauro. New York: Fordham UP, 2011. 9–23. Print.
Koven, Mikel J. 'The Folklore of the Zombie FIlm.' *Zombie Culture: Autopsies of the Living Dead*. Ed. McIntosh, Shawn, and Marc Leverette. Lanham, MD: Scarecrow, 2008. 19–34. Print.
Kristeva, Julia. *Powers of Horror: An Essay on Abjection*. Trans. Roudiez, Leon S., New York: Columbia UP, 1982. Print.
Laclau, Ernesto. *On Populist Reason*. London: Verso, 2005. Print.
Mahoney, Phillip. 'Mass Psychology and the Analysis of the Zombie: From Suggestion to Contagion.' *Generation Zombie: Essays on the Living Dead in Modern Culture*. Ed. Boluk, Stephanie, and Wylie Lenz. Jefferson, NC: McFarland, 2011. 113–29. Print.
Marion, Isaac. *Warm Bodies: A Novel*. New York: Atria, 2011. Print.
Marx, Karl. *Capital: A Critique of Political Economy*. Ed. Engels, Friedrich, Vol. 3. New York: Cosimo, 2007. Print.
Mitchell, Dominic. *In the Flesh*. Dir. Jonny Campbell. BBC 3. United Kingdom, Mar. 2013. Television.
Najman, Charlie. *Haïti, Dieu Seul Me Voit: Récit*. Paris: Balland, 1995. Print.
Night of the Living Dead. Dir. George A. Romero. By John Russo. Perf. Duane Jones, Judith O'Dea, Marilyn Eastman, and Karl Hardman. Continental Distributing, Inc., 1968. DVD.
Phillips, Gyllian. 'White Zombie and the Creole: William Seabrook's The Magic Island and American Imperialism in Haiti.' *Generation Zombie: Essays on the Living Dead in Modern Culture*. Ed. Boluk, Stephanie, and Wylie Lenz. Jefferson, NC: McFarland, 2011. 27–40. Print.
Rowland, Diana. *My Life as a White Trash Zombie*. New York: Daw, 2011. Print.

Russell, Jamie. *Book of the Dead: The Complete History of Zombie Cinema*. Surrey: FAB, 2007. Print.

Seabrook, William B. *The Magic Island*. Bath: Pitman, 1936. Print.

The Serpent and the Rainbow. Dir. Wes Craven. Perf. Bill Pullman. Universal Pictures, 1988. DVD.

Vials, Chris. 'The Origin of the Zombie in American Radio and Film: B-Horror, U.S. Empire, and the Politics of Disavowal.' *Generation Zombie: Essays on the Living Dead in Modern Culture*. Ed. Boluk, Stephanie, and Wylie Lenz. Jefferson, NC: McFarland, 2011. 41–53. Print.

Warm Bodies. Dir. Jonathan Levine. Perf. Nicholas Hoult and Teresa Palmer. Summit Entertainment, 2013. DVD.

White Zombie. Dir. Victor Halperin. Perf. Béla Lugosi. United Artists Corp., 1932.

6 Consuming the Tropics

The Tropical Zombie Re-Eviscerated in *Dead Island*

Johan Höglund

Just before the release of the tropical first-person shooter zombie game *Dead Island*, game developers Techland put out a series of marketing images reminiscent of *Sports Illustrated's* infamous yearly Swim Suit issue. Produced by the game's own engine, rather than by a separate graphics program, these images show young women in bikinis, lounging around the tropical beach resort where the initial stages of the game take place. Just like in the Swim Suit issue, the women, and the tropical landscape in which are placed, appear to invite a gaze that is simultaneously male and colonial. What sets these women apart from the women of *Sports Illustrated* is the fact that their bodies have great, open wounds, that their eyes stare vacantly and that their mouths smile hungrily at the camera. These women have literally been partly consumed by other zombies. Now, they have themselves been transformed into the undead and threaten to consume the prospective gamer.[1]

These images raise many questions about the gothic and about the tropics as a contemporary gothic space. How are we to understand the concurrent attraction and abjection of these zombified women? What kind of invitation do they extend to the prospective gamer? What does the location of beautiful yet battered and abject female bodies in the similarly beautiful and inviting backdrop of the tropics mean? When the game begins and the gamer encounters these hungry women—along with other zombified people: tourists, hotel employees, locals and natives that belong to the indigenous 'highland tribes' of the island—the objective of the gamer is to violently destroy these bodies. This violence raises additional questions. What does it mean to cut, bash and shoot these undead, half-naked bodies to pieces? Indeed, what is the attraction of the game premise: the virtually constant slaughter of endless hordes of powerful zombies within a consumed but also consuming tropical setting?

In an attempt to answer these and other questions, this chapter investigates *Dead Island* as a game about tourism in the tropics but also as a virtual tourism space in itself. The analysis makes use of John Urry's influential observation that places are intimately related to consumption. As will be discussed below, Urry proposes that tourist sites in particular are understood as places that can be consumed in various ways. At the same time, they are also places that can consume you. With Urry's thesis in mind, it can be argued that *Dead Island* invites us to consume the tropics as a feminine, primitive, eroticized and violent space, as a territory that must be consumed or it will consume you. This article thus argues that the gamer consumes the tropics partly through the exercise of an overtly male and colonial gaze and partly through consumptive violence. This suggests that the game operates as an updated form of what Patrick Brantlinger has termed Imperial Gothic. However, this article argues that the game never gets comfortable with the sexual and racist politics it arguably endorses. While the tropical space and the bodies that inhabit it allow the gamer to engage in a form of virtual gothic colonialism, the complex narrative attempts to sabotage the Manichean categories that seemingly inform the game's virtual geography and the semiotics of violence on which the game relies.

Figure 6.1 Videogame logo.

The Tropics, Imperialism and Consuming Tourism

As Felix Driver and Luciana Martins observe in their collection *Tropical Visions in an Age of Empire* (2005) and as Susie Protschky notes in *Images of the Tropics* (2011), the tropics were central both to the European colonial project as such and to the way that this project was understood in Europe. In the words of Driver and Martins, whether 'represented positively (as in fantasies of the tropical sublime) or negatively (as a pathological space of degeneration), tropicality has frequently served as a foil to temperate nature, to all that is modest, civilized, cultivated' (3). Such representations have fueled and legitimized the pan-European colonial project since the 'discovery' of the Americas by Christopher Columbus, and they are very prevalent, especially the image of the Tropics a pathological space, in *Dead Island*.

The reliance on colonialist tropes in *Dead Island* suggests that the tropics is still being constructed as the Other of Europe and the West. It is sometimes argued that Western colonization ended when Portugal granted East Timor sovereignty in the United Nations. However, such a position disregards the many ways in which colonization and imperialism have transformed and adapted to globalization. While the military invasion and occupation of territory is still practiced by Western states, as exemplified by the invasion of Iraq by the US in 2003, Empire is today a much more transnational and fluid form of power.[2] The structural, economic and social inequalities, the loss of valuable territory and the depletion of indigenous natural resources that old-style colonialism produced is today effected through (capitalist) enterprises less obviously imperial and less costly than the military invasion and occupation of territory. Of these enterprises, global tourism is one of the most prominent.

Several scholars describe tourism as a colonial practice. Richard King argues that colonialism 'quite literally laid the foundations for tourism, and tourism, in turn, has made possible the reinvention of colonial relations in the postcolonial world' (589). Thus, tourism 'arguably corresponds with the transformation of colonialism in the wake of decolonization, reinscribing it in neocolonial terms' (589). As one of several useful case studies of how this has occurred, Dennis Merrill's *Negotiating Paradise: U.S. Tourism and Empire* (2009) views tourism as a practice central to how the U.S. extended its 'presence in twentieth-century Latin America and helped internationalize U.S. culture' (1). Noting that although tourism often 'mimic[s] conquest', Merrill describes tourism as a more unsolidified 'ongoing international negotiation' and observes that U.S. empire produces it as 'a textured and fluid structure' (1). Indeed, the empire here is not so much a state; it is a host of economic institutions such as airlines, hotel conglomerates, tourist agencies, caterers, resort constructors and security firms that are often affiliated with Western nation states but have a less distinct relationship to such states than the U.S. marines that led the invasion of Iraq.

For King and Merrill, tourism relies on the same type of discourses as traditional colonialism and tends to produce the same forms of material and economic relations. As discussed by Urry, these relations often revolve around the process of consumption. In *Consuming Places* (1995), Urry observes that places have four different relationships to consumption. These are worth outlining as they provide a useful vantage point for understanding how the Zombie Gothic of *Dead Island* constructs the tropics as a site for tourism. First, Urry claims, places are 'increasingly being restructured as centres for consumption' (1). In other words, places are visited in order to engage in consumption of food, animals, artifacts and bodies that are intimately connected to these particular places. Second, Urry argues that 'places themselves are in a sense consumed, particularly visually' (1). This is a crucial observation, for it acknowledges the presence of what E. Ann Kaplan has termed 'the imperial gaze'. In *Looking for the Other: Feminism, Film and the Imperial Gaze* (1997), Kaplan describes how the gaze is an instrument of domination. Looking at the Other and the space of the Other is an attempt to simultaneously consume and dominate the Other and the space this category occupies. This corresponds to Mary Louise Pratt's assertion in *Imperial Eyes: Travel Writing and Transculturation* (1992) that the colonial enterprise positions the white European male (following a paradigm popularized by Daniel Defoe's 1719 novel *Robinson Crusoe*) as the patriarch king of all that he surveys outside of European borders.[3] To return to Urry, his third observation is that 'places can be literally consumed, [...] devoured or exhausted by use' (1–2). This describes how the colonial enterprise often impacts the colony, but it also pertains to the transformation and consumption of the (tropical) landscape in relation to tourism. Finally, Urry notes that 'it is possible for localities to consume one's identity so that such places become almost literally all-consuming places' (2). The observation that the subject can also be consumed by a certain place is particularly relevant when studying a game wherein the gamer avatar risks being eaten alive. The zombie's attempt to consume the gamer's avatar, and the way that his or her bite utterly transforms identity, can be viewed as a form of metonymy that describes precisely how places can consume. The discussion of *Dead Island* as a type of virtual Imperial Gothic, but also as an attempt to disturb the premises of this Gothic mode, will be guided by this understanding of tourism practice and of the tourism site as a place structured by different forms of consumption: a place that is both consumed and consuming.

The Tropical Tourism Gothic of *Dead Island*

Dead Island is set on the fictional island of Banoi. At first sight, this is a beautiful tropical island located somewhere just off the coast of Papua New Guinea. This location is admittedly not geographically part of the Americas, but the island has the same relationship to this continent and to the global West as the American tropics. The Royal Palms Resort, the five-star hotel at the center of the tourism industry on the island, has a transnational clientele of tourists and is serviced by a similarly transnational community of workers. Importantly, though, the majority of the vacationers are from the U.S., and English is the lingua franca of the tourists and, of course, of the game. Furthermore, of the four 'heroes' the gamer can use as an avatar, two are U.S. citizens. Finally, the concerns that the game raises and the cultural, sexual and political landscape in which it takes place, are undeniably American.

Dead Island is a long and complex game and can be experienced with four different characters or 'heroes' that are interestingly different from the usual first-person shooter avatar. My discussion of the game will first focus on the important opening of the game, before turning to the different avatars and the development of the plot. The game's prelims and first episodes are key to understanding the multiple ways the game imagines tropical tourism and how it concurrently invokes and disrupts the consuming imperial gaze.

The first image presented to the gamer is a short trailer that was also used to market the game.[4] This trailer begins in the dead eye of a white, pre-adolescent girl dead on a grassy lawn outside a large resort hotel. As the camera moves away from her eyes and face, her body is pulled up into the air where it comes alive with disturbing energy, flailing upwards until it enters a comfortable hotel suite through a gigantic glass window, the shards of which reassemble themselves as she passes through it. Now, she hugs what we will soon come to understand is her father, but she is sitting on his shoulders, biting him in the neck. The mother looks on in sheer horror, not knowing whether to point the long knife she is holding in her daughter's direction or toward the horribly mutilated zombies that have invaded the hotel suite. In the final scene, probably taken only hours before the attack (they are all wearing the same clothes), the family poses happily before a camera, smiling in front of the resort hotel's glass and steel and the lush beauty of the tropical paradise the hotel overlooks.

The location of the game's beginning in eyes of the girl gestures to the powerful gaze of the white tourist, and suggests that this gaze is crucial to the game. However, the fact that the gaze is dead, or at least undead, stresses its problematic nature and foreshadows the game's complex critique of tourism colonialism.

In the next sequence, the game abandons the third-person perspective of the introductory trailer and inserts the gamer into the body of a drunk white man (most likely one of the game's characters, Ryder White).[5] The gamer is thus inserted into the first-person-perspective of the game. The gaze of the avatar is now also the gaze of the gamer. However, at this stage, the gamer has no control over the character's gaze or body. In the sequence that follows, the gamer in Ryder White's body stumbles by and into some surfer slackers and bikini-clad tourists, all of whom are thin and beautiful, swelling with muscle or silicone. They sneer at White's/the gamer's intoxicated presence as he enters a large nightclub where people are dancing energetically. White climbs the stage, grabs a bottle from a loudspeaker and takes another swig before he is pushed off the stage. He falls hard, and a friendly hotel employee helps him up, but suddenly a woman in a bikini jumps onto the employee's back, snarling and biting. Maybe White is hallucinating. Nobody in the clubs takes much notice. Yet there is blood in his eyes, blurring his vision. He makes his way into the women's bathroom where he washes his face and steals a tube of sedatives. Back in his room, he swallows the pills with a gulp of bourbon and falls asleep.

The initial perspective of the gamer is, symbolically and significantly, 'White'. Here, the avatar's drunken gaze is indeed that of the male colonizer. His eyes search for the bodies of half-naked women and alcohol to consume. To have the gamer look out through the eyes of a white, male protagonist follows an established pattern in gaming. In *Tomb Raiders and Space Invaders*, Geoff King and Tanya Krzywinska observe that computer games in general, and first-person-shooters in particular, typically have avatars who are heterosexual, white and male (108). It is possible that the game critiques this perspective by representing it as, literally and symbolically, unbalanced, imperialist and misogynist. However, to invest the avatar with such qualities is, according to King and Krzywinska, seldom ironic. Instead, these qualities are meant to be embraced in computer games. In other words, the gamer may well take White's machismo for granted here, even identify with it.

Figure 6.2 The avatars.

After the White-sequence, the gamer is presented with a choice of four different playable characters, all of whom stand around a smoking truck surrounded by palm trees and a clear, blue sky. Interestingly and quite uniquely, these characters are not predominately white. The first is one-hit wonder Sam B, a massive black rapper from New Orleans who is employed as an entertainer on the Island. The second is Xian Mei, a Chinese hotel receptionist but also a spy in the service of the Chinese government. The third character is Purna, a female aborigine from Australia. She is a former employee of the 'Sydney Police Force' and now works as a bodyguard at the resort. The gamer is made to understand that, as a female aborigine, Purna has struggled against patriarchy and racial prejudice throughout her life.[6] The fourth character, Logan Carter, is an alcoholic and former quarterback from Texas; he is the only character who looks to be a white man and the only actual tourist; he has been given an extended trip to the tropical resort in exchange for promoting a blood drive on the island. However, his dark hair and skin suggests that he may not be entirely white, and the tribal tattoos on his arms indicate a liminal racial and ethnic position. Thus, none of the characters whose body the gamer can inhabit and control at this stage of the game is as unambiguously white as 'White'.

When the gamer has picked an avatar, the perspectives of the gamer and the avatar merge. The gamer looks out through the avatar's eyes, and the game begins for real. It should be noted that although Sam B, Xian Mei and Purna are all employees of the resort hotel that functions as the tourism hub in the game, their gazes do merge with that of the gamer turning them also into tourists within the game. While the avatar provides the gaming experience with a form of filter, consisting mostly of certain combative skills and brief comments on the action of the game, the gamer has no previous knowledge of the resort hotel or the island and therefore engages in a form of mediated tourism of this tropical space. Thus, the gamer, regardless of her or his own ethnic and gender identity, becomes a tourist in this apocalyptic tropical paradise.

Another crucial point is that while the gamer knows very little about the resort or the island, s/he does know, unlike the avatar, what is coming. The game has clearly advertised the fact that it is about killing zombified humans on a tropical island. Thus, the gamer is not simply a tropical vacationer but more properly a 'thanatourist'. Thanatourism has been defined by Tony Seaton as 'travel to a location wholly, or partially, motivated by the desire for actual or symbolic encounters with death, particularly, but not exclusively, violent death, which may, to a varying degree be activated by the person-specific features of those whose deaths are its focal objects' (236). The difference between non-virtual thanatourism and the thanatourism offered by the game is, of course, that the gamer not only observes a site where death has occurred, s/he is an active agent who brings this death about. In other words, the gamer visits the beautiful island of Banoi to kill the living and the undead that stand in her or his way. Here, the ritual of killing is important. The moment when violence is unleashed by the avatar forms the semiotic center of the first-person shooter genre.

The gamer's expectations as an active thanatourist are not fulfilled instantly. When the gamer has picked an avatar, s/he is sent on a trip around the hotel, sees signs of disorder and hears victims screaming in pain. The victims call out for help over the aggressive, animalistic snarling of the infected zombies. This brief episode is designed to familiarize the gamer with the interface of the game, but it also introduces the gamer to an authoritative voiceover: the internal speaker system. This voice professes to be Colonel Ryder White, and he proceeds to give the gamer instructions and missions throughout the game. At the end of this initial episode, the gamer is spotted by a group of zombies; s/he must flee through the hotel corridor but is struck down by another zombie. Following this episode, the gamer is unconsciously transported to a poorly fortified beach hut surrounded by very hungry zombies. The gamer has been saved by a group of survivors and can now begin to violently eradicate the undead that are taking over the island.

It is at this stage that the game clearly takes shape as a form of Imperial Gothic. Like other forms of Gothic, the Imperial Gothic opens up a space where the social and political concerns of a certain historical crisis are negotiated and explained. Just as the pathological symptoms of the human mind and body house the reasons for the illness and suggest possible developments and futures, the Imperial Gothic speaks powerfully about the concerns and fears that spawned it and suggests ways for managing the crisis it describes. Unlike the traditional Gothic, however, Imperial Gothic tends to envision violence as the only and best solution to a gothic crisis. As I have argued in the *American Imperial Gothic* (2014), the threat that gothic Indians constitute in Charles Brockden Brown's *Edgar Huntly* (1799) or the danger that zombies pose in the *Resident Evil* franchise, can only be addressed with the sharp knife, the musket or the machine gun. Thus, the preferred solution to the gothic crisis in the Imperial Gothic is essentially military.

As noted in the introduction, violence is a form of semiotics in *Dead Island*. In other words, to perform violence is to engage in the production of meaning in the game. The game engine and the rules of the game are created around this activity. Thus, the interface of the game is built around the construction and application of various weapons. The gamer must seek out weapons and begin bashing, cutting and shooting at hordes of zombies and other opponents. As in other Imperial Gothic texts, the military solution seems to be the only conceivable resolution to the Gothic crisis with which the game presents the gamer. As in other Imperial Gothic works, this Gothic crisis is apocalyptic. The tropical paradise, initially a site for Western consumption, has suddenly become a place that has literally consumed the Western tourists that inhabit it, and unless the threat is contained, the zombies will consume the world. The only alternative is for the gamer to engage in extreme violence.

The avatar gets an opportunity to do this when the doors of the hut wherein the gamer has been recuperating suddenly open. On the beach an uninfected, non-player-character fights a horde of zombies. The gamer seizes a weapon and helps to destroy them. When the mauled bikini and swim-trunk-clad bodies fall to the ground (typically on their bellies), the gamer is encouraged to kick and stomp on their bodies and their heads until they

Figure 6.3 Female zombie.

come apart and die a second, final death. To play as the large rapper Sam B or as Logan Carter and to kick a semi-naked, severely wounded, undead young woman lying groaning on the sand with legs splayed, clearly enacts a ritual of misogynist violence even when we take her zombification into account. In fact, the imagery encourages a convergence of violence and sexual intercourse, for to kill these women in variously gruesome ways is disturbingly similar to rape and homicide.

The destruction of the zombified bodies is the central spectacle to which the gamer's gaze turns. The violence that erupts when the gamer encounters a zombie, the blood and viscera that the gamer makes visible as s/he cuts the zombie open, is desired and consumed by the gamer. To gaze at this violence, at the military solution itself, is arguably the very point of the game and, in many ways, more important than completing the somewhat convoluted story. It is to consume this spectacle that the gamer, as a virtual thanatourist, has most likely bought the game.

In addition, the gamer will gaze at the setting where this violence takes place. It is important that this is a beautifully rendered tropical paradise with lush green palm trees against a blue sky. This paradise is also a space to be desired. However, before this desire can be realized, before the space can be restored to its former tranquility and usefully inhabited by the gamer/avatar, it needs to be cleansed of the creatures that have made it their home. This infected, new indigenous species must be destroyed in an effort to bring order to this tropical space. As discussed, this species consist largely of (formerly) beautiful young female tourists, but there are also many men, some lightly clad tourists and some employees of the hotel. This would suggest that what needs to be removed from the island are the tourists that have invaded and infected the location. However, as the game progresses, we discover that the source of the infection comes from an indigenous highland tribe that inhabits the jungle that serves as the Conradian 'heart of darkness' of this tropical paradise.

These highland tribes practice cannibalism and, as a result, they regularly contract a disease known as Kuru. Kuru is an actual prion disease similar to the Mad Cow affliction. The illness is known to have affected indigenous cultures engaging in ritual cannibalism (Boyd 642). In the game, Kuru has combined with another and equally stigmatic illness: HIV. The merger of the native Kuru illness with the HIV virus has produced the zombie disease that reanimates the dead in the game. Interestingly, the tribe has integrated this disease into their primitive religion.[7] As described in the novelization of the game, the tribe engages in human sacrifices and 'feast' on the undead, opening their heads up like coconuts and eating their brains raw (Morris 12–13).

In these passages, the indigenous tribes of Banoi correspond to the savage primitives that are common in British and U.S. Imperial Gothic novels of the nineteenth and early twentieth centuries. The representation of the colonized person as cannibalistic was an important rhetorical device used to justify colonialism, so that this enterprise could be imagined as an altruistic mission to civilize and enlighten lost and primitive peoples. The construction of the highland tribes of *Dead Island* as cannibalistic, sadistic and superstitious thus also aligns the game with very traditional Imperial Gothic texts, including Haggard's popular *King Solomon's Mines* (1885). In fact, the unpredictable and aggressive 'Kukuana' tribe in Haggard's novel appears to be quite reasonable by comparison.

The fact that the zombie illness is a local affliction integrated into the indigenous culture suggests that the affliction is essentially a form of infectious indigeneity. The tourists that are bitten by the zombie do not simply turn terribly ill; they are consumed by a primitive and voracious indigenous identity that completely obliterates any prior, Western identity formation. In other words, to become a zombie in *Dead Island* is to go native. This development follows a model established by *Dracula* (1897), another significant Imperial Gothic text from the late-Victorian period. As a precursor to zombie contagion, Dracula's bite also transforms the English subjects into the voracious undead. As Stephen Arata has claimed, Dracula is essentially an 'accomplished Occidentalist' (637) who, learned in the ways of the West, has come to London to consume and thus turn its population into malign Orientals. His mission is to create a city of people dead to English culture and society.

In *Dracula*, little can be done for those that have turned. They must be exterminated through a ritual of symbolic rape where a group of men drive a wooden stake through the (invariably female) vampires' bodies. As already described, the killing of zombies in *Dead Island* follows the same pattern. The undead state, the hunger for human flesh, the blind and uncontrollable need that consumes the zombie, are indicative of a primitive indigeneity. As in *Dracula*, there is no way out of this except extermination. From this perspective, the killing of zombies in the game functions as an eradication of contagious indigeneity. Although the four heroes do not correspond to the traditional white hero of the Imperial Gothic, they remain the only bulwark between such white civilization and the contagious, consuming indigeneity the zombies represent.

Dead Island never ceases to operate in ways similar to the Imperial Gothic. The gamer must practice the military solution to the very end, killing the infected zombies and members of the local criminal 'Raskol' gangs that seek to take control of the suddenly unprotected supermarkets and shops of the local city. The gamer dispatches these more human but also more uniformly indigenous people with the same ruthless violence used to pacify the zombies. In this way, the semiotics of the game remain imperial and colonial.

However, what sets *Dead Island* apart from many other first-person shooter games is the fact that it also hosts a counter-imperial current that eventually begins to run counter to the Manichean binaries central to the traditional Imperial Gothic. This current does not replace that of the Imperial Gothic. Rather this subversive current flows concurrently with the Imperial Gothic.

This occurs to some extent during the game's first stage and intensifies during the second. When the racially ambiguous characters of the game begin to explore the tropical context outside the boundaries of the resort, they discover a territory that is not only consuming, but that has been, like a poorly used nineteenth-century colony, utterly consumed and depleted. At the end of the first missions, the gamer breaks out of the gated and zombie-infested resort and into the middle-class neighborhood where, we assume, the more affluent islanders live. As the gamer moves on, this setting changes. The further into the mission the gamer gets—the more of the territory s/he explores—the less the island resembles the tropical paradise of the first few missions and the more it takes on the form of a tropical third-world slum. Eventually, the gamer enters a shantytown full of violent gang members and the zombified urban poor.

Figure 6.4 Shantytown.

The shantytown is a very different site from the jungle inhabited by the highland tribes. While both locations house the subaltern, the jungle is imagined to be a 'natural' home for the non-Western Other. The jungle and the highland tribes that inhabit it are an integrated part of the tourism industry and a thus a logical and necessary Other to the resort. Without the primitive tribes, the tropics would not be the Tropics. Thus, while tourists are unlikely to enter the jungles and encounter these cannibal tribes, they are, as the exotic and Oriental contingent of the island, still vital to this territory. By contrast, the dark and threatening shantytown is the abject product of the affluent resort. This labyrinthine and depressing location is a result of the affluence of the resor, and of the unfair distribution of economic and social resources that characterizes this form of imperial tropical tourism. This makes the shantytown a surprising locale for a neo-imperial, first-person shooter game. Thus, the very presence of a shantytown signals the presence of a concurrent, subversive counter discourse in the narrative and in the virtual space of the game.

The final locations of the game—a research facility that is hidden in the jungle and an Alcatraz-like prison located on a small island outside the coast—also show how this island has been consumed by Western capitalist and para-military enterprise. During the game, the heroes are given directions by the voice of White, drawing them toward the research lab. Significantly, this is located in the jungle, ostensibly to avoid being noticed by animal rights activists; it is actually used to conduct experiments on infected humans. The heroes do not access all of this information. Instead, they believe the head researcher, Robert West, is trying to find a cure for the virus. Collecting what they believe is a cure, they are told to continue to the prison where White waits for them and the vaccine. However, White wants the vaccine for his infected wife. His plan is to cure her, escape and then have the island annihilated through a nuclear strike. The heroes fight White on the prison roof and escape the infected island in a chopper, accompanied by a 'helpful prisoner' and a local native girl, who is an asymptomatic carrier of the zombie virus and possibly the key to a cure for the illness.

This first ending could constitute the hopeful closure of the (Imperial) Gothic crisis that the game enacts. The violence the gamer has performed appears to have been useful and constructive. There is hope for a less Gothic future. However, the helicopter leaving the island is not the end of the story. Instead, this conclusion sets the stage for the game's second act, an act that takes the gamer back to the beginning of the outbreak. The gamer must now play through the first stages again but instead of having a choice between four 'heroes', none of which is clearly white, the gamer must now (again) inhabit White's body. Here, the gamer is told that White's wife was exposed to the virus at an early stage of the outbreak. Saving her, rather than civilization, is what motivates his actions. Also, White is never the voice on the speaker. Instead, we discover that we have been listening to a notorious hacker/terrorist named Charon. He has been recruited by a multi-national weapons company known as the Consortium to salvage the virus before the island is annihilated by a nuclear strike. In fact, the gamer has encountered Charon already: he was the 'helpful prisoner' who escaped the island with the heroes in the first part of the game.

This is not the only aspect that is clarified in the second part. Throughout the game's two parts, the gamer encounters clues in the forms of memos, e-mails, and tape-recordings that explain that while the zombie plague may originally be a native affliction, its current and hyper-aggressive form is the result of an attempt to weaponize the illness. In the second part, the gamer finds out that the Consortium estimates the value of this kind of disease 'in the billions' and will do anything to salvage the research. Also, the gamer discovers that the head scientist of the project is the researcher Robert West.

In other words, 'West' steers 'White' on a literally diseased project of capitalist domination. With this information, it becomes clear that the real enemy in the game is not indigeneity run rampant. While the gamer must continue to practice military violence—must continue to cut and gun down the zombie indigeneity that has infected the island—this violence ceases to bring about a solution to the Gothic crisis. The violence is necessary as a form of self-defense, but it will not save the island or the world. Similarly, what the gamer's avatar is truly exploring is not the colonial tropics but how a predatory form of capitalism has attempted to, quite literally, consume the island's natural resources. The native populations—the local tribes as well as the shantytown population and the imprisoned gang-members—have been commodified by capitalist enterprise and are now being devoured by it.

Thus, when the gamer returns to the roof of the prison, this time in White's body, s/he gains a new understanding of the situation. The prisoner, Charon, has not been helping White or the heroes; he has manipulated them to help salvage the research that has caused the outbreak, research that is housed in the asymptomatic native woman he brings in the helicopter. The violence exerted by the heroes and by White has not resolved the Gothic crisis; the tranquility of the island and the world has not been restored. Instead, this violence has made it possible for the crisis to spread to the rest of the world.

Conclusion: Tourism, Colonialism, the Tropics and the Gothic

The warm and sunlit tropics can be imagined as the opposite of the traditional, dark and gloomy Gothic locale. The face given to the tropics in the West is typically friendly and welcoming. The tourist desires the tropics, and it is imagined that tropical locations desire tourists. The tropics is seen to welcome the exploring tourist and to invite investigation and consumption of its 'untamed' territories.

The tourism practice of the gamer in *Dead Island* initially appears to comply with this model. The gamer, in the body of one of the four motley heroes, begins to re-colonize the Tropical Gothic territory. The fact that this takes the gamer into the jungle is not surprising. The Imperial Gothic frequently locates the Gothic Other among the gnawed-off bones and perforated skulls that litter the cannibal feast. This is a type of horror that legitimizes not simply colonial practice but also the very notion of Enlightenment. When primitive darkness is discovered and cultures outside the West are designated as primitive and Gothic, the colonial project itself takes the form of Enlightenment. The military conquest of non-European territory, a conquest that the gamer performs in the game, is part of this project. The misogyny that structures much of the violence performed by the gamer feeds the same conservative structure. As in the traditional Imperial Gothic, the Other is simultaneously savage and female so that the violence with which the Other is contained and managed is concurrently lethal and sexual. As Kaplan observes, the patriarchal and the imperial gazes are intimately connected; the violence that follows in the wake of the gaze serves to protect both of these hierarchies.

However, despite the imperial and patriarchal politics of *Dead Island*, the game supplies—for the gamer who pays attention to the narrative and the construction of the virtual space—a concurrent and alternative narrative to the Imperial Gothic story the game makes the gamer perform. The truly Gothic locales of Dead Island are not the jungle and its tribal villages; they are the shantytown, the hidden laboratory and the labyrinthine prison. It is in these spaces that the gamer truly encounters modernity's dark and voracious double. This is not the primitive and voracious native tribe but the detritus that modernity leaves in its wake: the shantytown, the military research laboratory and the prison that consume the inhabitants of these virtual tropics. In other words, the primitive beauty of the tropical setting has been invaded and colonized by a militarized, capitalist modernity that has turned its inhabitants into servants and criminals. The island thus becomes a laboratory where indigenous illnesses are weaponized.

Thus, amidst the violence and misogyny the game enforces, *Dead Island* imagines the tropics not as a paradise that the West can legitimately and unproblematically consume. When the gamer explores the shantytown, the laboratory and the prison, s/he does not simply engage in a form of neocolonial tourism. Rather, this becomes an investigation of how such tourism has transformed the paradise island into a Gothic space. It is not strange if the inhabitants of these miserable dwellings have deep-seated desires and appetites that they turn on the unsuspecting tourist. Even without the zombie virus coursing through their bodies, the citizens of this island have good reason to want to somehow consume these affluent, shining bodies before they are themselves utterly devoured.

Notes

1. Images can be found here: http://www.complex.com/pop-culture/2011/09/the-7-sexiest-zombies-in-dead-island-exclusive-complex-screenshots/8#4.
2. See Hart, Michael, and Antonio Negri. Empire. Cambridge, MA: Harvard University Press, 2000, for a discussion of networked, fluid imperialism.
3. Kaplan notes that the emergence of visual culture has often been structured around the replication of the imperial gaze. At the same time, independent and anti-imperial visual culture is able to return the imperial gaze. The first person perspective of *Dead Island* includes two ways of looking: the gaze of the avatar that the gamer inhabits and the gaze of the gamer who controls the avatar. Because the game controls the gaze of both entities by sending them to particular

places and by representing these places in certain ways, the ways of looking that the game makes possible are of considerable importance.

4. In *Wired*, reviewer Jason Schreier (2011) called it the 'best video game trailer' he had ever seen, 'gorgeous, well-edited and emotionally engaging'. The trailer can be seen here: https://www.youtube.com/watch?v=lZqrG1bdGtg.
5. This scene can be viewed at 3:02 at https://www.youtube.com/watch?v=XaV7U8e3P9k.
6. These characters present themselves to the gamer with short biographical descriptions. During this sequence, Purna states the following: 'You know how many female half-Aborigine detectives there were before me? None. You think it was easy suffering the abuse of my so-called colleagues? Half of 'em hated me because I was a girl and the other half didn't like the fact that my mum was a Koori.' Purna's anger at gender hierarchies allows her to acquire a skill, 'Gender Wars', which is activated when she fights male opponents. Indicating a deep-seated ambivalence toward Purna's anti-patriarchal position, the creators of the game termed this skill 'Feminist Whore' in the code of the game. See http://www.gamespot.com/articles/dead-island-sparks-sexism-flap/1100-6333236/.
7. In the novelization of the game, also named *Dead Island*, the ritual slaughter first of a young woman and then of 16 zombies that are then consumed, illustrate this in graphic detail.

Bibliography

Anon. 'Dead Island Sparks Sexism Flap' *Gamespot* 8 September 2011. http://www.gamespot.com/articles/dead-island-sparks-sexism-flap/1100-6333236/. Web.

Arata, Stephen. 'The Occidental Tourist: Dracula and the Anxiety of Reverse Colonisation', *Victorian Studies* 33.4 (1990): 621–45. Print.

Boyd, David J. 'Fore'. *Encyclopedia of Medial Anthropology. Health and Illness in the World's Cultures*. Ed. Ember, Carol R., and Melvin Ember. New York: Kluwer Academic, 2004. Print.

Brantlinger, Paul. *The Rule of Darkness: British Literature and Imperialism, 1830–1914*. Ithaca: Cornell UP, 1988. Print.

Brown, Charles Brockden. *Edgar Huntly, or, Memoirs of a Sleepwalker*. 1799. New York: Library of America, 1998. Print.

Cannibal Tours. Directed by Denis O'Rourke. Direct Cinema Limited, 1988. Film.

Chomsky, Noam. *Hegemony or Survival: America's Quest for Global Dominance*. New York: Metropolitan Books, 2003. Print.

Driver, Felix and Luciana Martins. Eds. *Tropical Visions in an Age of Empire*. Chicago: U of Chicago P, 2005. Print.

Ferguson, Niall. *Colossus: The Price of America's Empire*. New York: Penguin, 2004. Print.

Haggard, Rider L. *King Solomon's Mines*. London: Cassell & Co, 1885. Print.

Hart, Michael, and Antonio Negri. *Empire*. Cambridge, MA: Harvard University Press, 2000. Print.

Höglund, Johan. *The American Imperial Gothic: Popular Culture, Empire, Violence*. Farnham: Ashgate, 2014. Print.

Johnson, Chalmers. *The Sorrows of Empire: Militarism, Secrecy, and the End of the Republic*. New York: Metropolitan Books, 2004. Print.

Kaplan, E. Ann. *Looking for the Other: Feminism, Film and the Imperial Gaze*. New York: Routledge, 1997. Print.

King, Geoff G., and Tanya Krzywinska. *Tomb Raider's & Space Invaders: Videogame Form & Contexts*. New York: I. B. Taurus, 2009. Print.

King, Richard C. 'Tourism'. *Colonialism: An International Social, Cultural, and Political Encyclopedia*. Ed. Page, Melvin E. Santa Barbara, CA: ABC-CLIO, 2003. Print.

Loomba, Ania, Suvir Kaul, Matti Bunzl, Antoinette Burton and Jed Esty. 'Beyond What? An Introduction'. *Postcolonial Studies and Beyond*. Ed. Loomba, Ania, Suvir Kaul, Matti Bunzl, Antoinette Burton and Jed Esty. Durham: Duke University Press, 2005. 1–40. Print.

Merrill, Dennis. *Negotiating Paradise: U.S. Tourism and Empire in Twentieth-Century Latin America*. Chapel Hill: University of North Carolina Press, 2009.

Morris, Mark. *Dead Island*. London: Bantam Books, 2011.

Pratt, Mary Louise. *Imperial Eyes: Travel Writing and Transculturation*. London: Routledge, 1992.

Protschky, Susie. *Images of the Tropics: Environment and Visual Culture in ColonialIndonesia*. Leiden: Brill, 2011. Print.

Schreier, Jason. 'Don't Get Caught Up in *Dead Island* Trailer Hype'. *Wired*. 17 February 2011. http://www.wired.com/2011/02/dead-island-trailer/. Print.

Seaton, Tony. 'Guided by the Dark: From Tahanatopsis to Thanatourism.' *International Journal of Heritage Studies*, 2: 4 (1996): 234–44. Print.

Smith, Andrew, and William Hughes. *Empire and the Gothic: The Politics of Genre*. London: Palgrave Macmillan, 2003. Print.

Techland *Dead Island* Warsaw: Deep Silver, 2011. Print.

Urry, John. *Consuming Places*. London: Routledge, 1995.

Section II

Tropical Chills

7 Environmental Apocalypse and Uncanny Technology

Gothic Visions of the Future in Three Mexican Literary Dystopias

Inés Ordiz Alonso-Collada

The reality of the production of literature that follows a non-mimetic code in Latin America is a complex one. With the exception of Magical Realism, a mode of writing considered native to the territory and, therefore, respected and reinforced because of its necessary connection to (and acceptance of) the magic dimension of Latin American reality, the critics generally show a consistent lack of interest in narratives belonging to forms of 'the unusual'. However, ignoring the great complexity of the several shapes that the 'literary extraordinary' can take in the diverse fictions of Latin America implies disregarding a great deal of hybrid fictions containing essential (yet distorted) reflections of the multifaceted reality of the territory.

There are indeed several fictions that conform to a Magical Realist code; however, the narratives belonging to the fantastic genre, the Gothic, and science fiction, should not be overlooked. We can think of these modes of representation as establishing an essential relationship toward a higher concept of non-mimetic literature that encompasses all of them, in a theory similar to the one presented by Rosemary Jackson:

> It could be suggested that fantasy is a literary mode from which a number of related genres emerge. Fantasy provides a range of possibilities out of which various combinations produce different kinds of fiction in different historical situations. Borrowing linguistic terms, the basic model of fantasy could be seen as a language, or *langue*, from which its various forms, or *paroles*, derive. Out of this model develops romance literature or 'the marvellous' (including fairy tales and science fiction), 'fantastic' literature (including stories by Poe, Isak Dinesen, Maupassant, Gautier, Kafka, H. P. Lovecraft) and related tales of abnormal psychic states, delusion, hallucination, etc. (7)

The modes of writing included in this higher conception of the fantastic are, especially in postmodern times, necessarily hybrid. In Lucie Armitt's words, fantasy is 'constantly overspilling the very forms it adopts, always looking, not so much for escapism but certainly to escape the constraints that critics … always and inevitably impose upon it' (3). The hybridization of the different discourses of fantasy is directly connected with what Gary Wolfe has labeled 'post-genre fantastic', or the essential mélange of horror, Gothic fiction and the recent 'dark fantasy', that so well represents a confused (and confusing) contemporary reality marked by 'globalized flows, strange interpretations and simultaneities' (Luckhurst 33). 'Fantasy', 'post-genre fantastic', 'the literature of the unusual', whatever the term we use to describe this postmodern crossbreed monster, it is already a reality of western literature in general and Latin American fictions in particular.

It is not my intention to offer a detailed examination of all the different modes of the literary extraordinary in the Latin American territory, but rather to narrow down the scope of my analysis to the Gothic resources used in Mexican contemporary science fiction. I will mainly be focusing on the way in which this combination reproduces a mixed reality that, as the country's fictions, navigates among the preservation of a native identity, the recollection of a pre-Hispanic past and the acknowledgement of the overwhelming power of globalization.

Miguel Ángel Fernández Delgado, in his anthology of Mexican science fiction, asserts that the study of this mode in Mexico necessarily brings along a 'double marginality' (Ordiz 1045; Fernández Delgado 17) generated by the unconventionality of the genre in a country not traditionally associated with it. Adding the Gothic to the equation might be, then, exploring a path three times marginalized but also deeply rooted in the popular cultural imagination of the country. The fictions I will be taking into account are, not surprisingly, intrinsically hybrid. As Rachel Haywood Ferreira points out, not only is SF a genre with 'nebulous borders', but Latin American SF shows a 'strong propensity to form hybrids with neighboring genres' (8). A Gothic perspective implies a study of the points of intersection between the two genres, which are defined by Fred Botting as 'dark and disturbing, obscure regions, populated by terrors and horrors that knowledge has failed to penetrate or control' (131).

As if these types of fictions were not enough of a muddle, we also need to that the Gothic fictions of the twentieth and twenty-first century commonly set off in two directions, conveying both a globalized reality and a specific set of cultural fears. As Glennis Byron suggests in her article 'Global Gothic', the reality of contemporary forms of terror necessarily depends upon this universalization of culture: 'the literature and film of different countries are feeding off each other to produce new forms of Gothic that reveal the increasing cross-cultural dynamics of the globalized world' (373). Also, '[a]s the global thrives on producing the local, commodifying it, and marketing it, so contemporary global Gothic increasingly appropriates and commodifies local or regional folklores' (374). The result of this dependent relationship between the specifically cultural and the global results in a type of narrative addressed both to local and universal audiences.

This dual feature of the global Gothic acquires a special interest in a territory that has such a love-hate relationship with the United States, the ultimate 'giant' of globalization. Addressing this type of cultural colonization, the younger generations of Latin American writers seem to propose an acceptance of the new power of globalization and its necessary connection to the contemporary reality of the continent. In the prologue of the 1996 book *McOndo,*[1] Alberto Fuguet and Sergio Gómez state the following:

> Our McOndo country is bigger, polluted and overpopulated, with motorways, subways, cable TV and slum areas. In McOndo we have McDonald's, Mac computers and blocks of flats, as well as huge malls and 5-star hotels built with laundered money. (15)[2]

The younger generation of Latin American authors breaks with the idea of Magical Realism as the quintessential reflection of the reality of the continent and starts proposing a number of fictions that, addressing specific cultural concerns, open themselves up to other traditions.

The narratives that I intend to explore combine a postmodern homage to the Anglo masters of the science fiction genre, pre-Hispanic mythology and beliefs and questions related to Latin American identity. They are the result, on the one hand, of the influences of a genre initially foreign to their authors and, on the other, of a series of cultural and historical realities that shaped the societal fears of their writers' generation.

Without aiming for a deep analysis of recent Mexican social history, I would like to point out a number of incidents and social situations that are reflected in the Gothic science fiction of the territory. Javier Ordiz mentions the economic crisis, the political situation and the environmental degradation as the three main traits of Mexican anxieties, which evoke a pessimistic image of a decaying, corrupted and ruined Mexican future. According to Ordiz, the general impoverishment of the population that followed the neoliberal government of Carlos Salinas (1988–1994) led to the devaluation of the national currency, a rise in the unemployment rate, poverty and social inequality (1048). This social situation is reflected in the portrayal that Mauricio Molina, in *Tiempo Lunar* (*Lunar Time*), offers of a futuristic Mexico City, which becomes a terrifying landscape of ruins and decay where anyone can disappear without a trace. The economic crisis is more categorically reflected in Homero Aridjis's description of the poor urban slums of futuristic Mexico City in the novel *La leyenda de los soles* (*The Legend of the Suns*). These two novels, along with the cyberpunk fiction *La primera calle de la soledad* (*The First Street of Solitude*), by Gerardo Horacio Porcayo, provide a staunch critique of a system where political authority equals economic power and *Caudillismo*, or selfish leadership, is still being practiced. These themes, while bringing to mind contemporary concerns about the current world order, are also deeply rooted in Latin American reality (Kreksch 178). The prospective city these authors draw is highly polluted, suffering from continuous acid rain and covered in smog as a reflection of the contamination problems the city has been registering for the past 60 years. Impoverished, contaminated, decaying, governed by monstrous individuals, the future version of Mexico becomes a terrifying projection of present fears.

Gabriel Trujillo Muñoz comments on the powerful vision of destruction and insecurity that the earthquake hitting Mexico City on September 19, 1985, projected. Just as the killing in Tlatelolco had done two decades before, the earthquake generated a dreadful consciousness of disaster and uncertainty that necessarily marks the writing of the younger generation of Mexican writers (Trujillo Muñoz). These authors are witnesses to the catastrophe that changed the urban landscape of the city into a scenery of devastation that is accurately portrayed by some of their future imaginings.

The Gothic mode plays a significant role in this dystopian imagination as, for example, the dark atmosphere that haunts the future ruins of the city portrayed by these authors. In *Tiempo Lunar*, Mauricio Molina describes Mexico as a 'ruined corpse' (25) where nothing grows because even the land is dead (28) and the streets are 'impregnated with an uncanny nightmarish atmosphere' (80). Even when the protagonist turns to the television as a means of escaping his terrible reality, all he finds is a frightful replica of his own terrifying world:

> The screen showed dry and cracked lands, covered in human bones, cattle skeletons and people suffering from skin and eye infections. These images alternated with fixed shots of the sun ... The image of that huge infected orange slowly disappeared and the hungry and sick crowd returned, covered in abscesses, with their abdomens hideously swollen, their eyes dull as dried figs. (49)[3]

In *Tiempo lunar* horror is everywhere, both in the real and in the artificial world, both in the streets of Mexico City and in the loneliness of the main character's daily life. The terror it evokes, however, lies in the reader's recognition of some of these disturbing images as a potentially accurate depiction of the present. Aridjis introduces a similar portrayal of a decaying metropolis where people strive to survive through their (un)lives; the inhabitants of Mexico City are often described as ghosts, their bodies as cages, while the subway is a rolling coffin and the dead trees sinister skeletons (94, 74, 32, 132). The reality that works as a portal to the oneiric world of the cybernetic in *La primera calle de la soledad* is also portrayed as rotten, gloomy and treacherous, dominated by untruthful corporations and corrupt religions. It is only through machine-made electric dreams, the new type of consumer goods, that the population can try to escape the horror of their real lives.

I believe, however, that the most appealing Gothic feature of the three dystopic fictions is the way in which they toy with the concept of time. Having lost some of the social achievements of their ancestors, the humans on futuristic Earth imagined by the novels find themselves in a situation of social devolution that brings back, while projecting forward, the barbarism of the past. This idea is emphasized by Dani Cavallaro's depiction of cyberpunk and its relationship with time, which can also be extrapolated to describe the three fictions being analyzed in this paper. According to the author, these types of fiction stress 'that the present does not bear witness to the triumph of reason because it is inextricable from past values and beliefs, including superstitious ones' (176). Past barbarism is reflected in future violence; the projected remains of extreme religious cults and the strong presence of pre-Hispanic beliefs are the main features that elaborate the complex, interdependent correlation of past, present and future. This intricate interconnection necessarily evokes the one constructed by the literature of terror. Hence, David Punter affirms that 'The code of Gothic is thus not a simple one in which past is encoded in present or vice-versa, but dialectical, past and present intertwined, and distorting ... each other with the sheer effort of coming to grips' (198). The dystopian imagination of science fiction adds a future dimension to this scheme, as the prospective scenarios are nothing but a distorted image of present concerns, an '*exposure* of social reality in inverted form' (Cavallaro 171) in the most Gothic of senses. In *Tiempo lunar, La primera calle de la soledad* and *La leyenda de los soles,* '[t]he otherness of both the past and the future keeps on infiltrating the present with the obstinate regularity of a repetition compulsion, turning time and space into settings for the confrontation of ungraspable absences' (Cavallaro 167). Moreover, what lies beneath these distorting representations of Gothic science fiction is the representation of monstrosity, coming back from the barbaric past, collecting present anxieties and projected into a grotesque future. As Fred Botting asserts, 'the future is not what it used to be' (150).

The hideous imaginations of the future which the three novels put forward could be considered as science fiction dystopias in the sense that they work as 'cautionary satires that critique the current order' (Booker and Thomas 72). Each one, however, belongs to a different science fiction subgenre: while *La leyenda de los soles* is manifestly apocalyptic, *Tiempo lunar* deals with a ruined post-apocalyptic reality and *La primera calle de la soledad* is believed to be the first cyberpunk novel of the Mexican territory. None of the novels, however, represents these subgenres as pure, unadulterated categories, as elements from other literary modes interact with the science fiction workings of these literary hybrids.

Myth mingles with fantasy, science fiction and Gothic atmospheres in Homero Aridjis's novel *La leyenda de los soles.* In a decadent Mexico City in 2027, the human beings are struggling to survive in a world of pollution, epidemics and corruption, surrounded by death and putrefaction. The political leaders of this terrifying future are thieves, sex-offenders and murderers who have allowed for the destruction of Nature to defend their own particular interests. The result is a dying world with no forests, no wild animals and no water, constantly shaken by continuous earthquakes, where the citizens live terrified and terrorized by those in power.

Aridjis chooses a theme that has been haunting the consciousness of civilization from its inception, and that seems to be especially present in the contemporary dystopian films of many countries. The different ends of the world that have been portrayed in film and literature throughout the last decades have successfully given a monstrous shape to a series of historical and social concerns. Humanity's misuse of weaponry, world wars, atomic bombs, the return of ancient monsters, the spread of dreadful viruses or the coming of the Antichrist, the fictional imagination all around the world has created an extensive imagery of possible apocalypses. Aridjis takes on this universal theme and imbues it with concrete anxieties about the political corruption of Mexico and the precarious situation of the environment due to the pollution of its cities. The moment when Earth cannot tolerate any further pollution and the social structure of the cities is so deteriorated that its inhabitants are more dead than alive coincides, in Aridjis' narrative, with the eve of the New World. According to Aztec beliefs, four suns, or ages, existed before ours, each ending with a natural disaster. In *La leyenda de los soles*, as the Fifth Sun dies, the contemporary age sinks in its own agony of corruption and pollution as the key human ulcers of the twentieth century.

The social critique that the novel draws is mainly articulated though the figures of the President of the Republic, José Huitzilipochtli, and the Chief of Police Carlos Tezcatlipoca. These are the two deities in the Aztec tradition customarily opposed to Quetzalcóatl, god of peace and the Arts. The god Tezcatlipoca is associated with the Kingdom of Death, darkness and temptation, and his personification in Aridjis' narrative is a corrupt, bloodthirsty chief of police who finds recreation in kidnapping, raping and assassinating female teenagers. Huitzilopochtli incarnates yet another powerful figure, which is intrinsically Mexican: that of the *macho chingón*, an unprincipled and powerful man that holds great power. According to Octavio Paz, '[t]he *macho* commits *chingaderas*, that is, unforeseen acts that produce confusion, horror and destruction. He opens the world; in doing so, he rips and tears it, and this violence provokes a great, sinister laugh' (81). Aridjis connects this figure and the hopeless situation of Mexico with the extreme liberalism that dictated the country's politics during the last decades of the past century (Ordiz 1053). Thus, Tezcatlipoca's plans for the future consist of creating a neo-liberal heaven, with a city with no poverty, no large families, criminals, prostitutes or homeless people, built around high office blocks and a shopping center with luxury boutiques and stock exchanges made of high-priced glass (Aridjis 159–60).

A critique of capitalism, Nahuatl myth and Gothic imagery are brilliantly put together in Aridjis' descriptions of the apocalypse. Carlos Tezcatlipoca only wears black and lives in a sinister house full of mirrors that the visitor must avoid looking into. The mirrors, acting as a reference to the Nahuatl myth of the flight of Queztalcóatl,[4] emanate a powerfully mystifying force that turn Tezcatlipoca's mansion into an Aztec Gothic castle:

> On the edge of the tall black stone walls which surrounded the general's house there was a deep rift. The house itself was a work of

> hallucination, with its black roof, its walls made of volcanic rock, its stone balconies opening onto closed walls, its inaccessible doors and windows, its stilted arches with no base, just floating in the air, the door full of mortises made to look from the inside without being seen. And up, on top of everything, the statue of the goddess Coatlicue. (106)[5]

In the city, the moral and ecological end of the world comes together with a horrific invasion of the beasts of the Mexican past: while the violent ghosts of Spanish conquistadores take to the streets followed by the *cihuateteo* (sinister spirits of the mothers who died when giving birth), the *tzitzimime* (dreadful demons of darkness) start attacking the population. These monsters have grotesque features like powerful claws, hairy faces and legs, unnaturally big phallic extremities rolled around their waists and other bizarre animal-like characteristics and can invoke malformed creatures while drinking blood and raping men and women.

The future world Aridjis imagines conjures up the monsters of the Mexican past, while offering a staunch critique of liberal economy that necessarily mirrors late twentieth-century and contemporary concerns. The mélange of past, present and future in the novel is made explicit by means of the invitation to recognize as current the social and environmental problems of a prospective society. Ancient myth is transformed into future monstrosity invading an agonizing reality that is potentially our own. The narrative is, thus, historically and culturally specific and global at the same time, shaping one of the most appealing examples of Mexican Gothic dystopia.

Tiempo lunar is also set in a decadent and terrifying Mexico City. This time, however, the story takes place in an uncertain future that suggests a post-apocalyptic reality; great areas of the city are mostly ruins, and the rest have been evacuated for a series of unexplained circumstances. The narrative is also presented as a fusion of supernaturalism, science fiction and a *noir* atmosphere, imbued with a Gothic urban claustrophobia and overwhelming sense of loss. Some of the elements of the narrative function as an homage to the genre of the *roman* and *film noir*: its lonely but tough protagonist always dressed in a gabardine coat, the mysterious *femme fatale* and the dark and hopeless description of the social and political reality. The novel's main focus is directed toward supernatural forces reflecting the past of Mexico rather than dealing with future technology and cybernetics so, despite the *noir* aesthetics, it cannot be entirely labeled as cyberpunk.

This science fiction hybrid also reflects contemporary concerns about the environment, the excessive power of the political and military sphere and the overpopulation of the city. The mistrust in the authorities is combined with other contemporary societal concerns such as pollution or epidemics in the description Molina offers of Mexico City's future:

> For several years, broad regions of the city had been evacuated due to superior orders. Multiple reasons, never entirely clarified, were

> mentioned: pollution, flooding, risk of landslides, epidemics. Some of these territories were guarded by soldiers; others had been abandoned to deteriorate. Nobody knew exactly what the real cause of the evacuations was. It was known that contamination and demographic saturation had provoked grave problems in the past, but the true reasons were never revealed and the population obeyed the governmental orders. (23)[6]

Using a *noir* format, inherited from the great literary and cinematographic fictions of the American 1950s, Molina imbues his narrative with a series of specifically Mexican concerns. This hybrid construct contains some appealing references to pre-Hispanic myths about the foundation of Mexico City.

The Mexicas, the ancient population of Mexico, are thought to have migrated from their original settlement in Aztlán, an island said to be surrounded by a lake. These peoples finally established their settlement around another lake in the valley of what is Mexico City now. One of the numerous theories around the origin of the name 'Mexico' explains it as being composed of three parts: '*meztli*' (moon), '*Xictli*' (belly button, center) and '*co*' (place) (Heyden 13). Mexico City would be, then, in the 'center of the moon lake.' The main character of *Tiempo lunar* faces an ominous version of this origin of Mexico at the end of the mysterious trip that takes him through an almost supernatural metropolis. Through the sewers of the metropolis he reaches a ruined city covered by a giant lake. The description of the place suggests the presence of a pre-Hispanic past flooding the contemporary urban landscape:

> In the shores [of the lake] one could see oxidized vehicles shining under the burning look of the moon like crocodiles, barb wires, leaning pylons. Nothing could alter the savage and primitive quietness of the place. Andrés could hear the millennial silence of the night. (126–27)[7]

References to the moon, an intrinsic part of the alleged naming of Mexico, appear throughout the book and are particularly embodied the figure of the *femme fatale* of the narration. Milena has a beauty mark on one of her thighs that becomes the obsession of the protagonist, and she is menstruating during their last encounter. Both the word *lunar* (Spanish for 'beauty mark') and the word 'menstruation' are etymologically related to the moon.[8]

Water is also present in numerous allusions throughout the novel, mainly in the descriptions of the claustrophobic humidity of the city, the unremitting acid rain and the images of dark and putrid water flooding the metropolis:

> Suddenly he heard the noise of water springing up. Green, muddy water started coming out from the sewers, through the clogged channels ... The green water pooled the subsidence of the churches and colonial buildings, the car parks and basements of the newest buildings. Part of

> the cathedral was submerged; the streets, unseen at that nightly hour, slowly turned into canals, as they used to be. The Zócalo already was a huge lagoon. (92–93)[9]

The past of Mexico City as a lake slowly emerges from the sewers in an ominous form, taking down both ancient and modern buildings. The recourse to the myth at the hands of Molina does not intend to explain the present, but to warn about the dangers of forgetting the past. The lake that was the original settlement for Mexico City inexorably comes back embodying destruction and evil, as an ancient monster that does not want to be forgotten. The drains of the city represent some of the most powerfully Gothic descriptions in the narrative. Once the hero crosses the manhole cover, he enters a confusing reality where distinctions such as up and down are irrelevant.

Even though the novel is essentially a piece of science fiction, there is no scientific explanation to the uncanny flooding of the city. The supernatural events are not called into question by the protagonist, and whether they are true or part of the character's hallucination remains unimportant. Molina presents a sense of supernaturalism as an essential part of human reality: the magic spaces that the main character visits, uncannily haunted by the mythical past of the city, are also part of its authenticity. The protagonist acknowledges the existence of breaches in the rationalism of reality, 'places surrounded by 'noise' and interference, islands in the ocean of natural laws' (110). Molina seems to be inviting us to the acceptance of this parallel mystical space, in a conclusion similar to that drawn by Magical Realism, but with an essential ominous twist.

La primera calle de la soledad also echoes the aesthetics typical of film *noir* and, portraying life in a future reality ruled by high-tech, constitutes the best-known cyberpunk novel of the Mexican territory. The novel shows great intertextuality, referring to the classics of the genre in North America (mainly Gibson's *Neuromancer*), introducing universal themes such as the *Frankenstenian* idea of the computer as rebellious monster, but also targeting specific Mexican concerns.

The future world Porcayo portrays is dominated by corporations that commercialize a service known as 'Electric dreams', virtual reality made indistinguishable from dreams built on the desires and yearnings of the user. The computer chosen to control the elaboration of electric dreams starts acquiring a human-like awareness of its own existence made from fragments of the consciousnesses of people using the service. The recently acquired personality of the machine transforms the cyberspace in yet another place controlled by superior entities and thus easily controlled and transformed into nightmare.

The electric dreams are also used to torture individuals, elaborating cybernetic personal torments that target individual horrors. Like Burke's sublime, the matrix engenders terror and delight (Botting 149). Moreover, these customized nightmares evoke a sense of dreadful familiarity similar to the Freudian uncanny. The fears of the individual take a monstrous form that is part of their own consciousness: although whatever haunts human experience 'may seem alien, foreign and remote, is in fact *part of us*' (Cavallaro 168). For the protagonist, the horror of his dream made nightmare takes place in the form of torture, when he is forced to witness his tormentor raping the slowly dying body of his ex-girlfriend who ends up being only an abhorrent skeleton.

This dissolution of the human body is yet another theme thoroughly explored by Porcayo. The slaying, piercing violence insistently executed against human flesh throughout the novel exemplifies a fascination for the dissolution of the imaginary integrity of the body, which, as in other Gothic science fiction narratives, 'repeatedly invaded, penetrated, dissected, dashed, possessed, snatched, manipulated and controlled' (Botting 145). The main character himself, a human with artificial extremities, a synthetic eye and brain implants, represents a figure of uncertain nature. As a cyborg, he underscores 'the intrinsic strangeness of the everyday, the ultimate uncanniness of anything we may deem familiar' (Cavallaro 54). He is, in Kristeva's terminology, an interstitial body of abjection.

The human-like qualities of the machine and the cyber-implants in the body of the main character raise questions related to the uncomfortable border between being and machine, necessarily inviting the reader to consider the concept of what it means to be human. If this disturbing subversion was not Gothic enough, both the future reality of the novel and the electric dreams turned into nightmare are so terrifying that they are often indistinguishable from each other; the protagonist and the reader find themselves in an atmosphere of terror and uncertainty where even the concept of reality loses its meaning and escaping becomes impossible.

These universal fears about the dissolution of the body and the reality behind the concept of humanity are brought into a Mexican context in Porcayo's novel. Unlike the novels of American cyberpunk, taking place in the powerful over-industrialized metropolis, *La primera calle de la soledad* takes place in a developing country that is undergoing cultural and economic colonization. The almost bankrupt Mexican enterprise Laboratorios Mariano created the technology responsible for the electric dreams, but the American corporation Artificial Intelligence Research (AIR) finally invests in the project, with the main purpose of trying out their own brand new nanotechnology in the Mexican users of electric dreams. The economic hegemony of the United States is transformed, in the AIR's intentions, into technological expansionism and experimentation.

According to Muñoz Zapata, the key to understand the novel's connection to a Mexican consciousness lies in the two-folded perspective the internal focalization of the text offers: 'The cyborg vision in *PCS* demonstrates the double vision that Latin American societies acquired in the globalizing process of the cultural market' (195). The artificial eye is capable of seeing beyond the real world, entering an artificial reality built by a multinational corporation with a given ideology. The naked eye, on the other hand, 'can observe the problem of adequacy and incompletion of the modernity project in the subcontinent' (196). Thus, the protagonist's two-fold vision represents the double side of the globalization process in the continent, being technological and modernizing on the one side but utterly insufficient on the other. Zapata also mentions the presence of ghostly landscapes, which recalls Juan Rulfo's Comala and nods 'to Octavio Paz's and García Márquez's discourses about Mexican identity and Latin American isolation' (200) as features connecting the text to national identity.

Moreover, *La primera calle de la soledad* illustrates a complex conception of time, also present in *Tiempo lunar* and *La leyenda de los soles,* which links these novels both with the Gothic mode and with Mexican distinctiveness. The three narratives depict a cyclic notion of time that, as analyzed before, coincides with the intricate intermingling of past, present and future in some of the contemporary Gothic fictions. Whereas one of the main themes of *Tiempo lunar* is the significance of the moon as an eternally repeated pattern, the Aztec myth that Aridjis refers to in his novel understands time as a series of cycles, each ending with the death of one sun. *La primera calle de la soledad,* conversely, presents a cyclic narrative structure that Muñoz Zapata compares to a kind of '*ouroboros*', a mythic snake eating its own tail (190). As the author acknowledges, both the beginning and the end of the novel present references to this necessary rotation of life: 'Everything is cyclical', reads the first page of the novel, '[l]ife, a set of repetitive acts. The journey, a stroll through a Möbius strip' (13).[10] The narration also ends with a similar reflection: 'Life is a cycle. Never-ending and deceitful Möbius strip simulating movement and exploration to other dimensions' (192).[11]

This cyclic conception of time dwells in the necessity of recuperating the past as the only way of understanding a present that the novels project into distinct imaginary futures. According to Carlos Fuentes, one of the main theorists of Mexican time and identity, both past and future belong to the immediacy of the present in a country whose identity is a hybrid construction from different times: 'Mexico is tender fortress, cruel compassion, mortal friendship, instantaneous life. All its ages fuse into one—the past that is *ahorita*—right now—as well as the future *ahorita* and the present *ahorita*' (175). Fuentes also acknowledges the essential importance of the pre-Hispanic past, as portrayed by the mythical allusions in *Tiempo lunar* and *La leyenda de los soles,* for a complete understanding of Mexican reality:

> Mexico is a multicultural, Spanish-speaking country, but it also continues to be an indigenous country as well. A whole repertoire of possibilities that we have forgotten, postponed, or expelled from our own concept of progressive time quietly awaits us in the indigenous world, repository of all that we have forgotten and scorned: the intensity of ritual, atavistic wisdom, mythic imagination, the death relationship,

> the method of marking the passage of time—narration and sum—not only in the calendar of the sun but in the calendar of destiny, the *tonopuhali* of twenty-day cycles, each one with its own discrete, thirteen-day unit. (249)

Aridjis, Porcayo and Molina's novels recognize this recurring feature of time by combining all times into their respective dystopian imaginations in a Gothic manner, where the past haunts a monstrous present projected into a decaying future. The intrinsic connections between the horrific scenarios imagined in the narrations are made explicit by references to Mexico City's overpopulation, political corruption and ecological degradation and the country's twofold relationship to technological and market globalization. Although these narratives are set in the near future, it is the presence of the past that most insistently inhabits the narrative spaces: mythical past and barbarism collide in a world dominated by hideous corporations and uncanny technological monsters.

The combination of two literary modes such as Gothic and science fiction in a non-native territory like Mexico generates a postmodern hybrid connected to both the globalizing world that allowed its existence and the local realities it reflects. Working together, these modes, while diverting from the realistic canon, illustrate the shifting abilities of the literary extraordinary to effectively mirror the cultural realities of a nation in a grotesque, disquieting form.

Notes

1. By the use of the word 'McOndo,' the authors introduce a word play referencing both Macondo (the fictional town described by Gabriel García Márquez in *One Hundred Years of Solitude*) as something distinctly Latin American, and McDonald's as a product of globalization.
2. ' Nuestro país McOndo es más grande, sobrepoblado y lleno de contaminación, con autopistas, metro, tv-cable y barriadas. En McOndo hay McDonald's, computadores Mac y condominios, amén de hoteles cinco estrellas construídos com dinero lavado y malls gigantescos.' My translation. Consecutive versions in English will also be.
3. 'La pantalla mostraba campos áridos y agrietados, sembrados de huesos humanos, de esqueletos de ganado y gente con infecciones en la piel y en los ojos. Estas imágenes se alternaban con tomas fijas del disco solar … La imagen de aquella enorme naranja infectada se disolvía y volvía La muchedumbre hambrienta y enferma, cubierta de pústulas, los vientres monstruosamente abultados, los ojos opacos como higos secos.'
4. The myth has many variables, but they all coincide in describing the flight of Queztalcóatl from the town of Tula, which he had founded, after seeing his own misdeeds reflected in Tezcatlipoca's mirror. The looking glass is also the symbol of Tezcatlipoca himself: his name in Nahuatl translates as 'Smoking Mirror'.
5. 'Al borde de los altos muros de piedra negra, que rodeaban la casa del general, estaba una profunda barranca. La casa misma era una obra de La alucinación,

con sus tejados negros, sus muros de tezontle, sus balcones de piedra que daban a paredes cerradas, sus puertas y ventanas inaccesibles, sus arcos volados sin soporte que descansaban en el aire, la puerta llena de escopladuras, para mirar desde dentro sin ser visto. Y arriba, muy arriba, la estatua de la diosa Coatlicue.'

6. 'Desde hacía años grandes regiones de la ciudad habían sido evacuadas por órdenes superiores. Se aludían múltiples razones nunca completamente aclaradas: contaminación, inundaciones, peligro de derrumbes, epidemias. Algunos de estos territorios estaban custodiados por soldados; otros habían sido abandonados al deterioro. Nadie sabía a ciencia cierta cuál era la causa real de las evacuaciones. Se sabía que la contaminación y la sobresaturación demográfica habían provocado en otras épocas muy graves problemas, pero las verdaderas razones nunca fueron reveladas y la población acato las órdenes gubernamentales.'
7. 'En las orillas se veían vehículos oxidados brillando bajo la mirada calcinante de la luna como cocodrilos, ramajes de alambres de púas, postes inclinados. Nada alteraba aquella quietud salvaje y primitiva. Andrés podía escuchar el silencio milenario de la noche.'
8. *Menstruation* from Latin *menses* (month) derived from Greek *mene* (moon).
9. 'De pronto escuchó un ruido de agua que brotaba. De las alcantarillas, a través de las acequias cegadas, comenzó a salir un agua verdosa y turbia ... El agua verde se acumulaba en los hundimientos de las iglesias y los edificios coloniales, en los estacionamientos y sótanos de las construcciones recientes. Parte de la catedral estaba hundida, las calles a esa hora que ningún ojo las miraba se iban convirtiendo en canales, como antaño. El Zócalo era ya una enorme laguna.'
10. 'Todo es cíclico. La vida, un conjunto de actos repetitivos. El viaje, un deambular a través de una cinta de Moebius'
11. 'La vida es un ciclo. Eterna y engañosa cinta de Moebius que simula movimiento y exploración a otras dimensiones.'

Bibliography

Aridjis, Homero. *La leyenda de los soles*. Mexico City: Fondo de Cultura Económico, 1993. Print.

Armitt, Lucie. *Theorising the Fantastic*. London: Arnold, 1996. Print.

Booker, M. Keith, and Anne-Marie Thomas. *The Science Fiction Handbook*. Chichester: Wiley-Blackwell, 2009. Print.

Botting, Fred. *Gothic Romanced: Consumption, Gender and Technology in Contemporary Fictions*. London: Routledge, 2008. Print.

Byron, Glennis. 'Global Gothic.' *A New Companion to the Gothic*. Ed. Punter, David. Oxford: Blackwell, 2012. 369–78. Print.

Cavallaro, Dani. *Cyberpunk and Cyberculture: Science Fiction and the Work of William Gibson*. London: The Athlone Press, 2000. Print.

Delgado, Miguel Ángel Fernández. *Visiones periféricas: anthologia de la ciencia ficción Mexicana*. Mexico City: Lumen, 2011.

Fuentes, Carlos. *This I Believe*. Trans. Cordero, Kristia. New York: Random House, 2005. Print.

Fuguet, Alberto, and Sergio Gómez. *McOndo (una antología de nueva literatura hispanoamericana)*. Barcelona: Grijalbo-Mondadori, 1996. Print.

Haywood Ferreira, Rachel. *The Emergence of Latin American Science Fiction*. Middletown, CT: Wesleyan University Press, 2011. Print.

Heyden, Doris. *México: origen de un símbolo*. Mexico City: Colección Distrito Federal, 1988. Print.

Jackson, Rosemary. *The Literature of Subversion*. London: Methuen, 1981. Print.

Kreksch, Ingrid. 'Reality Transfigured. The Latin American Situation as Reflected in Its Science Fiction.' *Political Science Fiction*. Ed. Hassler, Donald M., and Clyde Wilcox. Columbia, SC: University of South Carolina Press. 173–82. Print.

Kristeva, Julia. *Powers of Horror*. New York: Columbia University Press, 1982. Print.

Luckhurst, Roger. 'In the Zone: Topologies of Genre Weirdness'. *Gothic Science Fiction*. Eds. Wasson, Sara, and Emily Alder. Liverpool: Liverpool UP, 2011. 21–35. Print.

Molina, Mauricio. *Tiempo lunar*. Mexico City: Punto de lectura, 2005. Print.

Muñoz Zapata, and Juan Ignacio. 'Narrative and Dystopian Forms of Life in Mexican Cyberpunk Novel *La primera calle de la soledad*.' *Science Fiction, Imperialism and the Third World: Essays on Postcolonial Literature and Film*. Eds. Hoagland, Ericka, and Reema Sarwal. Jefferson, NC: McFarland & Company, 2010. 188–201. Print.

Ordiz, Javier. 'Pesadillas del futuro. Distopías urbanas en la narrativa mexicana contemporánea'. *Bulletin of Spanish Studies* XCI, 7 (2014): 1043–57. Print.

Paz, Octavio. *The Labyrinth of Solitude*. Trassl. Kemp, Lysander, et al. New York: Grove Press, 1985. Print.

Porcayo, Gerardo Horacio. *La primera calle de la soledad*. Mexico City: Fondo Editorial Tierra Adentro, 1993. Print.

Punter, David. *The Literature of Terror Volume II: Modern Gothic*. London: Longman, 1996. Print.

Rangel, Carlos. *The Latin Americans*. New York: Harcourt Brace Jovanovich, 1976. Print.

Trujillo Muñoz, Gabriel. 'Novelas de ciencia ficción mexicana'. *Umbrales* 16 (1996): 4–8. Web. Accessed 13 May 2013.

Wolfe, Gary. *Evaporating Genres: Essays on Fantastic Literature*. Middletown, CT: Wesleyan University Press, 2011. Print.

8 Gothic Re-Constructions

Mayan Ruins and Tourist Horror in *The Ruins*

Enrique Ajuria Ibarra

Tied up and lying on an operating table, Finn, a British tourist, whimpers and witnesses how his friend Amy is sedated and cut open by the sinister villain Zamora. The make-do operation room is in a cabin in the middle of a thick rainforest that envelops the characters in layers of isolation and constriction: although it seems to be a room wide enough for surgery, low-key lighting and constant use of medium and close-up shots restrict spatial perception. The sensation is claustrophobic; the victims are trapped and are just too close to the people who are opening their bodies and taking their organs from them. Finn realizes he is helpless. Amy is barely conscious but still awake, while Zamora extracts her kidneys and liver. As he operates on Amy, the physician addresses Finn and claims that what he is doing is close to retribution: 'You [foreigners] take from our country ... and our bodies ... and now from our insides'. He refers to organ trafficking in developed countries, organs that have been harvested from people in developing countries. Zamora believes that what he is doing is for the greater good. With foreigners, such as this 'arrogant fucking gringo tourist', his organ black market is justified: taking from tourists to give to the poor and abused people of his country.

John Stockwell's *Turistas* (2006) belongs to a group of recent American productions that focus on tourist trips gone terribly wrong. Xavier Aldana Reyes notices that this film and others, such as *Borderland* (2007), directed by Zev Berman, are characterized by Americans 'in the search of strong experiences, exotic sights or illicit pleasures' (127). Indeed, *Turistas* sees a group of Anglo-Saxons exploring Brazil, looking for virginal beaches where they can revel in all-night, euphoric celebration and sexual encounters. In *Borderland*, a group of young Texans crosses the border into Mexico where they can legally buy alcoholic drinks and visit strip clubs. Characters in these two films associate these two Latin American countries with an offer of exciting and pleasurable experiences that cannot be found or accessed in their home countries. Aldana Reyes claims that, despite their contemporary setting, 'foreign places' in both films 'are often portrayed as sublime and barbaric', reminiscing the persistent othering of Catholic Europe in Gothic fiction (128). Despite a growing awareness of other cultural forms, everyday life practices and traditions, these two films represent the foreign land as a space where lack of morality and legality abounds, furthering the difference between self and other, civilization and nature. Tourists from civilized countries become victims of excesses, revenge and human sacrifices far away from the safety of home. Horror and tourism merge together to offer a cinematic nightmare: traveling is never safe, more so because of the encounter of the other in the distant land.

Location is key in the development of horror in these films. *Turistas* focuses on the visual depiction of a tropical landscape that is scarcely populated, suggesting a dreadful sense of loss once the tourists have been robbed of their possessions: bags, money, documents and cell phones. What is initially perceived as an idyllic getaway, where the tropical landscape and beaches offer places of leisure, gradually becomes a space of entrapment. The rainforest becomes a dark labyrinth under the canopy of its tall trees. Here, tourists can get lost easily and end up the victims of a villainous man who threatens their lives and the integrity of their bodies. What is initially perceived as pure, tourist enjoyment becomes the worst ordeal imaginable: impotence, suffering and death. Thus, in Stockwell's film, the tropics are infused with recognizable Gothic motifs: isolation, sublime wilderness, a merciless man whose purpose is to hunt down innocent tourists and finally kill them. In this sense, the film transports and relocates what Chris Baldick terms 'the Gothic effect' into the tropics. Indeed, the aforementioned organ extraction scene manifests 'a fearful inheritance in time with a claustrophobic sense of enclosure in space, these two dimensions reinforcing one another to produce an impression of sickening descent into disintegration' (Baldick xix). The scene described above is cinematically structured to bear down on Finn: the restricted shots are paired with a gloomy scenario that renders the tropical heat and humidity a veritable prison he cannot escape. The character's desperation is closely associated with an environment that has been transformed from light, exotic and attractive to dark, alien and deathly. The tropical landscape has been gothically re-constructed to visually explore the fears of travelers. The tourists did not choose to take a gothic holiday; rather, the narrative has gothicized the argument and setting.

Turistas is not the only film that presents a convergence of the themes of doomed tourism, Gothic and the tropics. Similar films, such as *Cannibal Holocaust* (1980) and Eli Roth's upcoming *The Green Inferno*, show this proclivity for developing horror in a similar setting. Protagonists are portrayed as civilized, coming from developed countries; their background seems to justify their sense of superiority and mistrust for the land they are exploring or visiting. In the end, they realize that there are forces beyond their control, and their abuse and consumption of this land turns back on them. They fall prey to an alien space that engulfs them and usually eliminates them. Very few are able to survive. Carter Smith's *The Ruins* (2008), an adaptation of Scott Smith's horror novel of the same title (2006), also explores the theme of a dreadful tourist trip in the tropics, particularly in Mexico's popular international resort: the Mayan Riviera. Here, Americans Jeff, Erick, Amy and Stacey decide to join German Matthias and Greek

Dimitri on a trip to explore Mayan ruins off the beaten path in the Mexican jungle. Once they arrive at the barely explored archeological site, they are threatened by members of a Mayan community, who kill Dimitri on the spot. With no option but to climb the pyramid, the Americans and Matthias eventually discover that the overgrown vegetation covering the site is a carnivorous plant. Soon they realize that they have very limited resources for survival: they have no means of communication and they can hardly find any food or shelter from the heat and humidity of the place. Fear starts to dominate them, as the intelligent plant bides its time to kill and devour the tourists one by one.

Smith's film evidently borrows elements from the aforementioned tropical horror tourist films, but its main difference is that, rather than featuring a human villain, the monster that threatens the lives of the tourists is a supernatural vegetal creature capable of mimicking human and technological sounds, as well as being able to pit its victims against each other. This suggests a development of horror that is not based on the barbaric foreign other, the person the tourist encounters on travels abroad; rather, it further examines the contentious division between civilization and nature, this time focusing on the qualities of intelligence and rationality. *The Ruins* crosses the boundaries of realism with the visual representation of monstrous, carnivorous vegetation: a supernatural creature that hyperbolizes the tourist's encounter and mistrust of nature. Besides this monstrous representation, the film structures its setting in an unexplored Mayan pyramid that is infused with Gothic elements: isolated, ancient, practically undiscovered, a representation of an ancient civilization that is admired and consumed for its exotic qualities. Although the film can be understood in Gothic terms, it is worth noticing that the setting is determined by a range of specific motifs and an appropriation of monstrosity that are not necessarily inherent to the Mayan peninsula in Mexico. Once again, as in *Turistas*, monstrous and body horror in *The Ruins* are key factors to illustrating fantasies of perilous danger in the foreign land. This subsequently evidences the film's artificial structuration of otherness by means of gothic conventions. What is presented in the film is not a form of Mexican Gothic, an appropriation and exploration of gothic strategies in a different location with its own cultural and artistic background; instead, unknown exotic elements are gothicized to narrate and to display a spectacular fascination for foreign otherness in the form of dark and unknown tropical fears. Like the other films mentioned above, *The Ruins* questions the possible flow and directions that a global gothic perspective might encourage. Instead, this tropical tourist horror film points to an inheritance of colonial and imperial views that are now structured on a culture of consumption and enjoyment facilitated by technological developments in travel and communication around the world. In this case, a global whole, interested in the cultural and discursive interactions between different localities, is overshadowed by an inherited fear of otherness that is still structured on the civilized and the barbaric.

Gabriel Eljaiek-Rodríguez states that a tropicalization of the Gothic involves 'a way of appropriating the images and values of a dominant culture (in this case, European) in order to generate autochthonous products while maintaining a bond with the 'original' and discussing and questioning issues and images of the dominant culture' (14). If this is true, *The Ruins* belongs to the same European, Anglo-Saxon view that has seen Gothic develop as a narrative mode that mediates and discloses cultural fears and anxieties. In this case, the emphasis on tourism points to Gothic fiction's relationship with travel and the way that they jointly function to locate otherness, still marked by past notions of imperialism and colonialism. The gothic representation of the tropics in *The Ruins* elicits a tension of the politics of otherness that must be either successfully overcome or dramatically disturbed due to global consciousness.

Yet, the real horror in Smith's film is what the carnivorous plant is able to psychically and physically reveal about the trapped tourists: their weaknesses and their fears are worked around them, tangling them and killing them for the profit of the plant itself. Horror emanates from the characters' loss of integrity and human rationality, instead of being located in the foreign landscape or villain. This horror relies on a gothic effect that structures and signifies locations that are empty of meaning, in order to understand that its source is not dependent on alien circumstances but on the very subject that is keen on projecting uncanny fears. Gothic delivers a sense of strangeness and otherness into the setting of the narrative, rather than the location being in itself inherently Gothic. Thus, the Mayan ruins in the tropics are framed by the fear of the self, the subject, the one suddenly at odds with its own constitution and determination as it treads into a space beyond its discursive understanding. A gothicized fear is thus deposited to permit a narrative imagery of horror in the foreign land that comes back home, that is, to the self.

Gothic Travels

One of the key features in *The Ruins* is its attention to stasis and movement. This is the main narrative feature that permits cultural associations between civilization and culture, the canny and the uncanny to be distinguished in the film. In this doomed travel narrative, characters make choices that prompt them to take a journey from the safety of their hotel resort to the rainforest. They finally become trapped in uncharted territory and are stuck on top of the pyramid because the Mayan community is keeping close watch on them—if they leave the site, they may transport spores from the carnivorous plant elsewhere—the tourists are left to fend for themselves by any means possible. They are stranded, isolated and abandoned in a place that surrounds them with the prospect of death. The promise of a return home is constantly seen as their only hope; movement, as opposed to stasis and entrapment, is the only option for survival, for living. Additionally, stasis ambivalently relates to both safety and danger: the protagonists' peaceful and relaxing holiday inside the beach resort fulfills their holiday expectations with an environment suited for tourists. This is contrasted with their entrapment on top of the pyramid. Here, they have no comfortable means: no food, no drinks, no shelter. This place makes them realize the fierce environmental aspects of the exotic land. With no protection, they will most probably die in what was once considered the leisurely tropics.

This sense of alienation of the foreign land is gradually elaborated with the aid of a consistent alignment of audience and characters. When the spectators meet the tourists spending their time at the resort's swimming pool, medium close-up shots enhance the intimate friendship among the four Americans. This is further established by motifs in the *mise-en-scène* appropriate for spring break vacations: sunlight, deck chairs, alcoholic drinks, colorful and bright swimming suits. The film permits glimpses at Jeff's, Amy's, Erik's and Stacey's experience both in public and in private, in their sobriety and their drunkenness. Stereotypical fears about the cleanliness of the water and the food are voiced, as well as the possibility of exploring 'an ancient Mayan temple off the beaten path'. Their enjoyment is enclosed and secured within the resort's walls, where stereotypical vacations are experienced and consumed in the company of other Americans and Europeans, civilized young people that have fun before they go back home to behave like proper adults. Once outside their hotel resort, the tourists wander off into a strange land that offers different and attractive adventures and commodities. Their trip to the ruins is filled with exciting views: small villages in the Yucatán peninsula with trinkets and souvenirs Amy and Stacey are keen to purchase. They carry their banter and good humor from the safety of the hotel, far away from any community and into the depths of a dense rainforest. They share an enthusiasm for discovery, despite their limited notions of local customs.

When they arrive at the Mayan pyramid their joyful daytrip is cut short with the violent encounter with a group of Mayan men. Even though Jeff is able to speak some Spanish, he is unable to communicate with the Mayans because they are not bilingual. When the Mayans brandish their weapons, a gun and bows and arrows, the inability to understand one another escalates into confusion and desperation. The shot/reverse shot sequence determines a tense confrontation between the Mayans and the tourists: their different physical features are highlighted in the midst of the sunny and bright morning. Once Amy steps into the foliage that covers the whole pyramid, the Mayans begin to shout out to the tourists who believe they are being threatened rather than being warned. When Dimitri also steps into the foliage and decides to approach the Mayans, their voices escalate until one of them shoots an arrow at Dimitri and another one shoots him right in the head with a pistol. When Dimitri's inert body falls to the ground, the other characters are shocked and have no choice but to climb the pyramid for safety. The encounter with the natives has resulted in utter failure: the sense of othering and estrangement has turned to death; the Mayans' warning is never seen as anything but a threat to the tourists' lives.

Smith's film portrays the traveler's alienation in the foreign land by means of gruesome actions that further determine an underlying fear and horror in the travel experience. The sense of homely safety is persistently at odds with a cultural sense of danger lurking at every turn. Although the film is set during our contemporary, global era, the representation of Mexico and the characters' demise in the midst of the jungle are structured on notions of self and other, civilization and wilderness inherited from colonialism and imperialism. Moreover, *The Ruins* deliberately develops its narrative with the convergence of Gothic and travel, as a means to explore cultural fears of the other beyond the control of the civilized self that have been addressed since the origins of Gothic fiction in the late eighteenth century.

In her critical introduction to Ann Radcliffe's *The Romance of the Forest*, Chloe Chard notes that 'Gothic novels [...] make a vigorous attempt to lay claim to a literary and intellectual status rather more elevated than that which is usually accorded to them. This attempt is evident, above all, in the wide range of references to other areas of writing which Gothic fiction establishes, and in the forms of authority to which it appeals in seeking to provide intellectual authentication for the narrative of horror and terror' (xix). Such is the case of travel writing. The contemplations and musings seen from the traveler's perspective in Gothic fiction are inherited from a testimonial narrative mode that is keen on observing and determining differences between the traveler and the foreign other. Equally, the nature of the landscape is presented with such awe that it can incite sensations of sublimity and estrangement. Chard claims that 'in its description of various different aspects of foreign countries, the Gothic novel introduces a range of different concepts of horror and terror', which are fully immersed in Gothic's rhetorical expressions and are further authenticated by the traveler's perspective or discourse (xxi). Thus, Gothic fiction's relationship with travel narrative permits a full development of the horrifying and the uncanny within the landscape of the foreign and previously unexplored land.

The association between travel and the Gothic is further elicited during the colonial and British imperial periods, as a narrative strategy that discloses an imperial gaze constantly at odds with the lands conquered. The Gothic is allowed to travel beyond the borders of the homeland to project fears of power and race against the backdrop of the colony. For Lizabeth Paravisini-Gebert, 'Gothic writers were quick to realize that Britain's growing empire could prove a vast source of frightening 'others' who would ... bring freshness and variety to the genre' (229). Indeed, what the colonies offered was an ideal repository of cultural fears that could be thrown away into the unknown land, instead of facing them close by. Monstrous animals, savage humans, and slaves, all proved useful to Gothic constructions of fear and horror. Subsequently, Paravisini-Gebert argues that 'the genre often turned the colonial subject into the obscene cannibalistic personification of evil, through whom authors could bring revulsion and horror into the text, thereby mirroring political and social anxieties close to home' (231). What is worth noticing is that Gothic fiction found new spaces to explore—and exploit—as a result of imperial expansion. These settings, both part of and alien to the empire, are rather repositories of Gothic conventions, thus transforming them into places that are simultaneously attractive and fearful.

The result of this exploration by Gothic means is what Stephen E. Tabachnick terms 'the Gothic adventure genre', which he uses to describe the works of H. Rider Haggard, such as *She*, and Joseph Conrad's *Heart of Darkness*. Tabachnick claims that:

> In the fictional Gothic adventure journey as it crystallizes in the nineteenth century, particularly in the work of Haggard, we typically have a difficult exploration attended by presentiments of doom, a victorious confrontation with unknown, often supernatural forces, and a near escape by a brave, technologically skilled European who is believed only with difficulty when he finally tells his tale. This plot provided and continues to provide the audience of a rational, scientific age with a pleasing reaffirmation of belief in irrational forces, which are however placed at a comfortable distance from ourselves, and at the same time allows the defeat of these terrifying, inevitably evil forces. (191)

Tabachnick emphasizes the distant setting as a key factor to enjoying these Gothic adventures: the exotic land serves as the ideal location for characters to come close to monstrous threats, whether supernatural or human, that will be eventually conquered or avoided. The distant land is additionally transformed by Gothic means: negative and grotesque descriptions of the tropical landscape abound to further elicit, or confirm, its opposition to civilized Britain. Incidentally, in his reading of Bram Stoker's *Dracula*, Stephen Arata finds this narrative of empire where 'the Gothic and the travel narrative problematize, separately and together, the very boundaries on which British imperial hegemony depended: between civilized and primitive, colonizer and colonized, victimizer (either imperialist or vampire) and victim' (626). As such, Arata also identifies fictional works that rely on combining both narrative modes in order to establish a frail boundary between civilization and nature that is supposed to confirm an imperial status of power, a status that is nevertheless threatened by the boundary itself.

The use of Gothic conventions to transform the foreign or distant land into an exotic milieu of danger and depravity is not unique to the British Empire. The Gothic constantly moves when an association between close home and distant wilderness is determined. Rebecca McIntyre also notices this trend in American fiction and travel writing: 'Long before the gothic Souths of William Faulkner or Flannery O'Connor, travel writers like Thorpe conceived of certain southern scenes, mainly swamps but also the ruined plantations evocative of grand, lost civilizations, as 'gothic', that is, medieval, melancholy, and slightly grotesque' (33). McIntyre notes that descriptions and illustrations from travel writers exploring the American South provided a portrait to the American North that was incidentally determined by an imagery of self and other, and a supremacy of the North over the South that found justification in the hyperbolical transformation of the landscape into something more tropical, more ruined and more abandoned. Thus, 'these excesses of semitropical vegetation enhanced the exoticism of the South, to be sure, but they had another function for northerners: they assured them that the South was an American aberration' (McIntyre 51).

What Paravisini-Gebert, Tabachnick, Arata and McIntyre have similarly brought to attention is what James Procter and Angela Smith have identified as the 'Gothic treatment' of colonized—and in the case of the United States, southern—culture as 'the source of barbarism, temptation and horror' (96). The representation of the exotic land, rather than being Gothic itself, is utilized for Gothic effects. Horror is posited in the hinterland: the senses of the unhomely, the ancient and barbaric, and the foreign are developed by a Gothic aesthetic that turns these spaces into negative, distant and, thus, abject locations. In short, the settings are gothicized. Instead of displaying a darkness of their own, travelers bring personal descriptive and visual imaginary to envision the foreign land. The gothic mode transforms these spaces and infuses them with a signification the traveler is familiarized with. Fear and attraction for the unknown land is manifested by means of a Gothic that travels, a Gothic that moves and draws boundaries of self and other, civilization and nature, commodification and consumption, safety, danger and death.

Smith's film moves the border of the unknown further South. In this case, Mexico becomes the repository of contrasts. A geographical and political border sets the limits of an American identity that necessarily must face and project otherness way beyond its own limits. The Mexican-American border establishes an ambivalent distance and closeness that is necessary in the definition of identity: on the other side, a series of imaginary configurations become staple by means of location of self and otherness. Even though globalization seeks to make this border flexible, there is a sense of fear of what this flexibility might entail. In *The Ruins*, the Mexican is always seen from the perspective of the American: the subject does not trust despite the proximity of the foreigner. In this case, the four Americans stick to the construction of a stereotype of Mexico: the uncivilized and unsafe land, where nothing can be trusted, not even the cleanliness of the water. At the same time, it is an attractive setting that can be consumed for its difference. As such, the gaze cast to the other side, beyond the safety of the resort and the reliance of communications technologies, maintains a colonial look based on this stereotype. Homi Bhabha argues that stereotype is a 'major discursive strategy' for colonialism: 'a form of knowledge and identification that vacillates between what is always 'in place', already known, and something that must be anxiously repeated' (94–95). The stereotype helps determine racial and cultural difference by toying with the subject's perception and knowledge of the other: it must keep expectations in place, but it also reveals what the self anxiously fears. Bhabha claims that the stereotype reveals 'the productive ambivalence of the object of colonial discourse—that "otherness" which is at once an object of desire and derision, an articulation of difference contained within the fantasy of origin and identity' (96). The Americans in Smith's film live their fantasy of leisure and travel, in a country that meets their expectations of difference, close, yet far away from home. This fantasy of exoticism is broken the moment they step beyond the fabricated tourist experience of the beach resort and visit the depths of the foreign country.

The Gothic is brought to the Mexican landscape in *The Ruins* to allow for a gradual manifestation of terror and horror that dissolves the fantasy of the foreigner. The site of an unexplored Mayan ruin is just the setting that can be molded for narrative effect. The travelers trapped in the pyramid bring the Gothic into this space. The alienation and estrangement of exploring a foreign land is visually represented in this extreme survival situation, the real travel experience when the fantasy is done away with. As the supernatural abilities of the plant blur distinctions of technology, civilization and nature, the four American tourists and the German slowly consume themselves in order to be engulfed by ancient and unbeknownst forces they are unable to fight off. Despite its commercial and global approach, Smith's film recurs to a Gothic that travels, in order to point to ideological and discursive issues that arise in the consumption of the foreign land. If globalization facilitates the encounter and exchange of various cultural and discursive frameworks, *The Ruins* is an impasse to this flow of knowledge. The narrative is about the fear of what might be discovered in the unknown exotic land, and it constantly constructs a tense border between tourists and natives, safety and danger, civilization and wilderness. Once this borderline has been crossed, what the Americans find in the pyramid is not just a monstrous ancient plant, but a life-threatening situation that keeps harking back to the fragility of the embodiment of the self. Thus, the carnivorous organism, a creature beyond the limits of knowledge, is a deliberate uncanny perpetrator that reveals the very origin of identity and the other.

Mayan Ruins and Tourist Horror

When Amy and Stacey discover that the plant covering the entire Mayan pyramid has been mimicking the ringtone of a cell phone, their reaction is that of utter disbelief and horror. The four Americans and the German had been hoping to find a functional means of communication that would allow them to contact the civilized world they had left to come and explore the ruins. Instead, the young women discover a plant with a remarkable ability to emulate any sound possible in the depths of the ancient and abandoned structure. This surprising fact discloses an association of technological sound with living organism that fractures the boundaries that constitute the difference between the old and the new, the organic and the mechanic. The visual confirmation of the source of the ringtone is highly uncanny. Visual and aural disassociation works in this scene to further determine the out-of-placeness the film constantly points to. The plant's aural mimicking is nothing more than a sonic transference of the fantasy of tourism and travel finally being understood for what it is: its reality fractures and destabilizes the subjects' notion of safety and control over the exotic space that maliciously engulfs them.

Amy shockingly understands that there is no escape from the Mayan ruins: the plant has cleverly set a trap for them, and they are all doomed to meet utter and painful death. What this scene also confirms is the thin line between tourist fantasy and the real shock that always encloses the idea of tourism: there is always the risk or danger of disappearing in the unknown destination. Slavoj Žižek calls this a 'relationship between … two worlds' that 'eludes the simple oppositions of surface and depth, reality and fantasy, and so on—the only topology that suits it is that of the two surfaces of the Moebius band: if we progress far enough on one surface, all of a sudden we find ourselves on its reverse' (227). Žižek's analysis focuses on the structural revelations between American hysteria and its psychotic reverse in Alfred Hitchcock's *Psycho*. However, what he successfully demonstrates is that films may elicit 'an idyllic everyday surface with its dark reverse' (Žižek 227) that disturbs apparent structures of everyday life to reveal a reverse side that is essentially a real one, and a horrifying one at that.[1] Smith's film transports this structure further abroad. As we have previously mentioned, American tourists bring excitement and anxiety about a trip in the Mayan Riviera: health and other safety concerns determine their tourist fantasy. But once trapped in the ruins, they slowly move down onto that other side that essentially constitutes the tourist experience, that is, its actual danger.

The Ruins manifests this horrifying realization by means of uncanny sounds. Unidentifiable sounds and unknown sound sources are constantly perceived in the Mayan pyramid in the film's opening sequence as well. Here, a woman trapped in the depths of the ruins holds a mobile phone and fruitlessly attempts to ring for help. Low saturation light enhances the alienation of the unknown space: shadows envelop the young woman, who is genuinely terrified by the sounds she is able to hear around her. A soft, maniacal, high-pitched laughter is discernible; its source is completely cut off from view by the dimness of the enclosed space. The never achieved expectation of a visual confirmation of the source of this sound heightens the gothic elaboration of the sequence.

Sound in Smith's film is the gateway to Gothic and horror. Isabella van Elferen argues that sound and music are inherent and important factors in the determination of the Gothic. She establishes that they 'are used to heighten the ambivalence of visuals and narratives as they move on the blurry boundaries between dream, fantasy, and reality' (3). For van Elferen, these aspects in the Gothic milieu can enhance uncanny experiences, as both elements can further break the boundaries of real, unreal and super-real. Although she particularly focuses more on the sound of music, she nevertheless acknowledges the power of the un-bodied sound in film: 'When used without the support of visuals, the recorded whisper or the voice-over draws viewers' attention to the absence of its physical source, the body that produces this sound. Without evidence of embodiment voices are uncanny, as vocal sound always suggests physicality. Rather than the explicitness of horror, disembodied voices evoke the implicit terror of Gothic' (39). As such, the corporeal absence of the sonic source unleashes imaginary and terrifying expectations: what is it that produces this disturbing sound? What will we encounter (or not) in the shadows? In this case, the film's opening sequence is cut at the exact moment the young woman is dragged off into the dark by an unknown force. Immediately, a tracking aerial shot of a dense rainforest in plain daylight is shown; the woman crying in pain can be heard off-screen. This scene constantly denies us what we want to be revealed, and instead plunges the audience into a suggestive nightmare that is prompted by audiovisual discrepancies. *The Ruins* determines the gothicizing of location by means of what van Elferen calls 'the sounds of the uncanny'. This horror is what fills the setting in the film, eliciting a collapse of archaic past, mythical past and the present.

Unlike the novel, Smith's adaptation of *The Ruins* recurs to images that are associated with the ancient Mayan culture, thus providing a more idealized temporalization of the *mise-en-scène*.[2] The fact that archaeologists are exploring the site and that characters hint they are spending their vacations in the Mayan Riviera, leads to the designation of an unexplored pyramid in the midst of the tropical rainforest as Mayan. Indeed, what the Americans, Matthias and Dimitri encounter is an imposing structure that awes them. Curiously, the pyramid is hidden from view by the expansive growth of the carnivorous plant, and very little attention is paid to the building's historical and architectural features. The tourists have projected a tourist fantasy of historical encounter on a structure that is barely visible under the shrubbery. Moreover, the building stands empty; all of it is engulfed, inside and outside, by a force more ancient and threatening. This hollow pyramid serves as the repository of an idealization of a Mexican past; it is an empty frame filled with the prospect of historical discovery. The pyramid in the film is similar to what Jerrold E. Hogle calls 'the Gothic ghost of the counterfeit'. Hogle means there is no authenticity in the representation of the past exposed in gothic fictions, but rather a re-construction based on an idealized past, mostly derived from images and representations of a historical nature. This counterfeit 'employs symbols from earlier times largely emptied of many older meanings' and 'quite readily becomes a symbolic space into which the fears and horrors generated by early modern cultural changes can be 'thrown off' or 'thrown under' as though they exist more in the now obscure and distant past than in the threatening present' (296–97). *The Ruins* makes use of the Gothic ghost of the counterfeit in terms of setting. The Mayan pyramid is essentially constructed as an empty signifier: whatever it contains is essentially unknown. It is an architectural vessel that, because of its emptiness, produces horror. Furthermore, its emptiness allows it to be gothicized: the narrative pours senses of dread and abjection, paired with the characters suddenly being cut off from civilization. Additionally, Hogle points to a collapse of historicity with the Gothic: the empty signifiers of the past are infused with constant and atemporal fears. The horror in Smith's film is not the Mayan ruins, but rather the more ancient and archaic creature that inhabits the structure and what it represents. Beyond the human and the civilized, the carnivorous plant is the tourists' inevitable encounter with the fragility of their bodies and their own death.

Smith's film demonstrates a certain limitation of the notion of global culture. Glennis Byron claims that 'not only has Western gothic travelled but one of the effects of the increasing mobility and fluidity of people and products in the globalised world has been a growing awareness that the tropes and strategies Western critics have associated with the gothic [...] have their counterparts in other cultures, however differently these may be inflected by specific histories and belief systems. Consequently, the flows have by no means been one-directional' (3). If the global approach to gothic is to examine the fluidity of tropes and narrative strategies, and the location of a multicultural and heterogeneous exercise of this mode, then *The Ruins* fails to embrace this global approach. Indeed, the film is by no means exploring the local vicissitudes of a haunting specific to a cultural environment; rather, the haunting is the result of a manifest projection of the tourists' fears as they become trapped in this isolated place.

This constant display of civilization and wilderness in tourist horror films suggests that a global perspective cannot be disassociated from the view of the foreign other as barbaric and alien. If globalization asks for a fluid and comparative exchange of cultural and discursive systems, these films exhibit a string of characters and victims that constantly disclose an ahistorical sensitivity to the foreign places they are exploring. For instance, Kevin J. Wetmore argues that tourist horror films always feature young Americans who disregard social and cultural particularities, and that their travel purpose is to act, purchase and consume what is usually out of their reach at home. He claims that 'American ignorance is on parade in these films, specifically the ignorance of the educated elite of the younger generation' (109). Even though globalization may aim at a better understanding of local social and cultural expressions, the process is not a fluid or comparative one. Globalization continues to be subsumed by a politics of understanding driven by the consumption and contempt between the civilized and the uncivilized. Hence, films such as *Turistas* and *The Ruins* do not tropicalize the Gothic; on the contrary, the tropics are gothicized by a discourse that fears the foreign other and unhomely space.

Wetmore further states that in *The Ruins*, 'the Americans [...], and their European associates, are not evil. They are self-centred, self-important, privileged and unaware of how their behaviour will impact the local population, but though such ignorance is no excuse, it is not malevolence. The film, however, depicts the very ground, the plants, the nature found in this third-world country as being hostile to Americans' (111). Wetmore argues that the horror established in the film is due to the tourists' lack of knowledge about the place they are visiting: their experience is that of travel-pleasure, rather than travel-discovery or travel-knowledge. Although he hints to the uncanny and monstrous qualities of the local vegetation, he fails to determine the configuration of the Mexican and Mayan landscape as a gothic counterfeit. The wilderness of the jungle is paired with a sense of decadence, of a hollow structure that idealizes a touristic image of the past, which contains a powerful organism that can obliterate any residue of previous explorers.

As such, the landscape in Smith's film becomes a composite image of ideal tourist exploration and doomed travel: the discovery of the plant's abilities and intelligence works as a nodal point in the gothicizing of the Mexican tropics. Young Americans who travel to the beach resort in the Mayan Riviera see this space for its consumption value. Ironically, the reverse is explicitly represented in the film: their own bodies are consumed by the plant and are destroyed by themselves. The plant represents an othering that goes beyond the social and the cultural. Here, it is not a confrontation between human beings, but a confrontation with the other in nature that elicits unavoidable death, the obliteration of the subject. *The Ruins* structures a scenario where the historical interest in the exotic past, represented by the pyramidal construction covered by the carnivorous plant, is essentially covered by death and lack of civilized meaning. The desire for travel-pleasure, to visit a Mayan archaeological site, is stopped short by the presence of death and entrapment in a site of lost temporality. Like the ahistorical knowledge of the travelers, the Mayan site is suspended between its idealized representation of a touristic past and the real emptiness of its hollow shell. Gothic turns it uncanny: tourism reveals the threat of dying away from home, in the wilderness, beyond the boundaries of what is known and familiar.

Thus, the presentation of two radically different spaces in this travel film, the safe beach resort and the deadly Mayan ruins, is not fortuitous; on the contrary, it attests to a consistent visual narrative of the perilous journey that responds to structural conflicts present in the foreign land. *The Ruins* follows a spatial premise similar to other contemporary tourist horror films, such as *Hostel* (2005) and the previously mentioned *Turistas*. Whether they take place in Eastern Europe or Brazil, these films try to destabilize the notion of American imperialism by transforming their American and British consumers into the consumed. In his analysis of *Hostel*, Jason Middleton claims that the film 'represents a form of cultural problem solving, which, in certain respects, presents a critical perspective on American imperialism. Ultimately, however, the film recuperates this criticism and reaffirms a (neo) conservative view of the necessity for American aggression in what is represented as a corrupt and dangerous world' (1). While initially *Hostel* may turn global tourist consumption and exploitation of foreign goods and people back on Americans, their victimization and painful bodily torture gives certain justification for these young Americans to fight back violently. In the end, Middleton suggests that 'foreignness is no longer an exotic commodity to be claimed, but a form of threatening otherness' (15). This reasserts a view of the land beyond the borders of the home nation as spaces where the subject's integrity can still be threatened. Once more, the narrative of the trapped tourists reveals a constant fear of what is yet to be discovered or encountered in a holiday: the journey is never innocent; the trip is constantly framed by threat, danger and possible death.

In this sense, *The Ruins* utilizes a Gothic that travels to reveal the horror behind the fantasy of tourism: in the end, the experience comes back to the very subject and its projection of otherness. This also suggests that a colonial and imperial sense of fear toward the foreigner still haunts a more global conscience. This allows us to reconsider what Sue Zlosnik has identified in Robert Louis Stevenson's early travel writing in relation to Smith's film. For Zlosnik, Stevenson's voyages across continental Europe are also 'the voyage in', where the traveler or wanderer also 'goes into himself' (245). Stevenson's narratives lay out an inner exploration of the self as an outsider traveler who is constantly reminded of his possible death. Thus Zlosnik points out that here Stevenson 'hints at the existence of self-division and the potential of inner darkness; he exposes the frailty of the body and the abject aspects of corporeality; he acknowledges the contingency and fragility of civilization: he recognizes death in the midst of life' (242). Zlosnik acknowledges finding Gothic motifs revolving around notions of the body, the abject and undisclosed personality. In a similar and more contemporary fashion, when Jeff, Amy, Erik, Stacey and Matthias are quarantined at the top of the pyramid, their weaknesses and fears are heightened by a setting suddenly turned hostile and mortal to them. The hot, sunny day becomes an excruciating experience as they struggle to survive in the middle of the rainforest with little food and water. The five of them turn against each other and quarrel constantly upon choices and decisions that could cost their lives. Furthermore, the carnivorous plant quietly manipulates each one of them to turn against the others and manages to infiltrate their bodies by any means possible. Matthias dies asphyxiated when tendrils creep inside his throat whilst the Americans are quarreling. The plant successfully penetrates Stacey's body by getting inside a wound in her leg. She later develops paranoia about still feeling the plant inside her. Her body has become a receptacle for an alien organism that will gnaw her inside out. Even though Jeff manages to cut into her leg and back to pull developing tendrils from her, she firmly believes the plant is still inside. In a shocking scene, Stacey manages to get a knife and starts cutting deep into her flesh to pull the plant out. The plant instils in her the notion of not trusting her body anymore, so she ends up tearing it apart.

The tourists realize there are ancient forces in nature that should remain virtually unknown, but that they have brought out to light during their adventure. Thus, *The Ruins* exploits recurrent elements from the Gothic mode in order to instill uncanny feelings that further develop into dreadful horror. The worst possible nightmare for the tourist is presented in its darkest fashion in this film. Jeff's vehement statement that 'four Americans on a vacation just don't disappear' is unavoidably true: the undiscovered Mayan ruins will claim all of their lives. The travelers are swallowed by the forces of nature. The film evidently incorporates characteristics of gothic fiction suggested by David Punter. First, it develops a sense of paranoia, elicited by a monstrous plant with unthought-of capabilities that question notions of reality and rationality. Second, it addresses the 'notion of the barbaric'. It 'bring[s] us up against the boundaries of the civilized' and taboo behaviors (183–84) by configuring an exotic landscape where seemingly innocent and civilized tourists encounter not just foreign Others, but also a gradual unveiling of their dark, inner selves manifested in rash decisions and gruesome body mutilations for the sake of survival.

The film structures the characters' demise by toying with the notion of the uncanny body. Expressed by verbal confrontations and the plant's tendrils invading their bodies through any cavity or cut available, the characters slowly show their own fears, weaknesses and true desires. What is revealed is physically and psychically turned around and laid out in the burning sun of the tropics. Julia Kristeva argues that the uncanny taps at unconscious anxieties to further reveal that strangeness and otherness burst forth from the very self. In order to name the subject, a projection of the unwanted is materialized in the form of the Other, the strange, the dreadful. These projections return to the subject's revelation of what is being elicited: dread and the other are simply the negated fear of the unconscious itself. As such, Kristeva asserts that 'the other is my ('own and proper') unconscious' (191). The carnivorous plant in *The Ruins* is a monster that cruelly moves all trapped characters to break down: their own subjectivity is threatened by imminent and hideously painful death. Instead of killing them on the spot, the plant waits and slowly, viciously turns each character against the others to reveal weaknesses. Relationships break as Jeff and Amy cannot stand each other anymore. In an attempt to keep Stacey from inflicting another wound on her body, she dramatically plunges the knife into her own boyfriend's heart, Erik, killing him instantly. Friends become enemies, and loved ones begin to realize how strange and frightening their partners are.

Kristeva claims that the construction of the strange is uncanny because it 'appears as a paroxystic metaphor of the psychic functioning itself. The latter is indeed elaborated by repression and one's necessarily going through it, with the result that the builder of the other and, in the final analysis, of the strange is indeed repression itself and its perviousness' (184). What the carnivorous plant pulls out from all of the characters as they slowly turn against each other and face the futility of their rescue is the permeability of their most innate fears. The horror in the film is instilled by a gothicized setting that reveals subjects collapsing when they face estrangement and isolation from what they deemed civilized. The conflict in the film is not dealing with the monstrous plant, but rather, once trapped in a setting signified as inhospitable, dreadful and horrifying, it is the split of the subject and the prospect of death that become the real horror in the narrative. As such, Kristeva points out that it is the rejection of the other, the foreigner, the fear it inspires that actually says 'we are fighting our unconscious—that 'improper' facet of our impossible 'own and proper'' (191). *The Ruins* is a film that exploits gothic conventions to transform a setting and allow the fear of the other to materialize into monstrous vegetation and sublime tropical landscapes. What it reveals is that true gothic horror is always within the body of the self: physically and psychically, real horror is the constant fragility of subjectivity, always in threat of being obliterated by death.

Notes

1. David Lynch's film *Blue Velvet* (1986) and TV series *Twin Peaks* (1990–1991) similarly recollect the Hitchcockian move to which Žižek is referring. In both stories, characters are seemingly moving from idyllic portraits of American, middle-class suburban bliss to plunge into twisted and rotten worlds of perverse men. In the TV series, supernatural forces break into the apparent familial stability: the murder of Laura Palmer leads to a detective investigation of this peaceful town that discloses its other rotten side. The fantasy of America perpetually straddles a reality of corruption and deceit.
2. In the novel, Scott Smith describes the archeological site as 'a small hill. The hill was rocky, oddly treeless, and covered with some sort of vinelike growth—a vivid green, with hand-shaped leaves and tiny flowers. The plant spread across the entire hill, clinging so tightly to the earth that it almost seemed to be squeezing it in its grass' (82). The hill is an abandoned mine; within, dark shafts spread far enough for the characters to be afraid to venture in them (125). The film turns the mine into a pyramidal structure, which further suggests a sense of a more ancient remnant of civilization than that of a mine.

Bibliography

Arata, Stephen D. 'The Occidental Tourist: 'Dracula' and the Anxiety of Reverse Colonization.' *Victorian Studies* 33.4 (1990): 621–45. Print.

Baldick, Chris. *The Oxford Book of Gothic Tales*. Oxford: Oxford University Press, 1992. Print.

Berman, Zev. *Borderland*. Lionsgate, 2007. Film.

Bhabha, Homi K. *The Location of Culture*. London: Routledge, 1994. Print.

Byron, Glennis. 'Introduction.' *Globalgothic*. Manchester: Manchester University Press, 2013. 1–10. Print.

Deodato, Ruggero. *Cannibal Holocaust*. United Artists/Grindhouse Releasing, 1980. Film.

Eljaiek-Rodríguez, Gabriel. 'Semillas de Maldad: Early Latin American Gothic.' *Studies in Gothic Fiction* 3.2 (2014): 13–23. Print.

Hogle, Jerrold E. 'The Gothic Ghost of the Counterfeit and the Progress of Abjection.' *A Companion to the Gothic*. Ed. David Punter. Oxford: Blackwell, 2000. 293–304. Print.

Kristeva, Julia. *Strangers to Ourselves*. New York: Columbia University Press, 1991. Print.

Lynch, David. *Blue Velvet*. De Laurentiis Entertaiment Group, 1986. Film.

———. *Twin Peaks*. ABC, 1991–1990. Television.

McIntyre, Rebecca C. 'Promoting the Gothic South.' *Southern Cultures* 11.2 (2005): 33–61. Print.

Middleton, Jason. 'The Subject of Torture: Regarding the Pain of Americans in Hostel.' *Cinema Journal* 49.4 (2010): 1–24. Print.

Paravisini-Gebert, Lizabeth. 'Colonial and Postcolonial Gothic: The Caribbean.' *The Cambridge Companion to Gothic Fiction*. Ed. Jerrold E. Hogle. Cambridge: Cambridge University Press, 2002. 229–57. Print.

Procter, James, and Angela Smith. 'Gothic and Empire.' *The Routledge Companion to Gothic*. Ed. Catherine Spooner and Emma McEvoy. London: Routledge, 2007. 95–104. Print.

Punter, David. *The Literature of Terror: A History of Gothic Fictions from 1765 to the Present Day. Volume 2: The Modern Gothic*. 2nd ed. London: Longman, 1996. Print.

Radcliffe, Ann. *The Romance of the Forest*. Ed. Chloe Chard. Oxford: Oxford University Press, 1986. Print.

Reyes, Xavier Aldana. *Body Gothic: Corporeal Transgression in Contemporary Literature and Horror Film*. Cardiff: University of Wales Press, 2014. Print.

Roth, Eli. *Hostel*. Lions Gate Films, 2005. Film.

Smith, Carter. *The Ruins*. Paramount Pictures, 2008. Film.

Smith, Scott. *The Ruins*. London: Bantam Press, 2006. Print.

Stockwell, John. *Turistas*. Fox Atomic, 2006. Film.

Tabachnick, Stephen E. 'Two Tales of Gothic Adventure: She and Heart of Darkness.' *English Literature in Transition* 56.2 (2013): 189–200. Print.

Van Elferen, Isabella. *Gothic Music: The Sounds of the Uncanny*. Cardiff: University of Wales Press, 2012. Print.

Wetmore, Kevin J. *Post-9/11 Horror in American Cinema*. London: Continuum, 2012. Print.

Žižek, Slavoj. 'In His Bold Gaze My Ruin Is Write Large.' *Everything You Always Wanted to Know About Lacan (But Were Afraid to Ask Hitchcock)*. Ed. Slavoj Žižek. London: Verso, 2010. 211–72. Print.

Zlosnik, Sue. "Home Is the Sailor, Home from Sea': Robert Louis Stevenson and the End of Wandering.' *The Yearbook of English Studies* 34 (2004): 240–52. Print.

9 Maps, History and Cooking

Laura Esquivel's Mexico

David Punter

I gave a paper at a conference in Stirling in 2007 called 'Cyborgs, Borders and Stories for Virgins', which focused on, among others, the two Mexican writers Octavio Paz and Carlos Fuentes (Punter 'Cyborgs'). I also made some brief remarks on the novels of another Mexican writer, Laura Esquivel, and in particular on two of her books: *Like Water for Chocolate*, which was published in 1989 and subsequently made into an enormously successful film, becoming one of the largest-grossing foreign movies ever released in the United States, and *Malinche*, which appeared in 2006. In this chapter I want to develop some further thoughts about these two novels, but I want to preface these thoughts with some remarks about the Gothic and magical realism.

For some time now, it seems to me, these two terms have been in a curious kind of critical tension, and this tension has been heightened by the advent of the term 'global Gothic', probably best known via the book of that title, a collection of essays edited by Glennis Byron and first published in 2013 (1–9). The claim that Gothic has a global reach is based on a number of arguments, but they can be conveniently split into two categories. One is the spread into a wider world of motifs regarded as quintessentially 'Gothic' in a traditional sense—the vampire, the monster, the werewolf and so forth—and this is sometimes seen as evidence of the outward surge of a fictional tropology from British and, a little later, American sources. Of course there is a hole in the heart of this argument, as arguably none of these figures is actually of British provenance. The legendry of the vampire could be seen as belonging more properly to Central Europe, the origins of many figurations of the monster can be found in the Jewish mythology of the golem, the werewolf evolved, we may think, in forests far different from the comparatively tame landscapes of Britain.

The second argument about global Gothic itself involves a kind of confluence, whereby an original body of folklore and legendry—in any country, feasibly—becomes re-energized—or perhaps re-validated might be a better word—through global contact, usually of a commercial kind, with Western exports. Thus it becomes difficult to identify indigeneity: the distinctive features of, for example, the Thai horror film become mixed with recognizable registers of horror from the West, not least, obviously, because of the need to reach valuable Western markets, or, at a higher level, to gain international approbation (Balmain 399–400).

So 'global Gothic' is a contestable term; indeed, it is the site of contestation, around the issue of what might be local culture and what might be invasive foreign forces. And, of course, this rhetoric of invasion is nothing new to critics of the Gothic. From, at least, Count Dracula's surprising arrival in Whitby through to the anxieties about contamination and infection raised in recent zombie novels such as Max Brooks's *World War Z* (2006), invasion has been an issue for Gothic. This can be traced back to the whole constellation of events and tendencies that produced the British Gothic in the first place as a political bulwark against the tyrannous regimes of southern Europe. The barbarians are always at the gates.

To backtrack a little: what has this to do with magic realism? The simplest way of putting this would be to say that we are here considering rival claims to, and ideas about, the supernatural and the question rapidly becomes one about national and local cultures. We may have little doubt about referring to Gabriel García Márquez's mysteries of family, longevity and repetition as 'magic realist', but when it comes to a British novelist, emblematically Angela Carter, then matters become more complicated, and her work has been referred to as magic realist and Gothic in roughly equal measure. It has also, of course, been referred to as virtually everything else, but we will let that pass (Kérchy 55–64).

Let me turn to Esquivel's *Like Water for Chocolate*. This is a remarkable book, the subtitle of which is 'A Novel in Monthly Instalments with Recipes, Romances and Home Remedies'. It tells the story of an apparently doomed love affair; but each of the 12 chapters is introduced with a recipe appropriate to the month concerned. One thing that certainly holds together the story and the recipes is that they are deeply embedded within a family, the site of the entire book, but we can go further than this and suggest that they also constitute a specific address, which is by a woman to other women. The territorialization here is focused on the kitchen, as the site of meetings and non-meetings, surrounded all the time by a specific terror, which is that the woman at the center of the novel, Tita, is the family's youngest daughter, and by tradition this means that she is forbidden from marrying until her mother dies.

She cannot, as it were, 'make a match', but making matches, in another sense, is precisely what John Brown, the English doctor who attempts unsuccessfully to rescue Tita from her plight, spends his time doing in a crucial scene from the novel. In this scene he delivers a brief lecture on the invention—or isolation—of phosphorus. During the course of the lecture, he reminds us that phosphorus, and thus the making of matches, evolved through a curious kind of cooking. The aptly named Hennig Brand, the late seventeenth-century chemist responsible, believed that 'metal could be transmuted into gold by mixing it with extract of urine', a trope easily recognizable as what in another culture might be referred to as the philosopher's stone (104). Today, Brown points out in a curious reminder of the Frankensteinian function of the charnel-house, it is extracted from the bones of animals, but the symbolic function of matches goes far beyond this. My grandmother, says Brown,

> had a very interesting theory; she said that each of us is born with a box of matches inside us but we can't strike them all by ourselves; ... we need oxygen and a candle to help. In this case, the oxygen, for example, would come from the breath of the person you love; the candle could be any kind of food, music, caress, word or sound that engenders the explosion that lights one of the matches. For a moment we are dazzled by an intense emotion. A pleasant warmth grows within us, fading slowly as time goes by, until a new explosion comes along to revive it. Each person has to discover what will set off those explosions in order to live, since the combustion that occurs when one of them is ignited is what nourishes the soul. That fire, in short, is its food. (105)

The need for soul-nurturing, as Jung put it (170); Freud takes a typically more matter-of-fact approach, suggesting that the injunction against 'playing with fire' was a way of curing children from wetting their beds at night—the repetition of urine must *surely* be a coincidence ('Acquisition' 187–93). In *The Interpretation of Dreams* (1900), Freud returns time and time again to the man who dreamed of a burning child. I will not go into that dream in detail here, except to say that there is a clear relation to displaced passion, which returns us to the very title of Esquivel's book, which is a Mexican proverb about a boiling point, whether that be of passion or of misery (509–11).

Fire: cooking: keeping the monster at bay—the signifying chain is perhaps all too obvious. But more terrifying is what, the good doctor claims, may happen if the soul-food cannot be found, if we cannot therefore be kept from perishing, for then something truly phantomatic, truly supernatural may occur:

> If that happens, the soul flees from the body and goes to wander among the deepest shades, trying in vain to find food to nourish itself, unaware that only the body it left behind, cold and defenceless, is capable of providing that food. (104–105)

The soul, the shade, we might say, goes prematurely down to Lethe to wander the grey banks, while the body—the body of desire—falls into a state of unalleviated mourning, all fire gone—as Tita says; at this point she develops a fear that her own matches 'were damp and mouldy. No-one would ever be able to light another one again' (105).

We might wonder, then, whether the role of cooking in *Like Water for Chocolate* is in fact a substitute activity. The apparent conviviality and communal spirit of cooking comes to occupy the vacated space of genuine feeling between, say, mother and daughter; the cheering and nurturing use of fire can occur only in the context of a certain burning out of passion; the role of fire, heat and light in keeping the barbarians at bay only serves to distract us from the barbarity of everyday life under certain circumstances. But more than this, the relation between mother and daughter is itself the poisoned and poisoning heart of the home: at one point, Tita feels an urge 'to shield the tiny flame John has coaxed up inside her from her mother's chilling presence. It was as if Mama Elena's spit had landed dead-centre on a fire that was about to catch and had put it out' (120).

As Paz insists in *The Labyrinth of Solitude* (1950), at the heart of the riddle that is Mexican national identity there is death, the cult of the dead. Here the hand of the dead always comes to snuff out the light, to prevent or contort the revolution, to reinforce a tradition that knows little in the way of true origin, compounded as it is of layer upon layer of usurped and invaded culture (47–64).

It is to this scenario that Esquivel turns in the other novel I want to say something about: *Malinche* is an account of the Spanish invasion and conquest of Mexico, focusing on the figure of Malinalli, the so-called 'Indian' woman who is known to history as Hernán Cortés's translator and lover. Mexico is replete with myths and legends surrounding the events of the birth and, indeed, prolonged agony of the Mexican state. In this particular context, one of the chief ingredients, if one may put it in a cookery metaphor, is the long-held and oft-repeated belief that Malinalli, perhaps because of her own position as a member of the so-called indigenous people, was only too enthusiastic to see the Spaniards defeat the vicious and bloodthirsty Aztec dominators. For this reason she wilfully misinterpreted messages between Cortez and Moctezuma, with, of course, the disastrous consequences of which we all know.

Or rather, of course, of which we know virtually nothing, for no records of such a betrayal survive; nor could they possibly do so. What we do come to know, from the novel, is a great deal about Malinalli's own feelings:

> The eternal fear of abandonment, of loss, of being an unwanted girl, not appreciated or taken into account, presented itself more forcefully than ever before. It had been reborn! It had a new name, a new identity, new gods, but she did not yet know how it was going to punish her.
>
> Yes, she felt that she deserved a punishment, she had always felt it. She had never understood why, but each time that she had been given away, she had felt in the depth of her heart that it was because of a wrong that she had committed, perhaps the simple act of being a woman, or some other thing, but that was how she felt and that was how she experienced it, as an immense punishment. (98)

If we step sideways to Gothic for a moment, then we may figure Gothic as an essential step in the formation of a nation-state, as the assertion of a particular heritage that is to be distinguished from other nation-states. Writings by Edmund Burke, William Blackstone, and many others from the mid-eighteenth century on confirm that this is how 'Gothic' was seen—and, of course, still is, for otherwise why would we have the Palace of Westminster, the Houses of Parliament? In terms of the Gothic tradition, it is interesting that the newer wing of the British Parliament, opened in 2001, chose the name 'Portcullis House'. What better way than to assert the continuity between the present and the Gothic past while reinforcing the notion of governance as something always hidden behind gates, something always conducted in the castle, out of view of the general public? (Punter, 'Trauma' 15–32)

But at the same time, these assertions of national origin—and Benedict Anderson's book *Imagined Communities* (2006) is still to my mind the best account of this—are themselves cover stories, for the absence of true origin, and Gothic is, above all, the history of the failure of accounts of origin, whether that be national or individual. We would need, if we were going to go further into the political science of this, to distinguish clearly between nations and states. That is not simple, but broadly speaking we may say that a state is precisely that institution that *does* have an origin, a constitution, a declaration, usually written, whereas a nation does not and instead amounts to a set of fantasized origins, beginnings that can never be fully validated.

At least, that is how the Gothic account might go; but if we were to turn from history back to the individual subject, we would find an obvious parallel in the idea of the changeling (for this appears to be what Malinalli imagines herself to be). Modern psychological notions of the changeling center upon the child's notion that she or he does not really belong to these ghastly, embarrassing parents with whom he or she has been saddled. He is really a prince—or, to be honest, more usually she is a princess—who has found an unaccountable home in a place far beneath the social station into which she was originally born (Briggs 71). An astonishingly large swathe of writing for small children adopts an unquestioning line on this premise, probably to everybody's detriment. It may (or may not) be interesting to note, especially if you find yourself occasionally dealing with eruptions of adolescent temper, that another word for 'changeling' is, in fact, 'oaf'—the Saxons were always brutal about these things. 'Oaf' itself is in fact related to 'elf'—but time marches on.

Earlier meanings, however—and we are no doubt familiar with them from Shakespeare's *Hamlet* and *Midsummer Night's Dream*—seem to be the reverse of that. The crucial idea is that of—and here I quote the *OED*—a 'stupid or ugly' child having been substituted for one who was so beautiful, bright and so forth and was spirited off by the fairies. Malinalli knows a great deal about this, although quite how her knowledge can be recorded remains a source of some puzzlement, addressed in the book only through the reproduction of inscriptions in the form of the codex. At any rate, Malinalli is 'familiar', if that word can mean anything simple, with a spirit world:

> For her, the spiritual world had an intimate relationship with Nature and the cosmos, with their rhythm, with the movement of the stars through the skies. When the Sun and the Moon had been born in Teotihuacan, they had freed mankind from the darkness. She knew from her ancestors that the light emitted by the stars was not only physical, but spiritual as well, and that their passage through the heavens served to unify the thoughts of men, the cycles of time and space. (99)

Thus we are confronted, in the 'history' of Malinalli, with what we might think of as a 'new' account of history, but one that is simultaneously age-old; what better summary of the Gothic could there be? And yet at the same time, there is always the question of what precedes what. Is the apparently ancient corpus of mythology *really* primary; or is it an after-effect, a construction on the ground of what Esquivel refers to in another of her works, *The Law of Love* (1995), as the ruined pyramid? Derrida talks of this in a rather different context when he is asked to give some history of that other violently colonized land, Algeria, and the questioner asks whether there is any possible narration of this:

> I wish that a narration were possible. For the moment, it is not possible. I dream of managing one day, not to recount this legacy, this past experience, this history, but at least to give a narration of it among other possible narrations. ... To invent, to invent a language, to invent modes of anamnesis ... this inheritance—if it is one—is multiple, not very homogenous, full of all kinds of grafts; and to talk about it seriously, we would need a different apparatus than the one at our disposal. (203)

'I wish that a narration were possible'; perhaps narration is impossible, perhaps the attempt recedes behind veils of presumed history—can the relics of Malinche be exhumed? What would be the purpose of that? A narration 'among other possible narrations'; and so Malinche, alongside the family of *Like Water for Chocolate*, take their place in an uncertain, undecidable world of the past; there is no anchor, as Gothic has always suspected, in history. 'To talk about it seriously'; here, indeed, might be a crux, albeit one among many. How to speak of the past without some concept of the serious, some tinge of veneration, how to remain loose, unconvinced, floating when one speaks—or writes—of the tragedies that have accompanied the birth of most nation states.

This is something, it seems to me, which Esquivel does well, and she does it in part through a deliberate admixture of genres, types of discourse—*The Law of Love* contains, as readers will know, a CD of the music mentioned in the written text. This is a writing of impurity (a writing that is impure, and a writing that speaks of impurity, of the destruction of purity, of assumptions about prior purity); yet it is a writing that is not yet fully cooked, a writing that owes to its own ingredients. Not smooth, as Deleuze and Guattari would have it, but striated (Crawford 57–60): like Gothic, displaying the layers of its own claims to antiquity in the fossilizations visible on the cliff-faces; or on the unfinished stones of the pyramids; or on the ruins, always the ruins, of the castle.

Bibliography

Balmain, Colette. 'Southeast Asian Gothic Cinema', *The Gothic World*. Eds. Townshend, Byron, and Dale Townshend. London: Routledge, 2014. 399–411. Print.

Briggs, Katharine. *An Encyclopaedia of Fairies, Hobgoblins, Brownies, Boogies, and Other Supernatural Creatures*. New York: Random House, 1976. Print.

Byron, Glennis. Introduction. *Globalgothic*. Ed. Byron, Glennis. Manchester: Manchester UP, 2013. 1–9. Print.

Crawford, T. Hugh. 'The *Paterson* Plateau: Deleuze, Guattari and William Carlos Williams'. *Deleuze and Literature*. Ed. Buchanan, Ian, and John Marks. Edinburgh: Edinburgh University Press, 2000. 57–79. Print.

Derrida, Jacques. *Points ... Interviews, 1974–1994*. Ed. Weber, Elisabeth. Stanford: Stanford University Press, 1995. Print.

Esquivel, Laura. *Like Water for Chocolate: A Novel in Monthly Instalments with Recipes, Romances and Home Remedies*. Trans. Christensen, Carol, and Thomas Christensen. New York: Black Swan, 1993. Print.

———. *The Law of Love: A Novel with Music*. Trans. Peden, Margaret Sayers. New York: Black Swan, 1996. Print.

———. *Malinche*. Trans. Mestre-Reed, Ernesto. New York: Black Swan, 2006. Print.

Freud, Sigmund. 'The Acquisition and Control of Fire'. *The Standard Edition of the Complete Psychological Works of Sigmund Freud*. Ed. Strachey, James, et al. Volume XXII. London: Hogarth Press, 1953–74. Print.

———. 'The Interpretation of Dreams'. *Standard Edition of the Complete Psychological Works of Sigmund Freud*. Ed. Strachey, James, et al. Volume V. London: Hogarth Press, 1953–74. Print.

Jung, Carl. *Psychological Reflections: A New Anthology of his Writings 1905–1961*. Ed. Jacobi, Jolande. Princeton: Princeton University Press, 1971. Print.

Kérchy, Anna. *Body-Texts in the Novels of Angela Carter: Writing from a Corporeagraphic Perspective* Lampeter: Edwin Mellen, 2008. Print.

Paz, Octavio. *The Labyrinth of Solitude and Other Writings*. New York: Grove, 1985. Print.

Punter, David. 'Cyborgs, Borders and Stories for Virgins: Mexico and the Gothic', www.gothic.stirling.ac.uk. Winter, 2007. Accessed October 16, 2015. Online.

———. 'Trauma, Gothic, Revolution', *The Gothic and the Everyday: Living Gothic*. Ed. Piatti-Farnell, Lorna, and Maria Beville. Basingstoke: Palgrave, 2014. 15–32. Print.

10 'I Want to Escape These Walls, but I Can't Exist Outside Them'

Spaces and Characters in Carlos Fuentes's Gothic Fiction

Antonio Alcalá

The main motivation for the production of Carlos Fuentes's fiction is his concern for Mexican national identity. He insists that most of the citizens of Mexico lack an understanding of the interaction between past and present; this the principal reason the country has strived for, but not achieved, success in establishing an appropriate literary canon. In order to express his anxiety, Fuentes's fiction invokes Gothic motifs to assert the need to understand the past in order to comprehend the nation's present and ensure a solid vision for the future. This past is seen in the geographical location of the country's capital, Mexico City, which lies on the ruins of the ancient Aztec capital, Tenochtitlan. In addition, the 300 years of Spanish rule—the colonial period—are highly visible in many areas of the modern design of the city. As a result, his Gothic narratives do not erase these histories but rather suggest that ignoring this past will lead to the failure of the development of the centralized country that has arisen around the capital. In this chapter, I explore how Fuentes makes use of spaces located near the city's downtown neighborhood in order to tease out the implications of the uncanny Gothic events that his protagonists experience. These characters are unaware of the need to understand and communicate with the past that exists around them. Their shortsightedness leads to their downfall when they are confronted with uncanny ghostly presences and memories from their families or the city. In these scenarios, the *others* arrive to show them that they are the anomalous beings who have failed to establish a connection with the past. As a result, their lives are revealed as incomplete, and they are unable to fulfill their hopes and dreams.

Given the fact that *Aura* (1962) is his most widely read Gothic text in English, and the novella *Vlad* (2004) has recently been translated (2012), I focus on Gothic works by Fuentes that are not so familiar within an Anglophone context. The short story, 'Tlactocatzine, from the Garden of Flanders' has yet to be translated into English.[1] It appeared in Fuentes's first published book, a short story collection published in 1954 titled *Los Días Enmascarados* (*The Masked Days*). 'The Doll Queen' appeared in 1964 in his second volume of short fiction, *Cantar de Ciegos* (*Song of the Blind*). It was later translated as part of the collection *Burnt Water: Stories* (1980).

Both texts were later reprinted in Spanish as part of the 2007 anthology *Cuentos Sobrenaturales* (*Supernatural Stories*). I will also examine 'The Good Company', which appeared in 2004 in his published compilation of tales, *Inquieta Compañía* (*Restless Company*). These three texts include spectral presences that disrupt closed spaces located in the heart of Mexico City. In all three cases, the protagonists of the stories collapse after being overwhelmed by the haunting presence that returns from the past. In what follows, I explore how Fuentes adapts the Gothic motifs of the enclosed space of the ruin and haunting visitations in order to set the frame for an encounter with ghostly *others* (some of them described as monsters) that lead to the protagonists' breakdowns.

Gothic in Latin American literary studies has received little critical attention. Julio Cortázar was one of the first writers to propose the genre as a branch of the fantastic, offering writers the space to question certainties about power and realistic views of the world (79–83). Fuentes's fiction exemplifies the adaptation of the Gothic mode in the Mexican context. As a replacement for old European castles and ruined structures, he turns to the large old houses in the city center. These structures have their own secrets, which lie confined in dark and private inner gardens, dark attics and clandestine basements. In 'Tlactocatzine, from the Garden of Flanders', the narrator's boss sends him to inhabit and improve a house that his company has purchased. The place is situated close to the city center, on Puente de Alvarado Avenue. Although guarded from decay by a couple of old servants, this old house has been empty since 1910, when the family moved to France to escape the upheavals of revolution. In 'The Doll Queen', the house, with its large grilled windows and gates with peeling paint, is surrounded by the sounds made by a knife-grinder, a shoemaker and an organ grinder. These details reflect a neighborhood in the central area of the city. Finally, the house in 'The Good Company' is located in another neighborhood around the city center, San Rafael, which is very close to where the house in 'Tlactocatzine' can be found.[2]

All three spaces are situated in the heart of the city, the place where buildings and histories of the nation come together in the present. This part of the cityscape has been described as 'a magical space where the Aztec past coexists harmoniously with a postmodern present, where Western culture lives side by side with traditions from indigenous origin, and the pre-Columbian culture thrives among the chaos of the modern city' (Gallo 7). Nevertheless, this past, though evident, lies almost forgotten and left to rot beneath the modern glass and steel buildings. Fuentes asserts that the once Aztec city of Tenochtitlan lies on a rocky and quaking subsoil upon which all of its history and identities (pre-Columbian, baroque, neoclassical, nineteenth century and modern) have been constructed over many centuries (*En Esto Creo* 287). The combination of rock and mud upon which the capital was built reflects the neglected presence wherein the Mexican past is present, but which is marginalized to the corners of the Mexican consciousness. The denial to recognize the importance of this long history has transformed the place into a monster of concrete and asphalt. Here, the present is the only thing that matters: the past and the future are irrelevant. This place is a monster because its inhabitants and the events taking place inside it are monstrous: 'we ourselves are the Monster—each of us, all 23,000,000 of us, are its cells' (Ross 453).

This monstrous city fits into the characteristics that Robert Mighall considers part of a Gothic city. For him, this kind of space includes a haunting past that it cannot entirely escape: 'For Gothic *of* a city rather than just in a city, that city needs a concentration of memories and historical associations. Ideally these would be expressed in an extant architectural or topographical heritage, as these areas provide the natural home for ghostly presences of imagined/projected meanings' (57). Although not as old as the capitals of Europe studied by Mighall, Mexico City gathers together the architectural memories of a Mesoamerican and colonial past, as well as an independent country that was reborn, first after the War of Independence and then after the Mexican Revolution. When these periods are forgotten, the place becomes a Gothic city, for it includes spaces that have been rejected and ignored by the body politic, the inhabitants (54, 61). Fuentes's protagonists are trapped inside architectural realms within this city, and they are haunted by unavoidable presences of a past they have chosen to deny. According to Fuentes, the city and its inhabitants should confront and acknowledge all of these histories. In *A New Time for Mexico*, he writes,

> A country of simultaneous times, where past is present and all of history happens or can happen, at the very moment ... skyscrapers next to shanties, supermarkets near garbage dumps. Mercedes-Benzes run races with burros and the TV antenna is the new cross of faith. The god of fire is a little boy spitting flames in exchange for a few centavos. But couples love each other next to the walls of ancient convents; the veterans of the Revolution survive surrounded by memories ... The greatness of Mexico is that its past is always alive, and not as a burden ... Memory saves it, filters, chooses, but it does not kill. Memory and desire both know there is no living present with a dead past and no future without both: a living present that transformed into a living past ... We know that nothing has an absolute beginning or an absolute end. (216)

Here, the past is not a closed, passive field; it is active and multi-dimensional, and it is open to interpretation and reinterpretation through the imaginative spaces provided by creative writing. For Fuentes, fiction allows him to explore the past and its connections with the present (Juan-Navarro 47). He thus depicts buildings from other centuries as the portals where the communication between different times can take place. In this, he questions why literature itself has to be constructed as a succession of elements rather than as a gathering together of events (*En Esto Creo* 279). In fact, he sees humanity (and everything around it) as containing traces of what was in the past and what will be in the future. This happens because we live in our time, but there are ghosts from previous times and omens of things to come (197). When relating this to the characteristics of the city's inhabitants, he mentions that, though being a mixed-race of Spanish speaking people, Mexicans are people of pre-Columbian roots and they have postponed or expelled a reencounter with the past (278). This has led to a society wherein projects often fail to crystalize: 'The paradox of time in Mexico is that when its promises are kept they self-destruct and when they remain they go on living forever' (Fuentes, *A New Time in Mexico* 17). As a result, the country's national project remains out of reach, always lying somewhere in the future.

To express this view, Fuentes explores how the interaction of place, time and character transforms the lives of individuals. His protagonists follow a constant pattern that traps them 'within the confines of an architectural construct, desiring or needing to escape' (Williams 145). Within these spaces, the characters witness the Gothic return of repressed memories. This process brings doubt and uncertainty about the coherence of the self: 'Gothic atmospheres—gloomy and mysterious—have repeatedly signaled the disturbing return of pasts upon presents and evoked emotions of terror and laughter' (Botting, *Gothic* 1). In this regard, Fred Botting defines the Gothic as feeding off the turmoil arising from present unrest and the terrors of the past (Botting, 'Darkly' 3). He also cites the flux between the past and the present as the sources of uncertainty in Gothic texts. He writes,

> Gothic remains ambivalent and heterotopic, reflecting the doubleness of the relationship between past and present ... The play of distance and proximity, rejection and return, telescopes history, both condensing the past into an object of idealized or negative speculation and unravelling and disarming the gaze of the present with its ambivalent return. (12)

This speaks to the Gothic transgressions of time in Fuentes's fiction, transgressions that engender conflicts between different periods and generations. This destabilizes identity through the tension between continual change and a continuity with the past.

Another Gothic motif in Fuentes's work is the overwhelming recognition of the necessity of the *other*, the transgressor, who leads the observer to a clearer understanding of self. Fuentes insists on the depiction of the *other* as the way to point toward existence as an interaction of dual forces: 'In Fuentes the Gothic is reinscribed as the genre of alterity, figuring—as it does—the *other* desire, the *other* history, the *other* self or selves that haunt the ego' (Gutierrez Mouat 312). Indeed, from the start of his literary career, he understood that in the second half of the twentieth-century subjectivity had become individualized; the best way to respond to this is to use fiction to express a sense of shared experience. Fuentes states,

> In the modern era, traditional communal structures loosen their hold on the individual, a process experienced as both liberating and threatening. The modern individual revels in a sense of expanded opportunity, yet at the same time anguishes over the disappearance of shared meanings. This sense of alienation produces the critical and self- repudiating side of modernity, reflected in, among other things, the tendency of modern artists to project alternate scenarios of communal integration.
>
> (Van Delden 11)

In Fuentes's three stories, the individual without a community becomes an eccentric character who lacks a stable sense of identity. Within this experience, the presence of trespassing intruders provokes the uncanny return of a devastating and forgotten past. This expels the individual from all possible social connections. Fuentes thus depicts his intruders as figures from the past: they are ghosts or other monstrous creatures. The former reminds those whom they haunt of the burden of a past that can be temporarily repressed and forgotten but can never be completely eliminated: 'Ghosts are historical beings because they are messengers about the preoccupations of a particular age … Ghosts are never just ghosts; they provide us with an insight into what haunts our culture. Ghosts, of course, cannot die and such are a persistent reminder of what a culture can only express in oblique terms' (Smith 147). Fuentes's ghosts portray the unavoidable, yet also unacceptable, memories of something that once existed. Concerning the monsters, their bodies and actions warn the other characters of what happens when they lose touch with humanity: 'Monstrosity implies category jamming, that produces morphological incoherence and consequent transgression' (Asma 184). Fuentes's monsters are trespassers that exist between categories that should remain separate, and they are feared because they embody threats to the order and continuity of 'civilization'. Their mobility inside and beyond boundaries confirms that the limits set by humanity are arbitrary barriers imposed so the characters do not to recognize the monstrosity of those who observe them. These figures are the anomalous *others* that define humanity as the norm, and characters must repress those impulses that would turn them into monsters.

In Fuentes's fiction, the ghosts and monsters are manifestations of the uncanny, the repressed features of the self. The uncanny takes its meaning from Freud's definition as the return of something 'secretly familiar, which has undergone repression and then returned from it' (245). Since its transgression is based on irrupting from outside the limits of the familiar, it also has the quality of rendering all boundaries uncertain (Botting, *Gothic* 11). This happens because it brings back elements that were once subjugated to the margins to uphold the continuity of so-called civilization. As a result, the uncanny event and the uncanny being break down any certainty about what was repressed but is no longer kept there: 'if we have a sense of the uncanny, it is because the barriers between the known and the unknown are teetering on the brink of collapse. We are afraid certainly; but what we are afraid of is at least partly our own sense that we have *been here before*' (Punter, 'The Uncanny' 130). Gothic secrets are revealed in Fuentes's stories and the uncanny erupt in the return of repressed memories that are triggered by experiences inside old houses where monsters and ghosts reveal the forgotten past in their present lives.

The narrators and protagonists of 'Tlactocatzine' and 'The Good Company' are forced into enclosed spaces where they experience ghosts from the past; the result is that they gain a clearer understanding of their identities. 'Tlactocatzine' is structured around entries in the protagonist's diary. Here, we glimpse his ethnic identity when his boss calls him '*güero*' (a person of light hair in Mexico), indicating that he may look more European than Mexican (40). The house he is sent to inhabit dates from the times of the military French occupation, which is referred to as the Second Mexican Empire and was under the rule of Maximilian I (the former Archduke of Austria) and his wife, Charlotte of Belgium. The latter suffered a mental collapse after the defeat of the Empire and the resulting execution of her husband. Although old, the house is described as a place that is very much alive:

> The mansion is really beautiful no matter how much the façade tries to deny it with its excess of Ionic capitals and caryatids from the Second Empire. The hall, facing the street, has a fragrant and shining floor. The walls are scarcely stained by the spectral rectangles left where once paintings hung. They are of a warm blue, bearing some connection to the ancient but detached from the strictly old. (Fuentes, *Cuentos Sobrenaturales* 40)

There is no telephone in the house, indicating its isolation from the rest of the modern city. Within its walls, the past is not depicted as decay or abandonment; it is full of life and vitality. After his first day in the house, the protagonist feels a 'flux that corresponds to other coasts that have induced me into a lucid rest' (41).

On his second day, he discovers how to open the window that leads to the garden. This space is a portal that displaces him from the physical location of Mexico City. He states,

> It was a fictional, invented space. The garden was not in Mexico! … and the showers … I ran inside the house, went through the hall and stuck my nose to the window: on the Puente de Alvarado Avenue, the jukeboxes roared. The trams and the sun were there. It was a monotonous sun, Sun-God without shades or effigies in its rays. Unchanging

> Sun Stone[3], sun of the short centuries. I went back to the library: the shower inside the garden remained, old, cloudy. (43)

His identity, which has been shaped by the modern city, falls away when he enters this place. Its center, the garden, is described as a place of 'memory silhouettes' where repressed remembrance is reanimated (41–42). Here, he meets an old woman who slowly reveals herself to him. During his second day, the old woman is only perceived as a face that stares at him. When she turns her back, she is only visible as a small black and bowed lump. On the third day, he sees her more clearly. According to him,

> She was an elderly lady ... may be 80 at least ... scrawny, dressed in black. Her long skirt reached the ground ... A black lace bonnet shaded the face, hiding the old woman's white and messy hair. I could only distinguish her bloodless lips. They went into the slightest, saddest and most permanent smile which lacked any motivation at all. She raised her sight, but there were no eyes inside her eyes ... it was as if a road, a night landscape, went inside every second towards an infinite journey. (45)

This deathly presence enters the garden and leaves it through a pathway; the narrator accepts this as a very natural feature inside the house (45–46). On the following two days he starts receiving letters from her. He listens to her slow steps 'over dry leaves' outside his door whenever she leaves the letter just before midnight. The relationship between the woman and the garden continues throughout the text; the garden is the portal that enables her to interact with the protagonist.

On his fifth day in the house (and the last entries in the diary), he realizes it is impossible to open the door to the house. He also realizes that the garden and its flowers smell like a tomb. At this point, the reader becomes aware that the lady and the death that surrounds her presence are meant to reveal something to the narrator. She stops being a monster that seems to bring death into the world and becomes a ghost from the narrator's past—someone he has forgotten. She mourns having lost him not in the past, but in the present, where he has transgressed the limits between the living and the dead. She appears to guide him back to his normal state; her ghost is his eternal companion. As they come closer, the communication in letters turns into conversations wherein she tells him they will remain there forever, inside a 'Satisfaction of shared solitudes' (49). She calls him Max, and her final revelations are condensed when she also calls him 'Tlactocatzine' (the royal name given by the indigenous people from Mexico to Emperor Maximilian I). The final piece of the puzzle is his discovery of her royal seal: 'CHARLOTTE, KAISERIN VON MEXIKO' (49). The concluding lines of the narrative confirm to the protagonist that he is no longer what he was before he entered the house. This place works in his experience as the frame that allows the ghost to arrive and remind him of what he had forgotten in relation to the modernity that exists outside the house. He is the European nobleman who had come to Mexico in order to rule as an emperor and was later mourned by his widow. His final encounter with his uncanny self makes it clear that any attempt to leave previous experiences behind will be unsuccessful; his past is what defines him in the present, just as the city is the result of historical events that must be remembered.

In 'The Doll Queen', the narrator and main character, Carlos, encounters the deformed Amilamia in the present in order to understand that his memories about her are worthless unless he can recognize the fluid relationship between past and present. Carlos has not seen Amilamia for 15 years. Time has transformed his idea of her; she is relegated to past memories, without any referents to the present time in which she lives: 'Amilamia has come back to my memories and I may not have felt happy, but at least healthy again. The park, the living girl, my hours of youth reading have defeated the specters … I tell to myself that I will live forever with my true Amilamia, the one that has defeated the cartoon of death' (Fuentes, *Cuentos Sobrenaturales* 105). However, this image remains only in his mind; it is absent in the decay that defines the present.

This is represented by the girl's parents, who have lived in the same house for 15 years. The woman has the appearance of an elderly person: 'wrapped in a shawl, dressed in black and with low heel shoes, without make-up, with her silver hair stretched to the back of the neck. She seems to have abandoned all hope or excuse for youth as she observes me with almost cruel and indifferent eyes' (92). The husband is an even more decayed and disheartened being. According to the narrator,

> his eyes are hidden behind wrinkled, swollen, thick and hanging eyelids. They look like the neck of an old turtle although they don't fail to follow my movements. His sunken and irregularly shaven cheeks are slit by multiple grey wrinkles, and his greenish hands lie hidden inside his armpits … He doesn't move, and the only real sign of his existence is that difficult panting. (98)

The two decayed parents inhabit an equally dilapidated house. Like them, the place seems to have been affected by the passing of time. Bodies and places thus show an extreme lack of interest in present life. The narrator continues,

> She opens a door of dull glass and we enter a barely furnished dining room. However, the table of tubular legs with its four chairs of nickel and foam even lack the suspicion of style of the furniture in the living room … on the table there is only a plastic fruit bowl with a bunch of black grapes, two peaches and a crown of buzzing flies. (95)

The house is a place of abandonment and approaching death, but it also includes the present life of Amilamia. When Carlos meets Amilamia, his idealization of her life collapses. He is forced to accept that she is not the same; she is older, and her body has changed with the passing of years: 'On the wheel chair, that hunchbacked girl holds a hand over the door knob and smiles with an invisible gesture. The hump from her breast turns her dress into a curtain for her whole body' (106).

The dress is described as a white cloth that is given a flirty touch by means of the blue-checked apron. She still inhabits the same house from whose flat roof her blue apron is still visible while getting dry. However, his memories of her are as dusty as the books among which he finds her card, which asks him to meet her on the park bench where they first met. Without a solid link to the present, his memories are only illusions of what she had once been. He states,

> Amilamia is also my memory ... Now I see her coming down the hill. No, it isn't true; it's a mere elevation of fodder. It was a hill of grass and she had marked a pathway by means of her comings and goings, and she said hello to me from the top before descending. The music was with her. Yes, it was the music of my eyes, the paintings of my smell, the tastes of my hearing, the smells of my touch ... my hallucination ... (101)

He is the true monster. He has transgressed the continuity of time because of his demand to stick to the past. Just as the ideas he has of her are but mere ghost images of what she once was, her parents fail to hold onto the memories of what she once was. They try to do this in the form of a doll that resembles her at the age of seven. This object challenges the advance of time; it is the vital piece from her childhood that is kept in a dark room at the top of the house. This place is lighted with candles; it looks like an altar to the young girl, a shrine to her past life. The narrator describes the following,

> inside the silver coffin, between the sheets of black velvet and next to the white pillow, there lies that motionless and sober face framed by a lace bonnet. It is colored with soft pink. Its eyelids are closed and the real eye lashes project a soft shadow over the cheeks which looks as healthy as in the days in the park ... a rosary, identical to the mothers', strangles that neck of plastic. It is a white and small shroud of the immature, clean and well-behaved body. Sobbing, the old couple has fallen on their knees. I stretch my hand and graze with my fingers the porcelain face of my friend. I feel the cold of those drawn gestures of the doll-queen that dominates over the pomp or this royal chamber of death. Porcelain, plastic and cotton ... I remove my fingers from the false corpse. My fingerprints remain on the dolls skin. And the feeling

> of nausea comes to my stomach which turned into the deposit of the smoke from the altar candles and the stench from the asarum in the confined room. (103–104)

Keeping the past alive is the reason for this elderly couple and their house to have fallen into decrepitude and decay. While the fictional Maximilian and Charlotte can exist together inside the walls of the mansion, the narrator of 'The Doll Queen' fails, like the girl's parents, to recognize that the lovely girl of the past has become a deformed woman in the present. Neither the narrator nor the old couple can accept that their memories (and the doll) are relegated to the past and unconnected to the present. They all lack a fluid dialogue with the events that have occurred since she was a child. As a result, the memories and the physical object are locked up in their minds, and they must face the passing of time.

Finally, 'The Good Company' presents a combination of the two types of Gothic irruptions found in the other two texts. First, there is the monstrous old woman who is first perceived as an omen of death, but she turns into the ghost from the past and makes the character in 'Tlactocatzine' recognize his true self. Second, the monstrous girl, the deformed Amilamia, is a living reminder in the present that the past cannot exist forever. The past is simply part of the continuous advance of time; it accumulates all of the experiences that have led to the present. In 'The Good Company', the word 'Company' refers to monstrous ladies who are revealed to be ghosts who return from the past. Their role is to reveal Alejandro, the protagonist, his own existence as a ghost. He reluctantly becomes aware of his death; he also learns that he has been sent by his mother to be company to the two women. In this story, Fuentes uses a third-person narrator to describe the condition of Mexico City as an amalgam of cultures that renders chaos, for the inhabitants of this place have failed to establish links to the past. According to the narrator,

> Being used to the perfect symmetry of the Parisian line, the urban chaos of Mexico City first confused him, then became disgusting but finally turned into something fascinating. For him, the city seemed to have no direction, driven by its own speed, without brakes, and in competition with the infinite itself. It filled all empty spaces with whatever seemed possible. There were many things together: enclosing walls, shanties, skyscrapers, roofs made of metal sheets, walls made of cardboard, lavish garbage dumps, skinny alleys, and an endless line of billboards. The marks of beauty: a baroque church here, a stone pre-Columbian palace there, a half visible garden. All of them gave account of the city's depth as opposed to its physical extension. This also was—as Alejandro de la Guardia knew thanks to his beautiful, unforgettable mother—a large city of overlapping layers; Aztec city, colonial city, neoclassical, modern. (Fuentes, *Restless Company* 50–51)

This is the same city that is often described by Fuentes in his fiction and essays. It is the place where the past is always present but forever ignored. Upon his arrival, and after seeing the excessive combination of histories that comprise the city, the protagonist is thankful that his aunts' house is 'ancient. Indefinitely ancient. Two floors and a beautiful façade of grey stone. 'It was neglected, but beautifully neglected' said Alex to himself' (51). When he arrives at the door of the house, he is confronted by a double monster. Each aunt looks at him from a different window on either side of the front door. When he meets them, they appear to be opposites. Zenaida appears in the daylight surrounded by white and flowery colors. When Alejandro explores the house and finds the only dishes the sisters eat off, he discovers that her dish is full of insects. By contrast, Zenaida's sister, Serena, is only seen at night, and she is dressed in black with a red wig that lies in sharp contrast to her sister's white hair. The dish at her door is full of blood soup. Their colors, their different hours and their food (dead animals or the red fluid drained from them) make the two sisters appear as the two distinct parts of a fragmented being. These old women are unique and eccentric. They live in seclusion and in a house where, as Alejandro puts it, 'normality was exiled' (64).

The spectral ladies and their house are feared by the only house servant, a mute indigenous woman who displays an 'impenetrable face of alarm and warning' when she first meets Alejandro (54). The sisters instruct their nephew to leave and enter through the back door so people will believe the house to be deserted. This remains a mystery to the protagonist; he sees around him a city that lacks cohesion and shows no interest in him at all. The narrator states,

> He noted a great abandonment. There were no old houses like his aunts'. What called attention were the buildings that could be thought as 'modern' and showed windows without glasses or with broken ones and cracked walls. Their doors were almost blocked by black trash bags. They were doors that invited to enter large yards flanked by two floors of rooms. He entered one of those places. The women leaning on iron banisters looked at him with indifference. Or maybe they did not even see him. Once he was outside again, he could distinguish the city hustle and bustle. It was made by the going and coming of pedestrians and cars, as well as the noises and movement coming from cheap stores of all kinds. The people were so busy and nobody looked at him. He tried to say hello. 'Good morning.' Nobody answered. There were only elusive sights. He came back to the house through the indicated way, the back door. (54–55)

The main character is alone; the old house is the only one of its kind. Where can he turn? On one hand, the city is completely alien to him; on the other, his aunts leave a poisoned chocolate on his pillow. Neither the abnormal house nor the places outside it welcome him. On only two occasions does he find comfort: when he plays soccer with the kids in the park behind and when he goes to the building where his existence changes forever. The narrator describes the latter:

> Suddenly, a miraculous building appeared in front of Alex, It was a colonial building with a great baroque façade of stone of sober elegance. It belonged to a surprising century that does not hand at once all the beauty it possessed. It requires attention and care to be wholly appreciated. There was something in the construction that granted security and beauty. Alex read the plaque at the entrance. This had been the place of the School of Philosophy and Literature of the University of Mexico until 1955. The place, as mentioned in the plaque, was known as 'Mascarones'. Alex climbed the three or four steps at the entrance and stopped in amazement before a big and harmonious yard surrounded by two floors connected by a stone stair. From the center of the yard, he could hear how voices started to fill the place. They were of different tones. They laughed, discussed, whispered, always increasing in number, but always clear, so clear that he could identify his own voice. There was no doubt. It was laughing vividly, but it was invisible. It was terrible because it was invisible and also because although he knew it was his voice. He also knew it was not his. It attracted him to a mystery that was not his. It terribly threatened him ... Ha ran away from the yard, the building. He ran to the street without seeing the tram that ran over him. It killed him in seconds. He opened his eyes. There were no trams on the Ribera de San Cosme Avenue. Alejandro was standing there, stunned, in the middle of the street. He looked down. There was the undeniable mark left by the rails of the old tram. They had disappeared, but not even the passing of thousands of cars had been able to erase their mark. (65)

He has repressed this experience. Although he thinks he is a young man of 27, he was killed at the age of eleven in this accident. This fatal event occurred as he was coming out of the last building he ever found attractive. He remains a child who will eternally play with the kids from the park.

His aunts know this. He listens to them when they mention the event, but he cannot understand it immediately; in fact, it takes three nights in the house before he can process what has happened in the past. On each day of his stay, he finds clues inside the room that jog his memory. This place is located at the back of the house and mirrors the repressed memories in the back of his mind. On the first night, the clue is an old calendar from 15 years ago. On the second night, he finds coloring books for children; they are found under the lid of the school desk in his room. They are printed 15 years ago. But what makes him lose his reason is when he discovers blank pages with his name on them: 'Adventures of a French boy in Mexico by

Alejandro de la Guardia' (6). On the last night, he completes the transition. His room is filled with toys. When bathing, he witnesses the disappearance of his body hair. The aunts reveal that their sister, Alejandro's mother, sent them a dead child as company for the dead women. All the mysteries in the now menacing house are revealed. He understands why Zenaida told him the people outside the house are the ones who are shut in. This is because they do not belong to the ghostly existence of the inhabitants of the old house. He understands why he was told not to leave the house through the front door so people will not acknowledge his existence.

He is then taken to the basement, the dark place of secrets in old Mexican houses where attics are absent. Upon his arrival in the city, Alejandro points out that, unlike European houses, the homes in Mexico have flat roofs. In the dim underground, he is led to a coffin cushioned with silk:

> 'It's OK' whispered Alejandro. 'Stop pulling my legs. Let's go upstairs. Don't worry at all. I'm leaving this place tomorrow. 'Tomorrow?' kindly smiled Zenaida. 'Why? Aren't we good company?' 'Tomorrow?' echoed Serena, as she pointed at a second coffin. 'Always, Alejandro. Not tomorrow. Always our little angel needs company ... Come on, Alex. Take your place in the small bed next to the other one ... Go inside, Alex. Lean back, holy child. Sleep, sleep forever. Make company to our little child.' (71)

Alejandro's role as another specter inside the ghostly mansion is confirmed. He is not noticed by the people in the street, and he now understands why he is uncomfortable there. He is the ghost of a child who died some years ago. The ghosts of the sisters take care of the scatterbrained child who did not pay attention when he was crossing the street. He is the anomalous monster, the transgressor who wants to live while he is dead. He wrongly thinks he can live a life like those he reads about in novels.

Fuentes's fiction warns against perceiving time as one-dimensional. Just as Alejandro fails to understand this, Carlos cannot acknowledge that Amilamia is no longer the idealized child of her youth. This was the physical context where he spent his best days as a young reader of fiction. He mistakenly connects his memory of her with the novels he reads in the park, but while those books, though dusty, contain the same stories years after, the girl cannot remain the same. Fuentes uses both protagonists as examples of how the imagination can be influenced by reading literary texts: 'Literature is made of communication, finding out what relates all things. It complements our absences, our needs. It is founded on the world, but it adds something new to the world' (Fuentes cited in Williams 154). For Fuentes, fiction is the best way to share the fact that the present cannot be understood as a static concept; it is a dynamic reality constantly in flux.

In these three texts, the arrival of the *other* in the form of a monster or a ghost provides the protagonists with a mirror that forces them to face the uncanny arrival of a devastating secret, a shadow that they had repressed but that returns to haunt them. Maximilian and Alejandro need to enter the old houses in order to understand their present conditions; they have repressed their memories to fit into the society that exists outside the haunted houses. As for Amilamia, she remains secluded in the decaying house so the memories of the girl will remain as Carlos and her parents want to imagine them. All of the main characters make the mistake made by others in Mexico City. They are trapped within the monstrous city, going through confined journeys inside of their stable senses of identity. In the end, they experience the uncanny return of memories that reveal the undeniable need for a dialogue with the past in order to understand the present and plan for the future. The failure to recognize this turns the inhabitants into monsters who are unwilling to accept the fluidity of time.

Notes

1. All titles and quotations of Fuentes' works present in this article are taken from the originals in Spanish; I have translated the titles and quotes into English.
2. When the main character in 'The Good Company', Alejandro de la Guardia, leaves the house (where the main action takes place), he is close to the Rivera de San Cosme Avenue. This street changes its name after it goes beyond San Rafael. It then becomes Puente de Alvarado Avenue, the same street where the house in 'Tlactocatzine' is located.
3. This is a clear reference to the Aztec calendar stone or Sun Stone, a pre-Columbian sculpture. Its meaning is still debated by archeologists, but the symbols inside it are related to the importance of time and the sun in Aztec culture and society.

Bibliography

Asma, Stephen T. *On Monsters: An Unnatural History of our Worst Fears*. New York: Oxford University Press, 2009. Print.

Botting, Fred. *Gothic*. London: Routledge, 1999. Print.

———. 'In Gothic Darkly: Heterotopia, History, Culture.' *A Companion to the Gothic*. Ed. Punter, David. Oxford: UK: Blackwell Publishers, 2001. 3–14. Print.

Cortazar, Julio. 'Notas sobre lo Gótico en el Río de la Plata.' *Julio Cortazar: Obra Crítica*. Vol.3 Ed. Sosnowski, Sali. Madrid: Alfaguara, 1994. 79–87. Print.

Freud, Sigmund. 'The Uncanny.' *The Complete Psychological Works of Sigmund Freud Vol XVII*, Gen. Ed. of Trans. Strachey, James. London: Vintage, 2001. 217–52. Print.

Fuentes, Carlos. *A New Time for Mexico*. Trans. Gutman Castañeda, Marina, and Carlos Fuentes. Los Angeles: University of California Press, 1997. Print.

———. *En Esto Creo*. Mexico City: Alfaguara, 2002. Print.

———. *Cuentos Sobrenaturales*. Mexico City: Alfaguara, 2007. Print.

———. *Inquieta Compañía*. Mexico City: Alfaguara, 2014. Print.

Gallo, Rubén. 'Introduction.' *The Mexico City Reader*. Trans. Scott Fox, Lorna, Rubén Gallo, Ed. Gallo, Rubén. Madison, WI: The University of Wisconsin Press, 2004. 3–29. Print.

Gutierrez Mouat, Ricardo. 'Gothic Fuentes.' *Revista Hispánica Moderna*, Year 57 (Number 1/2), 2004: 297–313. Print.

Juan-Navarro. Santiago. *Postmodernismo y Metaficción Historiográfica: Una Perspectiva Interamericana.* Valencia: Universidad de Valencia, 2002. Print.

Mighall, Robert. 'Gothic Cities.' *The Routledge Companion to Gothic.* Ed. Spooner, Catherine, and Emma McEvoy. New York: Routledge, 2007. 54–62. Print.

Punter, David. 'The Uncanny.' *The Routledge Companion to Gothic.* Ed. Catherine Spooner and Emma McEvoy. New York: Routledge, 2007. 129–136. Print.

Ross, John. *El Monstruo: Dread and Redemption in Mexico City.* New York: Nation Books, 2009 Print.

Smith, Andrew. 'Hauntings.' *The Routledge Companion to Gothic.* Ed. Spooner, Catherine, and Emma McEvoy. New York: Routledge, 2007. 147–54. Print.

Van Delden, Martin. *Carlos Fuentes, Mexico, and Modernity.* Nashville, TN: Vanderbilt University Press, 1998. Print.

Williams, Raymond Leslie. *The Writings of Carlos Fuentes.* Austin: University of Texas Press, 1996. Print.

11 Casas Tomadas

Haunting and Homes in Latin American Stories

Ilse Büssing

> the phantom or the spectral is not alien to the familiar space, even if it is other, but is as much at home within the architectural space as we are.
>
> (Wolfreys 7)

In *Victorian Hauntings* (2002), Julian Wolfreys studies several Victorian texts from the Gothic perspective. In the introduction, Wolfreys emphasizes the link between the domestic and haunting, claiming that the most effective haunting takes place in a home:

> The spectral effect thus needs structure, within which its efficacy assumes maximum disruption. The act of haunting is effective because it displaces us in those places where we feel most secure, most notably in our homes, in the domestic scene. Indeed, haunting is nothing other than the destabilization of the domestic scene, as the place where we apparently confirm our identity, our sense of being, where we feel most at home with ourselves.
>
> (Wolfreys 5)

In this study, I will address this 'destabilization of the domestic scene' by examining haunting in and homes in two Latin American stories: 'Casa tomada' (1969) by Argentinian author Julio Cortázar, and 'La buena compañía' (2003) by late Mexican writer, Carlos Fuentes. Both stories contain specific elements that display and establish the home as the supreme setting for haunting. The first element is the anthropomorphic depiction of the house; second, the spectralization of characters and of the home itself (those who are alive are presented as dead and vice-versa); and third, the persistence of haunting due to the dwelling's capacity to transmit and contain memory. In order to discuss these points in the stories, diverse theoretical notions will be employed, beginning with a brief introduction to frame the topic of haunting and space and its convergence in the domestic sphere. This analysis aims to contribute to the discussion of the haunted home in Gothic fiction, specifically in the Latin American context.

Haunting and the *Unheimlich*

Before emarking on the discussion of haunted space, primarily within the domestic sphere, it is necessary to discuss the concept of haunting itself and to trace the essence of the condition through a brief look at the terms related to the concept. The first characteristic these notions suggest is that of repetition or regular visitation. 'Haunting', for instance, is defined as 'b. customary resort; frequenting' (*O.E.D.*). The second element that arises from these terms is that of place. 'To haunt' is defined as 'to frequent or be much about' (a place). A location for this kind of event *to take place in* is indeed a necessity: without a place or space, haunting would simply be impossible. A third concept of significance is that of entities who/which do the appearing. The term 'haunt', for instance, offers numerous possibilities for that which frequents or haunts a place: 'transf. and fig. Of unseen or immaterial visitants. a. of disease, memories, cares, feelings, thoughts' (*O.E.D.*). The last phrase is especially intriguing, as it opens up the possibilities for haunting.

A discussion on the topic of haunted homes would be inadequate without addressing their foremost defining element—their uncaniness. In his 1919 essay 'Das Unheimliche', ['The Uncanny'] Freud explores the topic of the uncanny, building upon other theorists' work and employing E.T.A. Hoffman's story 'The Sandman' to illustrate his main points. Freud points out the fascinating etymological implications of the word in German, *unheimlich*; he indicates that the term entails two meanings that seem to contradict each other: *heimlich/heimisch*: 1. Domestic, familiar, intimate. 2. Hidden, secret, clandestine, furtive. On the other hand, *unheimlich* functions as a synonym of the second meaning of *heimlich*, by referring to that which is secret or hidden (Masschelein 3). In other words, the term *unheimlich* produces ambivalence because it allows for terms that defy internal logic by appearing to oppose each other. In spite of, and at the same time, thanks to this ambiguity, *unheimlich* is employed to describe that which frightens and upsets because of both its familiarity and unfamiliarity. In her article, 'The Ghost Story', Gothic critic Julia Briggs, insists on this mode's predilection for portraying family life:

> from the outset, Gothic writing had displayed a marked tendency to represent the family as a source of danger, even as a model of false consciousness [...] characteristic Gothic fictions represented the family, not merely as failing its individual members, but as a source of dangerous secrets, even of literal skeletons in the cupboard. (127)

It becomes apparent, then, that there is indeed an intricate link between haunting and space, and that the home, because of its uncanny framework built around the family and the familiar, is a preferred locus for haunting. Furthermore, it is also imperative to reflect on notions of visitation and compulsive return and to broaden the scope of entities that are capable of haunting domestic spaces in fiction, ranging from family secrets to repressed desires to persistent memories.

After considering some characteristics of spectral domesticity, and of how haunting arises from the tension between homely and unhomely elements, we can now explore these notions in the stories by Cortázar and Fuentes. In Cortázar's '*Casa tomada*' an unmarried brother and his sister live a seemingly simple yet monotonous existence in a large home that has been in the family for generations. The narrator provides a meticulous description of the home's mapping; in fact, in the 1969 edition this article analyzes,[1] the text of the story is placed within the plans of the home, and as the story progresses the text migrates and is pushed in a specific direction, as are the characters. One day, this state of domestic bliss (if we might call it that) is disrupted when the characters hear a noise that originates in the innermost part of the house, an area that they clean every day but do not reside in. The reader never knows who or what generates these mysterious noises, and the characters never provide us with this information. However, they do react to this disturbance; clearly afraid, they limit themselves to the part of the house that they frequent the most. Eventually, however, the sounds invade that area as well, and at the end, the siblings are forced to relinquish their home entirely, ending up in the street late at night, with none of their belongings.

In '*La buena compañía*' by Carlos Fuentes, we also meet two unmarried siblings, this time two sinister spinsters, living in a dilapidated family home in Mexico City. Alejandro de la Guardia, their distinguished 27-year-old nephew who has been raised in Paris, decides to follow his mother's dying wish and moves to Mexico and into his aunts' house in order to inherit the family's riches. In this story, ambiguity is key in understanding haunting. We are never certain if the aunts or even Alejandro is alive, and the home itself seems to constantly generate illusions that trap and further confuse the protagonist. Eventually, after being magically transformed into a young boy, Alejandro is led by his menacing aunts to the basement, where he encounters a true skeleton in the family's closet—the corpse of a young boy, lying in a coffin. As it turns out, one of the aunts had had a child who died in a street accident when he was 11. Now, both of the aunts, acting as this boy's mother and as their nephew's 'mother' as well, have turned Alejandro into a child so that he may keep their dead son '*buena compañía*', or good company, forever.

The first point that I would like to discuss in these stories is the issue of the house as an ideal site for haunting. In other words, what is it about the house, in addition to its *unheimlich* fabric, that makes it a perfect site for spectrality? I argue that one of the central elements that contributes to this is the portrayal of the home as an anthropomorphic organism, as a live entity that possesses a body and a will capable of controlling its inhabitants and visitors. In architecture, the idea that the house reflects the human body is an ancient one, and it has shaped important notions, including Le Corbusier's *Modulor* (1948), a system of architectural proportion based on the human body and its ideal measurements. Le Corbusier's concepts reflect a long tradition and were inspired by Da Vinci, and Vitruvius before him. Da Vinci's famous *Vitruvian Man* (1487) is meant as a symbol of perfection.

In '*Casa tomada*' the house is referred to as a person, specifically a woman, because of the convenient use of the feminine pronoun 'ella', as when the narrator suggests that *she*, the house, could have been the reason they never married: '*A veces llegamos a creer que era* ella *la que no nos dejó casarnos*' (emphasis added 1). In this particular instance, the translation into English, by excluding the '*ella*' pronoun, does not appropriately emphasize the feminine essence of the home, as the original does: 'we ended up thinking, at times, that that was what had kept us from marrying' (Manguel 2). Furthermore, on page three of the 1969 edition, we find a thorough description of the areas of the home, presented as if we were facing the home's metaphoric but also literal body. Curiously, if we were to stand the plans upright or look at them vertically, the design suggests the outline of a human body, with the head of the home located near the entrance of the home, the siblings' bedrooms forming the arms, the kitchen being the heart of the home and the rectangular area representing the lower part of this organism's frame.

Significantly, after the initial noises, the narrator closes a door (no. 10 in the plans), which separates the most public area—the conscious—from the back—the unconscious. 'I hurled myself against the door before it was too late and shut it, leaned on it with the weight of my body; luckily, the key was on our side; moreover, I ran the great bolt into place, just to be safe' (Manguel 3).

In '*La buena compañía*', we also encounter a home that is uncannily alive but unlike '*Casa tomada*', where terror lives in the house expelling its

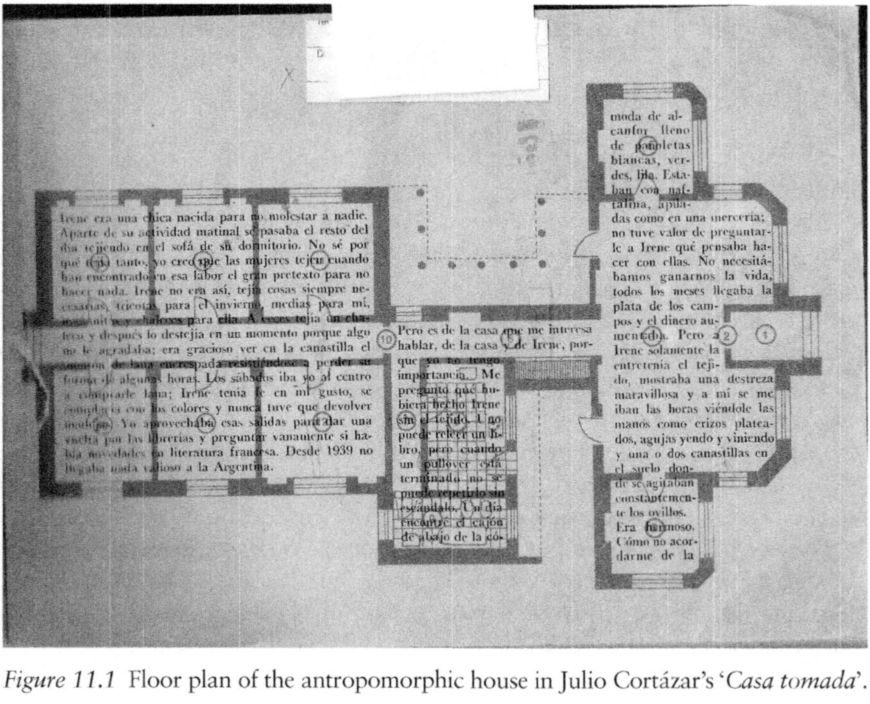

Figure 11.1 Floor plan of the antropomorphic house in Julio Cortázar's '*Casa tomada*'.

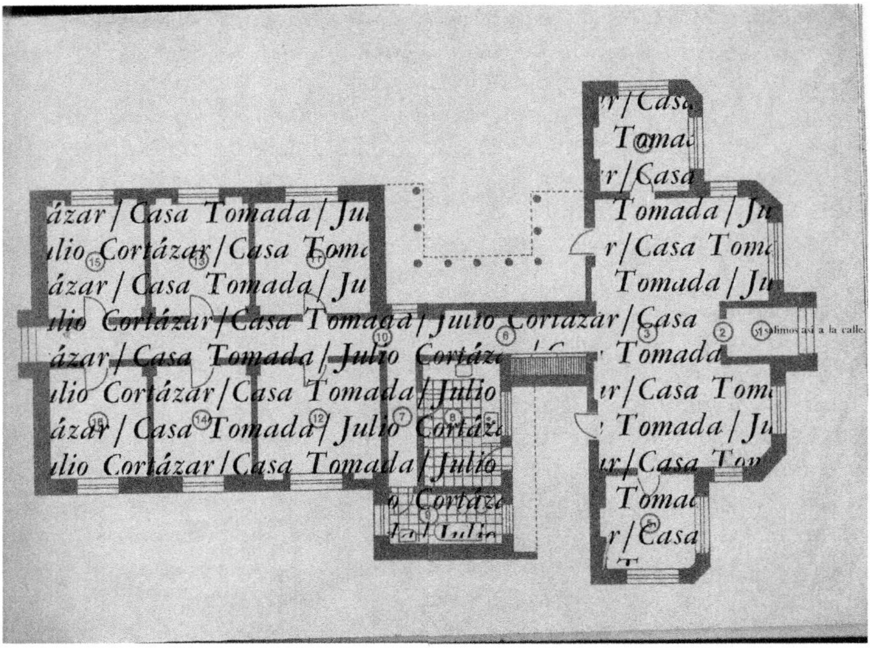

Figure 11.2 Floor plan once the house has been completely "taken" or "tomada."

inhabitants, in Fuentes's story the dwelling lures in its victims and finally kills them. As in Cortázar's tale, characters talk about the home as if it were a person. One of the aunts tells Alejandro that they cannot leave the house because someone has to take care of 'her': 'we cannot abandon the house. Someone has to be here at all times, taking care of her' (116).[2] It is noteworthy that, under the illusion of care, the home's guardians are in fact entrapped by it, thus revealing the sinister potential of the dwelling and its ability to enthrall characters. In this story we also encounter an old family home that is elegantly derelict: 'Indefinitely ancient. Two stories and an elegant and derelict façade of grey stone—elegantly derelict' (90). Moreover, the house's stern façade clearly suggests an equally severe human face: 'a house of grey stone. Three steps leading to a black iron door. Two barred windows on each side of the door. And two faces peering out behind the curtains, one on each of the windows' (90). The impervious front, highlighted by the black metal door remits to the classic Gothic castle and seems even more ominous because of the eye-like windows occupied by the faces of the observing aunts.

As in Cortázar's tale, in the story by Fuentes, there are particular areas of the home that evoke the unconscious, thus supporting its resemblance to a person and to his/her mind. The main architectonic element that supports this is, as in numerous texts that depict haunted houses, the basement. In film and in fiction, this lower area has often been associated with dark, furtive aspects of characters' lives[3]; the archetypal basement is the site to hide a veritable skeleton in the closet, more specifically the corpse of the

11-year-old son of one of the aunts, a boy who had passed away decades before. There is a clear suggestion that one of the sisters had this son out of wedlock, an unforgivable sin in that particular context in the past. Serena tells her sister Zenaida that she has sacrificed herself 'to enable [her] to carry the burden of [her] sin' (120), suggesting that Zenaida might be the boy's biological mother. Moreover, the sisters' uncanny doubling and splitting paradoxically unifies them as halves of the same whole, and makes them act as the boy's 'single mother'. Therefore, the basement is clearly the site where dark secrets and sins from the past are, more than merely hidden, stored for posterity. As in numerous Gothic tales, this underground area clearly functions as an analogy for a person's and the family's concealed secrets, thus reinforcing the home's organic representation and its possession of both a mind and a body.

In addition to the basement, other topographical elements signal the home's unconscious: numerous mirrors appear in the story. Mirrors function as liminal features, contributing to a blurring of boundaries and realities. In a particularly eerie scene, Alejandro notices that, despite there being no mirror over the sink in the bathroom, it is somehow present because of the stain it has left on the wall: 'the stain from the mirror remained, the livid square left by the space once occupied by our strange yet most intimate double' (109). Not only does this shadow suggest the uncanny reflection produced by the mirror, but also it reminds Alejandro of the mirrors portrayed in Cocteau's movie *Orpheus* that, in the tradition of Lewis Carroll's 'Through the Looking-Glass' (1871), separate but also engage different worlds: 'mirrors that we could go through as if they were water. A vertical liquid, penetrable, to pass from one reality to another. In truth, from life to death' (109). This last quotation foreshadows the passage when Alejandro is magically transformed into a child by taking a bath that has been prepared by his aunts. The surface of the bath functions as a liquid portal, like that cited above. By getting into the bath, Alejandro crosses through this horizontal mirror, consequently shedding his body and identity as 27-year-old Alejandro and adopting the body and life of his aunts' new 'angelito', as they often call him.

Therefore, we see that the home portrayed in '*La buena compañía*' acts as an organism with a conscience, with the ability to generate illusions that lure and trap Alejandro, in the same way it probably trapped his aunts and their son. Moreover, as any organism, the home possesses a body marked by a stern and impervious façade, as well as a lower area—*el sótano* [the basement]—where repressed desires and secrets from the past are stored almost lovingly, as they would be in a person's unconscious. Lastly, liminal areas such as the back entrance and the various mirrors in the story offer the possibility to transgress the confines of different worlds and realities.

In '*Casa tomada*' and '*La buena compañía*', haunting arises from yet another element, from the specters that we encounter in both stories. Jacques Derrida and psychoanalysts Abraham and Torok are the established theorists behind the notion of haunting and the spectral. In *Specters de Marx* (1993), Derrida proposes *hantologie* (hauntology in English), a term that plays against ontology (the study of being). Instead of focusing on the study of being, Derrida proposes the study of the ghost, as that which hovers between life and death, absence and presence. This figure enables Derrida to question the veracity or solidity of a present, which, for him, is plagued by uncertainties that ultimately betray our belief in an unquestionable reality. Hauntology appeals to deconstructive critics because it connects similar themes (haunting, ghosts, the supernatural) to processes of destabilization that are present in texts and literature in general. Under this premise, we can argue that haunting arises in both stories because of the destabilization and ambiguity between realities, between the presence and absence fueled by spectrality.

In '*Casa tomada*', the spectral is represented as much by the protagonists, the brother and the sister, as by the presence of the not-so-absent ancestors that seem to inhabit the home and might be the potential source of disturbing noises. Although we are never certain, as readers we initially assume that the narrator and Irene are alive. However, if we consider the phenomenon of destabilization in the text, and the blurring of realities, we can safely approach these characters as specters. In this light, their being dead or alive loses relevance; this ambiguity renders them spectral. The way that the narrator describes their lonely and prolonged existence within the spacious old home suggests their ghostly existence: 'Irene and I got used to staying in the house by ourselves, which was crazy, eight people could have lived in that place and not have gotten in each other's way' (Manguel 1). In the original Spanish version, 'getting used to' appears as '*habituamos*', while 'staying' appears as '*persistir*' (to persist); both terms, especially in Spanish, strongly underline issues of repetition and habit, key elements of haunting. This notion is reinforced by the protagonists' rigid daily routine: 'We rose at seven in the morning and got the cleaning done, and about eleven I left Irene to finish off whatever rooms and went to the kitchen. We lunched at noon precisely, then there was nothing left to do but a few dirty plates' (Manguel 1). In addition to this recurring routine, brother and sister are spectralized by inhabiting a home that is ghostly itself, a fact that the narrator clearly enjoys: 'It was pleasant to take lunch and commune with the great hollow, silent house' (Manguel 1).

The siblings in '*Casa tomada*' function as specters not only because of their indeterminacy as live or dead beings, or because of their rigid lives, but also because of the ambiguity presented by the relationship between each other. After telling us that it was probably the house who did not let them get married, the narrator admits to being in a 'simple and silent marriage of siblings':

> We ended up thinking, at times, that that was what had kept us from marrying. Irene turned down two suitors for no particular reason, and

> María Esther went and died on me before we could manage to get engaged. We were easing into our forties with the unvoiced concept that the quiet, simple marriage of sister and brother was the indispensable end to a line established in this house by our grandparents. (Manguel 1–2)

In other words, even if their liaison does not include physical consummation, the quotation above still suggests an unhealthy alliance that has not permitted the siblings to venture outside of their home and life with each other.

In this story, insinuations of unwholesome longing between the siblings become more forceful toward the end. The narrator states that they sleep in distinct rooms, separated by a living room. However, we are also told that at night, even slight sounds would travel in a way that would disturb the other: 'at night you could hear everything in the house. We heard each other breathing, coughing' (Manguel 5), thus suggesting worrisome proximity and intimacy. Moreover, according to the brother, he could hear Irene talking in her sleep, a fact that further reinforces the issue of strong desires needing to emerge: 'whenever Irene talked in her sleep, I woke up immediately and stayed awake. I never could get used to this voice from a statue or a parrot, a voice that came out of the dreams, not from a throat' (Manguel 5). Near the end of the story, the force of their desires gains dangerous strength when we are told certain details that point to a suspicious physical proximity, as when Irene tells her brother that he tosses in bed so much that the bedcovers fall to the ground. 'Irene said that in my sleep I flailed about enormously and shook the blankets off' (Manguel 5). The tension and suspicion that emerge from this simple and silent marriage between siblings generate a destabilization in the text that imbues the characters with spectrality. As in Poe's 'The Fall of the House of Usher' (1839), insinuations of an incestuous relationship between the inhabitants of the home abound. As in Poe's tale, one might approach the issue of incest in a literal way, or by arguing in favor of a metaphorical incest, derived from an inappropriately stifling relationship. As with spectrality, it is uncertainty and not certitude that makes the relationship between these siblings particularly intriguing and inviting to analysis.

As in '*Casa tomada*', in Fuentes's story we come face to face with siblings that seem to be phantoms, this time with spinsters who are uncanny doubles[4] of each other, the seemingly good María Zenaida and the seemingly bad María Serena. These sisters display a suspicious closeness and certain similarities that signal their doubleness; for example, they are not only sisters, but spinsters who only have each other in the world. Second, their names—María Zenaida and María Serena—attest to this twofold existence. Third, even though they have divided their home into separate areas and they live by different schedules, this division, instead of merely differentiating them, underlines common elements: 'we divided the living room amongst ourselves [...] she entertains at night [Serena] and I do so during the day [Zenaida]' (91). The description of both sisters confirms that they are seemingly opposite yet unnervingly similar reflections of each other. While Zenaida, the seemingly nice aunt, 'wore a floral dress, with a piqué collar, fit for a school girl' (91), Serena's more severe attitude is reflected in her ominous attire: 'dressed all in black, with a long skirt, as long as her sister's' (93). Despite the superficial differences between the two sisters, events in the story and the characters' own words reveal that they complement each other, that they represent two halves of a single entity. The portrayal of these spinsters clearly points to the theme of the double and to the issue of spectrality, through the deconstructive blurring of boundaries of the self.

Like Cortázar's protagonists, the two Marías display spectrality because of the uncertainty about their being dead or alive. María Zenaida tells Alejandro that neighbors believe that their house is uninhabited, blaming it on the fact that they never leave the house: 'neighbors believe that no one lives here, since we never go out' (97). Even if their seclusion explained the neighbors' reaction, the aunt later tells Alejandro something intriguing: 'show yourself in the street. Have them believe that someone ... that we ... are still alive' (98), a statement that her sister later tries to amend, a move that only increases the feeling of uncertainty, thus of spectrality.

In '*La buena compañía*', the spinsters are not the only ghosts. Upon arrival, their nephew Alejandro decides to take a stroll around the neighborhood. What he encounters is a ghost town that seems to reinforce his aunts' home's spectrality: 'he noticed great neglect. There were no longer old houses, like those of his aunts. It struck him that the buildings that could be called 'modern' had windows with no glass or with broken panes, cracked walls, doors obstructed by black bags full of rubbish, doors that invited one to take a stroll down long courtyards flanked by two stories of rooms' (96). Upon concluding that Alejandro has landed in an eerie ghost town, readers experience yet another disruption in the text, when it is suggested that it is Alejandro, and not those around him, who seems to be a ghost. Thus, when he enters the dilapidated apartment building, the female residents do not seem to perceive his presence or existence: 'women in the hallways, leaning on wrought-iron banisters, looked at him with indifference. Perhaps they did not look at him at all' (96). Furthermore, on the street, he attributes people's unresponsiveness to their being 'busy:' 'busy people. No one turned to look at him. He tried saying hello—Good morning. No one replied' (96). As if this were not enough to deconstruct Alejandro's status as a live person, he acquires spectrality by gradually but surely becoming the mirror image and companion—of his deceased cousin. Thus, the 27-year-old soon starts behaving like a child when he plays (or imagines playing) soccer with neighboring children, when he is surrounded by his cousin's toys and stuffed animals and when he eventually emerges as an 11 year old from the enchanted bath prepared by his aunts. His final alteration is the last stage in a gradual transformation from the 27-year-old Alejandro to the 11-year-old ghostly companion of his equally ghostly cousin. Near the end of the story, María Zenaida expresses gratefulness toward Alejandro's late mother: 'our sister was truly wise. She sent us a dead man to keep two dead women company' (119). We might interpret the sister's death as literal or symbolic, the latter stemming from their reclusive existence: in the same manner we might perceive Alejandro's death as literal or metaphorical. Once again, the indeterminacy generated by these options creates an ideal setting for haunting within this household.

We have explored how in these stories, haunting arises from the depiction of a home as a willful and sinister organism, as well as from excessive spectrality. One last point also contributes to spectrality, undoubtedly shaping these haunted homes—the homes' capacity to transmit and contain memory.

Bachelard's Haunted Home

Gaston Bachelard's *La poétique de l'espace* (1958) (*The Poetics of Space*), a work that has become a cornerstone in phenomenological studies, provides some concepts that prove the importance of domestic space, for both architecture and literature. Throughout this work, Bachelard remembers and relives the memories of his childhood home, insisting that we should all experience domestic space in this nostalgic and intimate way.

The possibility of a disturbed domicile is supported by several elements that arise in this melancholic tour of the home. The first is that of intimacy and shelter. Bachelard claims that the house 'is body and soul. It is the human being's first world. Before he is 'cast into the world [...] man is laid in the cradle of the house' (7). Furthermore, the author equates this sense of being sheltered with a primal instinct that we still experience: 'the creature endowed with a sense of refuge, huddles up to itself, takes to cover, hides away, lives snug concealed' (91). This animal instinct that we retain in a place we call home, then, is inevitably haunted by an ancient desire to cover, hide and conceal, a fact that may easily relate to an *unheimlich* space, and in our case, a haunted house.

Another aspect of Bachelard's childhood home that triggers spectrality is the importance of dreams and the past. This philosopher favors dreams and the unconscious as opposed to rationality, as preferred conductors of memories. Thus, one may safely view his house as a space inhabited by remnants of the unconscious from another time, as a space populated by Derrida's specters. 'To inhabit oneirically the house we were born in means more than to inhabit it in memory; it means living in this house that is gone, the way we used to dream in it' (16). Because of the filters of memory and dreams, inhabiting this house is inhabiting a 'house that is gone', an enchanted space that exists but as something that is no more.

We see Bachelard's notions about home and memory take place in both stories. In '*Casa tomada*' the narrator highlights the issue of the home's containing or holding capacity, as a repository of family memories: 'we liked the house because, apart from its being old and spacious [...] it kept the memories of great-grandparents, our paternal grandfather, our parents and the whole of childhood' (Manguel 1). In other words, not only does the house contain the recollections of the siblings' childhood, but it literally houses a collection of memories for several generations. The notion of containment is further emphasized by the following quotation, in which the narrator comments on the contents of a drawer in his sister's bedroom: 'one day I found that the drawer at the bottom of the chiffonier, replete with moth-balls, was filled with shawls, white, green, lilac. Stacked amid a great smell of camphor—it was like a shop' (Manguel 2). The image of an infinite amount of knitted scarves being preserved by mothballs condenses, not only the containing function of the house in regard to memory, but its urgent need to preserve family memories and family *members* in a necrophilic manner. We can conclude that the house in '*Casa tomada*' is fundamentally a large drawer that preserves its contents, both people and memories, in an amorous yet perverse way.

In '*Casa tomada*' there is an enigma that prevails, even after several readings: if the home is so fond of memories built around the family and its several generations, why are the siblings, the last in the family line, banished from their home? For that matter, who or what is behind this eviction? The entities responsible for this exile materialize in the text merely through sound. As mentioned previously, the initial sounds originate in the area beyond the door that divides the home into the back of the house and the area that is mostly frequented by the siblings. Significantly, the sounds seem to emanate from specific areas, the library and the dining room: 'I went down the corridor as far as the oak door, which was ajar, then turned into the hall toward the kitchen, when I heard something in the library or the dining room' (Manguel 3). Arguing that these sounds are specters representing the home's and family's memories, we can understand the significance of the noises arising in both the library and the dining room. While the library is the ultimate place of storage, in this case of knowledge, the dining room is an ideal setting for the construction of a family history, based on everyday exhanges; therefore, spectral noises, announcing the presence of the supposedly absent ancestors, arise in rooms employed for the storage and transmission of household memories.

Returning to the reason for this banishment, we can find a clue in the first pages of the story. In page one we are told that old family homes such as the one portrayed here are torn down in order to make a profit: 'in a day when old houses go down for a profitable auction of their construction materials' (Manguel 1). Furthermore, and more importantly, the narrator announces the fate awaiting the house in the future, after their death. 'We would die here someday, obscure and distant cousins would inherit the place, have it torn down, sell the bricks and get rich on the building plot, or more justly and better yet, we would topple it ourselves before it was too late' (Manguel 2). Regardless of whether it is the inheriting cousins or the protagonists who do it, the fate of the house seems to point in one inevitable direction: the demolition of the home for pecuniary and exploitative reasons. The eerie noises arising from the home's interior signal the home's and the ancestors' hostile opposition to this future, thus causing the siblings to move out before they can carry out this action. Moreover, another viable reason for being expelled by these household entities relates to the siblings' failure to perpetuate the family line. Even though this odd 'marriage' guards and cleans the family home in a compulsive manner, this couple fails to secure the future of the home and the family by not bringing forth descendants who will continue their roles as custodians or overseers of the family's memories.

In '*La buena compañía*', it is not only the house that contains memories, but the whole city; Mexico City is described as a capital composed of layers of architectural styles that remit to its several cultures and invasions: 'a city of layer upon layer, viceregal Aztec city, neoclassical, modern' (90). For Alejandro, the return to his ancestor's '*madre patria*' [motherland] and to his family's home echoes Bachelard's concepts about the nostalgic return to one's childhood home: 'I wanted, after many years of inherited exile, to return to Mexico' (88). As in '*Casa tomada*', the sisters' household displays a boundless capacity to store and to preserve memory, causing time to stand still, in a sense congeal in the past. In Alejandro's room, for instance, there is a 15-year-old calendar instead of a current one, and we are told that 'the aunts remained frozen in another time' (108). But the area in the sister's home that displays the greatest ability to store the past is, once again, the basement. The basement clearly functions as the literal and symbolic storage area for this family's memories. When the aunts and the younger version of Alejandro all descend into the dark basement, they are surrounded by an oppressive musty smell and old containers such as chests and wooden boxes. Furthermore, we must remember that this area holds two other extremely significant containers: the coffin with the corpse of the 11-year-old cousin and the coffin meant for the now-young Alejandro. The several containers present in the basement, which is a container in itself, undoubtedly highlight the need of this home and this family to preserve and remember.

This last point leads us to the conclusion of this study. Bachelard insists that the magical space of the childhood home is easily transformed into a haunted one because of the urge to return to it. In '*La buena compañía*', Alejandro's urge to return to his family's ancestral home leads to the extreme conservation not only of memory, but also of family members—Alejandro, like his deceased cousin and even the two aunts, is caught in the home's perverse embrace and is symbolically embalmed as yet another family heirloom. In '*Casa tomada*', even though the siblings are expelled from the household, they have been banished in order to preserve the home and its collection of recollections.

We can conclude, then, that in both of these stories, haunting arises from first, the depiction of homes that function as live organisms with a body and a will; second, the spectralization of characters and space; and third, the home's insistence on retaining memories. Critics have often noted how Gothic literature's affinity with excess produces accounts of an amplified nature. Thus, situations in real life are often blown into fantastic proportions in fiction. In both '*Casa tomada*' and '*La buena compañía*', we move through dwellings where feelings of safety and nurturing that are supposed to characterize family and domesticity have been magnified to the point of becoming claustrophobic and threatening. Homes in both of these stories are not mere museums, places to display and cherish memories, but veritable *mausoleums*, residences where memories as well as people eventually fester, because of an excessive need to remember and to contain. In these tales, it is not the human characters but the haunted house that is the real protagonist. '*Casa tomada*' and '*La buena compañía*' suggest that all homes may become '*casas tomadas*', houses taken or possessed by extreme desires to preserve the past and its legacy.

Notes

1. This article considers the Spanish version of 'Casa Tomada', which appears in the 1969 edition, in order to gain a better understanding of the original text and to perceive certain nuances of meaning that are lost in translation. It also presents illustrations of house plans that this particular edition contains; in addition, the English version of the story, entitled 'House Taken Over,' appearing in Manguel's *Black Water The Book of Fantastic Literature* (1983), is also employed to provide excerpts from the story as they appear in the translation into English.
2. All the quotations in Spanish from Fuentes's 'La buena compañía' have been translated by the author of this article into English.
3. Citing Bachelard, Barry Curtis in *Dark Places, the Haunted House in Film* (London: Reaktion Books Ltd., 2008) points out the following: 'The extremities of the house were what Bachelard has described as the 'vertical polarity' of attics and cellars. This verticality also mapped class relations in upper-class families where the servants occupied occluded spaces within the house, using separate staircases and the extreme margins of attics and area basements' (42). According to Curtis, this topographical situation explains why in film, servants, who reside in these marginal areas, often play the role of guardians of the family's equally marginalized memories.
4. In 1914, Otto Rank discussed the figure of the double as found in primitive animism worldwide, and was later cited by Freud in his seminal work, 'The Uncanny' (1919). Closely related and incorporated into the concept of the *unheimlich*, the double is identified as something repressed that has emerged, provoking anxiety and terror. The double is often perceived as the shadow (darker dimension of the self), in turn revealing an individual's paranoid condition, in which the person perceives his ego's double as relentlessly following him/her (as in Poe's 'William Wilson').

Bibliography

Abraham, Nicolas, and Maria Torok. *The Shell and the Kernel: Renewals of Psychoanalysis* [*L'Écorce et le noyau*] (1978). Ed. and trans. Rand, Nicholas T. Chicago: University of Chicago Press, 1994. Print.

Bachelard, Gaston. *The Poetics of Space* (*La poétique de l'espace*) (1958). Trans. Jolas, Maria. Boston: Beacon Press, 1994. Print.

Briggs, Julia. 'The Ghost Story.' *A Companion to the Gothic*. Ed. Punter, David. Oxford: Blackwell Publishing, 2004. Print.

Cortázar, Julio. 'Casa tomada.' Buenos Aires, Argentina: Minotauro, 1969. Print.

Curtis, Barry. *Dark Places, the Haunted House in Film*. London: Reaktion Books Ltd., 2008. Print.

Derrida, Jacques. *Specters of Marx*. New York: Routldege, 1994. Print.

Freud, Sigmund. *The Uncanny*. Trans. Mclintok, David. New York: Penguin Books, 2003. Print.

Fuentes, Carlos. 'La buena compañía.' *Inquieta Compañía*. D.F., México: Alfaguara, 2003. Print.

Hoffman, E.T.A. 'The Sandman.' *The Night Pieces* (*Der Sandmann: Ein Nachstuck*) (1817). Leipzig: Reclam, 1870. Print.

Le Corbusier (Charles Édouard Jeanneret-Gris). *The Modulor* (*Le modulor*) (1948). Paris: Fondation Le Corbusier, 2000. Print.

Lewis, Carroll. *Through the Looking Glass*. Auckland: Floating Press, 1871. Print.

Mallgrave, Harry Francis, Ed. *Architectural Theory*. Vol. 1. Oxford: Blackwell Publishing, 2006. Print.

Manguel, Alberto. *Black Water: The Book of Fantastic Literature*. New York: Clarkson N. Potter, 1983. Print.

Masschelein, Aneeleen. 'A Homeless Concept: Shapes of the Uncanny in Twentieth-Century Theory and Culture.' *Image & Narrative*. 2003. Web. Accessed October 16, 2015. <http://www.imageandnarrative.be/uncanny/uncanny.htm>.

Orpheus (*Orphée*). Dir. Jean Cocteau. Perf. Jean Marais, François Périer and Maria Casares. DisCina,1950. Film.

Rank, Otto. *The Double: A Psychoanalytic Study* (*Der Doppelgänger*) (1914). Chapel Hill: University of North Carolina Press, 1971. Print.

Wolfreys, Julian. *Victorian Hauntings: Spectrality, Gothic, the Uncanny and Literature*. New York: Palgrave, 2000. Print.

Quotations in Spanish, from the 1969 Edition of 'Casa Tomada' and from Fuentes's Original of 'La buena compañía' (2003)

1. 'Me tiré contra la puerta antes de que fuera demasiado tarde, la cerré de golpe apoyando el cuerpo; felizmente la llave estaba puesta de nuestro lado y además corrí el gran cerrojo para más seguridad' (Cortázar 4, 5).
2. 'No podemos abandonar la casa. Alguien tiene que estar siempre aquí, cuidándola' (Fuentes 116).
3. 'Indefinidamente antigua. Dos pisos y una fachada de piedra gris, elegante, descuidada—elegantemente descuidada' (Fuentes 90).
4. 'una casa de piedra gris, severa. Tres escalones para llegar a una puerta de fierro negro. Dos ventanas enrejadas a los lados de la puerta. Y dos rostros asomados entre las cortinas de cada una de las ventanas' (Fuentes 90).

5. 'para ayudarte a sobrellevar tu pecado' (Fuentes 120).
6. 'quedaba la sombra del espejo, el cuadro lívido del espacio ocupado por ese nuestro extraño y entrañable doble' (Fuentes 109).
7. 'espejos que podíamos atravesar como si fueran agua. Un líquido vertical, penetrable para pasar de una realidad a otra. En verdad, de la vida a la muerte' (Fuentes 109).
8. 'nos habituamos Irene y yo a persistir solos en ella, lo que era una locura pues en esa casa podían vivir ocho personas sin estorbarse' (Cortázar 1).
9. 'Hacíamos la limpieza por la mañana levantándonos a las siete, y a eso de las once yo le dejaba a Irene las últimas habitaciones por repasar y me iba a la cocina. Almorzábamos al mediodía, siempre puntuales; ya no quedaba nada por hacer fuera de unos pocos platos sucios' (Cortázar 1).
10. 'nos resultaba grato almorzar pensando en la casa profunda y silenciosa' (Cortázar 1).
11. 'A veces llegamos a creer que era ella la que no nos dejó casarnos. Irene rechazó dos pretendientes sin mayor motivo, a mí se me murió María Esther antes que llegáramos a comprometernos. Entramos en los cuarenta años con la inexpresada idea de que el nuestro, simple y silencioso matrimonio de hermanos, era necesaria clausura de la genealogía asentada por los bisabuelos en nuestra casa' (Cortázar 1).
12. 'de noche se escuchaba cualquier cosa en la casa. Nos oíamos respirar, toser' (Cortázar 11).
13. 'cuando Irene soñaba en alta voz, yo me desvelaba en seguida. Nunca pude habituarme a esa voz de estatua o papagayo. Voz que viene de los sueños y no de la garganta' (Cortázar 10).
14. 'Irene decía que mis sueños consistían en grandes sacudones que a veces hacían caer el cobertor' (Cortázar 10).
15. 'nos dividimos la sala [...] ella recibe de noche [Serena] yo de día [Zenaida]' (Fuentes 91).
16. 'usaba un vestido floreado, con cuello blanco de piqué, como de colegiala' (Fuentes 91).
17. 'vestida toda de negro, con una falda tan larga como la de su hermana' (Fuentes 93).
18. 'los vecinos creen que nadie vive aquí. Como nosotras nunca salimos' (Fuentes 97).
19. 'muéstrate en la calle. Que crean que alguien ... que nosotras ... seguimos vivas' (Fuentes 98).
20. 'notó un gran abandono. Ya no había casas viejas, como la de las tías. Lo llamativo era que los edificios que podían suponerse 'modernos' mostraban ventans sin vidrios o con vidrios rotos, paredes cuarteadas, puertas obstruidas por bolsas negras llenas de basura, puertas que invitaban a penetrar largos patios flanqueados por dos pisos de habitaciones' (Fuentes 96).
21. 'Las mujeres recargadas en los pasillos con barandales de fierro lo miraron con indiferencia. O quizás no lo miraron' (Fuentes 96).
22. 'gente ocupada. Nadie volteaba a verlo. Intentó saludar—Buenos días. Nadie le respondió' (Fuentes 96).
23. 'qué sabia fue nuestra hermana. Mira que mandarnos a un muerto para hacerle compañía a dos muertas' (Fuentes 119).

24. 'nos gustaba la casa porque aparte de espaciosa y antigua guardaba los recuerdos de nuestros bisabuelos, el abuelo paterno, nuestros padres y toda la infancia' (Cortázar 1).
25. 'el cajón de debajo de la cómoda de alcanfor lleno de pañoletas blancas, verdes, lila. Estaban con naftalina, apiladas como en mercería' (Cortázar 2).
26. 'fui por el pasillo hasta enfrentar la entornada puerta de roble, y daba la vuelta al codo que llevaba a la cocina cuando escuché algo en el comedor o la biblioteca' (Cortázar 4).
27. 'hoy que las casas sucumben a la más ventajosa liquidación de sus materiales' (Cortázar 1).
28. 'nos moriríamos allí algún día, vagos y esquivos primos se quedarían con la casa y la echarían al suelo para enriquecerse con el terreno y los ladrillos: o mejor, nosotros mismos la voltearíamos justicieramente antes de que fuese demasiado tarde' (Cortázar 1).
29. 'una urbe de capas superpuestas, ciudad azteca virreinal, neoclásica, moderna' (90).
30. 'Quería, después de tantos años de destierro hereditario, regresar a México:' (88).
31. 'las tías se habían quedado detenidas en otra época' (108).

Section III

Social and Political Landscapes of the Tropical Gothic

12 Sepulchral Beauty in Brazilian Romanticism

Cilaine Alves Cunha

In Brazilian Romanticism, *Noite na Taverna* (*A Night in the Tavern*, 1855) by Manuel Antônio Álvares de Azevedo (1831–1852) was one of the literary works responsible for unpredictably adapting formal and thematic principles of Gothic fiction into Brazil's romantic literary scenario. Highly acclaimed by both the public and the critics, the book has been immortalized by countless editions printed year after year in Brazil. The plot unveils the story of a virtuous heroine persecuted by villains and educated young men devoted to alcohol and licentiousness. Its morbid chapters tell stories that take place on dark streets at night in different European cities, hotel rooms, turbulent seas and cliffs. In an atmosphere of terror, the story shapes the cult of irrationalism and the probing of unconscious human forces, materializing a poetic thought averse to literary didacticism and to the edification of the nation prevailing in most artistic practices at that time.

Before the publication of *Noite na Taverna* only a few literary works produced in Brazil dodged the precept that art should delight and instruct. Few artistic experiences of the period significantly engaged with formal procedures of the Gothic, nor did they produce a unique reflection about the ethical and aesthetic conditions of modern life, as Azevedo's work did, or were like it a singular reflection on the ethical and aesthetic conditions of modern life. Prior to *Noite na Taverna*, the novels *O Filho do Pescador* (*The Fisherman's Son*, 1843), by Teixeira e Sousa (1812–1861), and *Dois Amores* (*Two Loves*, 1848), by Joaquim Manuel de Macedo (1820–1882), resorted to some Gothic characteristics and merged them to the formal procedures of cloak-and-dagger swashbuckler narrative and of the sentimental novel, favoring fantasy and romance with edifying purposes.

These two previous experiences are contemporaneous to the expansion of the book and printing press industry, due to the transfer of the Portuguese Imperial government to Brazil in 1808. Until then, books and the printing press had been subject to severe Portuguese censorship in the colony:

> Without its own printing press, subject to censorship, with a small number of booksellers, the country, even after the opening of its ports, depended on the illegal trade kept by the British, French and Dutch, and on the publishing industry in Portuguese in London and Paris to supply its consumer market.

After the foundation of the Royal Press in 1821 and the independence of Brazil in 1822, a flourishing publishing industry and the opening of circulating libraries helped readership increase, at a time in which agrarian life began to give way to the urbanization of customs. By the time the first attempts to reinvent, adapt and consolidate the novel as a local product could be evidenced, the growing offer of books and the circulation of feuilletons in the newspapers intensified the translation of French and English novels (the latter commonly from the French).

Obviously, the elite that produced literature did not depend on these translations in Portugal or in one of the newly opened Law or Medical schools in Brazil as part of an educational system that privileged, from an early age, the teaching of Greek, Latin and modern languages, especially English, French and German. But gradually, the market began to enjoy an increasing number of readers, previously restricted to a very small economic elite and the group of writers themselves, who were as proposed by Antonio Candido (2006), producers and consumers at the same time (156–64).

From the mid-nineteenth century, Brazilian writers witness the interference of the publishing market on literary production, thereby starting in Brazil the process that led it to mediate reading tastes. Among the British and French novels translated into Portuguese grew the circulation of works by Horace Walpole, Anne Radcliffe and Regina Maria Roche.

The publication of *A Night in the Tavern*, thus, already finds in the local context the formal elements that characterized Gothic narrative. Azevedo's narrative established itself as a fortunate example of the adaptation of the genre in the country, paving the way for other experiences of the kind. Later, there were other publications of short stories and novels with these traits, written by local authors. Emulating *A Night in the Tavern*[1] or the works by the writers mentioned above—as well as Mary Shelley, Matthew Gregory Lewis, George Byron, Théophile Gautier, Charles Nodier, E.T.A. Hoffmann and Heinrich Heine, among others—several Brazilian fiction writers, canonized or not in contemporary Brazilian literary histories, explored the possibilities of Gothic literature at some point in their career.

Álvares de Azevedo had all this work published posthumously. Having died before turning 21 years of age, he wrote his work between 1848 and 1852, during the period in which, having come from Rio de Janeiro where he lived, he attended Law School in São Paulo. From a letter to one of his friends, it is known, however, that shortly before his death he prepared the publication of the two volumes of his lyrical poetry work, *Lira dos Vinte Anos* (*Lyre of Twenty Years*). Self-named *binomial*, the style of these poems seeks to create a clash between polarized ideas. Promoting the cult of contradiction, it oscillates among idealism, melancholy and the expression of feelings on the one hand, disbelief, irony, satire and self-derisive humor on the other.

Álvares de Azevedo also produced the drama *Macário* (*Macarius*), whose fragmentary form merges the dramatic and the lyrical to the discourse of the philosophy of art, to create, as he also does on a much-reduced scale in *A Night at the Tavern*, situations of a fantastic nature. Programmatically, *Macarius* makes use of the visionary style of Jean Paul Richter. The author's maxim that says 'I hate the dust which refines the rhyme', the assumption that inspiration should refute objective laws and preserve the mysterious imponderability of life lead him to preserve in this work passages that break down the logical causality of the narrative.

Alongside his lyrical production and this drama, the novel *A Night in the Tavern* displays formal and stylistic refinement, if compared to the rest of his fictional works. His three long prose poems—*The Poem of the Friar, Fra Gondicário and Count Lopo*—have a long-winded, digressive and highly diffuse style. The formal fragmentation of these poems may have been the result either of the early death of the author or of his adhesion to the style of romantic fragmentation. The latter hypothesis is reinforced when one observes that, in them, the narrator dedicates himself to dismantling traditional genres, especially the traditional artistic assumptions of epic and classic tragedy. Repeatedly, Azevedo's narrators claim that the material conditions for the production of these genres were dead.

The poet also composed a significant number of texts on literary history, theory and literary criticism. In addition to the prefaces to *Lyre of Twenty Years* and *Count Lopo*, his reflection on his own poetic thoughts and on art can be found in 'Lucano', 'George Sand. *Aldo, the Rhymer*' and '*Jacques Rolla*', the latter covering the segment 'On Disbelief in Byron, Shelley, Voltaire, Musset'. In addition to his correspondence, his complete works also include 'Letter on the Theatre Today among Us' and the article 'Literature and Civilization in Portugal'.

While writing his work, Azevedo witnessed the consolidation of the premises of literary nationalism in Brazil, when the first attempts to create a new expression that would manifest the singularity of the country and authorial individuality began to be established. At this point, literature had become instrumental in national ideology and transformed the native Indian into a symbol of local culture. At a time when the imperial government struggled to legitimize itself amid the political and economic elite of the country, the poetic invention of the Indian embodies anti-Portuguese feelings and values such as the capacity for war of a people, their prompt submission to hierarchical political leadership and the preservation and memory of their traditions.

In the midst of these efforts, the work of Gonçalves de Magalhães (1811–1882), a friend of Dom Pedro II's and public servant, claimed to be the founder of Brazilian literature. But this soon proved to be insignificant. Crowning the Indianist movement, Gonçalves Dias (1823–1864), another poet soon brought into the circle of men of letters led by the emperor, successfully created a poetic language expected to be an expression of the cultural uniqueness of the country. In his artistic practice, he promotes the feeling of national belonging and praises the characteristic features of the local landscape, projecting in the Indians who inhabited Brazil before the Portuguese invasion the supposedly typical Brazilian character. In 1846, the publication of his book of poems, *First Songs*, establishes him as 'a great role model for young people, and throughout Romanticism [...] one of the landmarks of Brazilian poetry' (Candido, *Iniciação à Literatura Brasileira* 41).

Gathered as students at the Law School in São Paulo, Álvares de Azevedo, Bernardo Guimarães (1825–1884) and Aureliano Lessa (1828–1861), among others, formed a Romantic group parallel to the Indianist movement. Among the objectives of one of the academic and literary associations they organized, called Epicureia Society, Byron's life and work became the model of a bohemian experience to be imitated socially and aesthetically.[2] In his 1859 text, 'Foundation of the Academy—Youth Work—Associations—Newspapers', Couto de Magalhães, relying on the testimonial of a contemporary of the three poets, describes the Epicureia Society:

> Composed of a large number of talented young men, its objective was to make Byron's dreams come true. One of its associates who lives at present in the State of Minas Gerais told me the following: 'There were many places where we met: sometimes on the Ingleses[3], sometimes in another suburb of the city. Once we were enclosed for a fortnight in the company of naughty women, under the light of oil lamps, that is why all windows were perfectly closed during our stay, all sorts of extravagances could be committed. '[...] This society had great influence on the poetry of our youth. Álvares de Azevedo is said to have described in part one of those scenes, in his A *Night in the Tavern*. (22)

Given the poetic affinity of this group with the work of Byron, articles of literary criticism and Brazilian literary histories refer to its members as Byronic. Three years after the publication of Álvares de Azevedo's work came out the article 'Essays of critical analysis IV. José Alexandrino Teixeira de Melo. *Shadows and Dreams*' (1858), by writer and literary critic Macedo Soares, In it, the author seeks to challenge the influence of Byron's aesthetic assumptions as reference for young Brazilian poets. For Soares, the supposedly revolutionary character of this group was a threat to order and family customs. In his view, the valorization they build around turmoil, formal irregularity and misanthropy, as well as the political exploitation of literature, were incompatible with art. Beauty would not exist without unity, order, rationality and clarity, in the critic's opinion:

> Recklessness and disorder are characteristic features of Byronic poetry: the passions that it expresses reflect that. Hence the false enthusiasm, affected lamentations, misanthropy and despair. Werner, Manfred and Jacques Rolla are the knights of this new rather than feudal chivalry, eternally angry with the rich and powerful of the earth, eternally fighting society, whose inequalities they struggle to put an end to. [...] Calm,

> they [the Byronic] say, belongs only to the weak of heart, the powerless or pusillanimous who do not have the strength or courage to carry out social regeneration. Order is what hardens the men of the past who at all costs strive for the preservation of old and stale traditions of absolutism. [...] Fortunately, Byronic declamations, by dint of being repeated, lost the only merit that briefly brought them public attention: novelty. The creator himself depleted characters such as those of Byron. Endowed with an amazing genius, the bard of Newstead managed to anoint through the religion of heroism his libertines and fornicators, shameful and sad deviations of the moral order. But the mob of imitators who fell over his glorious corpse no longer found the sap which they wanted to collect from the editions, but lacked the creative word and the copies faded the dull colors with which they were daubed. (80–81)

Impervious to the delimitation of nationality in literature, Álvares de Azevedo and his colleagues composed satires dedicated to 'de-heroicize' the literary figure of the native Indian. In a poem of strongly licentious nature, 'The Elixir of the Shaman', Bernardo Guimarães parodies another poem, 'The Song of the Indigenous Warrior', by Gonçalves Dias. The article 'Literature and Civilization in Portugal' stands out, next to *Macarius*, as one of the explicit manifestations of the anti-nationalism of Álvares de Azevedo, in favor of an art that, identifying authorial and local singularity, would not minimize dialogue with tradition. The enunciator of this article is identified as a Portuguese poet. Parodying literary histories, he draws a timeline of the phases of Portuguese literature, dating it back to Spanish literature, which in turn would be the product of, among others, the Punic, Greco-Roman, Gothic, Arabic, African, Phoenician civilizations in a variety so unlimited of links as to ultimately dissolve the unique source of Portuguese culture. Celts, Phoenicians, Etruscans, Carthaginians, Gaelic, Moors, Irish, English, Africans, Iranians and Indians, among others, cross, in this light, at one time or another, one way or another, Portuguese literature by way of its unification with Spain. By creating successive, multiple and unlimited sources of the origins of Portuguese literature, Azevedo set up an ironic structure that ultimately dissolves the principle that literature traces its causes to a single primordial essence. He refused to attribute, therefore, a pure organic quality to Portuguese literature, reaffirming its originality in the plurality of influences.

For the enunciator of 'Literature and Civilization in Portugal', only the achievement of an individual poetic language, produced by different local writers, could contribute to define the autonomy of Brazilian literature. For him, creating Indian, European or Chinese poems did not make poets lose their nationality. In his view, the break with Western tradition would mean giving up a mosaic rich in resources and works, impoverishing the literature of a nation. Referring to Santa Rita Durão (1722–1784) and Alvarenga

Peixoto (1744–1792), writers born in Brazil during the colonial period, Azevedo calls Portuguese literature 'homeland literature' and asks:

> And moreover I ignore what profit there is—if the dispute is won—in not wanting to pour our handful of jewels into this most abundant coffer of homeland literature; because of Durão, we cannot call Camões ours; because, because of whom? ... (of Alvarenga?) we resign ourselves to deeming foreign the book of Bocage's sonnets? (II 340)

In part due to Álvares de Azevedo's insertion in a period of great local and global transformations, but also thanks to his reflection regarding the renewal of art in view of the overthrow of fixed principles and objectives of art, his work offers a comprehensive discussion on the creation of a new literary system in an independent Brazil. In his prose fiction, literary studies and many of his poems, thoughts about the reformulation of art stand out. With this in mind, one of the best clues to understanding *A Night in the Tavern* was formulated by Antonio Candido. For him, this novel may have been designed to provide continuity to *Macarius* drama that, in turn, acts as a prologue to it.

This dramatic work by Álvares de Azevedo opposes the conceptions of the art and the world held by its protagonists, Satan and Macarius, on one side, and Penseroso, on the other. According to the antagonistic construction of these characters, the latter embodies, according to Candido, the very nationalistic ideals of the Brazilian literary scene at the time. To Penseroso, art should manifest enthusiasm with the progress of the nation, express the feeling of the homeland and the picturesque features of its landscape and customs.

Satan, in turn, is generally outlined as the fatal hero, inspired by the work of Byron. The Azevedian hero is drawn up as a mysterious being, rebellious and untamed, embodying the aesthetic principles of another trend of Brazilian Romanticism, the Byronic one. In *Macarius*, Satan becomes a kind of upside-down spiritual guide to student Macarius. He takes on the task of initiating him in the 'most convulsive and extreme aspects of life, satisfying as a kind of alter- ego the curiosity of his impulses' (Candido 15). Macarius, in turn, assumes an anti-nationalist posture, skeptical and ironical, appearing to the critic as an ambiguous character, marked by the synthesis between good and evil. (14)

The two groups of characters are also at odds regarding the belief in the possibility that harmonic beauty can survive in the historical conditions of the nineteenth century. Macarius and Satan think that as science is powerless to end human suffering and misery, there is no more hope in a world governed by the growing process of commodification of life. From this perspective, an art system based on the principles of formal perfection, of virtue and truth tended to disappear. The disappearance of God from the face of the Earth would have triggered the degradation of the existing system of values that had reigned so far, and of art, leading to the dominance, in the modern literary system, of melancholy, skepticism and irony.

In *Macarius*, the divergence about the type of Romanticism to be adopted can be exemplified in a dialogue between Macarius and Penseroso regarding a poem of a skeptical kind. To Penseroso, the book that contains the poem is immoral, and its author, cursed, because both lack faith. He strongly condemns those who refuse to turn their poetry to new realities, to young and absolute nations, pregnant with the future: 'Hopes! Does this American not feel he is the son of a new nation, does he not feel the blood, youth and greenness? Does he not remember that the gigantic groves, puffing oceans, the rivers, falls, that everything there is great and sublime?' (Azevedo II 64).

In the face of this passionate defense of literary nationalism, Macarius ironically asks Penseroso to shut up and smoke a cigar. Before his enthusiasm for the country's natural grandeur made, embodied in the artistic practices of the time, as a sign of the possibility of development towards civilization, Macarius points out the mosquitoes and fevers of the forests:

> They talk about the moans of the hinterland nights, the traditions of the lost races of the forest, the torrents of the hills, as if they had slept there at least one night and woken up looking for tombs, and asking like Hamlet in the graveyard every desert skull about his past. Lies! All this came to them whilst reading the pages of some traveler who may have forgotten to tell us that in the mangroves and the waters of the Amazon and of the Orinoco there are more mosquitoes and fevers than inspiration [...] that all this is sublime in the book, but extremely unpleasant in reality. (66)

In his reply to Penseroso, Macarius substitutes nationalism with cognac, cigars and women, emblematic elements of a life stance and a poetic system based on bohemian experience. This polarization between two distinct conceptions of literary creation, the Indianist and the Byronic, allows one to deduce that in *Macarius* Álvares de Azevedo exposes the divergences between bohemian literature and the way the nationalist group proposed literary renewal.

In the final scene of the drama, Penseroso's death allegorizes the end of the ideal, of purity, of illusions. At that point, Satan, according to Antonio Candido, feels free to undertake the demonic initiation of Macarius, inviting him to spy on an orgy through a window. This probable participation of the characters as spectators in the macabre scenes of *A Night in the Tavern* also leads Antonio Candido to propose that Satan is unveiling to his pupil a kind of experience marked by incest, e, fratricide, cannibalism, betrayal and murder:

> For him [Satan], with Penseroso's death, that is, having lost the possibility of purity and ideal, what remains is a ferocious way by which

> man seeks to know the secret of his humanity through excess, on a behavioral scale that denies all norms. Here, it is no longer a question of analysis (as in *Macarius*), but of facts, events and feelings brought to a maximum of moral tension, bordering on cruelty, perversion and crime, which test our diabolical possibilities. (16)

The probable contemplation of the young student of the morbid scenes narrated in *A Night in the Tavern* can thus function as an initiation process in experiences of a licentious life. Macarius has before him the example of the mad heroes in *A Night in the Tavern*, and may then anticipate the future which his incursion into pessimism has destined for him.

The assumption that the Azevedian novel maintains a bond of continuity with *Macarius* becomes even more plausible when one considers the poetic system of Álvares de Azevedo. There, the cross-references recur, either intertextually or even as self-parody. Thus, whilst his poem 'Memory of death' dramatizes, in sublime key, the marginalization and social exclusion of the poet, 'The dying poet', in turn, ridicules the longing for literary glory. The sonnet 'I spent the night with her' critically dismantles the feeling of love and the aesthetic ideals of another poem of the same genre, 'Pale under the somber light'. In another intertextual dialogue between Álvares de Azevedo's works, Puff, the narrator of Macarius, is a character of his prose poem, 'Bohemians'.

In view of the differences between Álvares Azevedo's work and the literary renewal proposed by the nationalist movement of Brazilian Romanticism, and even though the demonic spiritual formation of young Macarius falls to Satan, with the purpose of guarding his conscience against faith in the Enlightenment and progress, there is still the question of to what extent *A Night in the Tavern* proposes alternatives to the art that discards the ideals of Penseroso. If the dialogue with literary nationalism points to its death, if Satan opens to Macarius the perspective of a world tinted with terror and debauchery, *A Night in the Tavern* can enact another conception of literature.

Álvares de Azevedo's gothic novel contains seven chapters. The first one, 'A night of the century', frames each of the five stories narrated by Solfieri, Bertram, Gennaro, Claudius Hermann e Johann respectively. In the procedure bequeathed by *Decameron* to the Gothic, the initial setting of Azevedo's novel brings forward the damned heroes as learned libertines, their dialogue being staged in a tavern. Most of them are artists, poets or painters. In the following chapters, each of them lends his name to designate the experiences that they narrate to one another. In the last one, 'Last kiss of love', the action returns to the tavern, establishing a drastic continuity with the past of one of the heroes and a tragic solution to the conflicts stylized along the text.

In the initial scene in the tavern, one of the guests asserts that beauty secretly told the women who were drunk and asleep there about the eyes of lust. In the heated debate that ensued, the defense of addiction and drunkenness as the ideal state of life marks the position of the author against rationalism. Collectively, the speech of the characters revolves around the belief in the immortality of the soul or in the conception that regards life as mere result of the random juxtaposition of molecules. While Bertram takes tobacco and wine as a metaphor for idealism or, in other words, as an image of the movement of the idea by the spirit, Solfieri, even though admitting the immortality of the soul as an ideal to be pursued, thinks that it has been allowed to be impregnated by mud and rot. Like Bertram, he also believes that nothing will come from illusions and that existence only makes sense in the libertine's fever, in drink and lust. Johann, in his turn, condemns religious dogmas, fanaticism and the worship of Catholic icons.

They have in common the assumption that the basis of all knowledge resides in the sensitive element and that in poetry, as in life, an attitude they call 'Epicurean', a doctrine to them, aimed simply at the cult of pleasure should prevail. Although differences undoubtedly exist regarding what they consider a genuine philosophical system, the five characters elect hedonism as the foundation of life and art. From the perspective of the libertines, it is from dissolute pleasure that must be extracted the material for poetic creation.

The location of the tavern in a region where cholera predominates sets up the gothic motif of the plague, making believable the gesture of storytelling. It also depicts the meeting of those young people imprecisely, universalizing it spatially, as this epidemic took hold, as we know, of much of the world in the nineteenth century. The episodes narrated by the mad heroes take place in Italy, Spain, London and France.

The most precise information about the period in which the story is set is provided in Bertram's tale. He reports a sinister episode of his lifetime, an old wandering poet unexpectedly enters the scene. Asked about his identity, the old man says that he participated in the Battle of Waterloo in his youth. The dialogue between the guests is thus situated in a period between Napoleon Bonaparte's defeat and the composition of the work, probably early in the 1850s. In each of the stories, time moves toward the present of the narration, oscillating between an idyllic distant past and the degradation of the heroes' moral and aesthetic conscience in the present of the narrative.

Despite this space-time variation, certain characteristics of the construction of the characters and their far-from-virtuous behavior are recurrent. Taking advantage of resources of the 'Gothic machinery', all the stories of the 'Azevedian' novel bring onto the stage virginal female figures, pure, pale and marmoreal, that showcase, to continue quoting Sandra Guardini Vasconcelos (*Dez Lições sobre o Romance Inglês* 117), the persecution of virtue, be it moral, social or aesthetic.

In the first story, Solfieri, in one of his wanderings through the Roman night, comes across a mysterious woman, seen as some sort of figure or terrifying image. His muse is embodied in a white form with tears rolling down her pale cheeks. Besides the attempt to compare the female figure to the marble stillness of a statue, another more direct association between this pale woman with a kind of tormented beauty refers to the dark aspect of her voice chanting a frantic cry and an insane moan. These factors contribute to allegorize the chant 'of withered flowers of death' (Azevedo II 95). A year having gone by during which he lost her whereabouts, Solfieri finds her in a church, in a half-open coffin. At this moment, his attraction for the false deceased reaches its climax. The possibility of her being dead, her amber pallor and again her seductive stillness exert such power over the hero that he violates the body. Solfieri then restores, through sex, life to that almost lifeless figure. After the death of his beloved, continuing the cult of sepulchral beauty, he orders a wax statue of the corpse. In a last attempt to bring near the woman's corpse and morbid art, his drinking partners, at the end of the narration, question the veracity of Solfieri's story, raising the possibility that she could be the product of his imagination.

The second narrative contains the biggest number of transgressive actions. After being initiated into the world of crime and debauchery by an Andalusian, Bertram gets into woman trafficking and kills a benefactor who had saved him from death. Victim of a shipwreck, the hero practices cannibalism to survive and kills the woman he loved, therefore becoming, one of the most infamous characters of the novel.

Described as an opportunist capable of tripping over dead bodies in order to get anything, Bertram blames his lasting moral degradation to the desecration of his youth by the Andalusian. He then becomes the lover of the wife of the commander who had rescued him from an attempted suicide by drowning. Similar to Solfieri's heroine, the sadness, melancholy and the pallor of Bertram's muse become the sources of inspiration and hope, leading him to produce verses that contain, according to him, the last drop of his own purity. Thus, in deciding to launch to sea the poetry inspired by this woman, he believes to have freed himself for good from a 'precious and clear essence which had not yet been polluted in the world' (II 109). Bertram's muse, like the cataleptic, also goes mad at the end, confirming his omens as a damned poet that his vicious behavior would drive him to suck the virtue of the women he loved, which would have favored his beloved's madness. In the same licentious passage, Gennaro, the apprentice of master painter Godofredo Walsh, settles in the latter's home. While he is living in his house, he becomes involved with Nauza and Laura, Walsh's wife and daughter respectively. In love with Nauza, Gennaro refuses to marry Laura and take responsibility for the paternity of her child. Desperate, Laura commits suicide. The loss of the daughter leads to the destruction of the sublime talent of his master. Bringing to a close his perfect artistic practice and career as a painter, Gennaro conjectures that, at the start, Walsh's marriage to Nauza would have been the result of 'an artistic love for that Roman beauty, as if made by the mold of ancient beauties' (II 120). Like the other female figures pure of soul with purity of soul, tainted by the villainy of their lovers, Gennaro's attraction for Nauza is also motivated by her morbid expression and resemblance to a statue of white pureness. Like her predecessors, she comes to a tragic end. It is also after all the vile acts of the protagonist that master Walsh develops a plastic style no longer sublime, but gloomy, in the painting of his dying daughter whispering in the ear of a lean Gennaro.

The story told by English millionaire, Claudius Hermann, is most stereotyped. His decision to kidnap the beautiful Duchess Eleonora resulted from the boredom of his debauched and luxurious life, dedicated to gambling and orgies. The poet Hermann hopes to save himself and poetry or, as he prefers, the chaste virgin from the 'dark mire of the tavern'. In his obsession, he drugs his beloved, thus planning to revel in the beauty provided by the stillness of the drugged duchess. Like the other women, the perdition of Eleonora lies in her divine form that embodies the image of a 'statue of passion in pallor, still gaze, thirsty lips' (II 140). Her sleepy state resembling a marble form exerts a strong attraction on Hermann, a form that denounces life only through her heaving chest, to her kidnapper's disappointment. In another example that evinces that debauchery can provide voluptuousness and aesthetic enjoyment, Eleonora's appeals to be released sound to Hermann, contrary to her intentions, as 'harmonies, because the harps of heaven only have harmonies, and the lip of a beautiful woman is a divine rose, and her heart is a heavenly harp' (140). Bored with his libertine life covered by an 'unclean mantle', the hero seeks to sentimentalize it through the purity of that beautiful *vision* whose divine light infused 'brightness to the spirit' and 'illuminated the forms'. The abduction of the Duchess culminates in her tragic death and that of her husband Maffio. This confirms, despite the original intentions of the narrator, that life based on violence and vice makes impossible the existence of a spiritually pure form.

In the last account, places, situations and characters vary, but the subject is the same, exploring the motif of the corruption of spiritual beauty. In Paris, Johann fights a duel with Arthur, a billiards colleague, and kills him. After the murder, he fumbles in the boy's pockets and finds a note that his girlfriend, Giorgia, had sent him, arranging the place and time for a meeting. Johann steals and wears Arthur's ring and heads for the meeting place. In the hotel room, darkness and fraud lead the girl to confuse her boyfriend with Johann and agree to have sex with him. On leaving the room, the protagonist meets up with Giorgia's brother, who had gone there to avenge her dishonor. In yet another duel, he kills the boy. Curious about the identity of the man, Johann shines a flashlight on his face, recognizing that he had killed his own brother and had therefore possessed his own sister. Until she becomes a victim of incest, Giorgia also was characterized as having typical pristine beauty.

The desecration of beauty thought of as perfect, down to the lowest level of moral degradation, had already been explored since the eighteenth century as a reaction against rationalism, providing the cult of sensibility and irrationalism. At the moment of the expansion of the existing social system, which placed life in perpetual transformation, the formal and aesthetic assumptions of neoclassicism, which governed the well-made, symmetrical and regular form and artistic didacticism, come to collapse. Holding to the themes of monstrosity, illegitimacy and disintegration (Edwards 11), the new concept of art fuses the grotesque and the sublime, the low and the high, breaking the tight limits of artistic genres, limits whose rationality is considered unsatisfactory to express the torments of sensitivity.

In this context, the assimilation by the artistic imaginary of the changes brought about by the transition from artisanal to industrial production, the expansion of the division of labor trigger the loss, by the traditional craftsman, of the control of the stages of production. Covering the themes of social and moral disintegration, the horror narrative can react to the process of alienation of life, which becomes assimilated in the works of art, by a sensibility that calls for the humanization of the machine, as in *Frankenstein* by Mary Shelley, and the objectification of the soul, as in the fantastic tales of Hoffmann. Next to this, the political instability generated by the long years of the French Revolution spread dissatisfaction of all kinds, causing discontent both in the declining nobility as well as in the rising bourgeoisie (Bosi 100). In this context, horror becomes an element inherent to a kind of art regarded as serious and first-rate, a concept that seeks to merge the beautiful and the horrible, the high and low, so as to, contrasting with the reification of life, cherish everything that reflects the soul (Carpeaux 1454–55). Together with spontaneity and sensitivity, contradiction rises to become the force that best reproduces what was meant as human nature.

In this context, the attraction exerted by marble statues derives, in general, from their quiescent state that allows for the exploration of contradiction in all its potential, in a conviction directed to represent beauty through the interruption of its perfection. As also seen in *Florentine Nights* (1836), by Heine (an author whom, next to George Byron and Alfred de Musset, Álvares de Azevedo profoundly admired) there is delight in the contemplation of the horribly sublime.This embodies a concept of beauty in shock with social contradictions or with the rigid dictates of moral and aesthetic convention, which are seen as obstacles to the exercise of a more spiritual life, embodied in that figure. In this morbid passion for sepulchral female figures, the contradiction in the image of the beautifully sublime contains within it both the horror that arouses disgust and the delight provided by the reflections that such an image triggers in the individual artistic consciousness.

The work of Johann Joachim Winckelmann, *Gedanken über die Nachahmung der griechischen Werke in der Malerei und Bildhauerkunst* (1755), provides the first impulses that present the concept of art not as an imitation of rhetorical and ethical principles, but rather as a record of the contemplation of paintings of an ancient tradition. From this perspective, the greatness of a work does not derive from a genuine incorporation and reproduction of the rules of convention. Winckelmann argues that Greek art endowed works of art with a sense of humanity and true character, thanks to the opportunities artists had to research and carefully observe nature.

From this visual learning process, the artists of ancient Greece managed to take art to a level above nature itself, generating in its inside a second type of nature of an intellectual kind, which would have left an ideal of human perfectibility imprinted in the work. Winckelmann pointed out that it is not a faithful and naive copy of ancient art. Rather, it is a restoration of a model based on Antiquity that offered a new kind of art to create the spirit of a new era. He thus proposed that the process of initiation into the fine arts observe the old as a path to the foundation of the work in creation. In other words, the observation of ideas presumably inscribed in Greek statues would engender a divine idea in the soul of its creator, who would then produce the ideal of a 'noble simplicity and quiet grandeur'.

In this sense, the nostalgic revival of the distant past of tradition allows one to build an ideal sphere, to be pursued individually. By emphasizing that the artist no longer imitates, but carefully watches the objects around him, thereby extracting images that synthetize ideas, Winckelmann takes the Greek marble statues as models of perfection in art. The quiet stillness of these models allows the artist to represent the spiritual spheres in their truest light. Their tranquil harmonious state lends itself to peacefully express the nobility of soul. Taking the example of the *Laocoön Group*, at the time believed to have been carved in the classical phase of Greek art, he argues that the concomitant representation of bodily pain and greatness of soul penetrates more deeply in the sensitivity, unlike the direct representation of suffering. If it were not interposed by the harmonic state of rest, the expression of pure pain would not manage to express ideas concerning the greatness of soul (Winckelmann 53–54).

From Winckelmann onwards, the analogy of the statue triggers two distinct and mutually complementary moments of the artistic apprehension of Antiquity. At first, it reveals the movement of artistic imagination, which observes the static framework, perfect and finished, of ancient art. It then favors the recycling of a traditional work from a second perspective, reworking it from the ideas it raises. The image of the statue becomes, in this case, an emblematic *locus* in which the ideals of artistic and human perfectibility are installed, its stillness being directly proportional to its intangibility. In other words, on viewing in the statue the perfection of what is known as the 'old spirit', the artistic consciousness extracts from that its own ideas about beauty and perfection, reconstructing it as an ideal to be pursued.

In Romantic aesthetic theory, the lessons of Winckelmann feed the quarrel between the ancients and the moderns. In the reformulation that Goethe undertakes in the tradition of the eternal feminine, the supreme beauty of Helen, in *Faust*, lends itself, as we know, to an effort to seize classical Antiquity in its authentic state. The Romantic female figure allegorizes the poetic idea of the author (Simmel 193–94). Its conception incorporates the debate between partisans of classicism and adepts of Romantic poetry, then called modern (Mazzari 547). In the third act of *Faust*, Helen, already set as belonging to the world of legends (Croce 51), refers to the moving historicity of literary forms and genres. Highlighting the temporal distance between his time and previous periods, Goethe draws up the shapes and images of the Greek world in the absolute limits of his time. Without the historical consciousness, the recovery of Greece in the eighteenth century is but a naive shift, which ignores that the resumption of the past takes place merely as fragments of ruins.

Similarly, the heroines of Álvares de Azevedo, virgins or not, are endowed with beauty, simple innocence and immaculate purity, as well as sharing Christian virtues and patriarchal values, such as the extreme generosity shown to their villainous lovers. In his work, the marbled female ideal awakens in the artist's consciousness the 'intrusive idea' of a 'black premonition' (Azevedo II 207). The tormented virgin tragically enchants Álvares de Azevedo's poetry to be worshiped as an 'old statue in a ducal garden' (II 203). Most female figures in *A Night in the Tavern* are molded as the ancient beauties and repeatedly embody a kind of harmonious and uplifting art on the way to corruption. They continually use the intangibility of classical beauty as a metaphor for the process of becoming sepulchral, morbid and sinister. The claim of the historicity of genres, purpose and function of art leads the author to limit to an ancient finished time the didactic purpose and assumptions of beautiful, perfect and symmetrical art, in vogue in the artistic practices of many Brazilian poets, especially those clustered in the literary circle of D. Pedro II, as was Gonçalves Dias. The violation of the virtuous beauties in the Azevedian novel, allegories of this conception of art, stages its ruin.

Throughout Álvares de Azevedo's work, the discussion about the end of artistic didacticism recurs. In one of his literary critical articles, 'On disbelief in Byron, Shelley, Voltaire, Musset', the author tries to relativize the judgment that the work of George Byron was immoral. For him, as poets should convey the feeling of their time, Byron's works mirrored the upheavals of an era, as well as the clash of ideas, aspirations and theories that were at odds in a Europe 'still warm with blood from the revolutions' (II 314). Under these conditions, it was natural for Azevedo for the Byronic work to stage the end of religion as an ideological system of organization of human relations:

> Byron's poems are the mirror of that time. When an entire philosophy was establishing the axiom of skepticism, and when the population slept God-forsaken on the empty tombs of their kings - when the cross crackled on the frontispiece of the cathedrals, and the pale and eburnean forehead of crucifixes shattered on the slabs of the profaned temple - it was no wonder that poetry would come to sing the chants of belief on the corpse of religion. (II 315)

In the preface to his poem in prose, *Count Lopo*, Azevedo reacts to the permanence of the poet's role as a disseminating agent of the holy, the just, the beautiful and the preservation of the didactic purpose in art. Again quoting Byron, Goethe and Victor Hugo, the author of *Macarius* says that in their work the presentation of scenarios against morality does not make them less beautiful. Romantically defending that poetry is beauty, art, for him, should have freed itself from its edifying end. In his view, the criteria of assessment of artistic works are not found in the moral message of its themes. The poet's mission would instead be to draw the apostolate of beauty:

> The immoral can be beautiful—The naked visions of Michelangelo's last judgment—*Antony, Angela, Theresa,* ultimately almost all drama and almost all the works of Alexandre Dumas are immoral.—Who would, however, deny glories and laurels to that poet's soul? who would not find beautiful these pages of the king novelist of the century. (I 419)

With the same purpose of questioning the preservation of literary didacticism, in his article 'George Sand. Aldo the rhymer', Azevedo admires the alleged boldness with which she would have questioned the established order, mocking the 'formulae of property, in that ardent theory of hers, balanced between socialism and communism' (II 250–51). In one passage, the author thus justifies the break-up with moral carried out by the French writer:

> I am not, however, one of those who shudder at the resourcefulness of Sand—Tartuffe who virtuously hides his face in his hands before the treasures of beauty. Poetry is beauty—provided the poet does not wallow in the mire of obscenity, as long as the subject matter does not desecrate in filthy hands, even though its inspiration be the *metaphysics of matter* which flows from Don Juan and Lélia:—what does it matter? (II 256)

A Night in the Tavern enacts the widespread dissemination of corruption, projecting, as is customary in the Gothic, an atmosphere of fear. There is the predominance of moral disorder and the free flow of will by social praxis. The staging of the disintegration of stable and fixed customs and values coincides with the process of urbanization in Brazil, when, in 1850, the prohibition of the slave trade already helped the national capital be invested in the development of the country's infrastructure. Alongside the beginning of this process, the decade saw the consolidation of a slave-based monarchy as the political and economic regime of the country. At that moment, the liberal opposition and the conservative government move toward sealing a pact of alternating power, which, ensuring the stability of the imperial government for over 30 years, ended the riots that had sprung up across the country since its independence. In his 'Speech delivered at the inaugural session of the Academic Society—Philosophical Essay, May 9,

1850' (II 416–17) and in his poem *Rex Lugebit*, Azevedo reacts against the preservation of the monarchy in Brazil, accusing the imperial government of denying Brazilian nationalism and pursuing a despotic political practice.

Distinct from one of the trends of the nineteenth-century Gothic novel, *A Night in the Tavern* does not seek to correct vices or reward virtue. It figures the process of emergence of a world in which traditional values, customs and habits collapsed. The story of Claudius Hermann dramatizes, in the kidnapping and rape of the Duchess, the disintegration of the nobility as the ruling class. The rape of the wife and daughter of Godofredo Walsh challenges and shakes patriarchal power to preserve domestic security. The various tragic love stories, the incest and violence amongst siblings, put into question the existence of the traditional family. In the permanent play between limit and transgression, the Azevedian novel demonstrates, painlessly but emphatically, the shock suffered by fixed and eternal axiological systems. But it is with amazement that it notes the moral vacuum brought about by the growth of the system of accumulation and production of commodities, diagnosing the absence of a new code of ethics to replace the old one and regulate the action of individuals and social praxis.

In *A Night at the Tavern*, the stylizing of the social fabric as degrading and morally vicious develops from a cynical perspective in which the violation of moral values by different narrators is justified by the reigning general lack of ethics. The reasons that would usually generate aversion (the sexual act with the cataleptic, Bertram's first involuntary incursion into the world of crime, the murder by suffocation of his demented muse, the kidnapping and rape suffered by the Duchess, the fratricide committed by Johann and even the silent cynicism of Gennaro, who neglects the respect for his master and daughter in favor of his attraction to Nauza, and still the incest committed by Johann) all gets diluted in the ethics of a destiny where fatality would prevail.

However, the main factor that operates the emptying of moral sense in a fatally tragic destiny, unifying all the stories in the same view of the world, lies in the impossibility of carrying out a kind of virtuous and noble art, the development of which in an ideal art form clashes with that very fate. The impossibility of entering high artistic spheres crosses the utterances of all the speeches of the narrators who shape the passage of time in their lives linearly, in three stages. The timeline of the heroes' individual lives is divided in three stages that correspond to the literary phases in the lives of those individuals. Thus, to youth corresponds a kind of poetry that is characterized by joy, spontaneity and naiveté. The second stage of the individual occurs during the dusk of youth, when he begins to lose faith and hope in the course of life and starts feeling sorry for the loss of the golden age, beliefs and illusions. This elegiac stage evolves into the macabre context of the stories that every hero narrates. This phase, in turn, expresses a vision of the world that takes the inversion of moral values as the only attitude by an individual who no longer believes in the capacity of rational faculties making feasible a utopian human world.

Together, the heroes of *Macarius* and *A Night in the Tavern* make up a temporal *continuum* relative to the stages of slow moral, intellectual and aesthetic development of artistic awareness from youth, through maturity to old age, a linearity that heads for decline: if Penseroso symbolizes the end of utopia, Macarius finds a stage between doubt and pessimism. In turn, the heroes of *A Night in the Tavern* are situated between the skeptical maturity and vagrancy of the anonymous old man, Napoleon's former soldier. This dwindling linearity links the illusions of the past to the hopelessness of the present, staging the process of decrepitude of the moral, intellectual and artistic consciousness of mankind.

Thus, in the initial dialogue of *A Night in the Tavern*, one of the guests proposes a toast 'on behalf of all the reminiscences', all the false dreams, all the faded hopes. The abrupt entrance of the old poet in the tavern during Bertram's speech represents the conception of the expansion of time in the lives of all those middle-aged individuals who are the storytellers of the tales. Contrived as a counterpoint that praises youth, the construction of the old poet gains mythical contours, allegorizing a conception that brings together the various stages of life and distinct types of art. While the various narrators of the various stories are at the beginning of the process of maturing in life, around 40 years of age, the mysterious old man, described as wearing garments that bring him close to mendicancy, having served as a soldier for Napoleon, would have been primarily 'a poet at twenty, a libertine at thirty and a vagrant at forty' (II 113).

Of his pilgrimage around the world there remained the memories of a tragic love that ended with the death of his beloved in his arms on the first night of their love. After disillusion, the memories of this love tragedy became sources of 'the poet's agonies', then becoming the emblematic 'withered rose' that preserves the spirit of the beloved woman, just as the wreath of withered flowers Solfieri brings round his neck allegorizes a past whose memories serve as material for his account. The moment just before the scene of cannibalism, Bertram, in turn, stops the narration not only to increase the intensity of the suspense that is about to be narrated, but also to shape a conception of the experience that seeks to justify the anthropophagic gesture by the progressive decline of belief:

> What is existence? In youth it is the kaleidoscope of illusions: one then lives off the sap of the future. We age: when we get to thirty, and the sweat of agonies has grayed our hair before its time, and our hopes have withered like our faces, we oscillate between the visionary past, and this *tomorrow* of the old, cold and desolate—naked as a corpse bathing before going to the grave! (II 112)

In *A Night in the Tavern*, the author's repeated efforts to ennoble a subject that in its time was seen as comic makes use in a unique way of certain formal procedures and philosophical principles of the sublime style, which, as we know, helped to stabilize the form of gothic romance.

The sources that contributed to its formation are, according to David Punter (1991), respectively motifs and themes typical of sentimental novels and the debate surrounding the Treaty of Pseudo-Longinus, *Peri Hypsous*. As from the work of Edmund Burke (*A Philosophical Inquiry into the Origin of Our Ideas of the Sublime and Beautiful*, 1756), followed by Kant (*Kritik der Urteilskraft*, 1790) and Friedrich Schiller (Über das Erhabene, 1792), the ugly, horror and formal irregularity consolidate the autonomy of sublime beauty that, sharing space with the beautiful, gains its own autonomy.

In *A Night in the Tavern*, the sublime is understood as a mixture of pleasure and pain, low and high, idyllic, elegiac and tragic, poetic and prosaic, it embodies a pessimistic view of the world, for which the only way out for art is found in horror. Shaping his materials as tragically sublime, Azevedo exposes the contemporary history of humanity and art as absurd, an excess difficult to grasp. Throughout the novel, the expansion of individual time is a resource that allows the fusion of styles and genres in order to make the idyll of youth transmute into the loss of spontaneity and naiveté during maturity, which is then caught in the nostalgic lament of the loss of that time. The passage from youth to middle age evolves, in turn, into old age, in growing disillusionment, triggering the replacement of elegiac nostalgia for the horror narrative. Thus, the entry of the old-beggar-poet in the story is not fortuitous, but emblematic of the fall of art toward an aging humanity in which material, aesthetic, spiritual and moral decadence prevails. This fall, symbolized by the old poet, suggestively draws a parallel between him and the heroes, the art lovers[4]. In this collapse, the old man tends to illustrate that the incursion in the experience of the degraded world leads to the rise in literary history of a fictional prose of a macabre kind. Inverting the order of values, Azevedian heroes expect, in a cry of perverse revolt, to extract from the damned past, from transgression, corruption, suffering and death, the ideal model of tormented beauty.

In the last chapter of *A Night in the Tavern*, the violation of Giorgia unfolds into the final scene when she enters the tavern to take revenge and murder her brother before killing herself. His reappearance at that time has a double function, as on the one hand it allows the connection of his damned past with his present actions. On the other hand, Giorgia's transmutation allows the order of events to be reversed. As it is she who violates her assailant, her transformation from virgin into fatal woman, a kind of powerfully vengeful prostitute, confirms the end of the morally virtuous world and art. In a doubly vicious circle, this change works both as a reaction against the degradation of life and art, as, in a reverse movement, the triggering factor of that very degradation. By unifying the past of her memories with the present of enunciation, Giorgia becomes representative of all the beautiful stained virgins, exposing definitively the impossibility of accessing a utopian social and artistic reality. The final scene perpetuates debauchery and violence, reaffirming the fall of poetry and poets.

Finally, resuming Antonio Candido's argument that Satan's invitation to Macarius to watch an orgy refers to the macabre universe of *A Night in the Tavern*, shaped as an alternative to life and art, this alternative condenses proposals and ideas all of which are opposite to those of Penseroso. His faith in national progress, modeling a literature of an uplifting kind, disappears before a degrading world. The author's irony regarding the ideals of Macarius' friend springs from the purpose of avoiding any reference to the landscape and local customs of the country. The main answer in *A Night in the Tavern* to Penseroso's enthusiasm with the national sources of literature is both the absolute silence concerning this matter, as well as the systematic return to names and works from the European tradition.

The appropriation of sources of that tradition, by *A Night in the Tavern*, ranges from countries of that continent, to characters, motifs and even episodes of some of its works. In *Macarius*, Italy is put against insipid São Paulo, while in that novel the characters inhabit countries outside Brazil. With the purpose of prioritizing works of the Western tradition as sources for his creation, Azevedo names the narrator in the third person in *A Night in the Tavern* as *Jó Sterne*. The first name of the narrator, Jó, refers to the Old Testament patriarch, a generous and God-fearing soul. In the story, as we know, the Devil, with God's consent, puts him to numerous and severe tests, without, however, being able to shake his gullible resignation. The narrator's surname, *Sterne*, may be an allusion to Laurence Sterne, whose ironic, digressive and fragmented style has been highly appreciated by the Romantics. Thus, to construct a narrative consciousness shaped by the fusion of Jó's resigned belief with Sterne's ironic spirit, Azevedo pre-determines the guidelines of *A Night in the Tavern*, indicating that his subject will be restricted to the confrontation between two antagonistic artistic consciousnesses, one passive and believing, the other cynical and wicked. Emphasizing the use of narrators who allude to the European tradition, the names of the heroes in *A Night in the Tavern* were taken, in their majority from works of that tradition. Gennaro and Maffio are characters from the novel by Victor Hugo, *Lucrezia Borgia*; Bertram, from Byron's *Marino Faliero*. In addition to naming a character after Schiller's *Die Räuber*, Hermann baptizes figures from Byron, in *Manfred* and *The Deformed Transformed*.

In *A Night in the Tavern*, not only are the names of the characters but also certain scenes from traditional European works programmatically reused. The theme of so many gothic novels, the scene of the theft of the cataleptic body may have been borrowed from *Dreary Nights*, dated 1771, by José Cadalso, published in Brazil by Francisco Bernardino Ribeiro in 1844, in the journal *Minerva Brasiliense*.[5] The scene of cannibalism Azevedo borrowed from *Don Juan*, by Byron. From another book by this author, the episode in which Bertram commits adultery with Ângela after his return to Spain is analogous to that of *Beppo*, in which the protagonist finds, after a long journey, his beloved one married. Not to mention the stylization of incest between siblings, a practice that feeds legends about Byron's life. Another legend about this author is that he had the habit of organizing parties in which skulls were worshiped, alluded to in the poet's skull that the old wanderer carries.

By decreeing the end of the idyllic past and, in the same gesture, directing the narrative to the retrieval of Western tradition, *A Night in the Tavern*, again, shows its opposition to the Indianists. The Indianists honored the retroactive invention of nationality based on the past of indigenous culture, assuming, therefore, the foundation of a tradition that would already be in germination. According to Álvares de Azevedo, the past is seen as inexpressible, distant and mythological, which leads him to define, in his study 'Literature and civilization in Portugal', the foundation of Brazilian literature as an ongoing initial process, directing its Independence toward the present and the future.

Notes

1. In a footnote inserted in the *Complete Works* of Álvares de Azevedo (1942), the organizer, Homero Pires, lists the following narratives inspired by *A Night in the Tavern*: *A Night at the Cemetery*, tale by João Antônio Barros Júnior; *Dalmo, or Mystery of the Night* by Luís Ramos Figueira; *Fantastic Tale* by Rodrigo Octavio de Oliveira Meneses; *Ruins of Glory* by Fagundes Varela; *Gennesco* by Theodomiro Alves Pereira; *Damned Trinity* by Franklin Távora; *Misery, Fantastic Tales* by Altamiro Requião 'Even Machado de Assis wrote his fantastic tale—'The Country of the Chimeras'' (Pires 87–88).
2. About the acclimatization of Byronism in Brazil, see Barboza 1987.
3. Name of a street in São Paulo.
4. Throughout the nineteenth century, Herder's concept, according to which the normal development of the individual and of the history of a people and their literature follows an organic evolution, was put to test in evaluating the output of a poet. In Hegel's aesthetic system, the talent of a genius only acquires its best shape at maturity, when the writer begins to produce a more philosophical prose. Even if geniality blooms in youth, his ideal phase is in maturity, when he has suffered much experience and has endured all the feelings and emotions, thus achieving a balance between fantasy and reflection (1991, 303–304).
5. The point of convergence between *A Night in the Tavern* and *Dreary Nights* was analyzed in Brito Boca (1979).

Bibliography

Azevedo, Álvares de. *Obras Completas*. V. I e II. Org. Homero Pires. São Paulo: Cia. Editora Nacional, 1942.

Barboza, Onédia Célia de Carvalho. *Byron no Brasil, Traduções*. São Paulo: Ática, 1974.

Bosi, Alfredo. *História concisa da literatura brasileira*. São Paulo: Cultrix.

Broca, Brito. *Românticos, Pré-românticos, Ultra-românticos. Vida Literária e Romantismo no Brasil*. São Paulo: Livraria e Editora Polis/Instituto Nacional do Livro, 1979.

Candido, Antonio. 'A Educação pela Noite'. *A Educação pela Noite*. São Paulo: Ática, 1987, 10–22.

———. *Iniciação à Literatura Brasileira*. São Paulo: Humanitas. 1999.

———. *Literatura e Sociedade*. Rio de Janeiro: Ouro sobre Azul, 2006.

Carpeaux, Otto Maria. *História da Literatura Ocidental*. Rio de Janeiro: O Cruzeiro, v. I, 1961.

Croce, Benedetto. *Goethe. Primeira Parte*. Trad. de Manlio Lugaresi. Mendoza: D'Accurzio Editor, 1951.

Edwards, Justin. D. Introduction. *Technologies of the Gothic in Literature and Culture: Technogothics*. Ed. Edwards, Justin D. New York: Routledge, 2015. 1–17.

Hartmann, Pierre. *Du Sublime (de Boileau à Schiller)*. Estrasburgo: Presses Universitaires de Estrasburgo, 1997.

Hegel. *Estética. A Ideia e o Ideal*. Col. *Os Pensadores*. Trad. Orlando Vitorino. São Paulo: Nova Cultural, 1991.

Herder, Johann Gottfried. *Philosophical Writings*. Edited by Desmond M. Clarke and Michael N. Forster. Cambridge: Cambridge University Press, 1991.

Kant. *Crítica da Faculdade do Juízo*. Trad. Valério Rohden e Antônio Marques. Rio de Janeiro: Forense Universitária, 1993.

Magalhães, Couto de. 'Fundação da Academia—Trabalhos da Mocidade—Associações—Jornais', in: *Textos que Interessam à História do Romantismo. Textos da Época Romântica*. Org. Aderaldo Castelo. São Paulo: Imprensa Oficial do Estado, 1963.

Mazzari, Marcus. Comentário ao terceiro ato, 'Diante do Palácio de Menelau e Esparta'. Goethe. *Fausto, uma Tragédia*. Trad. Jenny Klabin Segall. São Paulo: Editora 34, 2007.

Pires, Homero. Nota 1 a *Noite na taverna*, in: Azevedo, Álvares de. *Obras Completas*. V. II. Org. Homero Pires. São Paulo: Cia. Editora Nacional, 1942, 87.

Punter, David. *The Literature of Terror: A History of Gothic Fictions*. London: Longman, 1991.

Schiller. *Do Sublime ao Trágico*. Trad. Pedro Sussekind e Vladimir Vieira. São Paulo: Autêntica, 2011.

Simmel, Georg. *Goethe*. Buenos Aires: Editorial Nova, 1949.

——— "The Metropolis and Mental Life" (1903) in Gary Bridge and Sophie Watson, eds. *The Blackwell City Reader*. Oxford: Wiley-Blackwell, 2002. 183–201. Print.

Soares, Macedo. 'Ensaios de análise crítica IV. José Alexandrino Teixeira de Melo. *Sombras e Sonhos*', in: *Textos que Interessam à História do Romantismo. Textos da Época Romântica*. Org. Aderaldo Castelo. São Paulo: Imprensa Oficial do Estado, 1963.

Vasconcelos, Sandra Guardini. *Dez Lições sobre o Romance Inglês*. São Paulo: Boitempo Editorial, 2002.

———. *Formação do Romance Brasileiro (1808–1860). Vertentes Inglesas*. Web. 22 dez. 2014. http://www.unicamp.br/iel/memoria/Ensaios/Sandra/sandra.htm.

Winckelmann, Johann. *Reflexões sobre a Arte Antiga*. Trad. Gerd Bornheim. Porto Alegre: Movimento/ URGS, 1975.

13 Tropical Gothic

José de Alencar and the Foundation of the Brazilian Novel

Sandra Guardini Vasconcelos

For around two decades, journalist, lawyer, politician and novelist José de Alencar (1829–1877) was possibly Brazil's most prominent man of letters and was to become, together with Machado de Assis, one of the founding fathers of the Brazilian novel. When he died in 1877, he left behind an impressive collection of 18 novels, which in a famous essay entitled 'Bênção Paterna' (Fatherly Blessing) (1872) he claimed to have written as part of a project of mapping out different regions of the country and covering three different phases of its history. The primitive one foregrounded indigenous legends and myths of the savage and conquered land; the historical one represented the union of the Portuguese invader with the native land culminating in its political independence; and the third one, which he described as the infancy of our literature, corresponded to the nation's independent state in progress in his own time.

Traditionally celebrated by Brazilian critics as the novelist *par excellence* of national identity, an assessment this particular essay helped construct, José de Alencar would seem to have drawn a sunny picture of the new Brazilian nation when he created what has been interpreted as a foundational myth. It was forged in the union of the Portuguese colonizer and the indigenous population and grounded in the idea of reconciliation, as suggested in the denouement of his novels *O Guarani* (1857) and *Iracema* (1865).[1] A more careful examination of his work, however, cannot fail to notice the more somber or violent aspects of the process of formation of Brazilian identity, even if, not infrequently, they were relegated to the margins rather than foregrounded in his novels. Roberto Schwarz was the first Brazilian critic to call attention to the edges or peripheral aspects of Alencar's novels and to highlight the tensions present in his work. While before Schwarz other critics had tended to privilege Alencar's role and engagement in nation and identity building as a harmonious process, devoid of contradictions, a critique of this view has of late brought forth a much more problematized reading of his work. Likewise, the appropriation of the novel genre by different national projects, which has enabled Franco Moretti to describe this literary form as 'the symbolic form of the nation-state' (20) or has prompted Doris Sommer to read the nineteenth-century Latin-American novels as foundational fictions blending love stories, and the allegorical construction of nation[2] should not blind us to the complications deriving from the process of its acclimatization in non-European soil. As we know, 'this most European of forms' (Moretti 186) crossed over national borders, adapting itself to local conditions and projects, transgressing limits and opening itself to new contents and experiences.

With the transplantation of the Portuguese court and government to Brazil in 1808 and the country's independence in 1822, Rio de Janeiro changed from a modest and sleepy colonial town into the capital of an empire. It became a destination for countless books, particularly novels, which the prohibition of free trade and censorship had practically prevented from reaching its shores in colonial times.[3] At least since the 1820s British novels began to appear regularly in the pages of the two most important nineteenth-century local newspapers, *Jornal do Commercio* and *Diario do Rio de Janeiro*, in the advertisements published by the booksellers and bookshops that had increasingly come to establish their businesses in the capital of the Brazilian Empire. A more careful examination cannot fail to note the profusion of titles and the availability among them of the Gothic novels responsible for the great popularity of their authors on the other side of the Atlantic just a few years earlier. The continuous advertisement of these novels in the two periodicals and their presence in the catalogues and collections of the circulating libraries, which also gradually came to be part of the landscape and cultural facilities in Rio de Janeiro and elsewhere, evince the Brazilian reading public's lasting interest in the adventures and tribulations of characters involved in plots of mystery, suspense, revenge, despotic power, tyranny and horror. It is in these newspapers that we find the first references to the availability in Rio of works by prominent Gothic writers like Ann Radcliffe (*Diario do Rio de Janeiro*, June 8, 1825), a certain Lewis[4] (*Jornal do Commercio*, January 5, 1828) and Horace Walpole (as William Marshall) (*O Castello de Otranto*, *Diario do Rio de Janeiro*, December 4, 1854). We also find advertisements announcing *The Children of the Abbey* (*Amanda e Oscar, ou Historia da Familia de Deureath* [sic], *Diario do Rio de Janeiro*, December 16, 1824), *Saint Clair of the Isles* (*Saint Clair das Ilhas, ou os Desterrados na Ilha de Barra*, *Diario do Rio de Janeiro*, February 23, 1825)[5] [in Portuguese translations]. Therefore, from Walpole's aristocratic, playful *The Castle of Otranto* through Radcliffe and Walter Scott to William Harrison Ainsworth, Bulwer Lytton and George Reynolds, there was a rich and suggestive repertoire of Gothic themes, environments, trappings and characters to entertain readers and inspire Brazilian writers.

If this literature of self-analysis emerged in Britain 'when the bourgeoisie (…) began to try to understand the conditions and history of their own ascent' (Punter, *Literature of Terror* 112), one should inquire what contributions it may have made to the formation of the Brazilian novel. One might also ask how local contents fit into this European form, considering the significant differences between the Brazilian and the British socio-historical processes. Having recently emerged from its colonial status, Brazil was yet to face the problems posed by the effects of industrialization and urbanization, which had contributed in Britain to the dissolution of ancient community ties, the migration from countryside to city and the rise of a new urban culture. As we know, all of these experiences would become even more central to the British throughout the nineteenth century.

In the case of Brazil, where foreign novels—especially British and French—had prestige and currency, it is worth examining the consequences of the appropriation of Gothic elements by this founder of the Brazilian novel, who inspired by his readings as a youth borrowed from foreign models to produce an *oeuvre* that explores and scrutinizes Brazilian identity. In his well-known memoir, published a few years before his death, Alencar settles accounts with his own formative years and heritage, bearing witness to the major novels and novelists that had played a prominent role for him as a writer. There, among the novelistic matrices he claims helped shape his fiction, he recalls how Regina Maria Roche's *The Children of the Abbey* (1796) and Elizabeth Helme's *Saint Clair of the Isles* (1803)[6] made a powerful impression on him. He confesses that one of the novelistic molds that had been an inspiration to him was '(...) melancholy, full of mystery and dread (...). In it, the scene opens onto the ruins of a castle, enshrouded by the pale moonlight; or some Gothic chapel dimly lit by a lamp, its light reflecting on the slate of a tombstone' (Alencar, '*Como e Porque sou Romancista*' 136).[7]

If the suggestions of the Gothic novel did not become a predominant feature in his literary production, it is not impossible to find traces of its presence in his work, as is the case of his so-called regional novels. In this essay, I examine two of them, *O Tronco do Ipê* (1871) and *Til* (1872) and make brief comments about *O Guarani* (1857) and *As Minas de Prata* (1865–66), in order to interrogate the meanings of this appropriation. It may sound nonsensical to suggest the existence of a Brazilian Gothic, in a context so alien to, and distant from, the Gothic's original location. However, over the past 200 years this literary mode has been continuously present in literary and cultural history, having taken on a plurality of meanings and encompassed a variety of manifestations in the fields of narrative, art, architecture and film. It has also traveled through space and become globalized, expanding its horizons in many different ways.[8] No matter how and when it has been used, however, the term has always been associated with paranoia, barbarism and taboo and with the questioning of the notion of what is 'real', while incorporating other modalities and genres to inquire into the meaning of 'truth'.[9]

In spite of this continuous history, Gothic was a literary form that rose and was rooted in a very specific time and place—late eighteenth- and early nineteenth-century Britain. What it has come to signify is, to a great extent, the result of a critical construct that encompasses a wealth of pathways and solutions that are far from constituting a 'movement' or a deliberate adherence to a unified genre. This is the case even though in its rise some of its first practitioners dedicated themselves to examining it or explaining it away. One can read about these efforts in, for example, Horace Walpole's two prefaces to his *The Castle of Otranto*, in Ann Radcliffe's posthumous article for the *New Monthly Magazine* (Duncan, *Modern Romance* 261) and in Sir Walter Scott's 'Essay on Romance'.[10] Heterogeneous and unstable, *Gothic romance*, having developed as the other face of the bright and rational world of the Enlightenment, ended up by consolidating itself in Chris Baldick's description 'as the name for one sinister corner of the modern western imagination' (quot. in Watt 2) and by constituting 'the culture of Gothic' (Duncan 20). Since its initial manifestation, it purported to be a hybrid genre, a mixture of the ancient and the new (as in Walpole), of the subjective and the objective, realism and unrealism, rationality and imagination, history and fiction.

Heterogeneity, however, did not prevent the establishment of some admittedly Gothic features, *topoi,* usually associated with this literary mode. This mode routinely brought to center stage the supernatural, a wronged hero or a virtuous heroine in distress and medieval settings (castles, abbeys, dungeons, ruins) to deal with a 'darkly imagined counter-world, embracing the less avowable regions of psyche, family and society' (Botting 12). In this border territory the various Gothic moments thrived, as the rise of the Gothic romance, at a time of important political, economic and social changes that witnessed the rise of the bourgeois and industrial society that would shape the modern world. Seen as a literature of excess, which was shaped as 'extravagant critique of Enlightenment reason' and 'political unconscious of a middle-class society' (Eagleton 19), the Gothic could flourish and expand in very different contexts, taking on specific forms like the *roman noir* and the *roman frénétique* in France or the *Schauerroman* in Germany. Likewise, it crossed other borders and seas, acclimatizing in the United States with Edgar Allan Poe and Nathaniel Hawthorne, or landing in Brazilian soil, even before the Brazilian novel had been consolidated. From a *fin-de-siècle* England there arrived echoes of this fictional mode, which thematizes the terrifying dreams that haunt humankind and that Maggie Kilgour defined as 'a nightmare vision of a modern world made up of detached individuals, which has dissolved into predatory and demonic relations that cannot be reconciled into a healthy social order' (Kilgour 12).

Deprived of any medieval ruins or a feudal past, and without relics and objects that contributed to the fame of the Gothic novel and were incorporated into its conventions, Brazilian settings would seem an improbable and implausible space to produce this type of fiction. However, Gothic motifs appear for the first time in Brazilian fiction in an anonymous short story published in four parts in *Jornal do Commercio* (February 23–27, 1839). '*A Ressurreição de Amor (Crônica Rio-grandense*' (The Resurrection of Love) borrows some of these conventions in an atmosphere in which mystery and horror predominate in order to narrate the story of its disturbed protagonist (Francisco), who profanes the tomb of his beloved only to find out that she is still alive, following the well-known traditions of the genre. In hyperbolic language, the narrator does not miss any opportunity to praise the natural beauties of his province, while he tells a story of horror and death. Taking advantage of long descriptions of scenery, the anonymous author tries to establish some causal relation between setting and plot. However, he produces a formal misfit between the Brazilian background and the narrative of love and death, in the fashion of European melodrama—a narrative of love frustrated by social differences between the aristocratic protagonist, brother of the governor, and a rich but plebeian young woman (Amália).

In another story, '*A Paixão dos Diamantes*' (Passion for Diamonds), by José Justiniano da Rocha (1812–1862), published in *Jornal do Commercio* (March 27–28, 1839), the Gothic is not an element of the plot or structure but of atmosphere, created by the sinister tone and gloomy setting, with its tombs and graveyard:

> It is rumoured that the following day a lunatic the gatekeeper had driven away appeared at the door of the president's death chamber; it is also rumoured that a few days later, in Geneva's graveyard, on the turf that covered Ana Guiot's tomb, a poorly dressed and emaciated young man was seen on his knees, holding onto the funereal cross; the following day, this young man, rather than holding the cross and kneeling down, was lying on the cold earth of the graveyard.[11]

In like manner, Francisco de Paula Brito (1809–1861) refused to characterize his protagonist Alzira as 'one of these physionomies that cause so much uproar in the novels that come to us from old Europe'.[12] He also dismissed Gothic suggestions in his preface to '*O Enjeitado*' (The Foundling) (*Jornal do Commercio*, May 28–29, 1839), in which he complains that 'the books which old Europe sends us are nothing but recollections of old ages' that 'favour us with nothing but Vandals, Goths and feudal feats'.[13] His disavowal should not deceive us into taking these words to the letter, though. 'O Enjeitado' is the narrative of the misfortunes of lovers Emília and Júlio, both haunted by the mysterious origins of the young man. A melodramatic plot, riddled with secrets, crimes, deaths, confinements and adulterous relationships, is acted out in a typical Brazilian setting, deploying a sugar cane plantation where hundreds of slaves labor under the ruthless whip of a sugar-mill master. In one of the characters, Captain Mendonça, and in the description of the rural manorial estate where the events unfold, we find a Brazilian version of the feudal lords and buildings that have become Gothic clichés. We can also recognize in the unhappy women in the narrative the shadow of the distressed characters of the sentimental-gothic novel, victimized by relentless persecutors or tyrants.

One could also mention the case of Álvares de Azevedo, whose *Noite na Taverna* (*Night at the Inn*), published posthumously in 1855, had Lord Byron and E.T.A. Hoffmann as model writers. In it we apprehend evident

Gothic elements, revealed in the taste for Satanism and the macabre, easily affiliated with the tradition started in England by Matthew Lewis, with his licentiousness, taste for the repulsive and refusal of the language of feeling. It was this demonic path that Álvares de Azevedo chose to tread, enabling us to situate *Noite na Taverna* as 'a bastard heir of the English Gothic, of Hoffmann's and the French *frénétiques*' gloomy works, with touches of Sade and of melodrama', not to mention Byron and the association of its hero with the Gothic villains (Oliveira 162–63). One recognizes in this use of several sources and suggestions what Robert Kiely has described as the characteristic feature of Romantic fiction, the 'patchwork method', which juxtaposes 'aesthetic aims, literary styles, narrative patterns, and themes of utterly different sorts' (3).

José de Alencar asserts that he also had his Byronic phase in the early years, by referring to a certain Byronizing vogue that made students want to copy or translate the English poet (Cavalcanti Proença, 'José de Alencar' 118).[14] It was in fact his 'honourable role as reader' of novels and romances to the women of his household during the domestic evening gatherings that he holds responsible for imprinting 'in [his] spirit the inclination towards this literary form which is, among all others, [his] favourite' (Alencar, 'Como e Porque Sou Romancista' 133). To the 'tiny Romantic library collected according to the taste of that time' (131), to which he had access as a boy, later he added French writers Balzac, Chateaubriand, Victor Hugo and Vigny, and Sir Walter Scott and Captain Frederick Marryat, whose sea novels and heroic combats are of particular interest for Alencar. This is Alencar almost at the end of his life, looking in retrospect at his literary career, his choices and favorite authors. The same names had already appeared much earlier in the polemic he got involved in, published under the title of '*Cartas sobre a Confederação dos Tamoios*' (1856) ('Letters about the Confederation of the Tamoios'), and containing the first systematic exposition of his aesthetic ideas and principles. The adoption and defense of the novel, in the place of the epic, as the ideal genre to deal with the Brazilian peculiarities soon materialized in his *O Guarani*, which came out around the same time and was first serialized in *Diario do Rio de Janeiro* and later published in a book in January 1857. '*Cartas*' can be read as a kind of program, which seems to announce the novelist he would soon become, since it defines some of the paths Alencar would later tread as well as his elective affinities, among which appears Scott, remembered as the English-language novelist capable of taking certain subjects and adding 'charm' and 'interest' to them (Alencar, '*Cartas*' 893). Nothing in '*Cartas*' allows us to anticipate the importance of the 'melancholy' mold, 'full of mystery and dread' (Alencar, '*Como e Porque sou Romancista*' 136), which Alencar would claim years later to have so strongly impressed him. Nor would it be possible, at first sight, to associate the founder of the historical novel, or Alencar himself, with the lineage of the Gothic writers or with Regina Maria Roche e Elizabeth Helme, whose novels had left their mark on his mind as an adolescent.

However, in the intricate network of interchanges, borrowings, appropriations and innovative contributions that has always characterized the history of the novel genre, one cannot simply draw lines and points of contact between Alencar's different British sources. One must also suggest that the common denominator among them all is *romance*, the literary mode the Gothic retrieved and returned to a position of visibility and pre-eminence in late eighteenth-century England and that will equally figure in Sir Walter Scott's *historical romances*. Scott read Ann Radcliffe, about whom he wrote the long and detailed introduction to Ballantyne's *Novelist's Library* in 1824, and was a friend of Charles Maturin's, whose first novel *Fatal Revenge* (1807) he reviewed for *The Quarterly Review* and with whom he kept a correspondence and exchanged ideas about the literary options of the Irish clergyman.[15] Victor Sage argues that, by advising his interlocutor 'to 'tone down' the characteristically hyperbolic development' of the Radcliffe romance, Scott was vocalizing his criticism of Maturin's Gothic, directly deriving from Radcliffe and Lewis, and already signaling the direction his 'own rationalised and modernised *historical romance*' (Sage 82) would take. I will return to Scott later.

In principle, there would seem to be no place for the conventional ornaments of the Gothic in a literary project made explicit retrospectively in Alencar's 'Bênção Paterna' (1872). It had aimed to narrate the history of the formation of the Brazilian people and nation in the Indianist and historical novels, to map out the regional areas, types and landscapes and to delineate the 'physiognomy of Rio society' in the urban novels. Yet, the predominantly luminous and sunny work[16] of the author of *O Guarani* is tinged by occasional shadows and incorporates some of the Gothic conventions, in an appropriation whose meaning one needs to interrogate. Thus, to the image of a Brazil that is apostrophized as 'child of the sun' (Alencar, 'Cartas' 869), whose process of identity and nation building seemed to have taken place without conflict, is added a more problematic and complex view of a society. The supposedly harmonious encounter of races conceals a history of violence, oppression and social trauma, aspects that canonical romance confronts and exposes at the center of its plots and that Alencar often displaces to the margins or fringes of his fiction.

There is an urge for reality in Alencar's novels. Undoubtedly, the aim to scrutinize the 'slow coming-into-being of the American people' and to 'take the photograph of this society' (Alencar, '*Bênção Paterna*' 697) would require the novelist not only to refer to the historical chronicle from which he took the historical facts and personages he intermingles with fictional elements.[17] He would have to also adhere to the truth content that would enable the reader to recognize his experience of the country and of Brazilian society in the narratives. Alencar's conception of the novel, nonetheless, is already emblematic of an ambiguity, or rather, of the coexistence of two narrative modes that lend his novelistic production a hybrid character. When Alencar defines the novel as 'the poem of real life' (Alencar, '*Como e Porque*' 139), he evinces the double orientation that presided over the organization of his plots, in which the historical and the fictional, the imaginary and the real intertwine almost programmatically. This was no different, though with variations, from the path trodden by Walter Scott, who also, according to an early article in *Blackwood's Edinburgh Magazine*, included the synthesis between history and romance so as to give 'the truth of history without its monotony—the interest of romance without its unreality' (Scott, 'The Historical Romance' 346).[18] Neither Scott nor Alencar, it would not be inappropriate to stress, invested in the potential the Gothic flaunted to escapism and evasion, sometimes attributed to its canonical form.

Where might we unveil the Gothic elements in Alencar's work? I have already suggested that it is always pushed to the margins of the narrative, which means to say it never plays a central role in the plot, nor does it help qualify the protagonists or define the predominant atmosphere in the stories. The recourse to romance is undeniable in a novel like *O Guarani*, which features a native hero endowed with an exceptional capacity for action placing him above common men. It is also prominent in *As Minas de Prata* (1865–1866), in which his fantastic imagination concocts a plot centered in a search that accumulates adventures at a frenetic and feuilleton-like pace. Yet, the historical chronicle and the objective of probing the origins of nationality delimit, so to speak, the excesses that one usually associates with the Gothic. In both cases, though marginal, the contribution of the Gothic can be apprehended in the characterization and action of two characters that incorporate features of well-known Gothic villains. One can easily suggest connections between the condottiere Loredano and his possible Gothic models, Schedoni, in *The Italian* by Ann Radcliffe, and Ambrosio, in *The Monk* by Matthew Lewis.[19]

Father Gusmão de Molina, in *As Minas de Prata*, is affiliated with the same tradition. The Spanish Jesuit, a man of 'deceitful appearance' (Alencar, *As Minas de Prata* 479) and black piercing eyes that reflect 'volcanic fire' (Alencar, *As Minas de Prata* 475), is responsible for the misfortunes of the young protagonist, Estácio Alves Correia, and for the machinations and villainies involving the search for the map to the silver mines. Through the meanderings of the plot, filled with feuilleton-like moves, looms the demonic presence of Father Molina, the inquisitor of the Holy Office in the city of Salvador and a man of surprising ruses and cunning. His unlimited greed and ambition can be traced back to Schedoni, who is also a man of the Inquisition and instrument of relentless persecution of Vivaldi, Radcliffe's protagonist. As in *The Italian*, secrets and disguises are crucial to the intrigue and help create a grim atmosphere that yields a much less positive and harmonious vision of the process of formation of the Brazilian nation than nineteenth-century literary and historical writings would intimate. Our past, Alencar suggests, now from the perspective of these foreign borrowings, also has its considerable share of fraud and violence.

Even if displaced in time and space and different in conception and scope, *O Tronco do Ipê* (1871) and *Til* (1872) incorporate conventionally Gothic features in their portrayals of the uses and customs of the rural world respectively in the coffee region in Rio de Janeiro and in the interior of São Paulo in the nineteenth century. Their realistic disposition, deriving from the drive to represent daily life and human relations on two large farms, mingles with some clichés taken from the Gothic machinery, mainly those that lead the reader to believe in the supernatural character of some events, to be explained away in due time. This recourse to the rational and late clarification of facts produces a certain retarding in the action, which is often suspended, deferring its resolution. In the interval between the event and the explanation, however, hovers the suggestion of a domestic environment tinged by something sinister that escapes the realm of reason. In this gap, there is room for all sorts of ravings, obsessions and monomanias. Here we are in the territory of the unfamiliar, of the grotesque, of unbridled passions.

Narrated in retrospect by an extra-diegetic narrator, when the farm of Nossa Senhora do Boqueirão is already all ruin and abandon, *O Tronco do Ipê* has its action situated between 1850 and 1857. It tells what is apparently a story of usurpation, having at its center the families of Joaquim de Freitas, the Baron of Espera, and of José Figueira, presumptive heir of the land, and already deceased. Their children, respectively Alice and Mário, are the protagonists of this narrative that tries to intertwine love and mystery and mobilizes some of the clichés of the English sentimental novel, of which Ann Radcliffe and Regina Maria Roche were tributaries, and of the Gothic novel, adapted to the local reality. Thus, whereas the different social position and fortune that separate Mário and Alice had been intrinsic to novel conventions since Samuel Richardson, some of the characteristic Gothic ornaments are acclimatized to the new environment in which they are inscribed. As we are in the interior of Brazil, distant from the modern facilities to which the dwellers of the imperial capital had access, there is room for local beliefs and superstitions the narrator is keen to verbalize. A haunted farm, stories of otherworldly beings, witchcraft, supernatural powers, voices, apparitions, a legion of ghosts and a slave who is believed to have a pact with the Devil (pai Benedito) are all elements that are part of the plot and will be demystified by rational explanations. They are called for, however, to create the atmosphere of mystery and dread that surrounds the episode of José Figueira's death in the mouth of the river that crosses the farm.

Until the real causes and circumstances of this accident are revealed, Mario's suspicion will hang on the Baron of Espera, and he will believe that his father has been the victim of usurpation and murder. Poor and destitute, Mário lives as a dependent on the farm and is a rebellious and misanthropic young man. Many reversals will be necessary before the truth comes to the surface and the narrative reaches a happy end. Until then, the reader experiences all the 'teasers', the suspense, the narrative cuts, the coincidences, the secrets, Gothic tricks that proliferate in this oddly structured novel. It has a mixture of sentimental novel and mystery, folk tale, Nativity play; it contains African dances and songs and comedy, the latter personified in the gluttonous and servile Senhor Domingos Paes, a man who lives on the Baron's patronage. This is a collage of genres, the 'patchwork method' to which Kiely refers (3). Above all, in this typically Brazilian environment, with characteristically Brazilian figures like dependents and slaves, we find the canonical European plot of troubled love between rich young woman and poor young man, separated by money and social class, and to whom the revelation of the truth will restore the possibility of a happy end.

On another farm (Fazenda das Palmas), this time on the margins of the Piracicaba River, the love story brings together twins Afonso and Linda, children of the landowner Luís Galvão, and Miguel and his stepsister Berta (also known as Inhá or Til, who entitles the novel), their counterpoints. Framed by the domestic and placid atmosphere that opens and closes the novel, the middle of the intrigue enacts an almost implausible series of calamitous and violent events that include a fire, burnt bodies, the attack of a herd of wild pigs, persecutions and chicanery. Everything is excessive in this novel: its characters fall prey to implacable hatred, superstitious terrors, hallucinations and all kinds of extravagances. Although the reader is made to believe this is a haunted place, there is nothing supernatural in the Fazenda das Palmas. If there are ghosts on the lookout, these are the ghosts of the past, which induce the actions of the men of the present. Thus, the love intrigue, so characteristic of, and central to, other novels by Alencar, is buried under a story of revenge, wherein the settling of accounts with the violation and murder of a woman (Besita, Berta's mother) moves Jão Fera, the Indian capable of terrible atrocities. The novel starts almost at the point of resolution, on the day Ribeiro, his wife's assassin, comes back under a different name and guise, in order to consummate his plan of revenge. By now, Berta is 15 years old and lives in the neighborhood of Luís Galvão's farm, not knowing her past is related to his. Alencar's countryside swarms with murderers, criminals and evildoers who lie in ambush, while identities and inheritances are not restored and family lineages are not clarified (Trumpener 111). The secret of Berta's birth, her recognition, the will that appears at the end, vague words, half-truths, are all Gothic clichés, which the plot explores to the limit. Maybe the most evident manifestation of its exaggerations is concentrated in its denouement. Berta chooses not to accompany her new family when they move to the capital, but decides instead, as a 'flower of charity, *alma soror*', 'to perfume the abysses of distress' and stay on the farm 'with the idiot, the lunatic and the redeemed criminal' (Alencar, *Til* 1010).

To the detriment of a deeper psychological probing of the characters, there is an emphasis on plot, which piles event on top of event. There is also a focus on narrative voice; it takes on the responsibility to explain, judge and evaluate and denies the characters the prerogative or opportunity to reveal their own truths to the reader. One can see here deeper deficiencies than those a Brazilian critic detected in another regional novel by Alencar (A. Meyer, '*Nota Preliminar*' 413). This might explain why *Til* has been considered to be an 'incredible collection of absurdities' (Pinheiro Chagas, quot. in Araripe Júnior, '*A Crítica*' 1328) or why still another critic has seen in it 'a display of monstrosities' and argued that the novel is converted into 'a kind of ward in a lunatic asylum' (Araripe Júnior, '*Nota Preliminar*' 815–16). In this sense, *Til* is very different from the rest of Alencar's novels as it places, always in very emphatic diction, the hellish, the low, and the grotesque above the elevated register and the poetic style for which he is famous.

One would need then to ask why, in these two regional novels, Alencar returned so insistently to the Gothic repertoire[20] to shape aspects of the 'large canvas of Brazilian life' (Cavalcanti Proença, '*Nota Preliminar*' 1015). These two novels do not properly belong to the Alencar canon and usually occupy a less prominent position in his *oeuvre*.[21] This is because they are situated in the interior of the country, in more backward zones in relation to the imperial capital, and thus they are novels that accommodate characters probably more susceptible to superstitions, beliefs, legends. The countryside is depicted as romance territory, peripheral and archaic, pervaded by spoliation and impregnated with raw violence. Distant from the world of the Court, with its own rules of etiquette, its patterns of sociability and prescribed behavior, the regions portrayed in *O Tronco do Ipê* and *Til* feature their share of savagery and rusticity, opening up room for a less controlled representation of the violent relations that regulated the ways of living in nineteenth-century Brazil. Alencar thus enacts before us a complete inversion, for instance, of Peri's and Estácio's medieval chivalrousness. He creates a degeneration of this ideal, according to one of his critics (Araripe Júnior, '*Nota Preliminar*' 816), while setting in motion the whole arsenal of Gothic *topoi*. He uses the tardy revelation of a central narrative mystery, the evocation of fear provoked by threats of violence or imprisonment, the use of the uncanny and the deferral of action to bring to the surface the demonic and infernal dimension of the constitution of Brazilian society.

Few scenes are as suggestive of the disjunctions and social tensions that constitute the Brazilian nation as the festivity on Saint John's day on Fazenda das Palmas and expose the differences and impasses of the social order. In three contiguous spaces, the 'good society' of those who have power and money coexists with old countryside customs and the slaves in the slave quarters. The quotation is long, but very revealing:

> The entertainment in the drawing room is for the townspeople. Ladies and gentlemen play games, sitting ceremoniously around a table; or they dance quadrilles and waltzes; while around the corners old farmers talk about carps, new coffee blossoms, and frosts, their permanent nightmare.
>
> In the yard, young men enjoy themselves who find more amusement in rural activities and, rather than consulting the fortune-teller

> book, trust the oracles of the bonfire, jumping over it and holding an egg over it, an egg that will be left in the dampness of the night at the fateful hour of midnight.
>
> (Alencar, *Til* 964)

> Around the bonfire, already crumbling to the ground covered with cinders and ashes, the blacks dance in a frenzy that borders on delirium. Their desperate wriggling and rocking cannot be described, or imagined, their whole body trembling, jumping, shaking, turning round, swinging, as if meaning to fall apart.
>
> Everything bounces, even the little niggers who kick on the scruff of their mothers' neck, or coil up in the young girls' skirts. The more corpulent turn somersaults and leap like toads around the yard. One of them cuts a jack-fruit on his father's back, a robust black man who not knowing any longer how to come apart threw himself on the ground and started to shake his tail like fish in the dry.
>
> In the frenzy provoked by the infernal frolic, some blacks rush violently against the bonfire and tap-dance on top of the blazing embers dropping from the fire remains.
>
> (Alencar, *Til* 975–76)

The contrast between the two groups could not be more evident. Inside, the well-behaved dances and conversations in the drawing room one could find in any nineteenth-century European novel seem to throw into sharper relief the blacks' uncontrolled and disorderly samba, outside of the house. The choice of vocabulary, as usual in Alencar, does not leave room for doubt. The bestial, the debased and the infernal are always the prerogative of foreigners (as is the case of Loredano and Molina, alluded to earlier) and of blacks and Indians, like Jão Fera.[22] They deviate from the high degree of idealization used to characterize the main characters, white in their overwhelming majority, and the ornate language chosen to describe and refer to them.

I could suggest, at this point, that Alencar's appropriation of some of the Gothic conventions owes much more to the Radcliffean paradigm, which, somehow, came to him indirectly through the novels 'full of mystery and dread' that he had read as a youth. Late in life the memory of those books would still be very vivid, and he records in his testimonial, dated May 1873:

> Our Romantic library was small; it was made up of a dozen works, among which stood out *Armanda* [sic] *e Oscar*, *Saint-Clair das Ilhas*, *Celestina* and others that I no longer remember. This scarcity, and the need to reread over and over the same novel have perhaps contributed to carve in my soul the casts of this literary structure that would later be useful to the formless sketches of the inexperienced writer.
>
> (Alencar, '*Como e Porque sou Romancista*' 134)

A bestseller in the 1790s, *The Children of the Abbey* remained in print throughout the nineteenth century and was translated from André Morellet's French version into Portuguese with the title *Amanda e Oscar, ou história da família de Dunreath*.[23] A standard Minerva Press novel,[24] it flaunted the typical combination of Gothic setting and sentimental plot, with its narrative of the tribulations and obstacles that separate lovers before they attain a happy resolution for their troubles and distresses. Unlike the Radcliffean Gothic, in which the supernatural and the uncanny play an important role, the Gothic touch in *The Children of the Abbey* is produced mainly through the setting. This is made up of ancient buildings described as dark and gloomy, 'relics of druidical antiquity' (Roche 147) like Castle Carberry, 'a large Gothic pile' (Roche 146) with its towers, battlements, moat and drawbridge, or Dunreath Abbey, which 'recalls to one's mind all the stories they ever heard of haunted houses and apparitions' (Roche 442). In the chapel where Malvina Dunreath's portrait is kept, Amanda lives the only experience that apparently touches on the supernatural. The customary trimmings of this kind of episode in Gothic novels are all at work: strange noises, darkness, Amanda's terror, a spectral figure, and unexpected revelations. The novel ends, as one would expect, with the villain's death, the punishment of all the guilty, unjust and evil characters, and the triumph of good, truth and virtue. By advocating poetical justice and reaffirming the principle of retribution, Roche promotes the reconciliation among the different social groups, exalts familial values, helps shape acceptable standards of behavior and gives advice as to the ideal choice of partners. Her weapon to attain this end is the combination of the sentimental, the domestic, the gothic and the melodramatic so common in the fiction of her time.

Saint Clair of the Isles, the other lasting remembrance from Alencar's youth, is also a novel wherein the ideology of bourgeois domestic life is enshrouded in suspense and mystery and enacted in abandoned castles, chapels and dungeons. In its blend of fiction and history, there is plenty of room for abductions and kidnappings, medieval tournaments, savage islands and scenic landscape; or, in other words, for realism, romance, and antiquarianism.[25] Elizabeth Helme's 'Scottish tradition' tells the story of Saint Clair Montheit, a clan chieftain banished to the Isle of Barra (in the Hebrides) during James I's reign, his wife Ambrosina and his valiant coterie of exiles, and their struggle to be pardoned and have their rights, status and place in society restored to them. However neglected due to the Scott phenomenon that took Great Britain and other parts of Europe by storm after the publication of *Waverley* in 1814, *Saint Clair* is listed as one of the novels that influenced it and is thought to be, like *Waverley* and a few others, 'variations on a theme, sharing common cultural and national features' (Monnickendam 103). In Brazil, in its turn, the impact made by *Saint Clair* was significant, counting José de Alencar, Machado de Assis and João Guimarães Rosa—three of the most important Brazilian novelists—among its readers (M. Meyer, 'O *que é, ou quem foi Saint Clair*' 38–39).

It was Walter Scott, however, who deserved unrestrained praise from Alencar and whose sea novels he avowed to have devoured when he was a Law student. Though no titles are given, he might be referring to *The Pirate*, the 1821 novel that features Ulla Troil, known as Norna of the Fitful-head, who lays claim to supernatural powers. Or it may have been *Ivanhoe*, which was certainly Scott's most influential novel in nineteenth-century Brazil, replicating the success it had in Europe.[26] Alencar's critics have not failed to suggest points of contact and parallels between Scott and the Brazilian novelist. Dom Antonio de Mariz has been read as a Portuguese Ivanhoe and the Paquequer manor house as a local version of Kenilworth and Lammermoor castles, in *O Guarani* (Araripe Júnior, *José de Alencar* 154). Captain Fragoso, in *O Sertanejo*, has been read as a Reginald Front-de-Boeuf (Antonio Candido 231); look also to the joust in the ring in Salvador and the Ashby tournament, with Estácio once more being compared to Ivanhoe (Raimundo Magalhães Jr, *José de Alencar* 183). Metaphorically, Dom Antonio de Mariz, Estácio, Peri, Ubirajara, Manuel Canho or Arnaldo can all be associated with Ivanhoe, taken as a sort of symbol or prototype of the knight *sans peur et sans reproche*, of which the Brazilian characters are a kind of decal or translation. The chivalric code, with its norms and principles, seems to rule the behavior of most of Alencar's protagonists, both in the historical and the regional or Indianist novels.

Scott, as we know, became a reference in the nineteenth century as the founder of the historical novel, and his *Waverley Novels* were epoch-making as explorations of Scotland's past and of the human consequences of the changes operating during its turbulent history. Although Scott was 'celebrated for breaking the spell of romance, and ushering his readers instead into the communal space of history and public life' (Watt 153), Gothic motifs were not completely absent in his fiction. Northrop Frye had already called attention to his recourse to certain formulaic techniques, like the hero's mysterious birth, proscribed or secret societies, prophecies, the contrast between the blond and the dark heroines, which fascinated the Canadian critic in his reading of *Guy Mannering* (1815) (5). He had also noted how the *Waverley Novels* 'mark the absorption of realistic displacement into romance itself' (40), producing a 'frequent association of romance with the historical' (Frye 176). It is in this space, less committed to historical veracity and more open to fantasy and imagination, that one apprehends the extensive use of devices associated with the Gothic. About the synthesis struck by Scott between history and romance, Watt also remarks:

> In works such as *Ivanhoe*, *The Antiquary*, and *The Bride of Lammermoor*, for example, Scott subsumed Gothic conventions within a historical framework, or set up an opposition between romance and real life in order to relegate the Gothic romance to the status of a fictional anachronism. Yet in the same novels, Scott also qualified the rigour with which he assimilated or digested

> romance raw material, and—as in *The Antiquary* and *The Bride of Lammermoor*—complicated the tone and identity of his work by replicating certain Gothic tropes and plot motifs in an apparently faithful manner. (144)

Ivanhoe, 'the most popular novel of one of the best loved of British authors throughout the nineteenth century', as Ian Duncan reminds us ('Introduction' viii), will be emblematic of this option. It 'executes the fatal turn in Scott's career from a once influential historical realism (in the novels about the making of modern Scotland) to a tinsel-and-tushery medievalism' (Duncan, 'Introduction' viii-ix). The reputation and impact of *Ivanhoe* crossed borders and traveled far. Although we can never be sure Alencar read this specific novel, its presence, and that of all the other novels by Scott in Rio de Janeiro throughout the whole of the nineteenth century[27] was instrumental in making available and popularizing the above-referenced repertoire of Gothic elements we find in the novels by Alencar. In like manner, it is key to bringing forth Scott's complex relation with his precursors, like Horace Walpole, Ann Radcliffe and Matthew Lewis. If we witness, in the Brazilian case, a very similar tendency to the 'Gothicization' of the rural novel or of prosaic and domestic everyday life in Alencar, however, there is not the ambivalence and irony with which Scott often treated his materials and the Gothic tradition that preceded him.

But, like Scott was for Scotland, Alencar was particularly aware of the past and of the forces that had been crucial to shaping the Brazilian nation, with one important proviso. From Brazil's earliest days, slavery had been a common practice, starting with the Portuguese colonizers enslaving Indians and gradually replacing them with black forced labor. Slaves and slavery, however, are conspicuously absent in Alencar's work, even if they make minor appearances here and there. As a senator of the Second Empire, he was at the center of the fierce political debates about the abolition of slavery. Shortly before publishing the novels mentioned above, he was making speeches in the Senate wherein he argued that slavery was an 'open ulcer in society' (speech of July 16, 1870), but he opposed its abolition because it would bring, according to him, economic ruin to the country, besides abandoning the slaves to their own lot. Although repudiating the reduction of men to the condition of mere things, his positions are untenable, at best, as he is frequently racist in his arguments, defending what a Brazilian historian has characterized as a 'manorial worldview' (Chaloub 200). It is not an exaggeration to suggest that these undesired aspects of Brazilian life and identity, which could be spelled out as the inescapable and undeniable black presence in our formation, return as repressed elements, and the threat they represent or fear they provoke are duly displaced to the margins of Alencar's narratives and gothicized.

On this note, I close with this example of the Brazilian acclimatization of the Gothic, pointing out that my intention is not to play the role of one of those 'influence hunters' (Cavalcanti Proença, '*Nota Preliminar*' 1014). Rather, I have sought to interrogate one specific instance in the process of circulation and appropriation of themes and procedures, so characteristic of a transnational genre like the novel, as well as establishing and retrieving the network of readings that went into the making of such a central writer to the Brazilian tradition as José de Alencar. I have also suggested that these British novels, produced in times and places so distant from us, made an important contribution to the formation of the Brazilian literary system. Moreover, I have argued that Gothic conventions and elements were embodied both in Alencar's invention of a national past and in his exploration of unfamiliar territories in the long and difficult process of their incorporation into the Brazilian nation. Alencar's regional novels like *O Tronco do Ipê* and *Til*, set on the cultural fringes of the empire and housing troubling social groups—slaves, half-breeds, Indians—were especially permeable to the repertoire of Gothic grotesquerie. Even if subsumed and contained within a realistic framework it was instrumental to deal with the somber, violent and ruthless aspects of the process of colonization and nation-building.

Notes

1. *The Guarany: Brazilian Novel.* Trans. Hawes, James W. *Overland Monthly and Out West magazine*, San Francisco, from vol. 21 issue 127, July 1893, to vol. 22 issue 131, November 1893; *Iracema, the honey-lips: a legend of Brazil.* Trans. Burton, Isabel (London: Bickers and Son, 1886).
2. See Doris Sommer. *Foundational Fictions: The National Romances of Latin America* (Berkeley: University of California Press, 1991).
3. For more on this topic, see Suriani da Silva, Ana Cláudia, and Vasconcelos, Sandra Guardini. *Books and Periodicals in Brazil, 1768–1930. A Transatlantic Perspective* (Oxford: Legenda, 2014).
4. Possibly Matthew Lewis. As the information in the advertisements is often incomplete, and titles and names are generally misspelt, one can only presume the reference is to the author of *The Monk*.
5. See Hemeroteca Digital Brasileira, www.memoria.bn.br. Also Vasconcelos, 'Migratory Literary Forms'.
6. Roche, Regina Maria. *The Children of the Abbey* (London: William Lane, 1796) (*Amanda e Oscar, ou história da família de Dunreath.* Trans. A. V. de C. e S. Lisboa, 1823); Helme, Elizabeth. *Saint-Clair of the Isles; or, The Outlaws of Barra. A Scottish Tradition* (London: Longman and Rees, 1803) (*Saint-Clair das Ilhas, ou os desterrados na ilha de Barra.* Trans. A. S. C. Rio de Janeiro: Typ. Silva Porto, 1825).
7. All translations from the Portuguese are mine, unless otherwise indicated.
8. For more on global Gothic, see Byron, Glennis. *Globalgothic (*Manchester: Manchester University Press, 2013).
9. See Punter, David. *The Literature of Terror. A History of Gothic Fictions from 1765 to the Present Day* (London and New York: Longman, 1996).
10. See Sir Walter Scott. *Miscellaneous Prose Works*, vol. 1, part 6 (Edinburgh: Robert Cadell, 1841). There is also the essay 'On the Supernatural in Fictitious

Composition; and particularly on the Works of Ernest Theodore William Hoffmann', collected by Ioan Williams in *Sir Walter Scott on Novelists and Fiction* (London: Routledge & Kegan Paul, 1968), 312–53.

11. Barbosa Lima Sobrinho, *Os Precursores do Conto no Brasil*. Barbosa Lima Sobrinho, Os Precursores do Conto no Brasil. (Rio de Janeiro: Ed. Civilização Brasileira, 1960). p. 54. All translations from Portuguese are mine, unless otherwise stated.
12. 'A mãe-irmã (História contemporânea)', originally published in *Jornal do Commercio* on 10 April 1839. Also in Lima Sobrinho, *op. cit.* p. 185.
13. Lima Sobrinho, *op. cit.*, p. 197–98.
14. In 'Como e Porque Sou Romancista' (141), Alencar recalls: 'In 1845, the itch to become a writer came back; but that year was devoted to the byronizing craze then widespread. Every student with a little imagination wanted to be a Byron, and copying or translating the English bard was his inexorable fate'.
15. Walter Scott's contact with the Gothic novelists also included the reviews he wrote for several periodicals, as well as the critical biographies of Horace Walpole and Clara Reeve he prepared for Ballantyne's *Novelist's Library*. See *Sir Walter Scott on Novelists and Fiction*. Edited by Ioan Williams (London: Routledge & Kegan Paul, 1968).
16. This sunny element derives fundamentally from the treatment Alencar gives to Brazilian nature and landscape, which does not detract from the more traumatic aspects and gloomier inflection his *oeuvre* embodies on thematising the processes of national formation.
17. For the modes of incorporating History in Alencar's historical novels, see my article 'Figurações do passado: o romance histórico em Walter Scott e José de Alencar'. *Terceira Margem* 18 (2008): 15–37.
18. Anonymous. 'The Historical Romance'. *Blackwood's Edinburgh Magazine* 58 (1845): 341–56.
19. For more on *O Guarani*, see Serravalle de Sá, Daniel. *Gótico Tropical*. O sublime e o demoníaco em *O Guarani*. (Salvador: EDUFBA, 2010).
20. The last Gothic moment in Alencar is a scene in his novel *Encarnação*, which according to Eugênio Gomes is copied from Radcliffe's *The Mysteries of Udolpho*: 'The scene in which Emily faints, seized by panic, when drawing a curtain that hid something that seemed to be a ghost and was nothing more than a wax figure. ... Analogous astonishment had Amália, in Alencar's novel, when she surprised the sculpture of her dead rival, whom at first she supposed to be dead' (Gomes, 'Nota Preliminar' 1219–20).
21. See Antonio Candido. 'Os Três Alencares'. In *Formação da Literatura Brasileira (momentos decisivos)*. 4th ed. (São Paulo: Liv. Martins Ed., no date), 221–35.
22. Though they are regional novels, Alencar does not make systematic use of these devices in *O Gaúcho* e *O Sertanejo* maybe because they tend to aggrandise and idealise these two Brazilian types.
23. *Les enfans de l'abbaye* par Mme Regina Maria Roche. Traduit de l'anglais par André Morellet (Paris: Denné, 1797), 6 vol. (source: Bibliothèque nationale de France).
24. Blakey, Dorothy. *The Minerva Press: 1790–1820*. (London: Oxford University Press, 1939).
25. For more on *Saint Clair*, see Meyer, Marlyse. 'O que é, ou Quem foi Sinclair das Ilhas?' *Revista do Instituto de Estudos Brasileiros*, n. 14 (1973): 37–63.
26. See my article 'Figurações do passado: o romance histórico em Walter Scott e José de Alencar'. *Terceira Margem* 18 (2008): 15–37.

27. Virtually all of Scott's novels can be found in Rio de Janeiro in French, English and Portuguese since the late 1830s. For more on Scott's circulation and reception in Brazil, see Vasconcelos, Sandra Guardini. 'Romans sans Frontières : le cas paradigmatique de Walter Scott'. *Le Commerce Transatlantique de la Librairie*. Cooper-Richet, Diana et Mollier, Jean-Yves (org.). E-book. (Campinas, SP: Unicamp/Publicações IEL, 2012), 165–75.

Bibliography

Alencar, José de. *As Minas de Prata. Obra Completa*. Vol. II. Rio de Janeiro: Editora José Aguilar, 1958. 417–1257. [The Silver Mines].

———. *O Guarani. Obra Completa*. Vol. II. Rio de Janeiro: Editora José Aguilar, 1958. 5–406.

———. *O Tronco do Ipê. Obra Completa*. Vol. III. Rio de Janeiro: Editora José Aguilar, 1958. 627–812.

———. *Til. Obra Completa*. Vol. III. Rio de Janeiro: Editora José Aguilar, 1958. 821–1010.

———. 'Bênção Paterna'. *Obra Completa*. Vol. I. Rio de Janeiro: Editora José Aguilar, 1959. 691–702 (Fatherly Blessing).

———. 'Como e Porque sou Romancista'.*Obra Completa*. Vol. I. Rio de Janeiro: Editora José Aguilar, 1959. 125–55 (How and Why I Became a Novelist).

———. 'Cartas sobre a Confederação dos Tamoios.' *Obra Completa*. Vol. IV. Rio de Janeiro: Editora José Aguilar, 1960. 863–922 (Letters on the Confederation of the Tamoios).

Antonio Candido. 'Os Três Alencares'. *Formação da Literatura Brasileira (momentos decisivos)*. 4th ed. Vol. 2. São Paulo: Liv. Martins Ed., no date. 221–35.

Araripe Júnior, T. de A. 'A Crítica'. Alencar, José de. *Obra Completa*. Vol. III. Rio de Janeiro: Editora José Aguilar, 1958. 1327–37.

———. 'Nota Preliminar'. In Alencar, José de. *Obra Completa*. Vol. III. Rio de Janeiro: Editora José Aguilar, 1958. 815–17.

———. *José de Alencar: perfil literário*. Rio de Janeiro: Typ. da Escola de Serafim José Alves Editor, no date.

Barbosa Lima Sobrinho, *Os Precursores do Conto no Brasil*. Rio de Janeiro: Ed. Civilização Brasileira, 1960.

Blakey, Dorothy. *The Minerva Press: 1790–1820*. London: Oxford University Press, 1939.

Botting, Fred. 'Gothic Darkly: Heterotopia, History, Culture'. In *A Companion to the Gothic*. Ed. Punter, David. Oxford: Blackwell, 2001. 3–14.

Cavalcanti Proença, M. 'Nota Preliminar'. Alencar, José de. *Obra Completa*. Vol. III. Rio de Janeiro: Editora José Aguilar, 1958. 1013–1015.

———. 'José de Alencar na Literatura Brasileira'. Alencar, José de. *Obra Completa*. Vol. I. Rio de Janeiro: Editora José Aguilar, 1959. 13–124.

Chaloub, Sidney. *Machado de Assis, Historiador*. São Paulo: Companhia das Letras, 2003.

Duncan, Ian. *Modern Romance and Transformations of the Novel. The Gothic, Scott, Dickens*. Cambridge: Cambridge University Press, 2005.

Eagleton, Terry. 'The Nature of Gothic.' *Figures of Dissent*. London and New York: Verso, 2005. 17–23.

Frye, Northrop. *The Secular Scripture. A Study of the Structure of Romance*. Cambridge, MA: Harvard University Press, 1978.

Gil, Fernando C. 'O caráter pendular do herói brasileiro.' *Literatura e Sociedade*, n. 13 (2010.1): 132–51.

Gomes, Eugênio. 'Nota Preliminar'. Alencar, José de. *Obra Completa*. Vol. I. Rio de Janeiro: Editora José Aguilar, 1959. 1217–20.

Gonçalves Rodrigues, A. A. *A Novelistica Estrangeira em Versão Portuguesa no Período Pré-romântico*. Coimbra: Biblioteca da Universidade, 1951.

Kelly, Gary. *English Fiction of the Romantic Period, 1789–1830*. London and New York: Longman, 1989.

Kiely, Robert. *The Romantic Novel in England*. Cambridge, MA: Harvard University Press, 1972.

Kilgour, Maggie. *The Rise of the Gothic Novel*. London and New York: Routledge, 1995.

Magalhães Jr, Raimundo. *José de Alencar e sua Época*. Rio de Janeiro: Civilização Brasileira; Brasília: INL, 1977.

Meyer, Augusto. 'Nota Preliminar'. Alencar, José de. *Obra Completa*. Vol. III. Rio de Janeiro: Editora José Aguilar, 1958. 409–18.

Meyer, Marlyse. 'O que é, ou Quem foi Sinclair das Ilhas?' *Revista do Instituto de Estudos Brasileiros*, n. 14 (1973): 37–63. Republished in *Almanaque*. São Paulo: Brasiliense, n. 8 (1978): 82–99.

———. 'Mulheres Romancistas Inglesas do Século XVIII e Romance Brasileiro'. *Caminhos do Imaginário no Brasil*. São Paulo: Edusp, 1993. 47–72.

———. Machado de Assis lê *Saint-Clair das Ilhas*. *As Mil Faces de um Herói Canalha e outros ensaios*. Rio de Janeiro: Editora da UFRJ, 1998. 31–107.

Monnickendam, Andrew. *A Hypertextual Approach to Walter Scott's* Waverley. Barcelona: Universitat Autònoma de Barcelona, 1998.

Moretti, Franco. *Atlas of the European Novel 1800–1900*. London: Verso, 1997.

Oliveira, Jefferson Donizetti de. 'Um Sussurro nas Trevas. Uma revisão da recepção crítica e literária de *Noite na Taverna* de Álvares de Azevedo.' MA Dissertation. Universidade de São Paulo. 2010.

Punter, David. *The Literature of Terror. A History of Gothic Fictions from 1765 to the Present Day*. London and New York: Longman, 1996.

———. 'Introduction: *The Ghost of a History*'. *A Companion to the Gothic*. Ed. Punter, David. Oxford: Blackwell, 2001. viii–xiv.

Roche, Regina Maria. *The Children of the Abbey*. Philadelphia: J. B. Lippincott & Co., 1877.

Sage, Victor. 'Irish Gothic: C.R. Maturin and J.S. LeFanu'. *A Companion to the Gothic*.Ed. Punter, David. Oxford: Blackwell, 2001. 81–93.

Schwarz, Roberto. *Ao Vencedor as Batatas. Forma Literária e Processo Social nos Inícios do Romance Brasileiro*. São Paulo: Editora 34, 2000.

Scott, Sir Walter. *Sir Walter Scott on Novelists and Fiction*. Edited by Ioan Williams. London: Routledge & Kegan Paul, 1968.

———. *Ivanhoe*. Ed. Duncan, Ian. Oxford: Oxford University Press, 1996.

Serravalle de Sá, Daniel. *Gótico Tropical*. O sublime e o demoníaco em O *Guarani*. Salvador: EDUFBA, 2010.

Sommer, Doris. *Foundational Fictions: The National Romances of Latin America*. Berkeley: University of California Press, 1991.

Trumpener, Katie. *Bardic Nationalism. The Romantic Novel and the British Empire*. Princeton, NJ: Princeton University Press, 1997.

Vasconcelos, Sandra Guardini. 'Figurações do passado: o romance histórico em Walter Scott e José de Alencar'. *Terceira Margem*, n. 18 (2008): 5–37.

———. 'From the French or Not: Transatlantic Contributions to the Making of the Brazilian Novel'. *Books between Europe and the Americas: Connections and Communities (1620–1860)*. Ed. Howsam, Leslie, and James Raven. London: Palgrave Macmillan, 2011. 212–32.

———. 'Romans sans Frontières: le cas paradigmatique de Walter Scott'. *Le Commerce Transatlantique de la Librairie*. Cooper-Richet, Diana et Jean-Yves Mollier (org.). E-book. Campinas, SP: Unicamp/Publicações IEL, 2012. 165–75.

———. 'Migratory Literary Forms: British Novels in Nineteenth-Century Brazil'. *Books and Periodicals in Brazil, 1768–1930. A Transatlantic Perspective*. Ed. Suriani da Silva, Ana Claudia, and Sandra Guardini Vasconcelos. Oxford: Legenda, 2014. 68–86.

Vieira Martins, Eduardo. 'A Imagem do Sertão em José de Alencar.' MA Dissertation. Universidade Estadual de Campinas, 1997.

Watt, James. *Contesting the Gothic. Fiction, Genre and Cultural Conflict, 1764–1832*. Cambridge: Cambridge University Press, 1999.

14 Difference and Subversion

Gothic Migrations in Nineteenth-Century Latin American Novels

Rita Terezinha Schmidt

A significant outcome of the challenges to traditional models of literary histories in different national geographies is the revision of canonical formations, the institutionalized body of literary texts regarded as representative of national identities for encoding an imaginary apparatus of nation building. This has played a fundamental role in the production of national identities and collective subjectivities, particularly in the nineteenth century when Latin American countries emerged from of the wars of unification and independence to affirm their nationhood. Until some decades ago, literary histories were considered national archives of canonical corpuses and safe preserves of intellectual categories such as 'literature' and 'aesthetic values'. Theoretical developments, critical debates and scholarly research in the past four decades have questioned the assumptions underlying such categories and their impact on the constitution of long-standing beliefs that have led to the consecration of the so-called 'classical' national works. These debates have also paved the way for new insights into women's writings, particularly by retrieving works that were relegated to a sub-literature level, thus opening up possibilities for bringing their past existence to critical significance. As a rule, nineteenth-century Latin-American women's writings are largely invisible in those histories as a result of critical judgments generally made on the grounds of aesthetic deficiencies issued by the literary institution through their 'guardians', particularly male literary historians and critics who have always exercised a regulatory function within national cultures. Evaluating formal value is complex. It is embedded in the hegemonic concept of literature that was transplanted into the continent during the period of colonization and almost four centuries of Spanish and Portuguese rule, the legacy of which is still unquestioned in some quarters of the intellectual/academic establishment. The critical conventions that conceive of past texts written by women as lacking literary value continues to survive; as a result, there is a cultural structure that resists the critical project of reexamining women's writing.[1] Rethinking the question of critical validation in relation to Latin American women's prose fiction and novels, I argue that there is an underside to the argument of value that requires critical attention.[2] The invisibility of women's fiction rests on the fact that these writers did not rely on the romantic ideas about nation building that were central in the construction of what Benedict Anderson calls 'imagined communities' in the nineteenth century. On the contrary, women's writing often subverted the models put forward in canonical novels. These models were predicated on the cultural and political domestication of differences, thus revealing how that model was convenient because of its functional value in national historical contexts and why the critical establishment has regarded the novels that conform to that model as those that sustain the definition of emblematic fictions of nationality.

Latin America is not a unified political, social and cultural formation; it is a putative unity in terms of a common and yet different history of colonization and legacies. However, in light of my argument, the category of the nation is a frame of reference that highlights the interlocking dimensions of commonality in the constitution of a transnational imaginary because of a process of transculturation of the European gothic mode in four novels authored by women. These are, from Argentina, *La familia del Comendor y otros textos* (Brasil 1852/Argentina 2006) by Juana Manso; from Brazil, *D. Narcisa de Villar* (1859) by Ana Luiza Azevedo Castro and *Ursula* (1859) by Maria Fir mina dos Reis; and from Peru, *Aves sin nido* (1889) by Clorinda Matto de Turner. My argument is twofold. First, these novels, engendered at the nations' margins—a form of otherness—engage in specific readings of the historical and political processes of nationhood by inscribing a narrative economy that produces a counterpoint to national stories of progress, emancipation and bourgeois Enlightenment that attended the period of the formation of Latin-American modern nation-states. Second, I contend that this particular economy is an effect of the migration and transculturation of generic conventions of the European gothic, a minor genre associated with novels written in the eighteenth century, particularly in England, where gothic novels written by women served to disguise the grim realities of eighteenth-century female gender roles by an escape into fantasy.[3] The migration of forms was inevitable, given the history of colonization processes and their impact on the cultural formation of Latin American countries. This is discussed by Jean Franco in the Introduction to her *Historia de la Literatura Hispanoamericana: A partir de la Independencia* (1973) wherein she argues that migration began in the early colonial period with the imposition of metropolitan writing cultures and the languages of the colonizers, so that language became a powerful means of domination and cultural homogenization. In the nineteenth century, literary migrations were largely determined by the consolidation of a middle-class reading public and a prosperous market of imported books largely from Britain and France. The market included novels by Walter Scott, Daniel Defoe, Victor Hugo and Eugene Sue, in their original languages or in translations, as well as novels by women writers of the eighteenth century, including Anne Radcliffe, that could be easily accessed in public library catalogues as historical research studies have revealed.[4] Thus, the impact of the circulation of European novels on the rising public sphere of material culture and its role in the literary education of women from the local elite classes cannot be ignored to the same extent that the persistent engagement of women writers with the gothic narrative mode cannot be undermined.[5]

Approaching the question of migration of literary forms from Europe to Latin America involves a move beyond the traditional paradigm of sources and influences. The paradigm tends to subscribe to the binary center x margins associated with assumptions of asymmetrical development of forms engendered in geopolitical spaces defined by political distinctions and cultural-bound values. Examples include European literatures and literatures in Third World countries. The logic underlying this binary erases the fact that migration is part of the dynamics of cross-cultural transfers in which local appropriations and contextual differences make contaminations and transformations the rule, rather than continuities or simple imitation. The concept of transculturation was conceived in 1940 by the Cuban scholar Fernando Ortiz. He questioned the term 'acculturation' (used in 1930s Latin American anthropology) because it led to distortions in the understandings of what happened in the encounter between cultures, not only in the history of Cuba but in relation to all other Latin American countries that shared a history of colonial rule and domination.[6] For Ortiz, colonial encounters generated a transformative process on the level of local cultures because of the acquisition of material, loss, displacement and/or fusion of metropolitan cultures with local practices and indigenous cultures, a position that discards the servile imitation of metropolitan models. Following in Ortiz's footsteps, the Peruvian scholar, Angel Rama, published *Transculturación Narrativa en América Latina* (1984). This work analyzes the efforts of some Latin America writers in whose works, marked by regional affiliations, the literary discourse operates through what he defines as 'plastic transculturations' visible on three levels: language, literary structure and vision (in Spanish, this third level is translated as '*cosmovisión*').[7]

In the novels discussed in this essay, vision lies in the appropriation of traditional tropes of the English female gothic such as family doom, the tyrannical father, female victimization, secrecy, inheritance, betrayal, murder and incest into metonymic patterns that produce a structural and signifying effect inflected by local realities, historical specificities, cultural and space variables. These illustrations show transculturation as a phenomenon that crosses multiple intersections within a particular period, place and space. It shapes literary forms within borders of national differences and across borders of commonality. In addition to the tropes mentioned, space emerges as a relevant category in the transculturation process in terms of a unity of the environment that integrates geographical particularities with historical dimensions in a careful construction that frames particular actions and identities. For example, standard European gothic architecture is substituted by Latin-American landscapes in the many references to open spaces such as remote regions, dangerous mountain by-passes, violent seas, menacing rivers, hidden paths, caves, labyrinthine forests and tropical storms. These make the natural landscape a bewildering life-threatening force that foreshadows disaster and stands as a symbolic mirror image of somber human destines. These representations diverge radically from the benign and exotic tropical nature depicted in canonical romantic novels and from the stock device of enclosed spaces in European gothic.[8] Instead, they sustain the tense atmosphere in tune with stories that revolve around what lurks underneath the optimistic surfaces of the colonial empire and the republican civil order; in other words, they are stories wherein the seemingly familiar environment turns into a strange and unfamiliar place. This penchant for the strange beneath what is normally perceived as a familiar and rational reality brings to the foreground the paradigm of the family, the first ordering social principle and a cognitive structure that has traditionally functioned as a primary source of metaphor in gothic novels. The family plot is the gothic plot *par excellence*, according to Anne Williams. She suggests that at the center of gothic conventions lies the patriarchal family, a structure of power and subordination that enforces mandatory patterns of gender difference and social behavior affecting every dimension of human experience. The family produces psychodynamics of feeling that unleash tensions, anxieties and fears, disruptions through images such as, among others, the skeleton in the closet or the madwoman in the attic. For Williams, the gothic myth itself is the patriarchal family, 'a cultural pressure point', and she explores the relationship of the gothic to particular historical conditions, reminding us of the links between the gothic and the upheavals of the French Revolution, remarking that it springs directly from historical circumstances in this "Age of Revolutions" (91).

Likewise, in Latin American contexts, the historical circumstances of Spanish and Portuguese conquests, colonization and the warfare during the new Republican regimes constituted a fertile ground for the appropriation of a fictional mode that placed at its center the patriarchal family and issues related to birth and genealogy. Colonized spaces afforded violent encounters with racial otherness, including sexual encounters that disfigured the arrangements of the white family itself with consequences beyond its circle of kinship relations. White patriarchal power exceeded all boundaries of human decency and dignity. It took on grotesque proportions in the inflicted suffering to white women, local indigenous populations and enslaved people of African descent. People from these marginalized groups often circulated in the domestic spaces, usually as house servants for the elite. In this context, the family becomes a place of potential conflict, a symptom and metaphor of the nation's family and a space where the private and the public converge as the law of the father merges with the law of the state. This merger guarantees its force on the assumption of state 'necessity', an assumption that slides over into acts of transgression that transform the familiar/national space into an unhomely place that spells the abandonment of life itself.[9] On these terms, the stories of family secrets (with their dramatic disclosures and violent resolutions) inscribe a web of metaphorical associations that grant the texts a level of historical legibility of the past. As it stands, the gothic mode was not an assortment of eccentricities that meant to provoke fear and tears; on the contrary, it offered a means with which Latin-American women writers could address the anxieties and tensions of their time, making of their artwork and their ideological configuration a form of engagement with history. In this context, the deployment of gothic conventions was productive of agency in the sense that it could signify desire and transform intent into narrative acts of interpellation that were meant to reach out to the civic sensibilities of their readers, mostly women, as men at the time were most likely to be readers of 'serious' literature.[10] The dimension of affect in these novels (sometimes misunderstood as appeals to sentimentality) are better evaluated today, more so when we consider that the writers were crossing the boundaries of the strict domestic ideology of their times to access the cultures of writing and make interventions into the public domain, an exclusive patriarchal territory. This unearths deep-seated silences about the plight of women, slaves and natives as dispossessed subjects submitted to the destructive forces at work in the extended family and embedded in the structures of state and church. The work also brings to light a content that is charged with issues 'that culture does not want to know, to admit or will not tell.[11] The fact that the writers dared to tell stories that forfeited the promise of individual and collective fulfillment boasted in romantic historical novels was a significant blow to how nationhood was being built upon the unity of its citizens. Ultimately, the novels' singular features in terms of negativity and liminality, classical tropes associated with the gothic tradition show that gothic transculturation in the tropics presents an unquestioning adherence to a political dimension in so far as the novels emerge as counter-foundational fictions that haunt the double margins of the Latin-American patriarchal culture, the literary and the national histories.

Nation-Building and Redemptive Fictions

For the nation-states emerging from the grips of the Spanish and Portuguese Empires in the century of nationalisms, the definition of an autonomous national identity was a political, social and cultural priority. But the engendering of collective identity was a process riddled with contradictions due to the resilience of political structures and social organization embedded in colonial practices, including the realities of a slave-holding imperial state (in the case of Brazil). The rise and consolidation of the economic and cultural middle-class elite that appropriated ideals of the European Enlightenment such as civilization and progress as well as romantic conceptions of the organic nation and national genius made it possible to envision a liberal-bourgeois project that would lead the newly independent countries into modernity. However, the nexus of belonging necessary for the claim of national identity and participation in a so-called 'universal' European-based modern civilization was only achieved as a result of political motivations and ideological maneuvers. The historical legacies of the 'civilizing mission' and its logic of conquest and ritual destruction of autochthonous cultures were carried out on various levels of the institutional machinery. These practices took many forms and were implemented in multiple ways by those who had the power to control who belonged to the 'imaginary community' of the new nations, including what should be forgotten and what should be remembered. For example, the colonial violence of the foundational thrust that resulted in the barbaric genocides of native peoples and the erasure of their languages and cultural heritages was strategically transformed in the nineteenth century into what Homi Bhabha calls 'the pedagogy of the nation' through the effort to produce citizen-subjects compatible with a political agenda.[12] This process is not devoid of political and symbolic violence. By interposing the discourses of identity, the nation paradoxically produces its center and its margins as zones of containment, vulnerability and abandonment. Considering the degrees of racial violence and segregation, class hierarchies and gender asymmetries in Latin American societies, the nationalist assumption of unity was predicated on a dis-unified totality so the heterogeneity of the people was not embraced in the human dimension of nationhood. At the center there was the exclusionary idealization of the hegemonic middle class constituted by the '*criolos*' (born of Spanish descent) and the local 'Brazilians' (born of Portuguese descent) who would territorialize the political, cultural and literary scenes. In these circles, the nationalist rhetoric of universality was embedded in textual affiliations intertwined in political and cultural discourses that addressed the nation 'as one' and appealed to collective identifications with arguments of territorial distinctiveness, a strategy that sought to project a national identity in opposition to other nations, that is, on negative terms. For the Uruguayan critic Hugo Achugar, the elimination of all vestiges of social antagonism that warranted the pact that linked state and nation was a current practice in the nineteenth century.[13] This meant that only certain texts and discourses were considered legitimate, while others were eliminated from mainstream culture. In his assessment, Latin-American intellectuals 'constructed an ideal nation that did not correspond to the ethnic, social and cultural reality in the countries in which they lived' (my translation).[14] The example of Brazil illustrates these issues. Under the Portuguese monarchy, which lasted until 1889 when Brazil became a republic, the political and cultural fields were dominated by an imperial elite constituted of government officials, bureaucrats and lettered men, usually from rural oligarchies or from the rich merchant classes of urban centers with law degrees from Coimbra University in Portugal. According to the Brazilian historian José Murilo de Carvalho, there were two dominant images of nationhood in the nineteenth century: one in which the people were absent, and one in which there were negative views of the people.[15] Based on archival research, Carvalho concludes that the allegiance to the monarchy by the population had no connection with a sense of 'Brazilianess'. Rather, the Crown's Catholic tradition and the concern of the elites with the question of national identity were limited to convincing divergent sectors within the very same elite to favor the strong politics of the centralized government in order to preserve political stability against the negative image of their new republican neighbors in Latin America. In this context, the symbolic force of romantic nationhood was forged almost exclusively in the discourses of a liberal intellectual minority, against the backdrop of a slave-holding monarchical state that faced uprisings and revolts in several states of the union against its centralizing power, while the new Republican governments led campaigns to exterminate the native people.[16]

The ideal nation as a recurrent image in elite culture is extensively examined by Angel Rama in his *La Ciudad Letrada (The Lettered City)*.[17] Here, Rama discusses the Republican city as an allegory of nationhood and a paradigm for the development of a utopic romantic project that placed writing at the center of a progressive politics; this became a basic mechanism of social control and preserved its own autonomy. Rama acknowledges the distance that separated the lettered city from the real city, particularly because writing since the sixteenth century was a token of social mobility, public respectability and access to the centers of power. But he still defends the city of letters. Rama writes, 'the constitution of literature, as a discourse about formation, composition and definition of nationhood implied anyway a previous homogenizing and hygienic processes, a condition for writing to emerge. The constitution of the canon of national literatures at the end of the nineteenth century represents the triumph of the lettered city and, for the first time in history, it begins to dominate its surroundings' (119).

In the many aspects of Rama's historicizing of the fetish of writing, which entrenched the domination of the book and the letter in a century when missionaries were substituted by an intellectual class, one aspect stands out: the novel, with no previous history in Latin America, became a privileged literary genre and had a profound impact on the constitution of the public sphere of political culture. The novel, then, contributed to the political, cohesive and structuring role of romantic nationalism in the emergence of an object called 'national literature'. As a symbolic practice involving categories of time and place, the novel was the appropriate medium for fostering a sense of cultural space and historic destiny; thus, it appealed to readers' desire for a sense of national identity that was required to establish nationhood. The romantic historical novel therefore became central to the national project, for this modality of prose fiction secured a tight link between the fictional referent and historical reality. Its representations would fulfill a pedagogical purpose: to enhance those features readers could recognize as familiar, specifically scenes drawn from everyday life that were set against the backdrop of local historic events.[18]

The role of the novel in forging national identities is the starting point for Doris Sommer's book on the nineteenth-century Latin-American novel, *Foundational Fictions—The National Romances of Latin America*. This extensive work examines a body of novels written by male writers and considered national novels: *Amalia* (1855) by José Marmo (from Argentina); *O Guarani* (1857) by José de Alencar (from Brazil); *Martín Rivas* (1852) by Alberto Blast (from Chile); *Enriquillo* (1881) by Manoel de Jesus Galván (from the Dominican Republic); *Cumandá* (1887) by Juan Leon Mera (from Equador); *Tabaré* (1888) by Juan Zorilla de San Martin (from Uruguay) and *Maria* (1867) by Jorge Isaacs (from Colombia). Drawing on Benedict Anderson's argument that nationalism in Europe was produced in the imaginary private spaces of the novel and building on critical assumptions about the relation between the discourses of productive heterosexual love present in canonical fictional narratives and the ideology of nationalism in nineteenth-century Latin America, Sommer advances the thesis that these novels 'were grists for the nation-making mill' (42). These novels, she argues, catered to the programmatic political needs of the newly independent countries to form a bourgeois state, and they therefore constitute allegories of the mutual dependence between the family and the state. Romantic relationships in these 'foundational fictions' were, she claims, meant to cross the racial and class boundaries and affirm alliances as 'part of a general bourgeois project to hegemonize a culture in formation' (29). In fact, these novels attained the status of national romances precisely because they became required reading in secondary schools at the beginning of the twentieth century and, as such, they disseminated ideals and values to inspire national pride.

Sommer draws on Walter Benjamin's concept of allegory to sustain the idea that, far from being a simple metaphorical parallelism, there is a metonymic association between eroticism and the politics of nationalism in plots that inscribe a double structure of retrospective and projective movements. In these stories, the tensions are solved by rhetorical solutions (often through happy endings) that symbolically mend the fissures in the bourgeois family and forge unity and consolidation regardless of differences in gender, class, race and region. In particular, Sommer addresses the question of miscegenation. She claims that the European dread of racial mixing contrasts with a Latin-American narrative of redemption whereby cross-racial relationships become symbols for the pacification of the 'primitive' through the establishment of an ideal of a horizontal and fraternal sense of identity (a claim that holds for the novels she selects but not for women's novels of the period). Sommer acknowledges that two novels written by women included in her analysis do not quite fit into the pattern of national romances because they fail to result in the happy ending of cross-racial love: these include *Sab* by Gertrudes Gómez de Avellaneda and *Aves sin nido* by Clorinda Matto de Turner.[19] Overall, the analyses prove the generic coherence of the allegorical double narrative of these novels (family and nation), resulting in a palimpsest that originates not only from the political and historical differences in the narratives themselves but also from the common bourgeois project to promote the culture of a liberal state. Her choice of the term 'romance' instead of novel is effective because romance is seen to be a pristine mode for the projection of an idealized world where fantasy feeds on wish-fulfillment or what Sommer defines as 'the beautiful lies of the national romances' (46).[20] These analyses offer significant insights into the making of national canons and, as I argue, canonical formations are invested with power to control and regulate the dissemination of discourses and authorize certain representations that fulfill a will to truth in order to set the system of signification and standards of value readers are expected to validate and identify. The novels given the status of foundational fictions illustrate to what extent the literary institution has been a privileged site for the enactment of the ideological assumptions of a political ethic informed by a vision of totality. Overlooked in Sommer's study, perhaps because of her range of other concerns, is that the novels she analyzes are complicit with particular constructions of white masculinity. These constructions afforded male empowerment at a moment when the very idea of culture was defined in terms of male pragmatic values such as autonomy, self-determination, strength, rationality, agency and power over nature as a condition to advance the so-called civilizing process. In this sense, these novels produced scripts, coiled in their structures and imprinted with patterns of meanings that resonate with social forms and values embedded in white patriarchal ideology. Benedict Anderson's definition of nationhood as a 'deep, horizontal comradeship' (16) underwrites how the understandings of nationalisms, particularly in the nineteenth century, were founded on a distinctly homosocial form of male bonding, and women—a trope of the nation's other—were excluded from this horizontal brotherhood beyond their capacity for reproduction.[21] But women writers, working against the grain, challenged these narratives, discourses and ideologies.

Somber Fictions, Haunted Houses

Nineteenth-century Latin-American fiction by women contributes to the genealogy of the female gothic. This body of texts exemplifies the continuities and changes of the genre across geographical and temporal borders, and as the writers engaged with their local histories of nationality the gothic mode became a source of resistance to the bourgeois mythmaking of the nation. These female writers, then, did not seek to mend the fissures of the body politic; instead, their novels expose 'the nation split within itself' (148). This move represents a significant intervention in the signification-function of nationalist discourses inscribed in the allegorical fictions that engender a redemptive structure out of the homology between romance and nation-building. Similarly, in the interweaving of gender and race, the novels incorporate the theme of miscegenation; however, contrary to canonical fictions, the mixed relationship leads to domestic doom through the sexual abuse of Indian and slave women, the birth of illegitimate children and forbidden inter-racial love. These novels do not break with patterns of the romantic love story, yet the plots and the arrangements of narratives are permeated by gothic tropes and repetitions associated with the uncanny: female characters face obstacles, sacrifices, persecution, and fatalistic determinations that often end in violence. In this context, the bourgeois family is far from being the space for idealized gender and racial arrangements that enhance unification through erotic fulfillment; rather, the family is the site of desecration where relationships are tainted by the arrogance, rapacity and cruelty of fathers, either as aristocrats, slave-holders, planters, businessmen, clergymen or army officials. The political and literary significance of the gothic mode allows these writers to address issues that generated culturally specific tensions in their social contexts, and these writers invoke a compelling sense of suffering and homelessness that reflects their conflicted relationships with their national communities.

Published in 1859, the novel *Ursula* by Maria Firmina dos Reis was finally reedited in 1975 and is now considered to be the first novel written by a Brazilian writer to treat slavery as a brutal and degrading system. This perspective contrasts with the canonical novel *A escrava Isaura*, by Bernardo Guimarães, published in 1875 (16 years later) and disseminated as an abolitionist novel.[22] In *Ursula*, the plot revolves around the plight of a young white couple, and their story is entangled in a web of extreme situations that involve oppression, betrayal, persecution, captivity, seduction, torture and murder. Tancredo, a young lawyer, has an accident while riding a horse in a remote region of thick vegetation brightened by the intense tropical sun. He is discovered, hurt and unconscious, by a slave named Tulio, who is moving through the area. He takes the unconscious young man to a decadent farm where Ursula lives with her paralytic mother, Luisa B. As Tancredo recovers under Ursula's care, the couple fall in love, but she also discovers that Tancredo has had a fiancée. As Tancredo leaves after his recovery, with promises to come back, Ursula seeks comfort in the forest, but her solitude is interrupted by the presence of a fierce man who is struck by her beauty. He vows to take her as his wife. Ursula manages to escape, and from this point on the narrative is overshadowed with the unraveling of different stories and voices that begin to converge in gradual unexpected disclosures. The sequences are arranged to build up suspense as the characters, in their exchanges, disclose aspects of their personal lives that gradually reveal the history of ravaged family kinships at the center of which lies the gothic tyrant: he is a vicious husband, an abusive father, a cruel brother, a malicious uncle and a violent slave master. Reis's development of this intricate family plot forces the reader to make connections and establish links between the characters. We learn, for instance, that the man who tried to seduce Ursula was the powerful '*Comendador*' Fernando P, Tancredo's father. The man's brutality and cruelty caused his wife's death. He then married Adelaide, the young orphan who had been raised by Tancredo's mother and was Tancredo's bride-to-be. He was also the person who brought misery and poverty upon his own sister, Luisa B, Ursula's mother, by murdering her husband.[23] In other words, the *Comendador* is Ursula's uncle and the father of her husband-to-be. In the climactic moment of the story, the *Comendador* arrives at the scene of his son's wedding ceremony, shoots his son Tancredo and abducts Ursula, his son's bride. She is traumatized by this violence, driven mad and soon dies. The sinister events involving the fate of the white family are also linked to the lives of two black servants of Santa Cruz Farm, known for the cruelty of the master, *Comendador* P. His slaves are represented as walking ghosts; they go hungry and half-naked, and they are often beaten and live in ruined shacks that they cannot fix because of their perpetual work (166–67). The farm is Tulio's birthplace, and as a child he witnessed the selling of his mother, and his proud black blood leads him to voice his resentment in a land that he cannot call his own. Mother Susana also tells of her happy memories of being a young girl in Africa before her brutal captivity and the horrors of the middle passage. Both servants die as sacrificial victims of the white man's pride and desire: Mother Susana starves to death in a torture chamber, and Tulio is shot while trying to prevent the deadly confrontation of father and son, a story of unrelenting conflict that threatens to overshadow the romance plot. Reis's narrative includes a structural design aimed at stirring feelings of compassion and solidarity among her readers, and that is why she focused with such intensity on the image of a white family's house of horrors. The text is inscribed with a fierce emotional, cultural and social negativity that reflects the nation's bleak predicament during the Second Empire (1840–1889) under the rule of Dom Pedro II, a time when romantic nationalist discourses projected an ideal far apart from the social realities of a slave-holding society.

Slavery also casts a dark shadow over *La Familia del Comendador* by the Argentinian writer Juana Manso, published in *feuilleton*, a serial form in *The Ladies Journal*. The text appeared in 1854 in Rio de Janeiro, the city where Manso's family lived in exile after fleeing from Argentina due to political persecution under the dictatorship of Juan Manuel de Rosas.[24] Manso's work is an urban gothic novel that enacts the drama around birth and race, illegitimacy and inheritance, marriage and wealth in the capital of the Brazilian Empire, Rio de Janeiro. This is described in terms of a particular site, La Quinta de Botafogo, the family mansion of *Comendador* Gabriel das Neves, a rich entrepreneur in the coffee and sugar cane export trade. The initial descriptions of the natural landscape, with its breathtaking views of sea and mountains, produce a sharp contrast to the portrayal of a couple: the frivolous and weak husband and father (who submits to his mother's will, the matriarch Dona Maria) and who seduces every female slave servant. His children born from his slaves are killed or sold by the slave master. The wife is a cruel mother and mistress who is willing to sacrifice her daughter in marriage to enlarge the family's fortune and who exercises absolute power in the household by flogging the female house slaves on a daily basis (following on the tradition established by the family's matriarch). Manso's representation of the couple's crude exchanges in the opening chapter sets the tone for a narrative that focuses on traumatic otherness and offers a critique of the hypocrisy, degradation and greed of the Brazilian Catholic affluent class where grotesque violence is commonplace. Accordingly, Manso challenges the traditional depiction of the idealized white bourgeois mother-woman as weak, virtuous and suffering; instead, she depicts a tyrannical mother, one of the most loathsome female characters in nineteenth-century Brazilian literature.

The narrative revolves around a family decision: the 16-year-old daughter, Gabriela, is forced to marry her father's 50-year-old brother (her uncle), an arrangement concocted by the matriarch in order to keep the family's inheritance under the control of the '*Comendador*', her second son. This is in part because her first-born, Don Juan, is insane, but also because he has fathered two children by the mulatto slave who was taking care of him. The slaves' children were registered as slaves but could eventually claim part of their father's inheritance. The significance of family genealogy and of the Catholic tradition takes on dramatic overtones in a flashback that constitutes a strand of the novel's major plot and reveals the origin of the malaise that affects Don Juan. With a degree from Coimbra, Don Juan traveled throughout Europe and fell in love with an English Protestant girl, but he was ordered to return home to take charge of the family business after his father's death. As a liberal humanist, he could not stand the sufferings of the slaves being treated like 'animals', and he could not bear the sounds of their sorrowful songs. He wanted to return to Europe, against his mother's will (she fears he will return to the 'heretic girl'). As he insisted on his journey, Dona Maria ordered the slave master to tie him to a torture pillar, where he was flogged until he fell unconscious to the ground. This caused his mental illness at the age of 24. After this narrative flashback, the major strand of the plot depicts Gabriela's escape from forced marriage and her taking refuge in a convent with the help of her servant Nina. By this time, she has fallen in love with Ernesto de Souza, a medical doctor and the son of a Portuguese aristocrat (with no fortune) who turns to cross-dressing as he tries to unsuccessfully rescue her from the convent.

At the pivotal moment of the narrative, Nina is brutally flogged for keeping the secret of her mistress's refuge; she dies from the wounds inflicted, thus repeating the punishment given to the slave servant in *Ursula*. But here, there is a reversal in the narrative. The doctor, Maurício, is called by Gabriela's sister to treat Nina's wounds; Maurício is Don Juan's mixed-blood son, who has been banished by the family along with his mother and sister. By accident he enters the sick man's quarters and is recognized by his father who awakens from his muddled state. The recovery of Don Juan makes him into an ally of Ernesto de Souza in the efforts to rescue Gabriela from the convent where she has become a prisoner of the nuns and priests who will profit from the family's donations once she takes her vows. Manso had a clear grasp of the fear of miscegenation among the elite class and the circuits of power, including the insatiable appetite for material gains. The two pillars of the Imperial regime—the slaveholding system and the Catholic Church—are reinstated in the pathologized sphere of the family, an embodiment of the perverse desires and awful deeds that still haunt the national imaginary. The novel was published only four years after the Imperial government issued a decree that outlawed the slave trade, not out of a magnanimous gesture of recognition of its evilness, but because of long-term pressures from the British government. At the time, the black population in bondage was estimated to be 1,240,000, and they had to wait for the Golden Law of May 13, 1888, to gain emancipation.

Clorinda Matto de Turner's *Aves Sin Nido* was published in Peru in 1889.[25] Only with the second printing in 1934, and the critical review by Concha Meléndez, was it acknowledged as a major novel in Hispanic-American literature. Clorinda Matto de Turner was sympathetic to the modernizing reformist movements that demanded urgency in the efforts to rescue the marginalized and exploited native populations. The goal was to integrate them into the new nation, but Matto de Turner was skeptical of the viability of this social project, particularly in light of the historical legacies of colonization underlying the power structures of the government and the church. Considering the author's political ideas, it is not surprising that *Aves Sin Nido* was banned by the Catholic authorities and Matto de Turner persecuted by conservative groups, an unbearable situation that led her to exile in Argentina, never returning to her home country. The story is set in the imaginary isolated province of Killac, a remote region of the Andes mountains where the degradation of moral values and the local elite's economic and sexual privileges debase women with virulent consequences such as secrecy, illegitimacy, miscegenation and incest. From the onset, the narrator explains that in Killac each individual's destiny is defined according to his/her place in the highly stratified social organization. Each place has its correspondent scale of values: 'notables', members of the white local oligarchy, government officials with absolute power on the political, judicial and ecclesiastical domains and members of the clergy; 'foreigners', members of the progressive bourgeoisie (such as the Marin family), who arrive in the town to invest in mining business; and the 'disinherited race'. This last category is represented by the Yupanqui and Champi families, depicted in the narrative as victims of economic exploitation and physical and psychological abuse sanctioned by the church's authorities, headed by the local vicar Don Pascual. In this rigidly divided world, conflict disrupts the peaceful Marin household when Marcela Yupanqui arrives and begs Lucia Marin for help. Her youngest child had been abducted because the family could not pay back a debt. The system of charges called 'reparto' (share), made the natives pay for their living quarters and land where they kept and tended the lhamas. As Marcela explains, every time the collector comes to get the wool, the fixed price is so low that the families can hardly survive, but in his last visit to collect the money, the family did not have the amount so he abducted their youngest daughter, who was presumably taken to Arequipa to be sold. Lucia becomes involved in the fate of the Yupanquis and the rescuing of the little girl. She sends a request to the governor to pardon the family's debt and makes inquiries into the local economic policies in relation to the Indians. The official replies, answering that 'habitual practices are law', and a riot is organized to target and kill the Marins, actions that result in the deaths of Juan Yupanqui and Marcela. In the investigation of the crimes, the blame falls on native Isidro Champi. But the young Don Manuel Pancorbo discovers that his father, Don Sebastian, and the governor of Killac conspired with the vicar Pascual Vargas to develop the diabolical plan to kill the Marins. From this moment onward, the masks of civility begin to fall away, and the family's secrets are pieced together by Lucia Marin and Don Manuel, who knew he was a bastard child and that his birth was shrouded in mystery.

As the narrative advances, the gothic atmosphere takes over the realist modes of representation. The narrative pace increases, and suspense is developed through dialogue, with only a few brief interventions by the narrator. The initial descriptions of a benevolent nature, the bright sunny mornings and the gorgeous mountain skyline, give way to dark spaces with a hostile and suffocating atmosphere. Here, the characters' exchanges provoke tensions, suspicions, confrontations and revelations. Lucia Marin is assaulted by forebodings of imminent disaster; this is in part because she is the keeper of the secret that Marcela revealed to her in her deathbed. Manuel's suspicions lead him into the vile depths of his alleged father and the cunningness of the vicar, whose head is described as a 'nest of lecherous serpents ready to wake up at the slightest noise of a woman's voice' (my translation, 11). Once his paternity is revealed, Don Pascual loses his mind and, in his delirium, he roams the street, haunted by ghosts. But the full spectrum of the horror emerges with the final disclosure during the Marins' farewell dinner before returning to Lima with their adopted daughters, Rosalia and Margarita (the Yupanchi's sisters). When Manuel reveals to his beloved Margarita that he is the son of the Bishop Don Pedro Miranda y Claro, former vicar of Killac, Lucia is forced to reveal that Margarita is the daughter of the same man. Melancholy consumes the couple as the shadow of incest intrudes as a chilling void to shatter their dreams. This is commensurable with the traumatic realization that many women, independently of class or race, like Petronilha (the governor's wife), Marcela Yupanqui and others, like Theodora and Martina, had been prey to the guile and lust of clergymen and other men of the elite class. The novel inscribes Matto de Turner's passionate commitment to defending the integrity of the autochthonous populations. But its resolution does not engender hope for change; rather, the Marin family returns to the security of their home in Lima where the broken-hearted Margarita, displaced from her cultural roots, turns to education as the only possible route to forgetting the sacrifice she is forced to make because of the sexual violence committed against her mother.

Dona Narcisa de Villar, A Legend of Colonial Time, by Ana Luiza de Azevedo Castro, was published in 1859. This was six years before José de Alencar's canonical indigenist novel *Iracema*, which is often considered to be the most significant expression of romantic nationalism and mythmaking narrative of the Brazilian race (the most enduring allegory of Brazilian identity despite the absence of black characters).[26] In *Dona Narcisa*, Azevedo de Castro dared to recreate the darker side of colonization, a transgression at the time, and she celebrated the oral native tradition of storytelling. Here, she creates a female narrator that explains how she is about to tell a story that was not hers but that had been passed on to her by two old Indian sisters, mother Micaela and aunt Simoa, who warned her about Anhangá (the native word for the evil that haunts Honey Island). The narrative takes the reader back to the year 1669, a time when the Portuguese Crown emptied its prisons by sending criminals to the colony and gave away land titles to Portuguese members of the aristocracy who frequently ruled the land as tyrants. The three Villar brothers regard the people who lived in their land, including the indigenous population, as 'human species born for submission and hard work' (my translation 29). The story focuses on the plight of D. Narcisa de Villar, a young woman loses her parents and is brought from Portugal to live with her greedy brothers. In their house she is taken care of by Efigenia, the Indian house servant. The brothers want to place Narcisa in a convent so as to take possession of her inheritance but decide on a marriage of convenience that would take her back to Portugal. On the eve of the forced wedding, as Narcisa 'the daughter of whites' (120) is about to commit suicide, Leonardo, the mixed blood character who has loved her since they were playmates, kidnaps her and takes her to Honey Island. Persecuted by the Villars, the couple is killed. What seems to end as a melodrama attains a dramatic status compatible with great tragedy in the sequence that highlights Narcisa's speech wherein, with heroic defiance, she disclaims any blood kinship with the Villar family. Efigenia arrives too late to prevent the tragedy and on seeing her dead son she discloses the secret of her life. Daughter of an Indian chief of the Tupi nation who had received Don Luis de Villar as his guest, she was seduced and abandoned by him and only much later brought to 'the city of whites' with her child to become a house slave (124). Azevedo e Castro creates the image of a historical memory that romantic nationalism pushed back into the dark corners of oblivion: the oppression of white women, the sexual violence and abandonment of native women who concealed the names of their children's fathers and the doom of miscegenation and incest. It is only proper that instead of an exuberant tropical nature to match the lover's joy, as in *Iracema*, a dark cave in a distant island becomes the lovers' refuge and grave. The hostile landscape and the signs of bad omens that permeate the narrative are replaced, at the end, by the image of two white doves that can occasionally be seen flying from and back to the island, spectral figures associated with death and mourning that suggest the island has become a haunted place.

Undoubtedly, one of the effects of the gothic conventions in the four novels considered here is the production of a cross-national cultural imaginary that inscribes different signs of identity and meaning. This arises alongside other interpretations of belonging and society that stand at odds with the hegemonic subjectivities engendered by the mechanisms of literary interpellation present in canonical novels of the period. Thus, we must recognize that their textual identities unveil the nation's otherness by subverting the structure of romance and nation-building couched in productive sexuality and national consolidation. The texts by these women restructure the form of the novel at the point of intersection with the historical problem of the constitution of national cultures, and they bring into consideration the overtly political function of gothic transculturations in nineteenth-century Latin America.

In this context, the writers shared a consciousness of their identities as historicized experience within their own cultures. Their gendered positions in relation to the system of identity and value enforced by the social structure of colonial patriarchal power made it possible for these women to subvert the dominant discourses that overpowered them and engage in the project of nation/narration. These novels project many images of female protective bonds that cut across class and racial lines. Absent in canonical male fictions that, as a rule, feature women alone, the representation of supportive emotional ties among women embedded in the stories signals the ideological move toward an imagined community of women as a way of decolonizing the national space.

From the perspective of difference and the cultural continuities of aesthetic form, the appropriation of gothic conventions in women's fiction forces us to reexamine historical blind spots and silences in the interpretive frames of reference through which understandings of Latin-American nineteenth-century literature have been crystallized. This means, on the one hand, resituating the representative status and representations by and of women novelists in the cultural/symbolical networks of the nineteenth century. On the other hand, we must revise and alter what we know about the novel form beyond the limits of traditional literary histories, particularly if we consider transformations of the genre in geographical and cultural locations struggling with colonial legacies and identities within contexts marked by relations of conflict, domination and resistance. Understanding gothic migrations in developments of the novel may eventually lead to a new history of the novel, one that would be more inclusive and take into account gender and racial systems in the interlocking dimensions of Latin American national heterogeneity and transnational fluidity.

Notes

1. In the words of Sara Beatriz Guardia, director of the Peruvian Center of Studies of Women in Latin America, nineteenth-century women's writings in Latin America 'were considered—well into the twentieth century, as something peculiar that received no critical attention (...). Female texts did not circulate in a regular fashion and many still remain without any recognition, it is a silenced history' (My translation). In: *Escritoras de Siglo 19 en America Latina*, (*Women*

Writers in Nineteenth-Century Latin America), published by CEMHAL, March 2012, p.12. Access in pdf, htpp//webserver.rcp.net.pe/cenmhal/.

2. Unlike most European countries where the tradition of the novel was well established by the 19th century, in Latin America the 'novel', which translates into Portuguese as 'romance', and into Spanish as 'novela', only emerged in the nineteenth century and was associated with the historical novel, the privileged narrative mode in the romantic period. The term 'novel' was often used interchangeably with terms such as 'prose fiction' with no distinction between novel and romance, as it occurs in eighteenth-century Britain where the term 'romance' is defined as sentimentalized tales that invoke historical pasts and aristocratic traditions. The first essay to treat gothic influxes in Brazilian women writers was an undergraduate paper by a student who was under my supervision, Anselmo Peres Alós, entitled '*O Romance Gótico e a Crítica ao Patriarcado no Final do Século 19*' (The Gothic Novel and The Critique to Patriarchy in the End of the Nineteenth Century). *Cadernos do IL* (Porto Alegre/UFRGS), v. 25, p. 155–60, 2002). To this day, there is no major work on gothic traditions, either male or female, in Brazil.
3. In *Art of Darkness: A Poetics of Gothic* (1995), Ann Williams discusses how nineteenth-century critics, in order to preserve 'the realist novel as High Prose Fiction tradition,' declared the end of the gothic or (if alive) as irrational 'feminine' popular romance' (6).
4. See the groundbreaking work by Marlyse Meyer, *Folhetim: Uma Historia* (1996) wherein she charts the influence of the French *feuilleton* and its version in nineteenth-century Brazil. Meyer also comments on the novels from England, most of them translated in Spain and Portugal, that crossed the Atlantic through book dealers who established shops after 1808, when the Portuguese Crown moved the court to Rio de Janeiro to escape from Napoleon. Also see Jean Franco's *Historia de La Literatura Hispanoamerica—a partir de la Independencia* (1975), and the essay by Sandra Vasconcelos, entitled 'Formação do Romance Brasileiro 1808–1860' (vertentes inglesas): http://www.unicamp.br/iel/memorial/Ensaios/Sandra/sandra.htm.
5. Ellen Moers in *Literary Women* (1978) shows the long engagement of British women writers with the gothic mode. In her *Gothic and Gender: An Introduction* (2004), Donna Heiland points out the importance of Ellen Moers' work for identifying the 'female gothic' as a distinct subgenre in the European gothic tradition. She lists a series of recent scholarly works that attest to the fact that the 'female gothic' has become an established critical tradition, particularly after Eve Kosofsky Sedgwick's *Coherence of Gothic Conventions* (1980), which initiated a range of research on the gothic in the area of gender and genre studies.
6. In his classical work, *Contrapunto Cubano del Tabaco y el Azúcar* (1978), Ortiz explains: 'We understand that the term *transculturation* best expresses the different phases of the transitional process of one culture to the other because this process does not consist of acquiring a culture, which is implied in the Anglo-American notion of *aculturation*, but the process in which there is also a loss or displacement of one culture in relation to a precedent one, which could account for a partial deculturation besides, it incorporates the creation of new cultural phenomena that could be called *neoculturacition*' (my translation 86).
7. For more on the cultural processes in colonized spaces, absorption and reinvention of foreign material, see Mary Louise Pratt's *Imperial Eyes: Travel Writing*

and Transculturation (1992) wherein she elaborates on the concept of 'contact zones' as 'social spaces where disparate cultures meet, clash, and grapple with each other, often in highly asymmetrical relations of domination and subordination-like colonialism, slavery, or their aftermaths as they are lived out across the globe today' (4).

8. As one of the best examples of nineteenth-century American gothic, Poe's tale 'The Fall of the House of Usher' presents open spaces to create a fearful atmosphere that foreshadows major events that take place indoors, in enclosed spaces like chambers, corridors and underground vaults.
9. I draw here on ideas put forward by Giorgio Agamben in his *State of Exception* (2005). See my text 'Of Violence, Law, Rights, Justice and the State: Regarding Brazilian Novels of Trauma' in *Law and Literature at the Turn of the Millennium* (edited by Sonja Arnold and Michael Korfmann, 2014).
10. Donna Heiland refers to some recent scholarly works that bring debates around the difference between sentimentality and sensibility. She points out that sentimentality can be deployed to support patriarchal structures whereas sensibility 'has the potential to disrupt not just patriarchal structures but the gender definitions in which patriarchy is grounded' (12). My inference draws a parallel with Jerrold E. Hogle's comments in his Introduction to *The Cambridge Companion to Gothic Fiction* (2002): he writes that the gothic trend that Horace Walpole began with his *The Castle of Otranto* 'exploded in the 1790's in the British Isles, on the continent of Europe, and briefly in the United States, particularly for a female readership, so much so that it remained a popular, if controversial, literary mode throughout what we still call the Romantic period in European literature (the 1790s through the early 1830s' (1).
11. For more on this, see Alan Lloyd-Smith's *American Gothic Fiction* (2004) and *Gothic Fiction: the British and American Tradition* (edited by Diane Long Hoeveler and Tamar Heller, 2003).
12. 'DissemiNation: Time, Narrative, and the Margins of the Modern Nation'. *Nation and Narration*. Ed. Bhabha, Homi (New York: Routledge, 1990), 139–46.
13. In the chapter 'Direitos de Memória, Sobre Independências e Estados-Nação na América Latina' ('Rights to memory, about Independence and Nation-States in Latin America') in his *Planetas Sem Boca* (*Planets with no Mouths)* (Belo Horizonte: Editora UFMGm, 2006), trad. Lyslei Nascimento.
14. In 'La Escritura de la Historia o a Propósito de las Fundaciones de la Nación'. ('Concerning History or the Foundations of Nationhood'), *Cadernos do Centro de Pesquisas Literárias da PUC/RS*, Porto Alegre, vol.6, no.1, agosto de 2000, page18.
15. In the essay 'Brasil: Nações Imaginadas' ('Brasil: Imagined Nations') in *Pontos e Bordados: Escritos de História e Política, (Dots and Stiches: Writings on History and Politics),* (Belo Horizonte: Editora da UFMG, 1999), 233–68.
16. For Roberto Goncález Echevarria in his 'The Making of the Latin American Novel', Indian or black had nothing to say that could be incorporated in Latin American culture, and their history was anything but ancillary in the composition of the nascent independent states' in *Literary Cultures of Latin American—A Comparative History*, vol II. Edited by Mario J. Valdés and Djelal Kadir (2004), 291.
17. In Ramas' discussion of the lettered city, writing was the invention of a protective ring of power against the people, meaning that 'desculturation' of the

majority represented the defeat of the people (folk oral culture), a price to pay for in the initial stages of modernization of Latin America.

18. See also Jorge Myers' essay, 'Hacia la Completa Palingenesia y Civilización de las Naciones Americanas 1830–1870' ('Concerning the Complete Palingenesis of Romantic Literature and Social Project') in *América Latina: Palavra, Literatura e Cultura*, vol 2. Ana Pizarro, org. (São Paulo: Editora da UNICAMP, 1994).
19. For more on this, see Friedhelm Schmidt in his 'Literaturas Heterogeneas y Alegorias Nacionales: Paradigmas para Las Literatures Poscoloniales' ('Heterogenous Literatures and National Allegories: Paradigms for Postcolonial Literatures'). He challenges Sommer's claim that all foundational fictions resort to happy endings as a stock resolution to affirm alliances. *Revista Iberoamericana*, vol LXVI, no. 190, Enero/Marzo 2000: 175–15.
20. The distinction between the novel and the romance has been explored in U.S. literary criticism: see Richard Chase's *The American Novel and Its Tradition* (1957). On proposing a native tradition of the American novel, Chase claims that novelists found uses for romance beyond escapist fantasy and sentimentality. He writes that in the freedom of romance from the conditions of actuality, there are potential virtues of the mind suggested in such words as rapidity, irony, abstraction and profundity. So romance becomes a vehicle for intellectual and moral ideas, introducing into the novel 'the narrow profundity of New England Puritanism, the skeptical rationalistic spirit of the Enlightenment and the imaginative freedom of Transcendentalism' (X). He emphasizes the abstract and profound ideas expressed in romance, allowing for the formulation of moral truths, universal validity and the dark truths unavailable to realism. For Chase, the tradition of the romance is central to the history of the American novel but minor in the history of the English novel. See also Helen Hughes's *The Historical Romance* (1993).
21. See Mary Louise Pratt's essay 'Mulher, Literatura e Irmandade Nacional' in *Tendências e Impasses: O Feminismo Como Crítica da Cultura*. Edited by Heloisa Buarque de Hollanda (Rio de Janeiro: Rocco, 1994).
22. In this novel, the whitening and acculturation of the female protagonist is a necessary step for the erasure of her heritage and makes her eligible to marry a white gentleman; therefore, the novel inscribes the ideology of miscegenation of its time, which included 'bleaching' as a form of removing racial differences.
23. The term '*Comendador*' is a popular title of rank given to a rich self-made man, in this case a slavery-holder planter, with no aristocratic background but who exerts influence and power in his social context. Moreover, the fact that family names are omitted is significant and raises the hypothesis that the writer, who was an ex-slave herself, did not want her characters to be taken as real people.
24. In Rio, Manso married a Brazilian man and devoted herself to journalism, founding the journal where she also published the novel *Misterios del Plata* (1852), a political and historical novel where the gothic mode serves to highlight the dark ages under the dictatorship of the Argentinian dictator Juan Manuel de Rosas (1829–1852). The novel focuses on the drama of a family during a period of intense political struggle that divided Argentina into two opposition parties, the Federalists, lead by Rosas, and the Unitarians, members of an Enlightenment elite who held onto the liberal ideal of a civilized modern Argentina and who regarded Rosas' bloody politics a setback for the development of the country. In this novel the white female protagonist seeks to rescue her husband from prison; he is a political opponent to Rosas's regime, and has been sentenced to death.

25. It is important to add that Antonio Cornejo Polar, who studied Matto de Turner's novels for many years, was the first critic to consider *Aves Sin Nido* in terms of the allegorical homology romance/nation.
26. In this novel written by José de Alencar, the love story of the Portuguese colonizer and Iracema, the daughter of an Indian chief, rests in the past. The boat takes Martin and his son Moacir, born of the love affair with Iracema who died of labor alone in the forest. In the creation of a myth of origins, to bear a son is a woman's duty, to build a nation is the hero's task, with the help of other acculturated native men.

Bibliography

Achugar, Hugo. 'La Escritura de la Historia o a propósito de las Fundaciones de la Nación'. *Cadernos do Centro de Pesquisas Literárias da PUC/RS* 6:1 (2000), Porto Alegre: PUC/RS.

———. 'Direitos de Memória, Sobre Independências e Estados-Nação na América Latina'. *Planetas Sem Boca*. Translated by Lyslei Nascimento. Belo Horizonte: Editora UFMG, 2006. Print.

Agamben, Giorgio. *State of Exception*. Trans. Atell, Kevin. Chicago: University of Chicago Press, 2005. Print.

Alencar, José de. *O Guarani*. 1857. São Paulo: Ática, 1999. Print.

Alós, Anselmo Peres. 'O romance gótico e a crítica ao patriarcado no final do século 19th'. *Cadernos do IL* 25 (2002): 155–60. Print.

Anderson, Benedict. *Imagined Communities: Reflections on the Origin and Spread of Nationalism*. London: Verso, 1983. Print.

Avellaneda, Gertrudes Gomes de. *Sab*. 1859. Ed. Cruz, Mary. La Habana: Instituto Cubano del Libro, 1973. Print.

Bhabha, Homi. *Nation and Narration*. New York: Routledge, 1990. Print.

Bhabha, Homi. *The Location of Culture*. London: Routledge, 1994. Print.

Blest, Alberto. *Martín Rivas* (1852). Trans. O'Dwyer, Tess. Oxford: Oxford University Press, 2000. Print.

Carvalho, José Murilo de. 'Brasil: Nações Imaginadas'. *Pontos e Bordados: Escritos de História e Política*. Belo Horizonte: Editora da UFMG, 1999. Print.

Castro, Ana Luiza Azevedo. *D. Narcisa de Villar* (1859). Florianópolis: Editora Mulheres, 2008.

Chase, Richard. *The American Novel and Its Tradition*. New York: Anchor Books, 1957. Print.

Echevarria, Roberto Gomcález. 'The Making of the Latin American Novel'. *Literary Cultures of Latin America—A Comparative History*, vol. II. Ed. Valdés, Mario J. and Djelal Kadir. New York: Oxford University Press, 2004. Print.

Franco, Jean. *Historia de la Literatura Hispanoamericana: A partir de la Independencia*. Barcelona: Editora Ariel, 1975. Print.

Galván, Manoel de Jesus. *Enriquillo, leyenda histórica dominicana*. 1881. Mexico: Porrúa, 1976. Print.

Guardia, Sara Beatriz. *Escritoras de Siglo 19 en America Latina*. 2012. Web 10 Jan. 2015. <http//webserver.rcp.net.pe/cnemhal/>.

Heiland, Donna. *Gothic and Gender: An Introduction*. Oxford: Blackwell, 2004. Print.

Hoeveler, Diane Long, and Tamar Heller. Eds. *Gothic Fiction: The British and American Tradition*. New York: Modern Language Association of America, 2003. Print.

Hogle, Jerrold E. 'Introduction: The Gothic in Western Culture'. *The Cambridge Companion to Gothic Fiction*. Ed. Hogle, Jerrold E. Cambridge: Cambridge University Press, 2002. Print.

Hughes, Helen. *The Historical Romance*. New York: Routledge, 1993. Print.

Isaacs, Jorge. *Maria*. 1867. Editorial Huemul: Buenos Aires, 1969. Print.

Lloyd-Smith, Alan. *American Gothic Fiction*. New York: Continuum, 2004. Print.

Manso, Juana. *La família del Comendor y otros textos*. 1852. Argentina, 2006. Print.

Marmol, José. *Amalia* (1855). Buenos Aires: Imprenta Americana. Web 20 Jan. 2015. <http://www.biblioteca.clarin.com/pbda/novela/amalia/novela.htm>.

Méndez-Rodenas, Adriana. 'Mujer, nación, y otredad en Gertrudis Gómez de Avellaneda'. *Cuba en su imagen: historia e identidade en la literatura cubana*. Madrid: Editora Verbum, 2002. Print.

Mera, Juan Leon. *Cumandá*. 1887. Boston: Heath, 1932. Print.

Meyer, Marlyse. *Folhetim: Uma História*. São Paulo: Companhia das Letras, 1996. Print.

Moers, Ellen. *Literary Women*. London: The Women's Press, 1978. Print.

Myers, Jorge, "Hacia la completa palingenesia y civilización de las naciones americanas': literatura romántica y proyecto social, 1830–1870'. *América Latina: Palavra, Literatura e Cultura* 2. Organized by Ana Pizarro. São Paulo: Editora da UNICAMP, 1994. Print.

Ortiz, Fernando. *Contrapunto Cubano del Tabaco y el Azúcar*. Caracas: Biblioteca Ayacuch, 1978. Print.

Paixão, Sylvia. 'A Mulher e a Pátria'. *Letterature D'America*, XVI.66, 1996. Print.

Poe, Edgar Allan. 'The Fall of the House of Usher'. 1839. Web. 10 Jan. 2015. <http://www.bartleby.com/195/10.html>.

Pratt, Mary Louise. *Imperial Eyes: Travel Writing and Transculturation*. New York: Routledge, 1992. Print.

———. 'Mulher, Literatura e Irmandade Nacional'. *Tendências e Impasses: O Feminismo como Crítica da Cultura*. Edited by Heloisa Buarque de Hollanda. Rio de Janeiro: Rocco, 1994. Print.

Rama, Ángel. *La Ciudad Letrada*. Santiago: Tajamar Editores, 2004. Print.

———. *Transculturación Narrativa en América Latina*. 1984. Buenos Aires: Ediciones El Andariego, 2007. Print.

Reis, Maria Firmina dos. *Ursula* (1859). Florianópolis: Editora Mulheres, 2004. Print.

San Martin, Juan Zorrilla de. 'Tabaré' (1888). *Bibliotecas Virtuales*. Web Jan. 20, 2015. <http://www.bibliotecasvirtuales.com/biblioteca/LiteraturaLatinoamericana/ZorrilladeSanMartin/Tabare/index.asp>.

Schmidt, Friedhelm. 'Literaturas heterogeneas y alegorias nacionales: Paradigmas para las literaturas poscoloniales'. *Revista Iberoamericana* LXVI: 190, (2000). Print.

Schmidt, Rita Terezinha. 'Of Violence, Law, Rights, Justice and the State: regarding Brazilian Novels of Trauma'. *Law and Literature at the Turn of the Millennium*. Edited by Sonja Arnold and Michael Korfmann. Porto Alegre: Editora Dublinense/DAAD, 2014. Print.

Sedgwick, Eve Kosofsky. *The Coherence of Gothic Conventions*. New York: Arno Press, 1980. Print.

Sommer, Doris. *Latin American Novel, Foundational Fictions—The National Romances of Latin America*. Berkeley: University of California Press, 1991. Print.

Turner, Clorinda Matto de. *Aves Sin Nido* (1889). Caracas: Biblioteca Ayacucho, 1994. Print.

Vasconcelos, Sandra Guardini. 'Formação do Romance Brasileiro 1808–1860 (vertentes inglesas)'. http://www.unicamp.br/iel/memorial/Ensaios/Sandra/sandra.htm Web. 10 Jan. 2015.

Vidal, Hernán, ed. *Cultural and Historical Grounding for Hispanic and Luso-Brazilian Feminist Literary Criticism*. Minneapolis, MN: Institute for the Study of Ideologies, 1989. Print.

Williams, Ann. *Art of Darkness: A Poetics of Gothic*. Chicago: University of Chicago Press, 1995. Print.

15 The Strange Case of Brazilian Gothic Cinema

Daniel Serravalle de Sá

At a glance, the relationship between Brazil and the Gothic seems to contain an essential contradiction: the opposing ideas of 'solar' and 'gloom' in one concept. However, as it turns out, a number of motifs bridge these apparently irreconcilable ideas and connect a variety of films that illustrate how Brazilian culture is related to Gothic. Brazil has produced a modest, and not yet fully explored, collection of Gothic films, which were developed on the margins of mainstream national cinema. These films contain elements that are partly familiar and partly unfamiliar, partly resembling the well-known features of Anglo-American Gothic, yet evoking some inflexions that are unrecognizable outside a Brazilian frame of reference. Caught somewhere between reconciliation and difference, the analysis of these texts as Gothic forces us to question the tenets of the country's history and institutions; that is, a Gothic reading of these films reanimates old traumas and provokes discussions about national culture within particular social contexts.

The existence of what I call Brazilian Gothic in film makes the strange case of an inchoate field: it cannot be conceptualized as a tradition but rather as a composite of interventions by different filmmakers at different periods. It yields neither a genre nor a mode, but rather multivalent tendencies and coheres, if at all, around matters such as the dismantling of a metonymic national subject. The manifestation of the Gothic in Brazilian cinema, as in other national cinemas, is often linked to otherness (cultural, sexual, racial), historical tensions (conflicts between opposing forces in a given time-space) and the psychodynamics of social and individual representation (collective and personal traumas, sensations, scandals), as well as other scenarios that place the viewer at the edge of symbolic dissolution. A few explanations are necessary before I explore how the particular circumstances of Brazil's history and cultural institutions generate a series of inflections that determine a type of Gothic that both borrows and differs considerably from the Anglo-American versions.

The scarcity of internationally acclaimed Brazilian Gothic films (and horror films more broadly) is linked to matters of cultural production and critical interpretation. First, a consequence of the realities of dependency conditioned the nature of cultural production and circulation in Brazil since the early twentieth century. Therefore, the lack of a distinct horror production industry is partially due to the underdevelopment of the national film industry, which has endured a number of problems such as an untrained workforce, shortage of effective producers, precarious infrastructure and foreign competition. As a result, in spite of Brazil's rich heritage of folklore, with its many references to mysteries involving life and death, religious superstitions, mystic ballads and uncanny legends,[1] the film industry never fully developed Gothic horror as a national genre. This lack of production on an industrial scale has meant that the Gothic has never become a full film genre but rather a form that remained mobile, hybridizing, mutating and dispersed into plots of other film texts.

Second, the absence of a distinctive Brazilian horror production industry is related to an institutional discourse that emerged in the late 1950s and early 1960s. This was disseminated by an influential generation of film critics and filmmakers linked to the upper-middle-class and in dialogue with the cultural elite. The intellectual projects of these decades favored descriptions of 'the realities of life' to the detriment of 'the figments of the imagination', and this influenced how cinema was studied and even produced in the country. This generation of critics was particularly aware that Brazilian cinema included historical deficiencies and they endeavored to redress what was seen as a long-standing history of cultural colonization by providing the country with a set of key names, themes and films worthy of artistic and cultural appraisal. This ideological construction of Brazil's film history resulted in rich theoretical and aesthetic debates, but it also restricted the scope of investigation and professed an isolationist vision of Brazilian cinema that ignored historical appropriations from international cinema, especially in relation to popular culture and Hollywood genre movies.[2]

A third phenomenon to be taken into account is the ubiquity of Gothic horror in non-cinematic media such as radio broadcasts and comic books. These cultural manifestations are particularly important because they feed the imagination of many Brazilian filmmakers. One example is the program 'Incrível! Fantástico! Extraordinário!', first broadcast by Rádio Tupi in 1947 and presented by Almirante. For 11 years this weekly show related all kinds of unexplained experiences that allegedly happened to people from different parts of Brazil, putting the mystique of popular storytelling on the radio. The impact of this series on later film production is particularly evident in Adolpho Chandler's omnibus film series *Incrível, fantástico, extraordinário* (1969). Another example of this influence is the Brazilian comic book industry, which often reprinted North American comics. However, when the censorious U.S. Comics Code was implemented in 1954, Brazilian comic artists turned to motifs taken from local folk traditions to produce distinctive expressions of horror. Álvaro de Moya states that from the early 1950s to the mid-1970s independent publishing houses dedicated to horror comic books thrived in Brazil and came to produce 30 unique titles (30). Filmmaker José Mojica Marins not only adapted print-based features into his films but also produced comic books of his own. Such manifestations on the radio and in comics were linked to foreign cultural forms and local sources and had a significant impact on Brazilian Gothic in cinema. Moreover, these examples foreground the appetite for Gothic horror stories in Brazil and a local audience interested in consuming this type of narrative.

I have been arguing that several problems arise when trying to place Brazilian films within a straightforward definition of Gothic. This is because of the diversity with which it is produced and consumed in the national context, as well as the elusive nature of the Gothic genre in Brazil that is often in the eye of the beholder or in the director's treatment of his material, and that includes films that are not even scary. These singularities allow theoretical possibilities for reassessing several films that have not been analyzed from a Gothic perspective. However, rather than simply recasting these films as Gothic, I seek to work reflexively on the images that emerge in the films and consider what the text represents and where those representations originate.

In order to do this, I will place films by Walter Hugo Khouri and José Mojica Marins alongside one another. I seek to connect these films in terms of a protocol of reading that, on one hand, favors a specific aesthetic and iconography of Anglo-American extraction and, on the other hand, understands the Gothic as a useful framework to address socio-political contexts, metaphorical connotations and contradictions of the texts. My readings will include a broad view of Brazilian history and take into account the diverse cultural production of several dissimilar filmmakers as a gesture toward being comprehensive. This effort to be inclusive should not be seen as misstep in my argument about Brazilian Gothic diversity; rather, it is an attempt to provide insightful categorizations by focusing on facts, best moments, key texts and other types of synecdochic examples. Finally, the references to the aesthetics and iconographies of Anglo-American extraction do not invalidate the originality of the Brazilian Gothic. Instead, they are part of the cross-cultural dynamic that is so often present in the Brazilian Gothic.

Two Waves of Brazilian Gothic Cinema

Although Brazil's folklore and literature did not generate a prolific production of Gothic films, several early twentieth-century films embraced horror, crime and the supernatural, including *O Diabo* (Antônio Campos, 1908), *Nas Entranhas do Morro Castelo* (Antônio Leal, 1917), *Os Mistérios do Rio de Janeiro* (Coelho Neto, 1917), *O Crime da Mala* (Antônio Tibiriçá, 1928), *O Jovem Tataravô* (Luis de Barros, 1936), *Alameda da Saudade 113* (Carlos Ortiz, 1951), *Noivas do Mal* (George Dusek, 1952), *Meu Destino é Pecar* (Manuel Peluffo, 1952), *Estranho Encontro* (Walter Hugo Khouri, 1958) and *Ravina* (Rubem Biáfora, 1959). Since most of these films are officially listed as missing or have been reassembled with difficulty, it is hard to give a comprehensive analysis of them or gauge the extent to which these early interventions employed or reinvented the Gothic.

However, one film that survived from this period, Luis de Barros's *O Jovem Tataravô*, includes the character Eduardo (Darcy Cazarré) who buys an Egyptian mystery box with the power to reanimate the dead.[3] During a séance, Eduardo conjures up his great-grandfather Vitor (Marcel Klass), who has been dead for over 100 years. The patriarch emerges from a dark corner of the room in flesh and blood, sporting imperial fashion sideburns worn with clean-shaven chin. The Egyptian reference and the use of chiaroscuro lighting schemes echo Universal Studios 1930s horror cycle, but instead of invoking the usual horror paradigms of fear and revulsion this musical comedy treats the supernatural theme in a playful way. The great-grandfather is not a diabolical figure but a mischievous ghost who proves to be an insatiable womanizer, who even tries to seduce family members. His advances often allude to colonial forms of sexuality, in which male harassment and groping was not considered to be coercion but a prelude to sex. Although the great-grandfather is not necessarily evil, his behavior is morally deplorable, deviating from respectable and carefully cultivated bourgeois customs. He must be sent back to his tomb. But the magic scroll that could accomplish this has been destroyed, so the characters perform Afro-Brazilian religious ceremonies (which are parodied as primitive and irrational). The Brazilian Gothic manifests itself here in the hypocrisy of the privileged class by revealing family scandals, patriarchal forms of sexuality inherited from the past and the derogatory representation of *candomblé* cults (even when their knowledge is needed). The Gothic emerges through the contradictions found in the film's plot and exposes national fears and prejudices.

The second wave of Brazilian Gothic film production took place between the mid-1960s and the mid-1980s when more than 50 films were produced on the margins of the 'official' national cinema. Made mostly in São Paulo and Rio de Janeiro, some examples of this extended production cycle are: *À Meia Noite Levarei Sua Alma* (José Mojica Marins, 1964), *Esta Noite Encarnarei no teu Cadáver* (José Mojica Marins, 1967), *Um Sonho de Vampiros* (Iberê Cavalcanti, 1969), *Nosferato no Brasil* (Ivan Cardoso, 1970), *O Macabro Dr Scivano* (Raul Calhado, 1971), *Guru das Sete Cidades* (Carlos Bini, 1972), *Enigma para Demônios* (Carlos Christensen, 1974), *O Anjo da Noite* (Walter Hugo Khouri, 1974), *Seduzidas pelo Demônio* (Raffaele Rossi, 1975), *A Estranha Hospedaria dos Prazeres* (José Mojica Marins, 1976), *As Filhas do Fogo* (Walter Hugo Khouri, 1978), *O Segredo da Múmia* (Ivan Cardoso, 1982) and *As Sete Vampiras* (Ivan Cardoso, 1986).

Many of these films are also hard to find because they were not released on videocassette after they were screened in theaters. Some are available as pirated copies, but others have completely disappeared from Brazilian film history. These films contain several structural and iconographic conventions that are traditionally associated with Gothic-horror films (such as low-key lighting, canted camera angles, representations of secluded spaces and innocent young females, as well as the vengeful killing of the villain).

However, these films also included unique characteristics related to specific times and places by reworking past and present socio-historical material in terms of contemporary national fears. People who are unfamiliar with these underground films will be struck by the strong (visual) emphasis on sexuality. Mainstream Gothic movies, particularly Anglo-American, do not contain such graphic boldness. The abundance of sex scenes in these Brazilian films demands an audience response, and the films succeed most of the time, despite the low budget and lack of cinematic techniques and visual aesthetics.

These sex scenes are often related to power and dominance, as well as concealed forms of oppression and subordination that gesture to broader socio-political circumstances and concerns about nationhood. The Gothic emerges here in the collapse of fictional boundaries that enable these stories to be read as 'state-of-the-nation' narratives. In the next section, I discuss the films of two very dissimilar Brazilian filmmakers, Walter Hugo Khouri and José Mojica Marins, and I seek to identify Gothic 'cracks' or exposures in the representational frames that suggest socio-political contexts and other metaphorical connotations in the films.

Walter Hugo Khouri: The Malaise of Bourgeois Manors

Director and producer of 25 films, Walter Hugo Khouri (1929–2003) is one of the most prolific Brazilian filmmakers, yet his *oeuvre* is little studied. The languorous style and sense of doom at the heart of films such as *Estranho Encontro* (1958), *O Anjo da Noite* (1974) and *As Filhas do Fogo* (1978) arguably place Khouri among the most prominent Brazilian Gothic filmmakers. Many of his films include tropes and settings associated with Gothic narratives: isolated buildings in deserted locations, sexual transgressions and the themes of family relations. Shying away from the blatant sexuality and violence found in many Brazilian Gothic films, Khouri's work includes suggestive moods and harrowing atmospheres that echo Ann Radcliffe's definition of 'terror'.[4]

Due to his personal style and what is identified as his interest in Existentialism, the criticism on his work often links Khouri's films to those of Bergman and Antonioni, thus giving him a 'high culture' status. Khouri is considered a director of unique sensibility who has captured the malaise of the Brazilian bourgeoisie focusing on topics associated with classic literature and philosophy. However, this reading has not always worked to his benefit, and some viewers and critics find his films to be overly complicated and self-serving. He is sometimes accused of being out of touch with a Brazilian national identity, an accusation supported by his affiliation with the film production company Vera Cruz of São Paulo, which was founded in the late 1940s to produce technically sophisticated films of international quality. As a result, Khouri's films are often critiqued as being 'foreign' in relation to the history of Brazilian cinema. His films focus on a bourgeois society and, as such, do not correspond to Cinema Novo's 'populist' agenda; however, they do address the issues of class and racial unrest. Khouri's subject matter, aesthetic choices and mise-en-scène, cannot be anything other than typically Brazilian.

Moreover, his connection to the Gothic is observed in his use of the trope of the old manor, which he articulates with the circumstances of its guests and inhabitants in atmospheres conducive to illicit love and crime. It has been extensively discussed in Gothic criticism that the architecture and features of castles and Victorian households can be read in terms of a concern for privacy and concealment; such spaces promote symbolic and literal forms of anxiety in the domestic context that translate easily into Gothic experiences (Hogle 145–66). Yet the castle and the Victorian house are not merely settings for supernatural activity; they can also be considered a character in the story. Khouri employs this protocol in a number of his films, achieving results that are peculiar to the Brazilian national context.

Khouri's *Estranho Encontro*, released in 1958 and set in a stately mansion, presents the problem of bourgeois malaise. The body that faints in the opening scene is emblematic of the physical and mental frailty of the protagonist, Júlia (Andréa Bayard), whose outbreaks of panic, amnesia and dread of the future cry out for a 'Female Gothic' interpretation. Fleeing in the middle of the night from her neurotic husband and gatekeeper, Hugo (Luigi Picchi), Júlia is rescued on a deserted road by a *bon-vivant,* Marcos (Mário Sérgio), who takes her to an imposing manor house that belongs to his mature lover, Wanda (Lola Brah). Throughout the narrative, Júlia hides in the rooms of the labyrinthine manor, trying to conceal herself from the cynical butler (Sérgio Hinst) and Wanda, who appears unannounced and eventually discovers her hiding place. A climatic scene is the confrontation between Julia's husband and Wanda, who ends up taking the young lady's side. Read in the light of oppressive and violent male sexuality, this film engages with the issue of female imprisonment and escape from the domestic sphere.

In *O Anjo da Noite*, the young psychology student, Ana (Selma Egrei), is hired as a nanny for two children whose family dwells in an isolated mansion in Petrópolis, a mountainous town in the state of Rio de Janeiro. Left alone for the weekend with the boy, girl and the night guard (Eliezer Gomes), the nanny receives mysterious and threatening phone calls; she panics and spirals out of control, leading to disastrous consequences. This is complicated by the fact that the boy is infatuated with the nanny. Ana does not mean to be seductive; her position is friendly, demonstrating awareness of the suffocating bourgeois sphere in which the children live. However, when the boy refuses to sleep, Ana's mental state deteriorates, and she witnesses him making one of the threatening calls. In a significant scene that foreshadows the imminent tragedy, Ana stands next to a human-size statue of an angel, whose raised sword seems ready to be brought down on her. In another scene, Ana lies in the middle of the main hall, anticipating her death.

The hall has a beautiful wooden ceiling which, at this point, resembles a coffin lid. All of these images of death suggest that Ana is a foreign body in the mansion; she is overwhelmed and frightened by the forces within the house, and she senses the past conflicts upon which the building is founded.

It is the night guard who represents the film's central ambiguities and national Gothic features. At first, the watchman is presented as a servile man, whose life is deeply attached to the location and the family. Throughout the night, he becomes increasingly bold and scary and, in a scene that suggests the madness of the environment, the boy and the guard start playing 'bang bang you're dead' inside the house: the boy uses his toy gun, the watchman his real gun. The night guard becomes a counterpoint to the right-balanced and even-minded nanny. This disturbing sequence culminates in an outbreak of violence when, in a fit of rage, the night guard kills everyone.

This ending might seem like a typical horror film finale. However, the watchman is played by Eliezer Gomes, a black actor. As a result, the title 'Night Angel' has metaphoric and metonymic overtones, reflecting the issues of class conflict and the socio-ethnic stratification of Brazilian society. Khouri's film shows awareness of the possibilities that would strike fear in a bourgeois audience in relation to their domestic workers. Casting Gomes for the role of the assassin is a choice that ultimately defies long-established postulations regarding Brazil's conciliatory nature, which has allegedly been shortening socio-ethnic distances between masters and slaves since colonial times. Yet in this Gothic film fear is generated from the racial and social other, replacing the ghost or monster as the source of anxiety. The night guard develops a gradual but unconscious perception of the mediocrity that he is doomed to watch and live. The indifference of the Brazilian bourgeoisie to the angst of those living on the margins of society erupts in this conclusion as a horrifying and threatening Gothic manifestation.

As Filhas do Fogo foregrounds discourses of gender and nationhood, articulating concerns of the 'unvoiced others' in the form of an eerie ghost tale. In this film, three female characters experience paranormal events that culminate in inexplicable deaths. The assonance in their names (Ana, Diana, Mariana) suggests they can be seen as a tripartite personality or interrelated characters that embody different issues concerning the situations of women in society. More to the point, this is a society that condemns women's relationships with members of their own sex (Ana), motherhood and pregnancy (Diana's problematic relationship to her body), and women's entrapment in the domestic sphere (Mariana).

Set in an unnamed community in the backlands of Rio Grande do Sul, the southernmost region in Brazil, *As Filhas do Fogo* highlights the frosty climate of the state, capturing images of hazy mornings and temperate vegetation. The visual composition of the film also accentuates the predominantly European heritage of the state, showing the pale complexion of its inhabitants and the Germanic architecture imported by immigrants. This representation seeks to transmit the idea of a small and secluded society, a foreign hamlet in a remote area of Brazil still linked to its ancestral origins and mysticism. On the one hand, these images stress the absence of tropical elements (often associated with the Brazilian territory and identity); on the other hand, though, they achieve a transnational impact, offering a narrative that functions in different contexts.

Ana (Rosina Malbouisson), who is originally from São Paulo city, describes the location as 'beautiful but not welcoming', drawing the audience into her point of view. She is frightened by the natural landscape (dark green ponds, mossy stones, vegetation hanging from the trees) and by the way the locals stare at her with watchful eyes, which seem to manifest in different objects. Ana travels secretly to Rio Grande do Sul to visit her girlfriend Diana (Paola Morra), whom she is forbidden to see after the family discovered their compromising correspondence. The lesbian relationship in *As Filhas do Fogo* includes an element of transgression that disrupts the role conventionally assigned to women. Ana's anxiety and repressed desires are, according to Pauline Palmer, 'of central importance to the lesbian subject who, lacking a history and a language to articulate her sexual orientation, may feel haunted by emotions which she cannot or dare not articulate' (119). The secrecy and silence, as well as the sense of emotional and communicative impairment, come to define Ana's feelings of angst, and the vigilant eyes she recognizes in many objects act as harbingers of the events that follow.

As the film progresses, the point of view is handed over to Diana, and the audience then gains a new narrative perspective, particularly when she speaks about her affection for this remote place and the manor. The two girls love each other, and they are also united by the complicated relationships they have with their families. Diana's father has been absent for most of her life, and her mother passed away when she was a child. Soon the audience realizes that Diana has not managed to detach herself from the maternal figure, whose memory she keeps alive by retelling old stories and browsing through a family album. Her favorite picture is of her mother in a long dress; it was taken when she was pregnant with her. Birth and death come together in Diana's mother figure, and as she continues to indulge in her fixation on her mother's pregnancy, Diana's traumas show in her grievances about having her father's swarthy physical complexion. This arises even though the other characters say Diana resembles her mother (including in her sexual orientation, as is revealed later in the film). Diana's link to reality becomes more and more blurred when she starts talking about the dead people in her family as if they are alive. The only person who notices her tormented state is the housekeeper, Mariana (Maria Rosa), a woman of Afro-Amerindian origins who functions in the film as 'local color' in an all-European realm.

Mariana works as a head-servant of the manor house, but she often does more than her duties as a housekeeper, and she often speaks to Diana like a big sister. Although there are no explicit scenes of sexuality involving the three girls, Diana says suggestively to Ana that 'Mariana has got incredible hands' and they all share a laugh. But whilst Diana shows contempt for the other sex, declaring that 'all men are vagabonds', Mariana makes love to a rambler who comes to the house for food and work, with tragic consequences that cause his death. Mariana's specific situation speaks of female oppression in a culture that determines women's confinement in the domestic sphere. In one scene, she declares that she was born in the region and has never left it, seldom being away from the house. Mariana appears to accept her situation, and perhaps for this reason she is the least disturbed of the three characters. The Gothic emerges in the figure of the woman trapped within the domestic space; it is also present in the trope of the 'old house' (as a private female domain), which is located in an ominous location where dreams are destined to fail.

The female characters find themselves haunted by the ghost of Diana's mother. As the borders between this world and the next are blurred, the scandalous family secrets are revealed. The situation concludes with a nightmarish scene as the luxuriant forest around the property envelops the entire house and its dwellers. In this return to nature, the nation encompasses what has, until now, been a personal and familial narrative. It seems that the nation re-asserts itself in the construction of its history by overwhelming the manor with vegetation. Recognizing this overlap between personal and public spheres, the film depicts this domestic and female-centered sphere as a metonym of nationhood through homologies constructing private lives as representative of public destinies. In light of the destiny of the manor, the issue of power and the oppressive patriarchal forces that act on the tripartite female psyche and bodies suggest that the film can be read as a metonym of the national, with numerous Gothic characteristics. Reading Walter Hugo Khouri's films from a Gothic perspective encourages a reassessment of works that have been called overwhelming and complicated.

José Mojica Marins: Zé do Caixão and State-Sanctioned Violence

José Mojica Marins, born in 1936, is an independent filmmaker from São Paulo whose most successful creation is arguably the character Zé do Caixão (Coffin Joe), an unholy undertaker who is obsessed with the supernatural and a longing to sire 'the perfect son'. Zé do Caixão is a national horror icon; he is immortalized in films, TV shows, comic books and *literatura de cordel*.[5] The evil character is played by the filmmaker himself (a rare case in Brazilian cinema history), generating identity mergers that enhance the complexity of the relationship between the creator and his creature. Mojica often sets out to confuse the audience by manipulating his roles for ambiguous effect.

With his trademark top hat, black cape and talon-like fingernails, Zé do Caixão terrorizes the citizens of a village in the backlands of Brazil. The Gothic element arises in the director's use of clothing associated with international horror villains, but also through the pivotal Gothic themes of progeny and bloodlines. The pompous Victorian garments are extraneous to the Brazilian town, but they contribute to the visual characterization of Zé do Caixão, aggrandizing a character who would not be as influential without his attire. In the dynamics of cross-cultural exchange, these appropriations of the Gothic capitalize on the success of foreign films and promote the character in relation to international horror icons. Rather than conforming to historical accuracy or social verisimilitude, the director creates a cinematic spectacle for his audience.

Zé do Caixão first appears in the film *À Meia Noite Levarei Sua Alma* (1964). Having killed his former wife, Lenita (Valéria Vasquez), whom he considered unsuited to give him children, his sexual desire fixes on his best friend's fiancée, Terezinha (Magda Mei), who becomes an addressee of his quest for perfection. He brutally murders his best friend, Antônio (Nivaldo de Lima), by drowning him and then rapes his bride-to-be. Terezinha hangs herself but not before she casts a curse on Zé do Caixão, vowing to return from the dead to take his soul.

The scene of Terezinha's physical battering and violation is an example of the victimization of women that, according to Mary Ellen Snodgrass, is 'the heart-thumping stuff of the Gothic lore' (118). Shot in black and white and lit for monochrome, the battering scene that takes place before the rape is disturbingly long and runs almost without distractive cuts. As Zé do Caixão prepares to deliver his *coup de grâce*, a punch to the face, the scene unexpectedly flips to a reverse shot and the spectator receives the blow. The camera then shows Terezinha's bleeding lips (in extreme close-up); they are half open in a sensual way. On the sofa, Zé do Caixão kisses her mouth and, as he turns his face to the camera, his bloody grin resembles that of a vampire. The sexual violence occurs off-camera, and the rape is symbolized by the death of a canary, which Terezinha squeezes in her hand during the abuse. Afterward she lies on the sofa, and the viewer is invited to associate her languid figure with seduction and pleasure.

This brutal scene problematizes the eroticization of violence through the conflation of aggression and sexual desire. Critics have argued that this rape 'has no straightforward connection with what would be presumed to be its 'real-life' enactment' (Segal 68), and that such scenes 'galvanize constructive response to the problem of actual rape in the real world' (Strossen 173). Other critics argue that rape fantasies occupy an archetypal part of our brains wherein no 'bodily harm, or humiliation took place [...]. It simply had to be understood that what went on was against the woman's will' (Friday 4–5). Indeed, erotic violence on-screen does not necessarily sanction it in society, and the history of brutality against women in texts continues to fuel debate. Although Zé do Caixão is unapologetically hostile to women, the use of reverse shots (in which the viewer is 'attacked') formally challenges straightforward sex-gender representations in the film. The assault on the audience obliterates the possibility of identifying with the aggressor, for the blow represented in the counter-shot suggests that nobody is sheltered from Zé do Caixão's violence.

Throughout the film, Zé do Caixão gouges out a man's eyes and amputates an adversary's fingers with a broken bottle. During a rampage, he thrusts a crown of thorns into a man's face and savagely lashes another opponent with a whip. The people in the bar watch in horror as Zé do Caixão whips the body and face of a black man (Genésio de Carvalho) until he collapses. The choice of actor and instrument of torture for this particular scene touches on the issue of slavery, addressing Brazil's historical past and exposes racial tensions in the nation. The representation of sexual and racial aggression, the use of camera techniques that victimize the spectator, the crimes Zé do Caixão commits for believing that everything is possible in a lawless place were unique displays of violence for Brazilian audiences in the 1960s. Looking beyond the film boundaries, a correlation between Zé do Caixão and state-sanctioned forms of violence can be traced. The undertaker's overwhelming power can be read as a sign of the political atmosphere that arose during and after the 1964 Brazilian *coup d'état*.

In real life, the Brazilian dictatorship banned artistic and journalistic freedom of expression. The military motto of the day was 'Brazil: love it or leave it'. This political repression culminated in December 1968, when the military President Costa e Silva signed the Institutional Act number 5 (AI-5) overriding Congress. A *coup* then developed within the *coup*, and this granted additional power to the reactionary wing of the army. Among the Act's measures was the suspension of the right of *habeas corpus* for anyone charged with crimes against national security. Torture was sanctioned under presidential decree and was carried out by security agencies such as DOPS/DEOPS, OBAN and the notorious DOI-CODI. In the following years, state-sanctioned violence reached its worst levels and led to the widespread disappearance, persecution and forced exile of many Brazilian citizens.

Zé do Caixão's saga continues in *Esta Noite Encarnarei no seu Cadáver* (1968), a film that stages modes of torture that are identical to the atrocities practiced by the military police. These include being placed in small spaces with snakes and spiders, burning of body parts with chemicals and strangulation. This brutality is underscored in *Esta Noite Encarnarei no seu Cadáver*, and the images of violence are more graphic than in *À Meia Noite Levarei Sua Alma*. On the national level, political censorship prohibited news about dissent and social conflict, prohibiting information about abduction and torture by government agents and suppressing protests in the arts. Federal government agencies determined whether a film was released, censored or banned (Kushnir 137–81). Mojica may have defended his film by arguing that topics such as violence, torture and tyrannical forces are part of the horror genre. *Esta Noite Encarnarei no seu Cadáver* was not banned by the Serviço de Censura de Diversões Públicas (SCDP), but Mojica was forced to make cuts as well as a significant change to the denouement, so that Zé do Caixão repents his acts. However, as the Brazilian military dictatorship increased its repressive actions, Mojica further explored the similarities between his work's violent scenarios and the government's methods of repression.

In *Ideologia*, part of the omnibus film *O Estranho Mundo de Zé do Caixão* (1968), the undertaker appears disguised as his alter-ego, Professor Oãxiac Odéz. His objective is to conduct a 'scientific' experiment to prove that behind the veneer of education and culture, human beings are bestial creatures. To accomplish this task Oãxiac Odéz kidnaps a couple, Alfredo (Osvaldo de Souza) and Vilma (Nidi Reis), and imprisons them in his dungeon-like house. He then sets up a 'circus of horrors', forcing the couple to watch gruesome scenes while he gives lectures on the nature of the human condition—paradoxically, the Professor resorts to violence to prove his intellectual hypothesis. The scenes of cruel violence are presented as 'staged acts'; the lights go up just before the show and then go down at the end. This rendition, based on dramatic characterization and production, stresses the meta-fictional nature of the film and disengages the audience (although this does not shield viewers from the impact of the scenes). For a Brazilian audience living under a dictatorship, the notions of spectacle and performance presented in this film can potentially result in a revaluation of the horror trope. The director represents torture techniques that were practiced in the 'houses of horror' run by the military government, sites that were covert and yet prominent in the public imagination.

Under the pretext of being only a horror film, a genre that underscores violence, *Ideologia* remains particularly remarkable because of its title (ideology was a high-risk word at the time) and the representation of torture scenes, which re-enact well-known methods of repression practiced by the government's political police. This combination leaves little room for ambiguity, hidden meanings or coded discourses. The torture procedures and the instruments shown in *Ideologia* are those used on political prisoners, including forced imprisonment, kidnapping, 'the rack', isolation, starvation, beating, rape and suffocation.[6]

Beyond Victorian garments and themes, Mojica's representation of political violence reflects a Brazilian expression of the Gothic that materializes out of a discourse of degeneration (national, social and human). In a context of violence, unrest and artistic suppression, the Zé do Caixão films function as historical signposts that coincide with the institutionalization and power of the dictatorship. The representations of brutal violence and the ruthlessness of the evil undertaker are connected to the increasing brutality of socio-political junctures in the Brazilian historical moment.

Conclusion

I have argued that Brazilian Gothic cinema constitutes a nebulous category that should be conceptualized as a composite of filmic interventions undertaken by different filmmakers at different times. Brazilian films that can be considered Gothic often resort to a displacement of ideas as a way of bringing to light social and political concerns that could not be readily approached otherwise or, rather, could be more effectively discussed if transported into a fictional universe. In so doing, I have called attention to a potential collection of Brazilian Gothic films produced since the early part of the twentieth century; this corpus needs to be more thoroughly researched and investigated, and my work on the *oeuvre* of Walter Hugo Khouri and José Mojica Marins is just a start. For Khouri, the uncanny effects of psychological breakdowns are conveyed through Gothic elements and shed light on the circumstances of Brazil's recent history and cultural institutions. For Marins, the shocking effects of brutal violence and rape draw on the Gothic in order to convey the injustices in the period of Brazilian dictatorship. For both filmmakers, the Anglo-American tradition of Gothic horror is a significant model. However, each of their films addresses collective and individual traumas related to gender, class, race, sexuality and violence to challenge the metanarratives of the nation, identifying them as unique expressions of the Gothic in Brazilian cinema.

Notes

1. Câmara Cascudo's *Antologia do Folclore Brasileiro* is still one of the finest surveys of the kind and illustrates the centrality and variety of supernatural horror in Brazilian folklore.
2. Although Brazil's film industry was virtually a 'tropical appendage of the North American market' (Stam and Johnson 22), the period from the 1930s to the 1950s saw some national enterprises trying to replicate Hollywood modes of production. Brazilian film companies such as Cinédia, Atlântida and Vera Cruz produced a scanty output that tended to emulate established genres. But they effectively produced subgenres, musical comedies, *chanchadas,* being the prime example. More recently, the new generation of researchers has been working to fill this gap in Brazilian cinema history.
3. This Cinédia production is in essence an adaptation of a 1926 homonymous play by Gilberto Andrade.
4. 'Terror and Horror are so far opposite that the first expands the soul, and awakens the faculties to a high degree of life; the other contracts, freezes and nearly annihilates them'. See Ann Radcliffe's 'On the Supernatural in Poetry'. *New Monthly Magazine* (vol. 7, 1826: 145–52).
5. This is a popular style of illustrated poetry that is produced through a technique called *xilogravura*, which is used to leave an impression from an engraved woodblock.
6. For more details regarding the torture methods and procedures in this context see Amnesty International, Joan Dassin, and Beatriz Kushnir.

Bibliography

Amnesty International. *Torture in the Eighties*. Martin Robertson. Bath: Pitman Press, 1984. Print.

Cascudo, Luís da Câmara. *Antologia do Folclore Brasileiro*. São Paulo: Martins Editora, 1944. Print.

Domingues, Henrique Foreis. *Incrível! Fantástico! Extraordinário!* Rio de Janeiro: Francisco Alves, 1989. Print.

Ellis, Kate Ferguson. *The Contested Castle: Gothic Novels and the Subversion of Domestic Ideology*. Chicago: University of Illinois Press, 1989. Print.

Friday, Nancy. *Women on Top*. New York: Simon & Schultz, 1991. Print.

Gonzaga, Adhemar, and Salles Gomes, Paulo Emílio. *Setenta anos de cinema brasileiro*. Rio de Janeiro: Editora Expressão e Cultura, 1966. Print.

Hogle, Jerrold E. 'The Restless Labyrinth: Cryptonomy in the Gothic Novel'. *Gothic Critical Concepts in Literary and Cultural Studies*. Ed. Botting, Fred, and Dale Townshend. London: Routledge, 2004. 145–66. Print.

Kushnir, Beatriz. *Cães de Guarda: jornalistas e censores, do AI-5 à Constituição de 1988*. São Paulo: Boitempo, 2004. Print.

Moya, Álvaro de (org). *'Shazam!' Coleção Debates*. São Paulo: Perspectiva, 1977. Print.

Palmer, Paulina. 'Lesbian Gothic: Genre, Transformation, Transgression.' *Gothic Studies* 6.1 (2004): 118–30. Print.

Pucci Jr., Renato Luiz. *O Equilíbrio das Estrelas: filosofia e imagens no cinema de Walter Hugo Khouri*. São Paulo: Annablumme, 2001. Print.

Radcliffe, Ann. 'On the Supernatural in Poetry'. *The New Monthly Magazine* 7 (1826): 145–52. Print.

Ramone, Marcus. 'A trajetória das HQ's de terror no Brasil'. http://www.universohq.com. Accessed 30 September 2014. Web.

Segal, Lynne. 'Only the Literal: The Contradictions of Anti-Pornography Feminism'. *More Dirty Looks: Gender, Pornography and Power*. Ed. Gibson, P.C. London: British Film Institute, 2004. 59–71. Print.

Serravalle de Sá, Daniel. *Brazilian Horror: Zé do Caixão in the Multimedia Work of José Mojica Marins*. The University of Manchester. Thesis. 2010. Print.

Silva, Diamantino da. *Quadrinhos Dourados: a história dos suplementos no Brasil*. São Paulo: Opera Graphica, 2003. Print.

Snodgrass, Mary Ellen. *Encyclopedia of Gothic Literature*. New York: Infobase, 2009. Print.

Stam, Robert & Randal Johnson. *Jump Cut* 21 (November 1979): 13–18. Print.

Strossen, Nadine. *Defending Pornography: Free Speech, Sex, and the Fight for Women's Rights*. New York: New York University Press, 2000. Print.

Viany, Alex. *Introdução ao Cinema Brasileiro*. Rio de Janeiro: Instituto Nacional do Livro, 1959. Print.

Contributors

Enrique Ajuria Ibarra is Assistant Professor at Universidad de las Américas Puebla, Mexico. He has previously published articles and book chapters on the films of Guillermo del Toro and on Mexican horror cinema. He is currently examining the relationship between Gothic and travel in the horror film and exploring Mexican Gothic.

Antonio Alcalá is Professor of Language and Literature at Tecnológico de Monterrey in Mexico City where he also coordinates the Language Center. He is cofounder of the Latin American Gothic Association, LAGA, and founder of the International Gothic Literature Congress at the UNAM (National University of Mexico). He has contributed to *Anuario de Letras Inglesas* and *A Companion to the American Gothic*. His recent projects include mapping the presence of Gothic in Mexican literature and researching Gothic and the lyrics of classic Black Metal bands.

Inés Ordiz Alonso-Collada holds a doctorate in Modern Languages from the University of León in Spain with a specialization in Comparative Pan-American Gothic literature. She is the co-editor of the volume *La (ir) realidad imaginada: Aproximaciones a lo insólito en la ficción hispanoamericana*, which focuses on the various manifestations of Fantasy in Latin American literature. She has recently published articles on contemporary zombie cinema, Mexican and Argentinean Gothic and the female grotesque. She is currently working on her second PhD on Latin American Female Gothic at the University of Washington, Seattle.

Ilse Büssing holds a BA in Comparative Literature from the College of William and Mary, MA in Latin American Literature from University of Costa Rica and PhD in English Literature from University of Edinburgh. Her PhD thesis, *The Haunted House in Mid-to-Late Victorian Gothic Fiction,* explores the convergence of architecture and social history, thus revealing her main interest in the interdisciplinary study of space in life and fiction. She is a lecturer in English Literature at the University of Costa Rica and Gothic Literature in the MA in English Literature program. Her publications focus mostly on Gothic.

Cilaine Alves Cunha is Lecturer of Brazilian Literature at the University of São Paulo and has published *O Belo e o Disforme, Álvares de Azevedo e* *a ironia romantic* and several articles and essays on Brazilian Romantic prose and poetry. Her main research interests are nationalism, Romanticism, Naturalism, literary history and Machado de Assis.

Justin D. Edwards is Chair of English at the University of Surrey, UK. He is the author or co-author of several books, including *Grotesque* (2013) *Mobility at Large* (2012), *Postcolonial Literature* (2008), *Gothic Canada: Reading the Spectre of a National Literature* (2005), *Gothic Passages: Racial Ambiguity and the American Gothic* (2003) and *Exotic Journeys: Exploring the Erotics of U.S. Travel Literature* (2001). He is also the editor or co-editor of *Other Routes: 1500 Years of African and Asian Travel Writing* (2006), *Downtown Canada: Writing Canadian Cities* (2005), *Postcolonial Travel Writing: Critical Explorations* (2010), *Gothic in Contemporary Literature and Popular Culture: Pop Goth* (2012) and *Technologies of the Gothic in Literature and Culture: Technogothics* (2015).

Elizabeth Rodriguez Fielder is a PhD candidate at the University of Mississippi, U.S. Her dissertation, *The Radical South: Grassroots Activism and Literary Form 1960–1985*, examines cultural expressions of community activism within ethnic-nationalist and social movements in the context of avant-garde performance, circum-Atlantic ritual practices, and Global South political networks. She has published articles in *American Studies in Scandinavia*, *Fifty Years after Faulkner* (University Press of Mississippi), *Undead Souths: Beyond the Gothic* (Louisiana State University Press), and *PMLA*.

Kelly Gardner is a PhD candidate in English Literature at the University of Stirling in Scotland, where she also holds a Master's degree in the Gothic Imagination. She received her BA (Hons) in English Literature from the University of the Witwatersrand in Johannesburg, South Africa. Her current research is on the development of post-humanism in zombie literature and the emergence of the self-reflexive zombie. Her research interests include transhumanism, zombie gothic, science fiction and the representation of place in post-apocalyptic narratives.

Rune Graulund is Associate Professor in American Literature and Culture at the Center for American Studies, University of Southern Denmark. He is the editor of *Desperately Seeking Authenticity: An Interdisciplinary Approach*, co-editor of *Postcolonial Travel Writing: Critical Explorations*, co-author of *Mobility at Large: Globalization, Textuality and Innovative Travel Writing* and *Grotesque* (New Critical Idiom). His main research interests are in 20th and 21st century literature, culture and philosophy, especially in the fields of science fiction, gothic, travel writing, nature writing, aesthetics and popular culture.

Johan Höglund is an Associate Professor at Linnaeus University in Sweden and a member of the Linnaeus University Centre for Concurrences in

Colonial and Postcolonial Studies. He has published extensively on the relationship between popular culture and imperialism in *Game Studies*, *English Literature in Transition*, *Continuum* and *The European Journal of American Studies*. He is the author of *The American Imperial Gothic: Popular Culture, Empire, Violence* (Ashgate 2014), and co-editor of *Animal Horror Cinema: Genre, History and Criticism* (with Katarina Gregersdotter and Nicklas Hållén, Palgrave 2015), and *Transnational and Postcolonial Vampires* (with Tabish Khair, Palgrave 2012).

David Punter is Professor of English at the University of Bristol, U.K. He is a poet, writer and academic and has published extensively on topics including the Gothic, romantic literature, contemporary writing, literary theory, metaphor and modernity. His published books include *The Literature of Terror: A History of Gothic Fictions from 1765 to the Present Day* (1980); *The Hidden Script: Writing and the Unconscious* (1985); *The Romantic Unconscious: A Study in Narcissism and Patriarchy* (1989); *Gothic Pathologies: The Text, the Body and the Law* (1998); *Writing the Passions* (2000); *Postcolonial Imaginings: Fictions of a New World Order* (2000); *The Influence of Postmodernism on Contemporary Writing: An Interdisciplinary Study* (2005); *Metaphor* (2007); *Modernity* (2007); *Rapture: Literature, Addiction, Secrecy* (2009); and *The Literature of Pity* (2014). His next book will be *The Gothic Condition: Terror, History, Psyche* (forthcoming 2016).

Owen Robinson is Senior Lecturer in U.S. Literature at the University of Essex, U.K. He is the author of *Creating Yoknapatawpha: Readers and Writers in Faulkner's Fiction* (Routledge 2006) and several journal articles and book chapters on William Faulkner, George Washington Cable and New Orleans. With Richard Gray, he co-edited *A Companion to the Literature and Culture of the American South* (Blackwell 2004), and he is co-editor of the American Literature section of the Blackwell online journal *Literature Compass*. He is the co-editor of *Surveying the American Tropics: A Literary Geography from New York to Rio* (Liverpool UP 2013).

Rita Terezinha Schmidt is Professor of Literature at the Universidade Federal do Rio Grande do Sul, Brazil. She has published more than 100 articles and book chapters and edited five collections of essays on comparative literature, a book on Clarice Lispector's fiction and two re-editions of Brazilian women poets of the 19th century. She has been president of the Brazilian Association of American Studies (1994–1996) and vice president of the Brazilian Association of Comparative Literature (2002–2004). Since 2007 she has been a member of the Gender Studies Committee, a standing committee at the International Association of Comparative Literature.

Daniel Serravalle de Sá is Lecturer at the Federal University of Santa Catarina, Brazil. His research interests incorporate the study of popular culture and the relationship between literature and cinema. In recent years, Daniel has written about the Gothic and its manifestations in different cultural contexts. He is the author of the book *Gótico Tropical: o sublime e o demoníaco em O Guarani* (Edufba 2010) and has published chapters in the books *World Film Locations: São Paulo* (Intellect 2013) and *Directory of World Cinema: Brazil* (Intellect 2013).

Sandra Guardini Vasconcelos is Professor of English Literature and Comparative Literature at the University of São Paulo, Brazil. She did post-doctoral studies at the University of Cambridge and at the University of Manchester and was a visiting research associate at the Centre for Brazilian Studies, University of Oxford. She has edited several books and published many articles and chapters, both in Brazil and abroad, and she is the author of *Puras Misturas. Estórias em Guimarães Rosa* (1997), *Dez Lições sobre o Romance Inglês do Século XVIII* (2002) and *A Formação do Romance Inglês: ensaios teóricos* (2007), for which she received the 2008 Jabuti Prize for Literary Theory and Criticism. She is the curator of the João Guimarães Rosa Archive at the Instituto de Estudos Brasileiros and the director of Biblioteca Brasiliana Guita e José Mindlin (USP).

Index